Adventuring in the *Rockies*

JEREMY SCHMIDT

SIERRA CLUB BOOKS • SAN FRANCISCO

Copyright © 1986, 1993, 1997 by Key Porter Books Limited, Toronto

LIBRARY OF CONGRESS CATALOGING-IN-PUBLICATION DATA
Schmidt, Jeremy, 1949–
Adventuring in the Rockies : the Sierra Club Travel guide to the Rocky Mountain region of Canada and the U.S.A. / Jeremy Schmidt—Rev. ed.
p.   cm.
ISBN 0-87156-946-9
1. Rocky Mountains—Guidebooks. 2. Outdoor recreation—Rocky Mountains—Guidebooks.   I. Title.
F721.S34   1993
917.8'0433-dc20   92-34644

All text photographs by Jeremy Schmidt with the exception of the following: p. 98, 107 (top), 116, Colorado Tourism Board; p. 307, Environment Canada; p. 233, Montana Travel Promotion Unit, Department of Highways; p. 296, 298, Travel Alberta; p. 156, Wyoming Travel Commission.

Cover photo by Carr Clifton
Cover design by Bonnie Smetts
Book design by Amy Evans
Maps by Wendy Schmidt

Printed and bound in Canada

10   9   8   7   6   5   4   3   2   1

Contents

Introduction

THE ROCKY MOUNTAINS present an unexpected puzzle: just where, exactly, are they? At first, it seems a silly question to ask. If you approach them from the east, driving across the plains of Colorado or Alberta, the issue is as clear as it could be. The Rockies rise with shocking abruptness. One moment you are on the plains, and a mile farther you are in the mountains. Seen from an airplane, the transition is even more dramatic. The careful geometry of western wheatfields gives way to the complex uplift of the mountains as definitively as a coast gives way to an ocean.

But just have a look at a map, or better yet several maps of different scales, by different publishers, and the confusion becomes apparent. On one map, sprawled across the entire western part of the continent from Alaska to Central America, you find huge letters spelling Rocky Mountains, as if it were the only range in North America. Although a different map might label a few other ranges—the Sierras or Cascades, for example—it's hard to tell whether the map maker thought of these as subranges of the Rockies or as distinct entities. In fact, there is not a single Rocky Mountain in Oregon, but you cannot learn that from most large-scale maps.

Compare these with something on a smaller scale, let's say a map of Colorado, which is indisputably in the Rockies. However, you find that this map indicates dozens of other ranges. Instead of lumping all the mountains under a single name as the large-scale maps do, this one splits the state into a maze of subranges. The line of mountains above Denver are called the Front Range, with subcategories including the Mummy Range, Indian Peaks, the Never Summer Range and the Rampart Range. Marching off to the west, ranges and subranges carry the names of Sawatch, Park, Gore, Elk, Ruby, Flattop, San Juan and more. They vary in size, height, length, topography and almost any other parameter you can imagine. They are made of ancient granites over 2 billion years old, sedimentary sand- and mud-stones dating from 200 million years ago, and volcanic rocks so new they haven't had time to cool down fully. This is an endearing characteristic of mountains: the closer one gets, the larger and more complicated they seem. Every line of peaks requires a separate name. But which ones are the Rockies? Are they all the Rockies? Is there no standard for judging?

Much depends on your point of view. To many Europeans, the Rockies take up all of western North America (as to many of us, the only mountains in Europe are the Alps). People with wider geographical backgrounds know enough to distinguish the Rockies from the coastal ranges, such as the Sierra Nevada and the Cascades. But few people indeed would understand why residents of Kimberley, British Columbia, become indignant if some ignoramus fails to distinguish between THE Rockies, which form their eastern skyline, and the Purcells, which lie immediately to the west. In fact, the Purcells *are* distinct. They are much older than the neighboring Rockies, are made of different rock and are separated from them by a major thrust fault. "So what if they stand toe to toe for hundreds of miles?" a local person might ask. "Just because mountains come in herds doesn't mean they are all of the same species." It's a bit like equating England with Wales, or New Zealand with Australia. Does it matter? Be careful where you ask that question.

Such distinctions seem less important to people living on the U.S. side of the border. Central Idahoans will tell you that they live in the Rocky Mountains, even though their peaks (the Salmon River Mountains) are hundreds of miles from the Rockies of Montana. They don't seem to care about differences in rock type or geologic history. Nor would their distant neighbors in Denver or Santa Fe disagree. "Them's the Rockies, my friend—the Rocky Mountains every one of 'em. They's made of good hard rock, they stick up into that everlasting blue sky and ain't they just something to look at! Now don't trouble me with details."

Okay, I won't; but allow me just one more. There is, in fact, a reliable criterion for defining the Rocky Mountain Range. It is this: every one of these mountains, and all the separate chains in the Rockies, have come into existence as a result of a geologic event with the pleasing name of the Laramide Orogeny. This period of uplift began about 100 million years ago, spread throughout the region, and in some places is still going on. In combination with subsequent erosion, volcanic eruptions, additional uplifting and a recent ice age, it has built a great variety of landscapes, which despite their differences, are nonetheless considered parts of the same grand range. The Purcell Mountains are not a part of the Rockies, because they existed for many millions of years before the Laramide Orogeny began.

For the purposes of this book, I've opted for a generous approach to defining the Rockies, and have included a very large neighborhood indeed. From Santa Fe, New Mexico, at the southern end of the Sangre de Cristo Range, all the way to northern British Columbia, where the Liard Plateau meets the first (or are they the last?), low, pyramidal peaks of the Rockies, it is a land of great diversity, marvelous scenery, friendly people and unlimited opportunities for travelers. The Rockies span 2,000 straight-line miles and some 25 degrees of latitude. Tying all this together is a compelling natural delineation, the Continental Divide. It snakes along ridgelines the whole way, often on the highest peaks but not always. A whimsical traveler, its route is defined not by elevation, but by drainage. It twists around on itself like an old meandering river, and does a few surprising things. In Wyoming, it bifurcates around the Great Divide Basin, and farther north, in Yellowstone, the western slope actually faces east for a few miles. In New Mexico, it abandons the Rockies entirely, choosing instead to follow a westerly course, which takes it almost to the Arizona border.

Within this vast area are a number of cohesive subdivisions, reflected in the organization of this book. Beginning at the south end, the *Colorado Region* includes everything from Santa Fe, New Mexico, to the southern border of Wyoming. At that point there is a break—the Great Divide Basin, a high, cold desert with neither a drainage outlet nor a river to seek one. In central Wyoming, the Wind River Range marks the start of the *Yellowstone Region*, which, centered on Yellowstone National Park, includes all of northwestern Wyoming, southern Montana and a little of Idaho. Here the Rockies reach their widest extent. To the west is *Salmon River Country*, covering all of central Idaho and part of western Montana. It adjoins the *International Border Region*, straddling the U.S.-Canada boundary from the Idaho-Washington border to the eastern edge of the mountains. Then comes the *Canadian Rockies Region*, into which I have tossed wholesale the Purcell Range and parts of the Selkirk Mountains, just because it seemed like a good idea from a traveler's perspective.

Descriptions of these five regions make up the bulk of this book. For each, the reader will find a general discussion of the region's history, geology and natural history, along with an overview of recreational possibilities. Following the general discussion are separate sections devoted to specific parks, wilderness areas or wild rivers. These are most often organized by mountain range, not by administrative unit. For example, suppose you have an interest in the Wind River Range. By turning to the Yellowstone Region, you can find how these mountains fit into the general scheme of things. Turning then to the section on the Wind River

Range, you will find a discussion of the Jim Bridger Wilderness and surrounding areas, complete with a list of the best-known trails and campgrounds, access points, special regulations, permit requirements, if any,
and much more.

In giving directions to these places, I've taken a cue from the way
mountain residents see their surroundings. Westerners have a great affection for geography. They like to get a mental hold on the lie of the land;
to know how the place is put together. This may be only because there's
so much more geography to look at here than in other places, but I think
people who live with mountains get a deep sense of satisfaction from
knowing their neighborhood. They like to talk about it too.
Conversation is sprinkled with words like *bench*, *drainage*, *pass*, *plateau*,
ridge and *bottomland*. The words are spoken with warm affection for
what they describe. "The Rocking-J Ranch? Sure, Frank and Virginia's
place. Down the river about three miles, up on the bench at the mouth of
Hick's Canyon? I saw a herd of pronghorn out on the sage flats there the
other day; they must'a come down off the plateau early this year."
Listening to someone talk like that, you know that he can picture every
piece of the landscape, every turn in the road. He knows how the air will
feel along the river, how the sage will smell in the afternoon sun.

This book is written for people, westerners or not, who have that
same affection for geography. I've tried to convey a sense of how the
place is put together, a feel for the neighborhood, so to speak, which I
firmly believe is more useful to a traveler than any list of its parts could
be. So although this book is filled with specific, detailed directions and
descriptions, you won't find in these pages a comprehensive directory of
campgrounds, motels, restaurants, tour operators, scenic overlooks and
the like. I don't think such lists are necessary or desirable. Directories
encourage itineraries, and that's not the best way to travel in the mountain West. It's better to wander, to mosey along the byways according to
whim rather than schedule. You can follow any old road and find something interesting. The most important equipment for this sort of travel
is a good map, a healthy curiosity and a sense of how the land is put
together. Once you have that, traveling becomes a relaxed adventure.

If you stopped to ask a Montana rancher about campgrounds in the
area, he'd probably say something like, "Well, you can drive up Windy
Creek, there are two or three Forest Service campgrounds up there,
maybe ten miles from here. If you go a little farther, you can just pull off
down by the creek, nobody'll bother you there. Good fishin' too."
Those are the sort of directions this book gives. With this guide, both
experienced and novice mountain travelers should be able to choose a
destination and feel confident about making an initial visit to an unfa-

miliar area. Once there, you can use this book for directions to important points of interest. It will tell you where to find supplies, campgrounds, trailheads, visitor centers, advice, maps and further information. Going beyond that is a matter of personal discovery, or of obtaining more detailed guidebooks for specific places.

Let me give one example of why local guidebooks can be important. In this book's section on British Columbia's Purcell Range, you will find descriptions of several places of interest—the famous Bugaboo Spires among them—along with specific directions for getting there and other useful information. If you're interested in the Purcells, these are good places to begin, and this book will be sufficient to get you there. However, the range is big and complicated, with few developed or maintained facilities, but with lots of other places to go. For example, south of the Bugaboos is the St. Mary's Alpine Park, accessible only by trail and rarely visited. A local guidebook, *Exploring the Purcell Wilderness*, by Edwards, Morrow and Twomey, begins a trail description from White Creek as follows:

> There are no established trails giving access to St. Mary Alpine Park. Start on St. Mary Road; turn right onto White Creek Road at Mile 24.5 and follow it over two bridges for 9.5 miles to a washed-out bridge. . . . Three miles from this point by road is the junction of Spade Creek with White Creek. Park your vehicle here if you are not already on foot. Proceed left across Spade Creek, following an old logging road on the left (south) side of the creek to Spade Lake. Cross to the north side of the lake at the outlet and follow a game trail to the west end of the lake. The route to the upper lake climbs the steep slope between two streams to Huggard Lake 1,500 feet above. It is a difficult bushwhack through bog, alder and devil's club, and some cliff-scaling is necessary, but a fit and determined hiker can traverse this section in two hours.

The description continues in that vein. Such detail about the more obscure corners of the mountains, as invaluable as it may be, is best left to a local guide. I've listed such guidebooks at appropriate places in the text.

Preceding the regional information is a chapter devoted to the Rocky Mountains as a whole, with information that applies to the entire range. This includes background material on topics such as history, geology and climate. There are also sections of particular interest to travelers: sections on bears and other hazards, on recreational possibilities, on equipment needed for various activities, and so forth. It's best to read this part of the book first, and then refer to areas of individual interest.

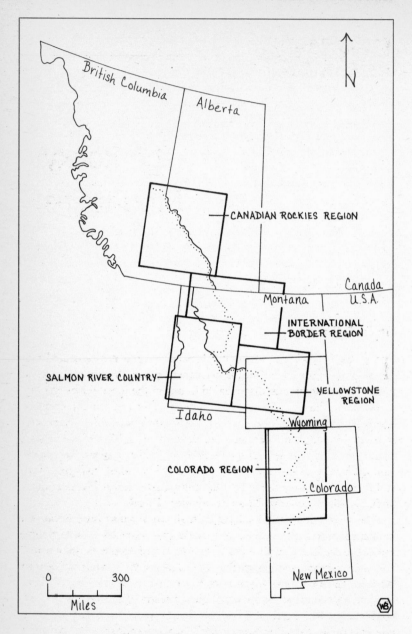

CHAPTER ONE

The Rocky Mountains

GEOLOGY

THE ERUPTION OF Mount St. Helens in 1980 demonstrated that mountains are by no means permanent things. In minutes, a great portion of the mountain disappeared in one of the most violent geologic events in history. Yet it was nothing compared to an event in Yellowstone some 600,000 years ago—the largest known eruption ever to occur. Hundreds of cubic miles of the earth were blown into the sky, settling in windrows several feet deep as far east as Kansas. The explosion left a caldera—a crater resulting from the volcano's collapse—measuring approximately thirty by fifty miles across and half a mile deep, an incredible excavation for a few minutes of work.

A more recent event must have been almost as impressive. Because it happened during the last ice age, there may even have been people around to see it, although unless they had ideal viewpoints, they would not have survived the experience. A tongue of the continental glacier blocked the flow of the Clark Fork River near modern Coeur d'Alene, forming an enormous lake which covered many of the valleys in western Montana to a depth of 2,000 feet. Ice, however, makes a poor dam, and eventually the river breached the glacier, causing a catastrophic flood. A volume of water sufficient to fill half of Lake Michigan drained westward in two or three days. Between eight and ten cubic miles of water per hour—ten times the total flow of all the world's rivers—raced at speeds of up to 45 miles per hour across Idaho and Washington. The devastation in its path was complete. This happened not once but many times, as the ice continued to advance, filling the lake again and again, only to be breached in turn.

Geologists tell us that the earth has been doing this sort of thing for billions of years. Some of what they say sounds incredible, as if they've been reading too much science fiction. They tell us of mountains rising up out of flat plains; of volcanoes exploding into existence in a matter of hours; of islands appearing in the middle of oceans; of the oceans themselves invading the land, staying for millions of years, and then retreating to leave behind vast deserts; of climates changing mysteriously from arctic to tropical, from ice cap to lush rain forest; and of whole mountain ranges sliding to one side like biscuits on a tilted breadboard.

And then they speak of destructive forces, of erosion by glacier, river, wind and gravity. As these forces go to work, all that new high ground changes shape. Valleys appear where there had been mere cracks, craggy mountains stand isolated against the sky, becoming defined in the same way that statues emerge from blocks of solid marble complete with piles of chiseled rubble around their bases. Complicating the image are the sudden breakthroughs of molten rock as volcanoes push up from underneath, building new mountains, filling valleys, creating vast plateaus, which in their turn would erode and vanish and be replaced. Terra firma say the geologists is anything but solid ground.

I have always found their arguments convincing. I've never had trouble accepting statements like "It was warmer here then," or "These mountains were once the sediments at the bottom of an inland sea." The evidence for these occurrences is overwhelming. You can stand on mountain viewpoints and watch erosion happening. You can see and hear the glaciers move, and recognize the shape of valleys which once held far greater glaciers. At viewpoints along the Banff-Jasper Highway, you can see mile upon mile of mountains made of tilted, bent, folded and broken layers of rock. Look closely at these, and you find ripple marks which could only have been caused by waves in shallow water. Embedded in the stone are seashells and the backbones of fish, among other fossils. Or visit Yellowstone National Park, where you can put your hands on the petrified stumps of California redwood trees. No one carried them there as a practical joke; they grew there at a time when the climate was similar to that of Big Sur, and were subsequently buried by ash from volcanoes.

Geologists are quite good at describing these events, at telling us when these things happened, and how thick the rocks are, and how old and so forth. But until recently, they've left one major aspect of the story a mystery. What caused the mountains to rise in the first place? Books always seemed to fall back on vague phrases like "forces deep within the earth" or "great pressure working against the rock." For all that was worth, they might as well have been telling us that a giant turtle lived down there, and occasionally it would stand up causing all sorts of havoc on the surface.

The Global Scene

Things have changed. Geologists now think they have an answer, a new theory which they say explains many of the old mysteries and adds a whole new dimension to our thinking. The relatively new science of plate tectonics, which studies the motions of continents, has stirred the soup. Essentially, this theory describes the earth's surface as a set of plates—seven major ones and perhaps a dozen smaller ones—covering the globe like huge, curved tiles. They float on top of the mantle, which, semimolten and fluid, is always moving the way chicken stew simmers beneath dumplings. As the fluid moves, so do the continents.

Recently published textbooks contain maps which show these motions as geologists think they might have happened over the ages, but without reading the text, you might never guess that these were maps of the earth. The maps show a planet; instead of a North Pole and a South Pole, this globe has a Pacific Pole and a Gondwana Pole. Strange-shaped blobs drift around from era to era, coalescing and dividing, coming together to form one great continent called Gondwanaland, then splitting into two called Gondwanaland and Laurasia, fragmenting yet again into many small parts only to recombine in a different configuration. Over the eons, it appears, continents have been moving around like bumper cars. The only thing that stays constant is the roundness of the planet.

Where I once pictured North America as a stable platform, its topography aging and weathering and being reborn, but maintaining its basic shape all the while, with Florida to the southeast and Alaska in the other corner, I must now think of the platform itself as being subject to change. At one time, it was upside down with its current arctic margin resting on the equator. South America was nowhere near, and a chunk of land called Ancestral Siberia drifted along the equator to the eastward as if enjoying a holiday in the tropics away from Mother Russia.

Eventually, on maps representing the Jurassic Period some 150 m.y.a. (million years ago), North America begins to look recognizable, located close to its current latitude and in its current orientation, although still firmly attached to Eurasia. This was the time of the great dinosaurs. After that comes the Cretaceous Period, during which the North

Atlantic Ocean is born. Greenland appears in the narrow rift between continents, and the Rocky Mountains begin to rise. Even as recently as 24 million years ago, with the dinosaurs gone and mammals dominating the scene—even then the world map is hardly recognizable. The Mediterranean is an inland sea, unconnected to the Atlantic, which itself is still a relatively narrow channel. Australia and New Guinea are one continent, snugged tightly against a compacted southeast Asia, and Greenland is still a part of Canada.

Geologists admit that these descriptions are in large part conjectural. Such events are too ancient and complex for the relatively new science of plate tectonics to have answered all the questions and put everything into a neat chronological scenario. But the principles, if not the specifics, are agreed upon.

The Creation of the Rockies

To understand the creation of the Rockies, we need to go back only about 100 to 150 million years ago, when the mid-Atlantic Ridge was born, and the North and South American plates began to push away from the Eurasian and African plates. As this motion continued, collision with the Pacific plate was inevitable. Under inexorable pressure, western North America buckled, broke and bowed upward along many fracture lines. The Rocky Mountains, at a relatively weak point in the crust, built up the way a pressure ridge appears in the middle of a frozen lake. All the while, the edge of the heavier and thinner oceanic plate was sliding beneath the continental plate—fully 1,500 miles of it and not finished yet. As it was pushed lower into the molten mantle, some of it melted, only to surge back to the surface as volcanoes at the borders of the plates. This happened on all sides of the Pacific Ocean, from the Americas across the Aleutian Islands to Japan, the Philippines and Indonesia. Geologists call this encircling band of volcanic activity The Ring of Fire. It accounts for the coastal ranges of British Columbia, Washington and Oregon. That includes Mount St. Helens.

Before the Mountains

The Rocky Mountains, then, appear to be collision damage; they began to rise about 100 m.y.a., and according to some geologists, the uplift continues even today. However, the story of the rocks that were exposed by the uplift goes back much farther than that, billions of years in fact. Previous mountain ranges have come and gone over the eons. It appears that one such range stood above the lifeless landscape fully 3 billion years ago. The evidence for this is in the so-called "basement" rocks,

Elk Lake lies at the base of the precipitous northern flank of Montana's Beartooth Mountains.

which outcrop here and there throughout the Rockies, and date from about 2.3 billion years ago. Their crystalline structure is that of rock subjected to the weight of mountains which have since disappeared. You can see these ancient rocks on the Painted Wall in Black Canyon of the Gunnison National Monument in Colorado, or in the Beartooth Range of Montana, among other places.

Between that time and the uplift of the Rockies, the continent went through a series of changes, with mountain ranges rising and eroding, and the sea rolling in only to drain away again. The region where the Rockies now stand was relatively quiet for most of those many years. Great layers of sediments built up in the inland seas, laid down in very orderly fashion to form a chronological record of geologic history. The rocks older than 600 million years are said to be from the Precambrian Era, the time before hard-shelled animals begin to appear as fossils. These rocks do contain signs of simple life-forms, such as the cabbage-shaped algae colonies seen along trails in Montana's Glacier National Park. But after 600 m.y.a., seashells and a large variety of other animal fossils started to show up.

When the western half of the continent began to lift for the final time, and the sea drained slowly away to the east, it left behind this vast thickness of undisturbed sediments, hardened into rocks. It is these layers that were first thrust upward to make the Rockies and that are still seen over much of the range—primarily in the Canadian and Montana Rockies. Down in Colorado, and the higher ranges of Wyoming, the sediments have virtually disappeared, stripped off by erosion to expose the hard, old, metamorphic and igneous basement rocks.

As the continent buckled and broke, it did so in a complex fashion. Erosion of the uplifted rocks happened in different ways, depending on such factors as local weather and the speed of uplift. Each individual range has its own history. For example, in Colorado the uplift began about 70 m.y.a., later than to the west and north. By 45 m.y.a., the mountains were mostly worn down to a broad upland with sloping sides. After that, about 40 m.y.a., the San Juans and other volcanic ranges came on the scene in a period of volcanism lasting some 15 million years. As it was winding down, another uplift occurred, which heaved the entire area 5,000 feet higher to its present elevation. As some blocks of the crust rose, others appeared to fall. (Actually everything was rising at that time; a block that appeared to sink did so only relative to adjoining blocks.) One of these was the Rio Grande Rift, a gash that now carries the Rio Grande River and that extends from central Colorado all the way to Mexico. It was caused by the pulling apart of two adjacent blocks. One became the Sangre de Cristo Mountains, while on the other side, through weaknesses caused by the faulting, volcanoes erupted. The largest of these, the Jemez volcanic field with its famous caldera the Valle de los Bacas, is on a major break, where the rift shifts eastward between Albuquerque and Espanola.

The Yellowstone Plateau, by contrast, is a massive upwelling of volcanic material as young as one million years old. Some of its adjoining mountains—the Absarokas, for example—are also volcanic, while others, such as the Tetons and the Beartooths, are uplifted blocks of basement rock. The story of each range is unique and worth telling; this book describes local geology at appropriate places in the text.

The Ice Age

The final, or we should say the most recent, chapter of the story began about 2 m.y.a. with the coming of the Pleistocene, or the Ice Age. During at least three episodes, vast glaciers covered most of Canada and reached a short distance into the United States. At the same time, glaciers grew on the summits of the Rockies, flowing down valleys to meet the continental ice cap, or, in southern areas, simply melting as they reached the warmth of lower elevations. The glaciers created a distinctive landscape in the Rockies, characterized by broad U-shaped valleys,

The Tobacco Root Mountains, Montana.

The Anaconda-Pintler Wilderness includes the easternmost extension of the Idaho Batholith.

moraines, cirques and knife-edge ridges called arêtes—features which soon become familiar to mountain travelers.

The last advance of the ice ended about ten thousand years ago. Since then, the glaciers have been shrinking. They have disappeared entirely from valley bottoms and from even the highest parts of the southern Rockies. Just in the last 100 years, glaciers in the Canadian Rockies have shrunk by hundreds of yards, a trend that is observable worldwide. At least one glacier, the Vaux Glacier in the Selkirk Range of British Columbia, has begun to advance once more, but no one can say what that means.

HISTORY

The human history of the Rocky Mountains begins in shadows somewhere before the end of the last Ice Age. Skeletal remains and worked flint found in California have been dated as far back as 50,000 years, but these findings are controversial. It is generally accepted that people were widely scattered over the continent 10,000 years ago, and probably somewhat earlier. The first people came from Asia, judging by archaeological evidence. Even today marked physical and cultural similarities exist between the native peoples on both continents. And they came by land. At the peak of the last glaciation, when vast quantities of water were tied up by continental ice sheets, the seas would have been as much as 300 feet lower than they are at present. A drop of only 150 feet would expose a land bridge across the Bering Strait between Siberia and Alaska more than 100 miles wide; with a 300-foot drop, the width would be 1,000 miles.

They had more than one opportunity to make the crossing. Geologists tell us that glaciers have advanced and retreated several times in the past 50,000 years, and that the Beringia Bridge, as they call this strip of land, has a history of repeated, cyclic exposures. For a time more than 35,000 years ago, it was exposed, then inundated until 25,000 years ago, then exposed for another 10,000 years, and flooded ever since. People may have crossed at any or all of those times.

They were nomads, hunter-gatherers who followed migratory beasts as they moved from place to place, going where the herds led them. They used, and left for archaeologists to find, a variety of stone tools, which closely resemble the sort used at the same time in eastern Asia. Then, about eleven to twelve thousand years ago, something happened. A new and elegant sort of stone spear point began to appear, one different from anything developed in the Old World, and distributed as far south as the Strait of Magellan. These points are called Clovis and

Folsom by archaeologists. They are different from each other but of the same time period and apparently used for the same purposes—to kill large game such as mammoths and the immense, long-horned bison.

The development of these stone points coincided with two other significant events. The first was a change in climate; the vast glaciers were in retreat. And second, a huge number of species disappeared from North America. Thirty-one separate genera, including mammoths, giant sloths, camels and other big animals—perhaps thousands of species in all—became extinct in a short time. We know them now only as fossils, as skeletons dug from riverbanks and frozen carcasses recovered from the permafrost of the far north. The coincidence of these three events—the Clovis and Folsom points, the end of the Ice Age and the mass extinction of so many large mammals—has touched off a series of unresolved, far-reaching questions. Did the animals die as a result of the rapidly changing climate? Was it the hunters, suddenly in possession of a new and more efficient weapon, who caused their extermination? Perhaps the new points were developed in response to diminishing numbers of animals and the need for a more efficient tool? Or was it a combination of these factors?

The answer remains a matter of theory, but evidence from ancient campsites describes an interesting sequence in the eating habits of these people. For about two thousand years after the new points appeared, the diets of their users were almost entirely meat, suggesting that hunting was easy. After that, people started eating more plants and fish, as evidenced by grain grinding stones and the location of camps beside rivers and lakeshores. Either they discovered fishing and agriculture, and adopted them as supplements to their hunting, or they were forced to develop new food sources, an idea that fits in with the concurrent die-off of so many species. Whatever the cause of the changes, agriculture became more and more important, until major cultures in the American Southwest, Mexico and Central America were based on domesticated plants and animals—especially corn, beans and squash, the vegetable triumvirate of the Southwest.

In the Rocky Mountains and adjacent plains, meanwhile, people kept to hunting and gathering as a primary means of survival, basing their cultures on the plains bison and animals such as elk and deer. They hunted on foot, with dogs as their only pack animals. Then Columbus made his voyage, and with the Spanish came horses. Native Americans immediately recognized the value of these animals and slowly, but with great determination, managed to acquire horses for themselves. By doing so, they revolutionized their lives, altered relationships among tribes, and developed into the powerful nomads who met the first travelers from the East Coast.

The first Europeans to see the Rockies were the Spanish in New Mexico. Coronado reached the Pueblo cities of the Rio Grande in 1540. He made little mention of what is now called the Sangre de Cristo Range and went no farther north than Taos. Spanish explorers after him showed the same lack of interest; but then, the Spanish were not fur traders, and their routes of commerce ran south of the mountains. Interest in the Rockies was stronger to the north, where the earliest reported sighting occurred in 1743. A French fur trader traveling from Canada, Sieur de la Verendrye, was trying to unravel the mystery of the Missouri River. He hoped to find a route to the Pacific Ocean, and although he came nowhere near the Continental Divide, two of his sons reported having glimpsed snowy mountains in the far distance.

Gradually, through the efforts of many explorers and adventurers, most of them involved with the search for furs and a feasible trade route to the coast, knowledge of western North America grew. Sailors brought back reports of their journeys along the Pacific coast. Shadowy stories circulated through the frontier communities of the Mississippi Valley, told by traders and travelers who had been varying distances up the Missouri River. In 1793, the great explorer Alexander Mackenzie pushed his way via the Peace River, in what is now northern British Columbia, all the way to the coast at Bella Coola. He was the first European to cross the continent. Although this was a major achievement, what his company needed was a shorter, more southerly route. Toward this end, the North West Company established Rocky Mountain House at the foot of the Rockies in 1799. But still, at the time of the Louisiana Purchase in 1803, the Rocky Mountain West was a great mystery. No one knew how far it was from the Pacific coast to the headwaters of the Missouri River, or where the Columbia River began, or even where the Spanish settlements of Santa Fe sat in relation to other features.

When he became president, Thomas Jefferson resolved to learn what was out there. The acquisition of Louisiana Territory merely added to his determination, and the famous 1804-05 journey of exploration by Meriwether Lewis and William Clark was the result. As much as anything, it was a commercial expedition, intended to assess the natural resources and trade potential of the Northwest, and above all, to find out if a feasible water route existed across the continent.

Their success, and the threat of American domination of West Coast trade routes, served to light a fire under the United States' northern neighbors. In 1806, David Thompson of the North West Company was instructed to cross the mountains, locate the headwaters of the Columbia River, and determine whether the river could be used to transport furs to the coast. He accomplished the job with characteristic panache and proved that the Columbia was indeed a feasible highway to the interior. This was the beginning of a long competition between the Americans, the Canadians based in Montreal, and the British of the Hudson's Bay Company, for control of the Rocky Mountain fur trade. It saw British posts as far south as the Snake River in southern Idaho, and British fur brigades in central Utah. It involved desperate struggles between Indian tribes trying to acquire rifles and trade goods, while preventing their rivals from doing the same. The Americans would encourage and equip one tribe; the Canadians another.

During this period, a new sort of frontiersman appeared on the scene—the mountain man. Until they turned their eyes toward the Rockies, companies acquired furs by building trading posts, filling them with things the local tribes wanted, and waiting for the Indians to appear with furs to trade. But in the Rockies, where mountain tribes were half-hearted trappers at best, and where competition between British and American concerns was intense, trapping developed into a profession engaged in by brigades of Americans or Canadians who were either employed directly by the trading companies, or were free trappers who sold their furs in exchange for equipment.

Thus began perhaps the most romantic period of Rocky Mountain history. For a brief 20 years between 1825 and 1845, the mountain men searched for beaver skins in every stream and mountain range they could find. Theirs was a hard life. Only a few extremely capable men survived the combined difficulties of isolation, weather, hunger, rivalry with native Americans, grizzly bears, accidental injury, and not by any means the smallest obstacle, the simple sheer hard work involved in trapping beaver for a living. To a few entrepreneurs, the fur trade was an opportunity to build fortunes (although more were lost than gained in the attempt), and the same motive—profit—was the ostensible reason for the mountain men to labor at their profession. Yet something in the life itself seems to have been a more compelling motive than money. Something about the West and its mountains and the freedom of unlimited horizons held an undeniable appeal for those who experienced it. Later would come the miners, the settlers, the military men, the politicians and all the others whose love for the geography, if they felt any attraction to it at all, was secondary to their aspirations of economic gain. By all accounts, the mountain men as a group were different. However great the disparity between their legend and their reality (and the disparity is great; these were hardly buckskin-clad knights of the Rocky Mountain Round Table), they truly seem to have felt a passion for the territory they so hungrily explored.

Jim Bridger, probably the most famous mountain man of them all, led, at one point, a brigade consisting of hundreds of independent trappers and camp followers, a virtual tribe of nomads who survived by the same skills and organizational structure as their native neighbors. Bridger eventually retired to Missouri, where he sat out his last years going slowly blind on a small farm. "I wish I war back thar among the mountains agin," he is quoted as having said. "A man kin see so much farther in that country."

It was a high life, but only for those who were capable. At its most active, the Rocky Mountain fur trade employed around a thousand nomadic trappers, along with their families and camp tenders; according to historian David Lavender, at least 182 of those were killed by Indians between 1805 and 1845. They had the run of the West, with not a fence or a road between Taos and the missions of California, not a settlement all the way from the mouth of the Columbia River to the lower Missouri River. With good horses and Hawken rifles, that entire magnificent stretch of geography was theirs to roam, for as long as they could stay alive and free enough of rheumatism and arthritis (occupational hazards for men who spent much of their time thigh-deep in the icy beaver streams setting and pulling traps) to keep on the move.

Romantic as their life may seem from our modern perspective, the mountain men were only the first of wave upon wave of migrants to the Rockies in search of something to exploit, to cut down or dig up and sell to consumers back east. For in truth, even the mountain men, for all their vaunted independence, were tied to the eastern and European market for beaver felt hats. Not only did the fashion turn eventually toward silk, but trappers themselves, in what has become a classic approach to making a living in the West, exploited their resource until beaver were too scarce for the effort. The mountain men in effect put themselves out of business and faded away to become guides, storekeepers, farmers or wanderers.

The first wave of settlers were people headed for Oregon and California—farmers looking for open lands. Their trail led them up the North Platte River and over South Pass to the Green River in Wyoming. Some headed south at that point, bound for California, the rest turned north across southern Idaho on their way to the fertile Willamette Valley. What began as a trickle became a flood. Driven from Missouri and then from Illinois, the Mormons came in 1847 seeking a place where they could be free of persecution. They had hardly put up a building when the California gold rush began, a lucky occurrence for the struggling Mormons. They made good money selling livestock and surplus food from their first successful harvest, taking in return a huge variety of goods, which the forty-niners were happy to be rid of at that point.

Central City, where the Colorado Gold Rush began in 1859.

It is ironic to think of how many westward bound settlers hurried past the Rockies, convinced that nothing of value lay there, that the mountains were nothing but immense barriers to be crossed and forgotten. Prospectors loaded with mining equipment rolled past streambeds that were later to yield millions. Settlers looking only for farmland struggled through some of the finest agricultural valleys in the country. Except for the Mormons, a few missionaries and the occasional solitary settler, travelers to the Rocky Mountains were transients in every sense.

That changed with the Colorado gold rush of 1859. It began a year earlier when Green Russell, a prospector from Georgia, dug into the bank of Cherry Creek at the foot of the mountains where Denver, Colorado, is now located. That digging produced a mere $600 worth of gold, which was no fortune even in 1858, but even so, the news of it set off an enthusiastic stampede by thousands of people willing to gamble that where a little had been found there must be plenty more.

They had reason to be excited. In 1859, the average daily wage for a laborer in the East was around a dollar—if he could find the work at all. A depression had hit the Mississippi Valley in 1857, leaving hundreds of unemployed, financially desperate men looking for opportunity. To their ears came the rumors of gold, and best of all, placer gold, which is the most easy to mine. Eroded from the bedrock by water and wind, it lies in the gravels and sediments of streambeds. Because of its weight, it sinks down through lighter materials, coming to rest against bedrock or in pockets created by large boulders. Any man with a shovel could get to it; then, by using a metal pan or a simple wooden sluice, perhaps with the addition of mercury to which gold dust readily clings, he could separate the gold from the gravel. All he had to do was get there, mark out a claim, throw up a crude shelter and start scooping up the gold.

It was indeed just about that simple, although for a brief time there were angry cries of hoax among early arrivals to the mountains. As it developed, Green Russell had been extraordinarily lucky; he found the only gold Cherry Creek was ever to produce. Quite a few of the 1859 stampeders took one look at the creek and turned back for home. These "Go-Backs," as those who remained called them in derision, spread their pessimism eastward as they retreated, convincing some of the other stampeders as they went. In all, perhaps fifty thousand set out for the mountains that year only to give up without really trying.

Many of them must have spent the rest of their lives wishing they had persisted, because at the very time the Go-Backs were feeling most injured, a man named John Gregory, while tracking a group of elk in the mountains above Cherry Creek, stopped to prospect on a frozen gravel bar of Clear Creek. He found gold, and after waiting long enough to assure himself that he had the best claim in the area, he let the news escape to the crowds then pouring into the infant town of Denver. Typically, word spread quickly. A wave of jubilant miners jammed into Gregory Gulch until all claims were taken. Miners kept coming, and when they saw that there was no room left for them there, they simply headed on into the mountains, panning as they went, and were rewarded. Creekbed after creekbed yielded rich, easily obtained deposits of gold.

Some of the gold strikes were truly fabulous, but not even the richest lode could match the ability of writers and storytellers to gild reality. An Iowa newspaper reported to its readers in 1860: "We learn from a man just returned from Pikes Peak [the name used then for the area around Denver, without regard for its location 50 miles north of the actual Pikes Peak] that gold there lies in bands or strata down the slope. The custom of the best miners is to construct heavy wooden sleds with iron ribs similar to a stone boat. These are taken to the top of the peak, several men get into each one and guide it down over the strata. The gold curls up on the boat, like shavings, and is gathered in as they progress. This is the usual method of collecting it."

Each time a strike was announced, mobs of miners would appear on the scene, getting there by whatever means they could command, be it on foot or on horseback, alone or in hastily formed companies. As soon as each placer bar was claimed to the limit, the hordes overflowed in all directions again, chasing the thinnest of rumors into unfamiliar country, from Gregory Gulch through central Colorado to Tarryall, Fairplay, Breckenridge and others.

From Colorado they poured northward into Idaho, where gold was found near Orofino ("Pure Gold"), and south into the Salmon River country, paying no heed to Indian objections to their trespass. Elk City and Florence exploded into existence, filled to capacity and overflowed toward Montana, where strikes at Deer Lodge led to better ground at Bannack, and on to Alder Gulch, where on May 26, 1863, the biggest placer source in the Rockies was found. With its 17-mile length, and eventual yield of some $35 million, Alder Gulch was claimed up in a matter of months, and the tide moved on north to Last Chance Gulch, site of modern Helena and more gold.

Meanwhile, in British territory, the scene was much the same, although British authorities were able to maintain order and avoid the vigilante violence of the American gold camps. Pay dirt was hit in 1858 in the Fraser River Valley, attracting mobs of Californians. As the Fraser looked to be played out, bigger scores were made far inland in the Cariboo Valley, and the crowds swelled in that direction as if magnetized.

It was a wild and frantic decade. Hundreds of thousands of hopeful miners swarmed across the West, their enthusiasm fueled at every turn by tales of sudden wealth. They heard about men who months earlier had never seen a mountain or a gold pan stumbling across placer claims where the gold was measured not in ounces or pounds but tons. They listened to each success story fully aware that they were playing a continental-sized game of musical chairs, with hundreds of prospectors vying for every available seat. The music, they knew, would stop soon enough; meanwhile, they all stepped a little faster.

A slim few ever turned a profit from their efforts. When the totals for that first ten years of excitement are added up, they are less impressive than one might expect. Colorado, by 1869, had produced $27 million; Idaho's count by 1867 was $45 million; and Montana, by the same year, had produced $65 million (compared with the California gold fields, which in their first ten years yielded $550 million).

Most gold miners had no interest in remaining in a place once the scent of gold was gone. The mountains to them represented an opportunity to strike it rich so that they could go back to their families and other ambitions. They were raiders in every sense, looters who ruthlessly tore from the earth anything they could find to sell, and with no concerns for how they did it. Historian David Lavender, explaining why people tolerated vigilante law in western mining towns, puts the issue in a broader perspective: "Since few of the stampeders expected to be around that long [long enough for the establishment of responsible authority, that is], why bother—any more than they bothered about fouled streams, burned forests, dead dogs in the streets, or lost gold in their careless mills? ... After all, each citizen had his work to do. If one value disappeared in order that another might be gleaned as quickly as possible, why, that was just one of the hard facts of the mountain present. The future would have to take care of itself."

Of course, the future did just that. By the early 1870s, placer mining was virtually dead. As easy gains disappeared, the territorial population of Idaho fell from a peak of over thirty thousand in 1863 to less than half that ten years later. Many of those who remained were Chinese miners who, through more careful work, gleaned a living from claims abandoned or sold cheap by white prospectors who were impatient with any but bonanza gains.

Not everyone fled from the mountains when the rush died. Many of the people who came in the path of the miners were merchants, newspapermen, professionals, farmers, land speculators and visionaries of every stripe. They made money supplying miners, building roads, running water supply lines, cutting wood, driving cattle and performing a variety of services. In doing so, they laid the cornerstones of a much broader, more lasting economy. Some of them, recognizing the long-term opportunities, decided to stay. Gradually, events justified their optimism. The first transcontinental railroad was built from both directions, west from Iowa and east from San Francisco, meeting near Ogden, Utah. That touched off construction of competing lines and of spurs to serve the bypassed cities of Denver and Salt Lake.

Things progressed more slowly in Canada, partly because until 1869 the Hudson's Bay Company owned the midsection of the country, and British Columbia was still a British colony. Nonetheless, events ran parallel in both countries. Canada acquired the Hudson's Bay Company lands and accepted British Columbia's bid to join the nation in 1871. The transcontinental line, after nearly twenty years of construction drama, was completed in 1886. The railroads of both nations were permanent developments, requiring not only supplies for construction but for operation as well. To pay for construction, the United States and Canada made massive land grants to the Union Pacific and the Canadian Pacific, respectively, with the expectation that immigrants would purchase homesteads and cities would sprout up as service and supply centers.

The other major factor in the development of permanent settlements in the Rockies was the shift from placer mining to hard rock, or lode, mining. This involved massive capitalization, many employees, smelters to handle complex ores and a gamut of support services from lumbering (for smelter fuel and construction) to ranching, farming, storekeeping and freight hauling, whether by muleback, wagon or rail. Not only did lode mines pay for these services, but their life expectancies were also long enough to justify major construction. The big mines during this period were at Leadville, Cripple Creek, Silverton, Aspen, Kellogg and Butte, among others. Silver, copper, lead, zinc and other lesser minerals augmented or replaced income from gold. Through boom and bust, through labor battles and international financial intrigue, the Rockies kept pouring out precious metal—building railroads, highways, towns and fortunes.

The towns built in this way were notorious for large populations of single men and the businesses surrounding their pleasures. For example, Wallace, Idaho, in 1890 had 28 saloons for 913 residents, plus miners from surrounding areas. Pretty serious drinking, but the Little League compared to Leadville, Colorado, which in 1879 boasted 10,000 people, 128 saloons, 115 gambling houses, 35 brothels, 19 wholesale liquor dealers, 51 groceries, 17 hardware stores, 12 shoe-stores, 4 banks, 3 newspapers, 9 book and stationery stores, and a music store. That was a typical list for mining towns of its day.

Even the hard-rock mines played out eventually, taking from 10 to 100 years to do so. As the veins ran out, or as world mineral prices fell, many towns died, or shrank drastically. Today, ghost towns litter the mountain states and provinces, and the decline continues, even where the veins have not been depleted. Butte, Montana, for example, still has ample ore, but the price of copper has fallen so low—telecommunications has eliminated much of the need for copper wire—that all mining and smelting activity has now ceased. With a population at its height of 140,000 people, Butte has shrunk to around 35,000.

These are the problems the West continues to deal with. Its economy has been based on the exploitation of primary resources, many of which are nonrenewable. When the resource is gone, or when the bottom falls out of the market, disaster follows. The lesson has been learned even in regard to renewable resources, which are capable of sustaining a more stable economy. In northern Idaho, for example, the gold rush was followed by a timber rush at the turn of the century, complete with claim jumpers and bloody battles. The logging industry reached its peak in the 1920s, with annual harvests in Idaho's St. Joe National Forest alone of 300 million board feet, most of it white pine. In the pattern established by the placer miners, loggers ruthlessly stripped away the most accessible timber, and when that was gone the mills closed, throwing even more unemployed men into the Great Depression. It still happens. Overgrazing, reckless timber cutting, poorly planned water projects and irresponsible mineral developments still occur and are the source of lively, sometimes heated controversy.

The pressure on basic resources can only increase as population grows. Throughout the mountains, change is happening at a dizzying pace.

The Rockies as Jim Bridger saw them remain, in many respects, just as we see them today. Mountains endure fairly well in the face of human impact. Yet the scale of change, when one stops to think that virtually every alteration has occurred in about a century and a half, is boggling. Every road in the region, every railroad track, every building north of New Mexico, every fence, every mine, every dam, every town, every map, in short, everything not done by native Americans before the advent of Europeans to the Rocky Mountains, has been done since the early 1800s, and by far the bulk of that has appeared in the last 50 years. Primary resources have fueled all that change. As they run low, the challenge for the West is to find more self-sustainable ways for its citizens to make a living.

CLIMATE

If there is any rule of mountain climate, it is variety. Mountains are large enough features that they can make their own weather, or alter what comes past them. A single range, or even a single mountain, might have any number of separate, distinct climatic zones distributed on its slopes. With altitude come changes in temperature, rainfall and wind velocity. As a general rule, mountains get colder, wetter and windier the higher you go. In addition, because of differences in solar exposure, prevailing winds or moisture retention, climate will vary from one side of the mountain to the other. It will vary even on opposite sides of a ridge, or a band of trees, or a boulder.

The differences are reflected by vegetation, and usually you can use the plants of a mountain as indicators of each particular climatic zone. For instance, spruce and fir trees indicate better soil and more moisture than ponderosa pine, while willows and cottonwoods grow only where the ground is saturated. Meadows of grass can be dry; meadows of sedge are always wet. You can walk along a ridge in southwestern Montana and find prickly pear cactus on one side and a lush forest of spruce and fir on the other. Undoubtedly, the cactus will be on the southern side, which faces the winter sun and dries out faster than the northern side. Within a hundred feet of each other are two very different climates, supporting very different biologic communities.

In a sense, the plants have learned the same lesson that experienced mountain travelers turn to their advantage: if you prefer a different climate from the one you are currently in, you have only to move—up, down or to the side—to find a more comfortable one. In the Midwest, if you find winter too cold, you must travel many miles and degrees of latitude to the south to get warm. In the mountains, let's say in Silverton, Colorado, which at 9,300 feet is a cold and snowy place, you have only to descend to Durango or Farmington, an hour or two distant. Admittedly, Farmington is not the tropics, but its climate is far warmer than Silverton's.

The same is true on a much smaller scale. I once lived in a cabin which stood at the edge of a large mountain meadow. The summit of the mountain was 4,000 feet above the cabin, and every night when the air was calm, I could feel the cold draining off the mountain like water flowing off a glacier. In the summer, this river of air brought cool fragrance with it. In the winter, it brought intense cold. The cabin had been built a century earlier by someone who understood the motion of air on that mountain. It was located on a small knoll at the very edge of the air drainage. After a hot day, I would walk 30 feet from the cabin and immerse myself in that coolness. A person thinking only in terms of summer might have been tempted to build the house there, but in winter, that spot would often be 20 degrees colder than on the knoll. I soon grew to appreciate the cabin's sensible location.

With a little practice, you can just about choose the sort of climate you prefer. When hiking, it makes sense to avoid south-facing slopes on hot summer days, but to seek them out in winter. A campsite is chosen to avoid cold-air drainage. The same concept affects other decisions: in July, wet areas are filled with mosquitoes, while in September, berry patches can be filled with bears. The decisions to avoid such places all come back to climate and the knowledge that just over the rise is a different one.

On the other hand, some trends are different from what you might expect. Everyone knows, for instance, that the farther south you go in the northern hemisphere, the warmer things get. For that reason, if you were interested in taking an early-season hiking trip in the Rockies, it would be reasonable to look to Colorado instead of Alberta. But you also have to consider a few other factors. The first is elevation. The mountains of Colorado are much higher than those of Alberta. Colorado's average elevation is 6,800 feet, a figure that includes the state's eastern plains. Quite a few of its mountain towns are over 8,000 feet high, and some are a good bit higher than that: Silverton (9,318 feet), Breckenridge (9,603), Leadville (10,152) and Climax (11,320). Compare these with the elevations in Canada, where Kimberley, British

Columbia, is billed as the highest city in the nation at just over 3,500 feet, and Banff (classed as a town, not a city) sits only a little higher at 4,538 feet. As a further comparison, Colorado contains every one of the 54 peaks in the Rockies that are over 14,000 feet high, including the highest, Mount Elbert, at 14,433 feet, whereas the highest peak in the Canadian Rockies is Mount Robson, at 12,972 feet.

This is not to say that the Canadian Rockies are somehow less grand than their Colorado counterparts. On the contrary, Colorado's mountains need every foot of extra elevation just to hold their own against the magnificent ranges located farther north. But their added height goes a long way to even out whatever climatic differences would be caused by being so much farther south.

The effect of latitude is obvious when you look at relative elevations of timberline. On Wheeler Peak, in the Sangre de Cristo Range of New Mexico (latitude 36 degrees), timberline is around 12,000 feet. On the U.S.-Canada border, with a latitude of 49 degrees, trees disappear above 7,000 feet. That figure comes down steadily as you continue north, until in the northern Yukon, in the true Arctic, the mountains have no trees whatsoever.

One other factor, besides latitude and altitude, affects mountain climate, and that is the effect of the earth's rotation on the density of the atmosphere. Our planet is not a perfect sphere. As it spins, it bulges a little at the equator and flattens in a corresponding manner at the poles. This is because centrifugal force is strongest at the equator, and the mass of the earth, being somewhat plastic, tends to flow in that direction. The atmosphere does the same, so that a barometer held at sea level on the Mackenzie River delta will record less pressure than a barometer on a ship in the Panama Canal. If the air feels heavier in the tropics, it may be because it in fact is.

The difference can definitely be felt on high mountain summits. Climbers say that an ascent of Mount Denali, 20,032 feet, (also called Mount McKinley after an American president who is most famous for having been shot while shaking hands with his assassin) is the equivalent in terms of climate and oxygen deprivation to a Himalayan peak measuring 24,000 feet but standing much nearer the equator. The atmosphere around Denali is that much thinner.

In the Rockies, then, you might head south looking for warmth only to find that changes in altitude have compensated for changes in latitude, and the snow is just as deep in the Jemez Range as it was in the Bitterroots of Montana. No one would argue that the seasons are the same. After all, winter days are longer in the south. Also, the Jemez have southern Arizona for a neighbor, while the town of Jasper cozies up against northern Alberta. But as a general rule, it seems that wherever you go in the Rocky Mountains, the seasons arrive at more or less the same time. What follows is a summary of an annual weather cycle.

The Mountain Year

Snow can fall at any time in the Rockies, even in July, but it never stays for long until some time in November. And then, usually by December 1 but some years a month earlier than that, winter—hard, solid, serious winter—comes to stay. It is, simply said, the most beautiful winter anywhere, winter the way it was meant to be, with sparkling blue skies, warm sun and powder snow. Generally, there's a lot of snow, with a few notorious places—Wolf Creek Pass in Colorado, Little Cottonwood Canyon near Salt Lake City, and Rogers Pass in the Selkirk Range of British Columbia—where the snow is measured in feet, not inches.

Temperatures *can* get terribly cold. The coldest night ever recorded in the United States outside of Alaska was -69°F in a remote basin of Utah. That was an extreme case, in which scientists placed sensing devices where they predicted the coldest air would lie: no one lives in the high basin they chose. Nonetheless, subzero nights are routine in the mountains. Thin air cools quickly, sending its heat into frequently clear night skies. Minus 40, whether Fahrenheit or Celsius, is no big deal. What makes the cold tolerable is that as soon as the sun appears in the morning, the air feels warm and before long icicles are dripping. The high altitude sun has great strength.

In many regards, mountain winters are milder than winters in the upper Midwest or New England. The infamous cold spells of the plains, caused by masses of arctic air which come south like glaciers to blanket the ground for weeks at a time, almost never have the depth they would need to surmount the Rockies. Out on the plains of Alberta, Edmonton suffers more from cold than Kimberley, British Columbia, located across the Continental Divide in the protection of the mountains. The same pattern occurs throughout the year. Nights are cold, days are warm, with rarely too much of either. This strong daily shift quickly becomes one of the most endearing qualities of the mountain climate.

Less endearing is the way winter ends. It goes out like the expiring hero of a melodrama. Just when you think it's down for good, up it crawls once more, dragging itself from its grave to dump another load of wet, sloppy snow in the middle of May. Or June. Or July. It was way back in March that you first felt a hint of spring. One warm day, gentle winds brought the fragrance of thawed ground from some distant valley. Somewhere, you knew, the snow on south-facing slopes was melting and plants were beginning to sprout. You felt a surge of desire for the end of winter and optimism that warmth and greenery were soon to come. By June you know it was a cruel hoax.

The truth is, winter never really leaves the Rockies; it just goes to sleep for a while. Residents are reluctant to talk about spring. Instead, they call it mud season, or late winter, or refuse to acknowledge that it ever happens at all (witness the Never Summer Range in Rocky Mountain National Park). The old saying that there are only three seasons in the Rockies—July, August and winter—says much about the emotional state of residents during the snowstorms of May.

Despite the jokes, spring *is* a distinct season, which lasts about two months: April and May in the valley bottoms, May and June at higher elevations. It is a season characterized by unsettled weather. Occasional sunny days feel warm but retain the sharp bite of winter. More common are the spells of rotten, cantankerous weather with low, cloudy skies spitting wet snow or sleet. In valley bottoms, winter snows have melted away, but the ground remains soaked, covered with sad brown vegetation which knows better than to send out new shoots until matters improve. In higher areas and on north-facing slopes, snow still lies deep.

It's possible to go hiking at this time of year, but high country snows make it hard. The only way to get around is by skis or by traveling very early each day—by moonlight even—and planning to sit still after the sun warms things up and the snow loses its crust. Few activities are so exhausting as postholing your way through hip-deep spring slush. On the positive side, you'll likely have the place to yourself. Not only do you reap the silence of solitude, but you'll soon notice that another sound—that of running water—is also missing. The quiet of a high frost-locked basin on a moonless night is positively eerie.

By July 1, summer is at last in full swing. Most trails are open, and if not snow-free, at least the snow is hard enough to walk on. Everywhere, meadows are filled with wildflowers. Streams burst with water at the height of the runoff. Birds sit on nests and the large mammals—elk, bison, deer—show up in park meadows with their increasingly capable newborns. Mountain summers are profligate times. To compensate for the short season, everything happens in a rush. All the flowers seem to bloom at one time, all the insects to emerge on the same day. Mountain towns swing into busy schedules of activities: music festivals, sports events, rodeos, barbecues and parades. For a time, life in the mountains is a carnival, with every living thing celebrating. Near-daily thunderstorms build in the afternoons and fill the evenings with electricity, adding to the festive atmosphere.

Yet for all of the pleasures brought by summer, it has its drawbacks.

This is the most crowded time of the year. Campgrounds, highways and trails, boat docks and fishing streams are all filled to capacity. To drive anywhere, you join a parade of motorhomes and station wagons. Walking on trails, you join foot parades. Tempers shorten in the heat and traffic jams. Every mountain town goes a little bit crazy by August, as people in the tourist business begin to wonder why they ever got into this business. They want to disappear as the larger animals have, off to the high country, or into the deep shade of the forest. What they really crave is autumn and the return of peace.

Partly for those reasons, the fall has become my favorite mountain season. September offers many of the same rewards as summer, without the frustrations. A few frosts have cut back the biting insects. Fewer people compete for road space and campsites. In parks like Yellowstone, the big animals reappear along the roads and in the middle of meadows, dressed in flashy new winter pelage, engrossed in the excitement of the breeding season. Nights are frosty, morning air is crisp, days are often warm with utterly blue skies. In the lower valleys of the western slope of the Rockies, all the way from British Columbia to southern Colorado, apples, pears, peaches, apricots and other fruits are being harvested and offered for sale at roadside stands. Aspens, spread throughout the ranges but reaching their climax on the broad slopes of central Colorado, turn their brilliant, translucent yellow with occasional startling patches of blood red. In Canada, alpine larch, a deciduous conifer, puts on an equivalent show. In Utah and Wyoming, the willows and scrub oak ignite marshland and hillsides, while everywhere, in lower, drier country along rivers, serpentine stands of cottonwoods toss their golden leaves into the wind.

September is the month of Indian Summer, a halcyon time during which you can sense impending winter and value the warmth all the more for what is coming. These days last well into October most years, and sometimes longer. There might be a week of storm, which for some reason often happens during the second week of September, but for almost two months, autumn is as you wished spring had been.

GETTING AROUND IN THE ROCKIES

Like most of North America, the Rocky Mountain region is set up for people with cars. Backroads, sunsets, campgrounds, unplanned stops and most trailheads are accessible only by private vehicle. An ordinary passenger car will take you most places, even on the majority of backwoods forest roads. A general rule is that if the Forest Service maintains a camp-

ground (indicated by signposts or by symbols on roadmaps) at the end of
a road, then that road is passable to ordinary vehicles. Four-wheel drive
is useful in places, especially early and late in the season, when a few
inches of snow or a muddy patch can be enough to keep you from getting over a pass. However, there is truth in the saying that the difference
between two-wheel and four-wheel drive is that the "Four-by," as westerners call it, will just get you further in before you get stuck.

Most backroads wander through lands administered by the U.S.
Forest Service or the Bureau of Land Management, or in British
Columbia and Alberta, by the provincial governments. These roads have
been put in over the past 50 years for logging, fire-control and mining
purposes, and the majority of them remain open. Maps, published by
the individual forests, show all of these roads in a given area and are
indispensable for anyone spending much time on them. In addition,
many of the backroads are marked with signposts at various junctions
giving road numbers, mileages and destinations. This book gives the
numbers of roads where applicable, along with approximate mileages,
but I highly recommend that you acquire the right maps if you plan
much backroad rambling. A discussion of maps is on page 73.

There is public transport in the mountains, but there seems to be less
of it each year. And because buses and trains run between population
centers, those who come to the mountains to find solitude will have a
hard time getting a bus to take them there. Trailheads of the Anaconda-
Pintlar Wilderness Area are not part of the Greyhound system.

There are, however, excellent alternatives to needing a car. In places,
notably the national parks like Glacier, Rocky Mountain, Banff and
Jasper, it's possible to arrive by public conveyance and then not look at
the inside of a vehicle again until you leave. Whether you camp out or
stay in lodges, you can walk each day on a different and rewarding trail.
If you want to see more of a given park than you can by walking, you
have the option of switching hotels or campgrounds part way through
your visit. For example, you could spend a week at the Many Glacier
area of Glacier National Park and walk a new trail or do a new activity each day. If you wanted to see more of the park, you could move on
to one of the other hotel complexes or campgrounds served by park
transportation. People happily spend entire summers in Glacier without
ever going more than a few miles at a time in a vehicle. Of course,
opportunities like these are limited to pretty heavily developed areas,
but there is much reason to recommend them.

Along the same lines, many mountain resort towns cater to the needs
of people who arrive without transport. Aspen stands out for its wealth
of opportunities, but others rival it: Banff, Jasper, Ketchum, Vail,

Telluride, Crested Butte and Estes Park among them.

Bicycle travel is getting more popular all the time, particularly with the recent development of mountain bikes. These look like reincarnations of the old American balloon tire vehicle of the '50s, but the resemblance stops there. With as many as 18 gears, special frames, beefed-up components, fat lugged tires and long wheel bases, mountain bikes are strictly high tech. They are also a new concept, for which forest managers have yet to develop regulations. In one view, mountain bikes are simply motorless dirt bikes; they may be quiet, but their tires are capable of doing the same damage as their noisy, prohibited cousins. Perhaps they do more damage, because they are easily carried past obstructions which stop heavier motorcycles.

Regardless of their future on foot trails, mountain bikes are here to stay as efficient vehicles for thousands of miles of dirt and gravel roads throughout the Rockies. You see these bikes everywhere now, with a few hotbeds of fat-tire fanatics. Crested Butte, Colorado, is fast becoming the world capital of mountain bikes.

Of course, the only way to really understand mountains is to walk in them. Get away from the insulated world of the vehicle and measure the trails with your feet, out where you can smell the air, feel the weather, touch the rock and get hold of elemental parts of yourself. Anyone can take a stroll in the mountains, to some degree, regardless of age, physical condition or even handicaps like wheelchairs. The mountains are jammed with places where even short walks—walks of a hundred yards or less—will transport you light years from the world of autos and roads and service stations. See the next chapter for information on hiking and backpacking.

MOUNTAIN ACTIVITIES

The Rockies are a friendly place, and easy to visit. No great mobilization is needed to make the trip, unlike a visit to Alaska or Africa or Nepal. You can drive your own car wherever you wish to go, or arrive at many locations by convenient public transport. You can camp out or stay in motels and lodges. You can cook over a campfire or take your meals at places ranging from hamburger joints to expensive French restaurants which advise you to make reservations a week in advance. You can spend upwards of $200 per day, or cruise along quite happily on less than $20. People with no outdoor experience whatsoever, and just a little prudence, have as much reason to expect a safe, happy holiday as the most experienced mountaineer. For in some way, the mountains are suited to everyone, whether you want to walk, float a river, stay with your family in one campground for two weeks, or just take a scenic driving tour.

Hiking and Backpacking

Of all mountain activities, walking is easily the most natural. It costs nothing; almost everyone can do it with no instruction (an increasing number of trails are negotiable by wheelchair); children do it as well as, if not better than, their parents; with the exception of birds and fish, all the other living things in the mountains get around by walking, which promotes the feeling that this is the natural thing to do; it leaves you feeling wonderfully healthy; and it requires no specialized equipment. Not even boots are needed, although if you're thinking of heading off trail or camping out, you obviously need more than if you're just out for a couple of hours of walking along a lakeshore. There are trails almost everywhere, some well maintained, others primitive or barely existent. Some are actually paved and as level as an urban sidewalk.

If you have done little mountain walking, it's wise to develop mountain savvy in places where trails are well maintained and routes are clearly marked by signs. That way you can learn about your stamina, your hiking speed, mountain weather, the effects of altitude, and so forth in a reasonably controlled setting. Such trails are found in national parks, which is one reason so many people choose parks as their hiking destinations. In some parks, you can register with the rangers and feel secure that they will come looking for you if you fail to show up at the end of the day.

Even if you aren't concerned about registering for safety reasons, it's a good idea to check with ranger stations whenever you have questions about trails. In national parks and some wilderness areas, permits are required for overnight stays, so you must see a ranger to get one. In other places, it helps simply to get an idea of what is available. The most popular trail may not be the best; rangers are more than happy to steer hikers to alternate places, thereby taking pressure off overused trails, and making things more pleasant for all involved. Most U.S. Forest Service offices keep on file complete inventories of trails, with descriptions and information pertinent to each. If all you get from a visit to a ranger station is advice about a footbridge that has washed away, along with directions to an alternate crossing just downstream, the time has been well spent. On the other hand, with budget cutbacks being felt at all levels of government, you might have to look hard to find a ranger with any recent knowledge of trail conditions. This is not usually their fault; they would like to be out on the trails, but paperwork takes precedence over fieldwork for many of them.

You can find somewhere to walk from April until late October. The season is longer at lower altitudes and in the southern end of the range, and much shorter in the high country, where snow sometimes keeps passes closed to the hiker until the end of June. Each year varies; the general rule for a mountain backpack trip is to plan it for no earlier than July and to look for snow by the end of September.

Wilderness areas are less regulated than national parks and are the choice of experienced hikers, but even these, particularly the more famous ones, are becoming crowded to the point of overuse; at least one, Indian Peaks Wilderness outside of Denver, already has a permit and quota system in effect. As alternatives, there are numerous de facto wilderness areas, which are neither officially designated nor supervised. Some of them are well worth visiting and are entirely uncrowded at the height of the season, pointing out that if you think creatively, you can find personal secret places.

No matter how crowded a popular place may be, it is usually possible to find solitude just a short distance from heavily used trails and campsites. Hikers like to think of themselves as independent souls, but they rarely seem to use imagination about where to go; instead, they follow the footprints of thousands who have gone before them, camping in the same sites, searching for wood in the same picked-over groves of trees. A statistic that is popularly cited by employees of Yellowstone National Park (and probably close to the truth) is that 99 percent of visitors never get more than 200 yards from their cars, and that 99 percent of those who do go walking never leave the trails.

There may be nothing wrong in that. Each summer season, more than two million people pass through Yellowstone, and from a strict management viewpoint, it's best to keep the traffic channeled, orderly, controlled and moving. A fleet of motorhomes and station wagons cruising past an alpine meadow on a paved road does far less damage to that meadow than all the passengers of those vehicles would if they parked (which would require a parking area) and walked through it sniffing the flowers and treading on delicate plants. In the same way, if hikers keep to the trails, their impact is limited to smaller areas than if they took off helter skelter across the landscape. If the trails are well graded and protected against erosion, then all the better. It seems to be what most people want.

Happily for bushwhackers, the alternative is always available. As of this writing, none of the parks or wilderness areas in the Rockies prohibit off-trail travel for properly equipped hikers and climbers (with the exception of certain limited, highly fragile places such as the geyser basins of Yellowstone, or archaeological zones such as the backcountry of Mesa Verde).

But the day of such restrictions may be approaching. Permit systems are on the increase, particularly in national parks, where the demand is greatest. Often there aren't enough permits to go around. On popular western boating rivers, the demand far outstrips the supply of permits; you could apply every year of your life for permission to float the Selway River in Idaho, and still the odds would be against your ever being allowed to make the trip. When, or if, the same sort of limitations will apply to certain popular hiking trails is a matter of conjecture. But when you consider the ever-increasing popularity of the country's wild areas, it seems that trail quotas and other restrictions are inevitable.

Where backcountry camping quotas are in effect, there are two systems. One is the zone system, under which a maximum number of hikers are allowed in a given valley or on the shore of a lake, but they are allowed to camp almost anywhere within that zone. The parks using this system encourage hikers to spread out, to distribute their impact lightly over a large area. In theory, this is fine. It works in some areas, and for hikers hoping for pristine surroundings, it is the preferred system. However, quite often hikers tend to choose the same places as people before them have chosen, and the end result is as bad or worse than the alternate system of designated campgrounds. Under this system, the wildness of each site is essentially written off, sacrificed to human impact with the expectation that the surrounding area will suffer less as a result. To this end, some parks have constructed picnic tables, outhouses, fireplaces and other "improvements" in their backcountry camps.

The idea behind permits is to limit impact on the backcountry, to screen out hikers who are ill-equipped or unaware of regulations, to collect statistics and to aid rescue efforts (rescuers know where to begin looking for lost campers). To a hiker, permits are a mixed blessing. If you can get one for where you want to go, it guarantees a reasonable degree of solitude. This, say the park managers who endorse the system, is the main reason: to preserve for the hiker a sense of wilderness, to preserve the aesthetic pleasures of the backcountry experience. Another benefit is that a marked campsite is a sure bet. If the ranger sends you to the shore of such-and-such lake, you can be fairly confident that camping is feasible there. You won't have to worry about thrashing around in the dark looking for a level place to pitch a tent.

On the negative side, permits can destroy the spontaneity of a backcountry trip, requiring you to go a certain distance despite the dictates of weather or personal inclinations. Many of the sites, because they are terribly overused, are unpleasant, sometimes dirty places to camp. Or they may be so poorly planned that they resemble the crowded auto camps in all their semiurban glory, packing far too many campers into a small area, destroying the very sense of isolation and contact with wildness that the planners were supposedly trying to preserve. Consideration for the quality of experience seems to have been put at the bottom of the priority list.

I know of far too many designated sites that seem to have been chosen hastily and with little regard for the aesthetic values of an area. One, in a mountain park, is located half a mile below a spectacular pass, in a boggy, windless, mosquito-infested hollow, which stays dank and muddy most of the summer and affords no hint of the magnificent view available on the pass. In glaring contrast, the pass is a particularly beautiful place, loaded with lovely, flat, sheltered campsites, each one with an unobstructed panorama of glaciers, deep valleys and ragged peaks. Until a few years ago, every hiker who came that way wanted to lay his bag somewhere along the pass, the better to see sunrise, sunset and moonlight on the mountains. To spend a night in that place epitomized the joys of mountain backpacking. I camped there quite a few times myself over the years, each time thinking that a night spent on the pass was the climax of the five-day hike which took me over it. As a friend whom I took there once said, "Not even Aristotle Onassis can afford a better view than that."

However, with the initiation of a permit system in that park, the pass was declared off limits. "No Camping" notices went up like so many Burma Shave signs. Hikers were assigned instead to the miserable hollow half a mile away, while people caught camping in the old places on the pass were issued citations, as if they had parked their cars on the White House lawn.

I understand the intentions of the park planner who made that decision. He was trying to restore and preserve the fragile vegetation of the pass, and in the process made a value judgment: it was better for campers to trample the ground in a nasty bug-ridden hollow, he reckoned, than to do the same on one of the most beautiful spots in the Rockies. As for myself, I think that before making the decision, he should have been required to live for a year in a city, doing some work that kept him far from his beloved wilderness park, and after months of organizing and anticipating, to finally hike up to that pass on a perfect summer evening, and only then decide where to put his sleeping bag.

On balance, for every uncareful planner there are dozens—maybe hundreds—of careless backcountry hikers who are blind to the damage their passing can do to the fragile mountain environment. Hikers have a responsibility to walk softly, to minimize their impact, perhaps even to go beyond what is required by regulations. Campfires and sanitation are the most important items for concern (see page 37).

Climbing

Mountains and climbing go together. Opportunities are everywhere, varying with rock type and mountain form. The Canadian Rockies, because of their rotten, sedimentary rock, are poor for rock-climbing but terrific for ice- and snow-climbing on their many glaciers. The best rock-climbing areas consist of harder rock: granite, gneiss, quartzite, metamorphosed limestone. In Canada, these sorts of rock are found in the interior ranges of British Columbia, such as the Purcells, where the Bugaboos are world-famous. In Wyoming, the Tetons can keep climbers happy for whole lifetimes; south of them, the Wind River Range has superb routes on some of the cleanest faces and pinnacles anywhere. And in Colorado, every other bump in the surface of the state cries out to climbers. Among the more famous places are Eldorado Canyon above the city of Boulder, and the Longs Peak Diamond in Rocky Mountain National Park.

It is not within the scope of this book to deal with technical climbing, beyond mentioning a few climbing schools at appropriate points in the text. If you are new to climbing and would like to learn, one of these schools is a good way to start. Self-instruction can be foolhardy.

River Running

The Rockies are home to some of the world's finest boating rivers, whether the crafts of choice are kayaks, rafts, canoes, dories or motorboats. Rentals are usually easy to find in resort towns, while outfitters and guides are everywhere. The season lasts from May through September, depending on levels of meltwater, and unless you have your heart set on rivers where use is restricted, you'll never want for boating in the Rockies.

Among the more famous whitewater rivers are the Salmon, the Clearwater, the Payette, the Kicking Horse, the Colorado and the Arkansas, all of them as wild as the mountains they inhabit, running for miles of water which is alternately white and green, rapids and deep quiet pools filled with trout.

Many other rivers flow peacefully for much of their length and make for pleasant boating in open canoes and rowboats. These stretches tend to run through wide ranching valleys between ranges, but not always.

The Snake River through Grand Teton National Park is a prime example of excellent canoeing water at the very base of the mountains. Even on these quiet streams, a certain degree of experience is important because of the hazards inherent in moving water as opposed to the quiet surface of a pond.

If you lack equipment or expertise (or for that matter, a permit, which in some places is the most essential item of all), you still have the option of going with a guided party. Virtually every runnable piece of river in the Rockies is served by private companies offering float trips in inflatable rafts. They provide a fine service. By and large, the boatmen, and boatwomen, are highly competent, interesting people. The rivers are spectacular and prices are reasonable. Many companies give you a choice of riding as a passenger in a raft rowed by a single boatman, or of joining a crew in a paddle raft, where everyone lends a hand. You get a bouncier, wetter ride in a paddle raft, and you have the pleasure of taking an active part in the adventure. You should expect a rafting company to provide everything necessary for the trip—the boats, of course, but also life preservers, wet suits if the river is cold enough to warrant them (most mountain rivers are), waterproof containers for your camera and other gear, and meals. For overnight trips, such items as sleeping bags and tents might be available optionally for a small surcharge.

Winter Activities

Skiing is the major nonmotorized winter activity, and although it does require special equipment, it's a natural extension of walking, especially if you choose cross-country touring gear (see page 44). In more and more places throughout the Rockies, cross-country trails are being marked out and groomed. This is being done by the Forest Service, provincial and state parks, and other agencies. Sometimes private groups provide this service, and trail systems change from year to year. In general, you can almost count on finding a system of set and groomed tracks near any mountain town. A fee may be charged, but never more than a few dollars. Forest Service offices and local ski shops are the best sources of information. Most downhill ski areas have cross-country tracks in their immediate vicinity as well.

Winter conditions are considerably more demanding than summer and capable of causing severe discomfort or death in a matter of minutes. Travelers really must understand frostbite and hypothermia, and how to treat them. Avalanches pose a much more complicated threat; avoidance of dangerous terrain is the best policy if you lack experience and local knowledge. Even people with extensive avalanche expertise know that asking about local conditions is essential to their safety. If you stray from well-traveled routes, you should know how to build emergency shelters and be prepared to spend a night in one. On anything but prepared and marked trails, have a map and compass and be aware that the weather here can close in at any time; white-out conditions can play havoc with one's sense of direction.

Also, if you are a skier, you know that snowmobiles are more common all the time. Many forest lands are totally open to machines, even places that are closed in summer to trailbikes. Locals can tell you where to avoid them. In the United States, detailed information is provided by Travel Plans, available at U.S. Forest Service ranger stations. Wilderness areas and most backcountry in national parks are closed to motors. However, and this is a large however, skiers must be aware of their own potential for impact, which can be larger than they care to admit. Because of their mobility, and tendency to go in unpredictable directions without the warning sounds of motors, skiers can in fact be harder on wintering wildlife than snowmobiles, that stay to marked routes.

TIPS ON LODGING

Grand Hotels

It's hard to overestimate the role of transcontinental railroads in the development of national parks in both Canada and the United States. Eager to promote travel on their lines, the Canadian Pacific, the Great Northern, the Union Pacific and other lines built spurs to the major parks—Grand Canyon, Rocky Mountain, Yellowstone, Glacier and Banff—and followed up with a series of magnificent hotels in choice locations. Chateau Lake Louise stands on the shore of perhaps the most beautiful lake in the Canadian Rockies. The Many Glacier Hotel occupies a site of rival beauty in Montana's Glacier National Park. The Old Faithful Inn, by a special act of Congress, was permitted a site just yards from the geyser for which it was named. Today, park managers rarely allow such large structures to be built so close to outstanding scenic areas, and when an exception does occur, it is roundly criticized. The emphasis now is placed on retaining as much of the natural scene as possible, even if that means housing visitors at some distance and requiring them to drive or ride a shuttle to popular areas. Despite the drawbacks of such a system, it is generally regarded as preferable to the transient cities that have grown up in places like Yosemite Valley and Old Faithful.

However, in defense of the big hotels, it should be remembered that they were built before autos were the prime means of travel to parks. Once a visitor arrived, he was expected to walk, or at most, ride a coach or a bus. The big hotels were built far too close to the landscape for modern tastes, but there were no parking lots or traffic jams in early days.

For better or worse, they stand today a select group, each with unique and interesting architecture, each in a prime location. If your plans include hotels rather than campgrounds, even for only a night or two, and your budget allows it, these are the lodgings of choice. Even hard-bitten backpackers will enjoy their spacious lobbies on stormy days.

Other Lodging

Otherwise, any number of choices exist. Motels are found in almost every city and town in the Rockies, and at many crossroads. Dude ranches provide rooms by the night or the week. More common all the time are bed and breakfast hotels operated from private homes as in the United Kingdom. Occasionally, you find a privately run campground where you can stay in a trailer or motorhome for the night.

In areas off the beaten path, you can wander along and be fairly sure of finding a vacancy late in the afternoon. But if you need lodging in more popular places, such as national parks, you need to arrive early in the day, or better yet, make reservations in advance. Complete lists of lodging facilities are available from state and provincial travel agencies. Most of these lists are in convenient booklet form, with information on price and relative quality. In some cases, you can call a central phone number for reservations; if your first choice is unavailable, they will try to find an alternate.

For budget travelers, there is nothing cheaper than a youth hostel. These are common in the Canadian Rockies, but less so in the United States. You don't need to be a member to stay in one, but it costs a little more if you're not. Nor do you need to be young; there's no surcharge for age. The only real drawback of hostels is their restrictive code of regulations. Hostels are run in the spirit of English boarding schools, with strict headmasters. You must be in by a certain hour, lights go off at bedtime, men are in one dorm and women are in another, but private family rooms can be reserved in advance. These rules, however, are not universal. I've been to hostels that are run just like hotels (in fact some are old hotels), and I can't imagine more pleasant places to stay. They are excellent places to meet other travelers, compare notes and hook up with rides or hiking partners. Handbooks listing all the hostels, their seasons of operation, facilities, rates, and other pertinent facts are available.

Memberships are $25 ($15 for 55+). Contact the following addresses for handbooks and membership information: American Youth Hostels, Hostelling International, 733 15th St. NW, Ste. 800, Washington, DC 20005 (tel: 202-783-6161); Hostelling International—Southern Alberta, Room 203, 1414 Kensington Rd. NW, Calgary, AB T2N 3P9 (tel: 403-283-5551).

Forest Service Cabins and Lookouts

Recently, the U.S. Forest Service has begun to rent cabins and lookout towers which are no longer used for management purposes, rather than tear them down or let them stand empty. Some are available in winter months only and are located several miles from plowed roads. For the most part, the cabins are old work centers or ranger stations in remote, sometimes very scenic places. Of course, the lookout towers, by their very nature, have wonderful views. Facilities are simple: bunks, tables, chairs, wood stoves, kerosene lanterns and outdoor toilets. Costs range from $10 to $30 per night, some with a limit on each party's stay. For example, the Weitas Butte Lookout Tower east of Pierce, Idaho, stands at the end of a 12-mile primitive road and rents for $50 for the first two nights and $8 per night thereafter. A complete listing of these cabins in the Northern Region of the Forest Service (Idaho and Montana) can be obtained from Northern Region Headquarters, P.O. Box 7669, Missoula MT 59807.

TIPS ON CAMPING

You can have almost anything you want in a campground. Facilities vary from the posh resort-like atmosphere of private developments (some with swimming pools, television rooms, laundromats, groceries and even restaurants) to the barest of forest clearings. National parks, national and provincial forests, state parks and other land management agencies all provide campsites with basic amenities—water, toilets, trash cans, picnic tables and fireplaces. Government campgrounds almost never provide utility hookups, and dump stations are provided only at the larger ones. Campers interested in traveling off the beaten path should be prepared to provide their own water and firewood or cook-stove, and to pack out their trash.

In this book, I've tried to mention specific campgrounds where such information seemed useful and appropriate. Also, I have included general descriptions of camping opportunities (for example, the book will tell you that campgrounds are located frequently along the Such-and-Such

Pass road, or that there is no campground at a certain trailhead). I have avoided trying to provide a comprehensive list, partly because there are literally thousands of campgrounds sprinkled throughout the Rockies, but also because there is no need. Campgrounds are easy to find, and you should have no trouble as long as you know in general what is available.

All national parks in the Rockies have campgrounds; the only exceptions are several national monuments in the United States, and I've noted those exceptions in the text. When you enter a national park, you are handed a map with campsites and other information clearly marked. At the entrance station, be sure to ask whether the campgrounds will fill up that night, and if so, how soon you must claim a site to ensure yourself of getting one.

U.S. Forest Service campgrounds are virtually ubiquitous and easy to find. The same is true of British Columbia Provincial Park campgrounds and Alberta Forest Service campgrounds. Many highway maps mark at least the important ones, and road signs along major highways are a big help. Best of all, maps put out by these agencies, and available locally or by mail (U.S. Forest Service maps cost $3), indicate every campground in a given forest. These offices also provide free lists of their campgrounds, including information on facilities, location, capacity, recreational features, access and more, so that if a boat ramp is important to you, or if you need potable water, you can know in advance.

As for other campgrounds, run by provincial and state parks or the Bureau of Land Management, or Indian reservations, information is available from any number of sources. Again, an ordinary highway map is useful; also, state and provincial tourist offices publish complete lists of all campgrounds within their boundaries—private, state, local, federal or whatever they may be. In the end, however, I should point out that it is quite feasible to travel through the Rockies without any sort of advance itinerary or any idea where the next campground will be. You can wander along in most places comfortable with the knowledge that around the next bend you'll find a pleasant place to pitch your tent or park your vehicle.

Campgrounds in national parks tend to be little cities, increasingly more crowded and less pleasant. Both Parks Canada and the U.S. National Park Service, in an attempt to centralize things, are gradually closing or limiting the season at smaller sites and herding visitors into mega-campgrounds, where four separate groups might find themselves within a hundred feet of one another. It may be that the huge and increasing demands placed on the facilities of national parks require this sort of approach; nonetheless, the effect at the height of the summer season is unfortunate. In Yellowstone in the middle of July, virtually all sites are occupied by 1:00 in the afternoon; it's common to see a line of vehicles at the entrance to a campground at 9:00 A.M. waiting to take the places of other people who are leaving that morning. No wonder campers who use these parking lots acquire vehicles with walls and controlled interior environments. Their city backyards are more spacious and more peaceful; maybe even safer from crime.

This is not to recommend against staying in them. They've become popular for good reasons, and some, especially the older ones in deep forest, or on lakeshores, or with only a few sites are a sheer pleasure. On the other hand, it's good to keep in mind that they are not the only ones. Just outside the boundary of a national park, you are likely to find several Forest Service campgrounds, which most travelers pass by.

Fees for national park campgrounds vary with services provided. In Banff National Park, for example, camping fees range from $10 to $22, the more expensive sites offering RV hookups and showers. Fees in the U.S. national parks are comparable, although I know of none that have showers in the campgrounds. At U.S. Government campsites, Golden Age Passports, given free to citizens over 62, entitle holders and their parties to a 50 percent discount on campsites. These are available at most Park Service and Forest Service offices.

Forest Service campgrounds are often more pleasant than those in national parks, if only because they are off the beaten path. Quite a few provide trash collection, drinking water from taps or hand pumps, and other simple amenities for a fee of about $5 per night. Many of the U.S. sites are cared for by volunteer camp hosts during the summer season— usually a retired couple living in their own travel trailer, who do this for the pleasure of living in a scenic, forested area for the summer. Other campgrounds, usually the more remote sites or the smaller ones, have no trash pickup or developed water source. These are free; the Forest Service asks only that campers keep them clean. A stay of 14 days is the maximum, after which campers must move to a different campground if they wish to stay in the area. Most Forest Service sites can be used at any time of the year, but water is turned off when it gets cold enough to freeze pipes. Some forests close their campground gates in the off-season, so ask at a ranger station or be ready to camp in an undeveloped site. There is no reservation system; in the high-use season, or on weekends, popular campgrounds might fill by noon.

Normally, marked and maintained campgrounds are accessible to passenger cars during the summer. Drivers with trailers and motorhomes should not automatically assume that they can negotiate a road marked as passable to autos; in doubt, ask first at a ranger station. Early in the season, snow may block roads, and mud can be a problem during thunderstorm season. Late in the year, travelers should watch for early snowfalls and hightail it out of remote areas if the snow starts to pile up. It has happened that imprudent people have had to abandon their vehicles for the winter when they ignored the message of an October storm.

Don't forget that except in certain restricted areas, most national and provincial forests are open to camping wherever you feel like stopping for the night. This open policy makes the forest lands wonderful places to wander in search of your own patch of privacy. Hand in hand with the freedom, of course, goes the responsibility to not damage a pristine area. It seems to be a part of human nature that once a set of tire tracks are visible across a previously unscarred meadow, a beaten road will soon appear. In a similar vein, if you see no fire scar, consider not building a fire there; where fire circles already exist, use them instead of making a new one. U.S. Forest Service regulations require that anyone camping from a vehicle and building a fire in an undesignated site is required to have a bucket, a shovel and an axe at the ready. Do be careful, if camping in this manner, that you are actually on forest, not private land.

Finally, there are commercial campgrounds, run by individuals or franchised by large chains. Even if they lack natural beauty (some do not), they do have the advantage of convenience. They are usually located along major highways, near freeway interchanges or on the outskirts of towns. Their business depends to some degree on visibility. Like motels, they cater to transient traffic and look mostly to people with trailers and motorhomes for their clientele. The facilities at these sites are often those of a resort: showers, swimming pool, gamesrooms, laundry, campers' store. For a small fee, you can get a shower even if you're not staying the night.

WALK SOFTLY AND CARRY A LITTLE STOVE

Mountain ecosystems, for all their apparent strength in facing the challenges of mountain weather, altitude and thin soil, are extremely fragile. Where winter lasts more than half the year, and where even summers are harsh, the margin of survival for living things shrinks to a hair's breadth. In alpine meadows, plants grow slowly; a tiny tree or heather bush hardly ten or fifteen inches in height may be centuries old, having been continually stunted by difficult growing conditions. Simply staying alive is challenge enough; they are unable to tolerate very much additional stress. Yet each tiny plant plays a critical role. Its roots hold the soil in place, retain moisture and provide shelter for even smaller plants.

If this mat of vegetation is destroyed, it might be years before the scar recovers, if it ever does. The Park Service estimates that where foot travel has stripped the vegetation and topsoil from areas along Trail Ridge Road in Rocky Mountain National Park, it may take 400 to 1,000 years for full recovery.

It's ironic that the most attractive places in the mountains are often the most fragile. Where you would most like to walk, or camp, or build a fire is where you should least do so. In the case of a trail above timberline, even light traffic keeps it open and subject to erosion, until in extreme examples what began as a footpath becomes a deep trench, or worse, a series of parallel trenches. If used carelessly or by too many people in too short a time, campsites on springy, fragrant meadows degrade into patches of dirt stripped of vegetation. Gnarled, weathered snags disappear into voracious campfires. Boulders, once decorated by colorful lichen, are blackened by the flames. Ash and half-burned chunks of wood litter the area, often peppered with bits of trash: twist ties, cigarette butts, scraps of plastic and unburned aluminum foil.

As use increases, it is more important for all of us to consider even the smallest details of our impact on the wilderness environment. Happily, modern equipment coupled with sensitivity and common sense makes it easy to travel in most places without leaving a trace.

Campfires

As pleasant as they may be, campfires are sometimes inappropriate, especially above or near timberline where wood is scarce and old snags complement the landscape. Well below the timberline, where wood is plentiful, fires may be acceptable. But even then, they should be small ones. (As the saying goes, an Indian stays warm by getting close to a small fire, a white man stays warm by chopping wood.) Try to use an existing fireplace rather than build a new one each time. If you are in a place that has never seen a fire, and are determined to build one, then follow this procedure.

Locate a bare patch of ground, one not covered with delicate green plants and with a low organic content (sand is perfect). Carefully remove the top two or three inches of earth to make a small pit. Build the fire in the pit, choosing small pieces of wood, generally no thicker than your thumb. These will burn hot and will do a fast job of cooking a meal. When you've finished with the fire, let it burn to ashes (another reason for using small pieces of wood). Black charcoal lasts for hundreds of years, while ash is quickly recycled. Stir the fire as it dies to encourage complete burning. The last step is to douse it thoroughly and stir it some more, ensuring that no embers remain hot. Then you can cover the pit with the topsoil you removed, pour water on that as well, and in a day or two it would take the skill of Tonto to know you had built a fire there. No blackened rocks, no half-burned logs, no circle of scorched vegetation. Of course, it might have been easier just to light a gas stove and leave absolutely no scar at all.

Sanitation

The manner in which you handle sanitation is more important than any other wilderness activity. It's really quite simple, which makes it all the more astonishing that so many people are so careless. A little consideration for those who follow is all that is needed. Human waste should be buried six to eight inches deep. Do not simply put a rock on top of it. You can carry an almost weightless plastic trowel to dig the required six-to eight-inch depth. An ice axe works just as well, if you don't mind dulling the adze. Toilet paper should be burned; keep matches or a lighter with the roll and ignite the paper before filling in the hole (DANGER! Fire Warning! In very dry conditions in dense bushes, carelessness can be catastrophic.) Believe it or not, marmots and other rodents gleefully dig this stuff up if not properly buried, liberating pastel ribbons of paper in the process. I prefer to see wildflowers, thank you. Another consideration is that colored paper contains potentially harmful dyes; use plain old white and burn it.

Also, latrines should be located well away from water supplies—at least a hundred yards. That should go without saying, but already, not a single source of surface water in the Rockies can be implicitly trusted. In the space of 30 years, the situation has reversed, from a time when we drank with pleasure directly from every rivulet, to the present, when prudence dictates purifying all water (see page 69).

Other waste, such as food wrappers and the like, must be carried to proper disposal sites, not buried to be unearthed later by other diggers. If you have a fire, you can burn some of your trash. Remember that plastic gives off deadly fumes when it burns and that aluminum foil does not burn. It's much easier to simply carry foil envelopes to a trash can than to fish around in fire ash to find the bits of metal.

Washing, whether of dishes, clothes or bodies, should be done away from lakes and streams. Cold, pure mountain water is very slow to decompose anything organic, including biodegradable soap. Spaghetti noodles last for weeks; contrary to an apparently popular myth, trout do not love Italian food. Instead of rinsing things in the lake, carry a pot of water some distance away and dump it, when finished, on an area of thick vegetation. Soap of all kinds can damage some plants. Use soap sparingly, or better yet, leave it behind.

Campsites

In some areas, campsites for hikers are designated. This does not mean, however, that you must put your tent in the actual campsite. On the contrary, in bear country it's advisable to use the site only for cooking and for hanging your packs. Then go off some distance from that source of odors, where previous campers might have dumped a skillet of bacon fat, and set your tent well away from trails or natural routes of travel. This has the added advantage of being able to choose a pleasant place to sleep, although it carries with it the responsibility to do no damage. This means no trenching (an archaic technique anyway) and attention to the ground over which you sleep.

Footwear

When walking on trails, be aware of erosion caused by feet in lug-soled boots. Sometimes there is nothing you can do; the trail is poorly constructed, or it's full of water and you are forced to make a new path to one side. Still, you can minimize the impact of your passing. On some trails, lugged boots are unnecessary; in fact they are a waste of energy where lighter footwear is adequate. In the spring, try to walk on snow or rock instead of soft thawed ground. Cutting switchbacks encourages erosion and saves little, if any, time and energy. When walking off trail, avoid going single file, which could create a path; if everyone in your group follows a slightly different route, plants can recover quickly. In the same vein, don't mark trees or leave rock cairns on wilderness routes. A major pleasure of wild country is the illusion that you could be the first person on the scene.

Please Don't Eat the Spring Beauties

There has been a recent surge of interest in edible plants. Books and magazine articles extol the pleasures of foraging for wild foods and living off the land. It sounds attractive but this sort of behavior is anathema to wilderness protection. As an example, one of the most often mentioned wild foods is the roots of spring beauties. These lovely little flowers, among the first of the season, bloom in moist areas throughout the mountains, sometimes covering whole meadows with their delicate nodding blossoms. The tubers are easy to dig, and quite tasty, as grizzly bears would tell you if they were so inclined. But to make a salad of these requires dozens of plants per person. When a group of hikers decides to collect a natural meal with ice axes, their desire to partake in the bounty of the wilderness yields results akin to strip mining in miniature.

The same goes for most other wild foods. Even if they can be collected without causing damage, any significant harvest of them deprives local wildlife of a needed food source. We've made it hard enough on wild animals as it is. On the other hand, I'm the last person to pass up a nibble of watercress or a handful of sorrel leaves for a sandwich. And I'd never suggest that hikers leave ripe strawberries and blueberries to dangle by the trail. But tasting a few and making a meal of them are two different things. Consider the story I read once about a prominent proponent of wild foods. He had taken a group of students into a desert region to teach them about edible plants. One in particular—a kind of tuber—he was eager to find. He remembered digging it in this area and was disappointed not to find any. The plant had become scarce, a shame because it was so delicious. Then, on the last day of the trip, having failed to find a single one, he discovered a survivor standing alone in a protected place. Promptly, he dug it up and ate it.

SOLITUDE IN THE CROWDS

> "If you want to get away from it all, consider visiting outside the Wilderness." *Kootenai National Forest publication*

Old Faithful, in Yellowstone Park, is the classic example of overcrowding in a national park. You hear it all the time: Old Faithful has a cloverleaf interchange, a divided highway, you can't hear the geyser over the thunder of 5,000 camera shutters, the parking lots are the envy of K-Mart, and so on. Well, all this is true. Old Faithful sees about twenty-five thousand visitors in a busy day. Even with the four-lane highway, there is still a traffic problem. If you went there in the middle of a July day, you would be justified in comparing the place to Disney World.

On the other hand, you would not be justified to discard Old Faithful just because you felt an aversion to crowds. On that same July day, at 6:00 in the morning, with the dawn light soft and warm, there were probably fewer than a handful of watchers around the geyser, and the parking lots were empty. Even in the evening, after the dinner hour, the crowds hardly deserve such a title. And in addition, dozens of other geysers in the immediate vicinity receive far less attention than Old Faithful. Most of them require some walking; if you are willing to walk a mile from your car, there's a good chance you'll have the eruption of Riverside or Daisy geysers practically to yourself.

This line of reasoning applies equally well to other less famous parts of the park. If silence and solitude are important to you, Yellowstone, despite its cloverleaf, is as likely a spot to find it as exists within the scope of this book. I know of a lovely mountain lake, which lies less than an hour's walk from Yellowstone's busy highway, yet as often as I've been there, and I've camped there half a dozen times, I have never seen another person on its shores. Nor have I seen any sign that anyone else knows about it.

This is true no matter where you go in the Rockies. Lake Louise, in Banff National Park, is usually jammed with people on any given summer day. Several extremely popular trails go along the lake or climb above it. The area deserves its popularity, but other places in the vicinity rival the scenery of Lake Louise and see far fewer visitors. Just over the mountain crest, in fact, lies one of the perfect gems of the Rockies, Lake O'Hara. Because the road is closed to private vehicles (you must ride a shuttle bus for a small fee, or walk), you leave behind the great mass of people when you spend a day, or longer, in this area.

It's all a matter of degree, of course. Lake O'Hara, although remote compared to Lake Louise, is visited by many more people than wilderness valleys not served by roads. But the point is that if you can find peace and quiet in such places as Banff and Yellowstone, you can find them anywhere. Here are some general principles for avoiding the crowds.

Rise early: early morning finds even very popular places nearly deserted. For two or three hours after dawn, most people are busily holding down their pillows, while outside, the light is ideal for photos, animals are more likely to be visible, and the air is fresh. Lucky for early birds.

Travel in the off-season: summer crowds reach their peak in the first week of July and continue until the first week of September, which usually coincides with the beginning of school. On the day after Labor Day in the United States, campgrounds and resort towns look like they've been hit by some sort of disaster. The streets are empty, the campgrounds shelter only a few survivors, the merchants and service industry people all show symptoms of shell shock after the long summer season. They soon recover, for autumn is their favorite time of year. It's also the favorite time for anyone able to travel after schools are in session—young people and retired people, for the most part, but never very many of them. Spring can be just as uncrowded, but the weather is potentially miserable.

Avoid the high spots: if a place is famous and accessible by vehicle (Trail Ridge Road in Rocky Mountain National Park, Old Faithful in Yellowstone National Park, Columbia Icefields in Jasper National Park, and so forth) it will be crowded from about 9:00 in the morning until sunset. If you wish to avoid people here during the day, you must go walking. Even a half mile away from the road will make the difference. All such places have trails, usually well-marked, and information centers where you can get suggestions and area maps.

Avoid the parks: national parks attract more people than any other areas. Often the forest lands immediately surrounding the parks are equally lovely and comparatively deserted. This applies to campgrounds, trails and other facilities.

Avoid designated wilderness areas: the designation labels these areas as special, attracting backpackers and fishermen, just as in the parks.

Choose alternate trails: in all parks and wilderness areas, some trails get most of the use. It might be that these trails are the shortest distance to a good fishing lake or a scenic valley, but sometimes they are simply the easiest places to drive to. To find which trails are less used, ask a forest or park ranger; they're invariably eager to take the pressure off overused places. After a few minutes of friendly conversation, a ranger is likely to tell you about some favorite, hidden place with the perfect, private campsite.

Get a good map: without a detailed map, you can't navigate the remote backroads or find your way to hidden backcountry spots. Most auto travelers carry nothing more detailed than a highway map, which means that thousands of miles of roads, along with lakes, campgrounds, trails and rivers, escape their notice. A surprising number of hikers rely on nothing more than trail signs, when a glance at a map would take them half a mile to a hidden lake. This book describes many backcountry roads and suggests less heavily used trails, but you'll find that supplemental maps are highly useful. See page 73 for information on these detailed maps.

TIPS FOR WINTER

Winter temperatures in the Rockies can be unbelievably cold. Just about every year we hear of nights in January when the mercury bottoms out around -60°F somewhere in the region. It makes national news, and rightfully so.

That sort of cold is a palpable force, a thing of oppressive weight, which affects everyone physically as well as mentally. The dangers are not simply frostbite (it is dangerous to expose skin to temperatures that low) but more subtle, psychic damage. I will never forget the winter of 1978-79, a record-setting season of intense cold when the ceramic sewer pipes in Red Lodge, Montana, froze solid at a depth of six feet. There was nothing for residents to do but stop using showers, sinks and toilets, and wait for warmer weather.

It wasn't much better anywhere else in the Rockies. The cold came in and stayed for the winter. At the beginning of the year, in December, people made their usual bad jokes about it. For a time, everyone enjoyed it; cold this persistent and this intense was phenomenal, worthy of attention, the subject of boasting. One morning in a small Montana town, I met a man walking down the street with the lever of his truck's gearshift in his hand. He had tried to shift gears at 55 below, and the brittle metal had snapped. He was delighted, if also dismayed: "Look at this, can you believe it? Well, I'll be go to hell."

That omigosh mood lasted a few weeks and then died. Silence replaced the banter. Earlier, everyone had been talking about the weather. Now, suddenly, it was a forbidden topic. People talked about anything else. Every day they fought against frozen pipes, frozen engines and ice dams on their roofs. Every time they walked outside, the cold clamped down, stiff and viscous, hard to move through, provoking feelings of claustrophobia and a sense that they were holding out in vain against an unrelenting force.

Finally, some began to give in to it. The strain showed on faces as marriages ruptured, as cattle were found frozen to death, as attempts to keep pipes and houses unfrozen finally failed, and as neighbors gave up and fled south. It was a hard winter.

It was also an unusual one. What made it so strange was not the intense overnight cold, but rather the way it stayed cold during the day. Even on clear days, the sun felt powerless and the air retained its bite. Normally, mountain days are not very cold, particularly when the sky is clear. The extreme overnight lows happen because in thin alpine air, the empty, black sky sucks heat from the earth at a frightening rate. But during the day, the sun, shining strongly and unimpeded by atmosphere, is quick to replace the warmth. It's not at all unusual for January temperatures to shift 50 or 60 degrees between 6:00 A.M. and 11:00 A.M. Mountain residents expect that to be the pattern. Clear nights are cold but clear days are warm. Cloudy skies bring only moderation, not extremes.

What happened that winter, said the experts, was that intense cold from the Arctic flowed south in such volume that it was able to breach the mountains, flowing up the valleys, inundating everything in subzero cold—a phenomenon that residents of the northern plains experience all too often, but that mountain dwellers expect to be protected from. Normally, those arctic air masses are too thin to blanket the mountains. Normally, winters in the Rockies are quite pleasant.

For the adventurous traveler, and especially for skiers, winter in the mountains can be sheer delight. Opportunities for any other non-mechanized activities—walking, boating, camping, relaxing in the sun—are just about nonexistent. Skiing is the whole show. Options range from established alpine resorts like Aspen or Lake Louise, where lift-serviced slopes and carefully groomed cross-country tracks combine with luxury lodging and restaurants, to a backcountry ski mountaineering trip. Between the two is a world of variation. Not all alpine resorts are big and expensive. Many western towns have their own family ski hills, which provide excellent terrain and snow conditions without the hype. An increasing number of lodges and resorts specialize in cross-country skiing. These may be posh or primitive, in luxury hotels or heated (sometimes) tents. Helicopters and snowcats shuttle skiers to remote slopes. Adventure guide services take parties on extended wilderness backcountry trips. The possibilities increase with each year.

A full review of winter recreation activities is beyond the purview of this book, but detailed information is available from the agencies whose addresses are listed in the text. In addition, a few words of general advice may prove useful.

Winter campgrounds are extremely limited. There just isn't enough demand to warrant plowing roads and winterizing facilities in most places. However, there are exceptions: Mammoth Hot Springs Campground in Yellowstone National Park, for example, or Wapiti Winter Campground in Jasper National Park. If you can sleep in your vehicle, the options increase. Ski areas have become used to having motorhomes and vans park in their public lots; they have designated areas for the purpose, and some resorts even keep heated restrooms open for parking lot campers.

Winter driving in the mountains can be intimidating if you haven't spent much time in snow. Descending a steep, icy pass with a thousand feet of air beyond the guardrail tries anyone's nerves. But with proper equipment and a little common sense, mountain roads are as safe as any others. A set of tire chains is mandatory; in some places you will not be allowed to proceed without them. Snow tires on the front and back wheels are almost as important, because much of winter driving is on hard-packed snow where chains are a bother but summer treads are insufficient. Winter driving is most hazardous when conditions are mixed, a common occurrence in mountains. With a gain in elevation, rain turns to snow. As you enter a shaded canyon, a dry highway suddenly becomes a sheet of ice. A light snowstorm can be a white-out blizzard in which the wind is channeled by the terrain. The worst of all might be what is called a ground-blizzard. The sun is shining, but stiff winds keep a sheet of snow moving across the highway, which packs hard under the wheels of traffic, making the road slick, and hides oncoming vehicles.

People who have lived in the mountains any length of time never make a highway trip without carrying emergency gear. This includes extra anti-freeze, flashlight, tools for repairing chains, a bag of sand, a tow-rope and a shovel. Also warm clothing, maybe a sleeping bag, fire-starter and food.

You want to be able to dig yourself out of a drift or a ditch, or if that is impossible, to survive a night waiting for someone to pass by and lend aid.

Weather changes with startling rapidity in the mountains. With experience, you can learn to predict the changes to some degree, but conditions will surprise even the most seasoned veteran. The idea is not to guess accurately, but to be prepared for anything which might develop.

As for off-road activities, preparation is entirely dependent on your plans. In developed places, you needn't go out equipped like Sergeant Preston of the Yukon. Ski resort boundaries are carefully marked and— theoretically—skiers within those boundaries are safe from objective hazards such as avalanche. If you have an accident, someone is there to help. Farther afield, you start needing more equipment and more expertise. Avalanche conditions are monitored by local agencies in many parts of the Rockies, but all you can expect from them are warnings of relative hazard levels: low, medium, high, extreme. No one but a fool would enter avalanche terrain when warned of extreme conditions, but even when the snow is relatively stable, you can find a dangerous place if you look hard enough. It's very important for winter recreationists who have a desire to explore the Rockies to have some knowledge of what causes avalanches and how to avoid them. Avoidance is not hard, if you know what to look for and are willing to go another way or to another place. Many times, you simply should stay away from certain valleys or slopes.

You can have a wonderful, worry-free time in the mountains, with no avalanche knowledge whatsoever, if you stay in developed areas and well away from slopes that might slide (such a slope can be very small, by the way). The alternative is to hire a guide or to study avalanches. To learn more, read a book on the subject. *The ABC of Avalanche Safety*, by E.R. LaChapelle, is a good start; *Wilderness Skiing*, by Lito Tejada-Flores, has a good section on avalanche safety. These will teach you less about prediction than avoidance, but that is the name of the game. In addition, avalanche safety courses are taught throughout the West, varying from occasional evening lectures to week-long field courses. Find out about these at any ski resort; their ski patrols are required to take courses and might even be providing them for the public.

BUGS, BEARS AND OTHER BOTHERS

Dr. Yogi and Mr. Hyde

Bears of the Rocky Mountains, in the popular imagination, are oddly schizophrenic creatures. On the one hand, we have Yogi the cartoon bear who, although he behaves like a juvenile delinquent, is at heart a lovable and harmless friend to everyone. His partner, Boo-boo, is even more so—small, furry and affectionate. Of course, they steal food from campers, but always with good humor and no real damage done. Yogi is a circus bear, a buffoon.

On the other hand is the Mr. Hyde of Yogi's Dr. Jekyll, the bear that appears on covers of men's outdoor magazines—a great slavering monster rearing on hind legs, towering over some valiant outdoorsman as he struggles to fell the beast with a knife or an axe. This is the grizzly bear of legend, *Ursus horribilis*, standing nearly seven feet tall on its hind legs (nine or ten on the magazine cover), weighing almost half a ton, astonishingly fast in reaction and powerful in rage, the most dangerous predator on the continent. Can this fearsome animal be in any way related to Yogi?

The answer is yes, but it has nothing to do with schizophrenia. Bears are intelligent, complex animals capable of widely various behavior. They can be perfect clowns and perfect devils, and this applies to both black and grizzly bears. Yogi was born, conceptually, from the behavior of black bears who used to frequent campgrounds and roadsides in Yellowstone Park (they still do in Yosemite). Quite often, their foraging after food produced hilarious entertainment for Yellowstone visitors. Accustomed to the presence of people, these bears were slow to provoke. They would calmly enter cars, tents and travel trailers, eat whatever they could find and leave by whichever exit presented itself—not always the door.

Accidents did happen in Yellowstone and continue in places that still have the problem. Campers were injured, some seriously, and some the result of their own stupidity. How else can we explain the actions of a man who smeared preserves on his child's face so that he could take a picture of the bear "kissing" the little girl? Or the man who lured a bear into the front seat of his car for a photo of it sitting beside his wife? Yet despite injuries, and the warnings of park rangers, few visitors were deterred; in Yellowstone, until severe control measures had their effect (the park still has bears, but now they live natural lives independent of human food), bears came to be regarded as part of the show, as important to a visit, and as reliable, as Old Faithful. Even when situations like those above ended in tragedy, people could find an element of dark humor in the stories and were eager to hear more. No matter that the bears were the true victims. After all, this was Yogi the clown, a hireling, not a wild animal.

No one finds humor, however, in a backcountry bear mauling. When these happen (not often, but always well publicized), they usually involve grizzlies, which are quite different animals from their cousins. This is not to downplay the power of a black bear; despite the ease with which black bears adapt to human presence, they remain formidable creatures. Yet an angry or frightened grizzly is a truly awesome animal and worthy of our sincere respect. A common reaction among park rangers and experienced mountain travelers, upon hearing of a bear mauling, is to ask, "What did this person do wrong?" Translated, this comes out, "What did this person do that I would not have done?" They want to know the details, not from any sense of morbidity, but because they feel that their safety in bear country depends on following a certain code of behavior. If it can be found that the mauling victim did something "wrong," then everyone breathes easier. The real object of fear is the anomalous bear, the one that breaks all patterns and behaves in a truly cantankerous, unpredictable manner—in short, a bear indifferent to the backcountry hiker's code. This code, described below, relies on bears to behave in accord with certain generalities, the most significant one being that bears do not want to attack people. Apparent attacks, according to generality, are actually defensive reactions, which can be avoided by following the code. And for the most part, this is true. Indeed, if bears hunted people with the same determination and skill that they use in pursuing gophers, the situation would be entirely different.

There's no question that bears are dangerous animals. Their behavior is unpredictable. Generalities often fail. Each bear is an individual, each encounter a new situation. By entering bear country, travelers tacitly acknowledge an element of risk just as they do when driving a car or flying in a plane. By normal standards, the extremely low probability of even seeing a bear, much less being injured by one, makes the risk acceptable. In Glacier National Park, where some of the most publicized attacks by grizzlies have occurred, fatal maulings make up only four percent of total park fatalities. Falls, drownings, heart attacks, hypothermia and auto accidents are far more common. What such cold statistics fail to say, however, is that death by auto crash, by the impersonal action of a machine, is somehow less horrifying than death under the hot breath of a wild animal. Perhaps this emotion is a part of our evolutionary heritage; all deaths are not equal.

Even when unprovoked, a grizzly has immense stage presence. My closest contact with a wild bear happened one night in Yellowstone when I was camped on a backcountry beach. A bright moon was shining, and I woke up when a shadow darkened the door of my tent. I turned to look and felt apprehension. Then I put on my glasses. With clear vision, apprehension turned to something more serious. For several long moments we both froze, three feet apart, I looking up, the grizzly looking down, his odor filling that small space, until finally he turned and wandered off along the shore. In retrospect, this was the perfect way to meet a bear. The surge of emotions, ranging from awareness to terror to relief to pleasure, has made the memory indelible. I'm grateful to have it, but I would never request a repeat visit.

Black bears are found throughout the Rocky Mountains, while grizzlies no longer live more than a few miles south of Yellowstone National Park. Their decline, from a range which in the 1800s covered most of the continent west of Ontario and north of central Mexico, has been dramatic. Some experts estimate a one-time population of one hundred thousand animals. Now, in the lower 48 states, there are fewer than a thousand, virtually all of them in Yellowstone and Glacier national parks and a few places between. The reasons for the decline are many, the most important one being the disappearance of habitat. Being adaptable animals, grizzlies could easily live in settled areas, feeding on domestic animals and garbage in addition to their more traditional foods. But this brings them into unavoidable conflict with human residents to the ultimate downfall of the bear. In order to survive, grizzlies require sizeable areas of wild country. Another of their problems is a low birthrate (as compared to, for example, coyotes, whose litters increase in times of low population). Female grizzlies do not breed until they are five to eight years old, and then only once every two or three years. Complicating the issue is the notorious difficulty of counting grizzlies. No one really knows how many there are, but neither does anyone contest that grizzlies are having a tough go of it.

Officially, grizzlies are listed as a threatened species south of the U.S.-Canada border. By law, human activities on land such as national forests, according to a Forest Service publication, must not "jeopardize the continued existence of the grizzly or result in the adverse modification or destruction of their critical habitat." What this means in relation to logging, mining, grazing and recreational developments such as alpine ski areas remains a source of heated controversy lacking clear definitions of what constitutes jeopardy to the grizzly. From the point of view of a wilderness traveler's behavior, however, things are relatively simple. The rules of conduct in bear country are well thought out, easy to follow and designed to protect both bears and people.

Avoiding Bears

The prime objective of travelers in bear country is to avoid bear encounters. Wild bears, as a rule, will give people a wide berth if they just have warning. Hikers do this by traveling in groups, making noise as they walk through areas of brush or forest. If you find the constant jingling of a bell annoying (I certainly do), then replace it with continual awareness of the trail ahead. At any blind spot, sing out a warning: "Hey bear, you there?"

Pay extra attention if traveling into the wind: bears rely on their keen sense of smell. Near rushing water or when trees are thrashing in the wind, you can't be sure your approach will be heard.

Keep an eye out for bear signs: droppings in the trail, fresh tracks and diggings. Never approach a bear, especially not its cub or (common in the spring) a carcass that shows recent activity. Cubs and protein are the two things about which bears are the most protective.

Women should know that the body smells associated with menstruation may have a connection in bear attacks. Some experts suggest that the odor of sexual activity may also provoke a male bear into attacking a man, as if perceiving the hiker as a rival in the bear's territory. Neither of these factors is likely to provoke an attack all on its own, but odors may worsen the outcome of an encounter caused in some other way. Additional provocations include pet dogs, which should never be in the backcountry, and strong-scented cosmetics.

When camping, remember that the main reason a bear comes around people is for food, and that bears are not a bit finicky. They will even try eating what we would consider nonfoods—aerosol deodorant, automotive grease and plastic bags that retain the smell of something edible. In car campgrounds, lock all food and cooking gear in your vehicle, preferably in the trunk. A cooler is no more than a convenient pop-top container for a bear. Keep cooking odors and food away from your sleeping area and tent. All garbage should go in the special bear-proof (actually bear-resistant) trash cans provided by the parks.

Backcountry campers should choose sleeping areas well away from trails and other natural travel routes. The shore of a lake or stream is not a good place to be. Nor is the bottom of a narrow canyon, or the low point on a pass, or a berry patch. Try to sleep in a place where neither you nor a bear would have reason to walk. I can offer no explanation for this, but without exception, fatal maulings involving campers in Glacier National Park have happened at night.

Everything said above about food odors pertains doubly to backcountry hikers. It may be foolish to carry and cook things like bacon and sausage, which spatter grease in all directions. Simple boiled meals using dried food are far less fragrant and pervasive. Whatever you cook, do it well away from your tent, preferably downwind, remembering that convection currents carry air downhill at night. Consider the next person to use the campsite. Just because you plan never to return to that site is no excuse for being careless with the disposal of food leftovers. With that in mind, pay attention to the condition of a campsite before you settle in. Is it dirty? Are there signs of bear activity? If so, find another place to sleep.

Before turning in, food must be well wrapped and hung with your pack high in a tree—not simply from a branch that a bear could get to and break, but out away from the tree trunk, preferably between two trees and 12 feet off the ground. A rope long enough to do this is as important a piece of equipment as boots. One hundred feet of eighth-inch nylon cord is usually adequate. Some hikers have taken to sleeping in clean clothing carried specifically for that purpose; clothing they have worn while cooking, fishing or picnicking, they hang with their packs. It should go without saying that all garbage must be thoroughly burned or carried out.

Confrontations

So what do you do if, despite precautions, you still encounter a bear? If distance permits, give ground and make a detour. Where detours are not possible, find a safe position, near a tree or several hundred yards away, and wait. If you let the bear know you're there, he'll likely go the other way. To see a bear under these circumstances is exciting and rarely dangerous.

The event to fear is the close encounter, when there is no room to flee, for either you or the bear. In this case, running is the worst choice. Bears are mighty fast, and by running you risk triggering a predatory reaction on the part of the animal. Instead, try to stay calm and motionless. A bear on its hind legs, with nose in the air, is not yet committed to action; standing up is a grizzly's normal way of assessing a situation, of trying to catch a scent or of seeing what you are. Not until it goes down on all fours do you need to react, so stand still or edge toward a tree if one is near, talk quietly and soothingly if you are able, and without any sudden motion, prepare to ease out of your pack. If you can reach a climbable tree, then go up it slowly and quietly, as high as you can. If not, then stand still. Chances are good that the bear will leave on its own.

A bear's preliminary aggressive behavior includes "whoofing," chomping its jaws, keeping its head low with ears laid back and advancing toward you. If a bear actually charges, the best advice is to play dead. Drop to the ground, face down, curl your knees to your stomach, put your hands behind your neck and stay still. Your pack may provide some protection. If this sounds like unreasonable advice, to lie still while a bear sniffs and paws, maybe even injures you, take heart in the knowledge that a number of people have survived such situations, and that fighting the bear or trying to run away would be worse than useless.

Bears' Rights

In confrontations between bears and people, the bear is virtually always the loser, particularly grizzlies, who tolerate human presence less well than black bears. Some hikers come to the mountains actually hoping to find bears, willing to risk the dangers of going quietly and

purposefully into bear habitat in the hopes of seeing and photographing one. They should keep in mind that when a bear is disturbed too
frequently (and no one can know when that might happen) his behavior changes. He leaves his feeding grounds, or worse, turns cantankerous. The first 100 times a hiker comes ding-a-linging his way through
the bear's meadow, the bear might run for cover; on the 101st, as if saying enough is enough, the bear might attack. Either way the bear loses.
If he starts attacking people, he may eventually be killed by rangers. If
he tries to change his feeding grounds, he does so by competing with
other bears on a range which cannot support all of them. One objective of forest and park managers in grizzly country is to monitor potentially hazardous situations and head them off before they reach a climax. Hikers may find areas and trails closed to use or there may be
warning signs posted in sensitive areas. For the good of the bears, as
well as our own safety, we should pay attention to the advice of rangers
and park wardens.

All through the Rockies, grizzly bears are in trouble. Their habitat
and their numbers are constantly shrinking. Over most of their onetime
range, they have disappeared entirely. Where this has happened, something greater is lost than simply a few half-ton hunks of wandering flesh
and fur. The mountains may look the same. But they don't feel the same.

Other Animals

Wild animals rarely attack people, but most will readily defend themselves or their young. The most ferocious attack I've experienced was
from a mother sage grouse who saw me as a threat to her chicks. She
attacked my legs in a rage, beating at me with her wings. Ounce for
ounce, I can't imagine even a sow grizzly putting up a stronger defense.

When it comes to larger animals, a little common sense goes a long
way. Early in the year, mothers are very protective of their young. In the
fall, the males can be irritable. Some old mountain hands count a bull
moose in rut as the single most dangerous animal in North America—
the same lazy fellow who a month earlier couldn't be bothered to get up
if you kicked him (please don't). In rut, hormones take charge. Moose
crash through the forest stopping for nothing, bulldozing substantial
trees and generally showing a bad attitude toward life. A person with
any common sense stays away.

Most of the time, a person sensitive to animals can approach fairly
close and be accepted as just another creature in the meadow. However,
this doesn't mean standing with your back to a bison grazing three feet
away so Martha can take a picture of you with the nice cow (two

Yellowstone fatalities). A good general rule for wildlife watchers is that when your presence affects the behavior of an animal—if it moves away, or gives you more than the casual glance, or shows a defensive posture— you are too close.

Snakes

Poisonous snakes are rarely seen at higher elevations. The climate is too cold. Where you might find them is on dry, southfacing slopes in warmer parts of the Rockies, along the Salmon River in Idaho, for instance, or on the Western Slope in Colorado. Their overwhelming desire is to avoid you; if you give them half a chance, they will do just that. Bites occur when people turn over rocks indiscriminately, or place their feet under an overhanging ledge instead of stepping over it, or climb a warm slope putting their hands on unseen ledges above. The best use of a walking stick is for poking ahead of you in suspect terrain.

Snake bites are not usually fatal. Even so, it's a good idea to read up on recommended first aid, if only because of all the false advice floating around. Some experts claim that more damage is done by so-called treatments than by the snake itself. Most hospitals have anti-venin available; if at all possible, drive to a hospital instead of slashing into a leg. All in all, snakes are a minor hazard.

Mosquitoes

Rocky Mountain mosquitoes come in a wide assortment, with 28 species in the Yellowstone region alone. Areas of greater ecological variety are blessed with a greater variety of mosquitoes. The far north, famous as it is for its limitless humming hordes, actually has only two or three species, while tropical rain forests have dozens. Their behavior is as diverse as their nomenclature. Some mosquitoes like shade, others prefer sun; some live at high elevation, others prowl valley bottoms. One type, *Aedes intrudens*, is relatively uncommon in the general population, but as its name implies it has a well-honed talent for finding its way inside buildings, where it becomes a major nuisance. Not all mosquitoes are interested in human blood; one species feeds only on cold-blooded vertebrates. What this all means to a traveler is that on the whole, mosquitoes are highly democratic: they'll get you no matter who or where you are, in the forest or on the tundra, in the middle of a lake or fast asleep in a mountain cabin.

It is true that only the female mosquito hunts for blood. Males are peaceful flower-lovers, living on nectar. If a female accomplishes a blood feeding, she can produce on the order of two hundred eggs, and she can repeat this several times in her short life span. However, contrary to what is often stated, females don't need blood to reproduce. If they are unable to obtain blood, they stop flying, digest their wing muscles and turn the protein into a much reduced number of eggs—perhaps only fifteen or twenty, but enough to carry on the common cause.

The most common sort of mosquitoes in the Rockies are called snow mosquitoes, because in order to hatch, their eggs must be frozen for a winter. When the snow melts in spring and summer, and the land is wet enough to support the aquatic larvae, the eggs hatch, and a few weeks later the air is filled with voracious blood-hunters. Now for the good news. Only one generation is produced per season. Once this first crop of mosquitoes dies (average life span of two to four weeks), there will be no offspring until the next year. If things don't seem to work that neatly in the mountains, this is because spring comes later to high areas than low areas, so not all mosquitoes of a given species emerge at the same time. Mosquito season works more like a time-release capsule. If you climb 5,000 feet from a valley bottom to a ridgetop, you're likely to come across newly matured and famished mosquitoes at some point in your hike. In general, however, July is the height of the season; by mid-August mosquitoes are a minor nuisance, while in September they are virtually gone.

A number of methods effectively cope with mosquitoes. Keep in mind that dark colors, warmth, carbon dioxide, sweet odors and dampness are attractants. Some people avoid eating bananas during mosquito season, or load up on vitamin B. Repellents work better than change of diet, especially those with *N-N-diethylmetatoluamide* as their active ingredient, a substance that dissolves plastic but apparently not skin. Use it sparingly. Usually a little on the backs of the hands, the neck and cheeks is sufficient. Loose-fitting clothing with a tight weave is a big help. In choosing campsites and rest stops, avoid wet, windless areas.

Other Insects

One hot summer day in Yellowstone, a man came into the ranger station pale and wide-eyed with his hand on the back of his neck. "I've been shot," he said, explaining that he had heard a gun go off, felt a pain in his neck and—look!—here was the blood to prove it. He wasn't joking, but he hadn't been shot either. He had been bitten by a buffalo gnat, a hump-backed little fly related to the blackflies of Eastern Arctic fame. As for the gun shot, the best guess was that a car had backfired somewhere in the area just as the fly found its mark.

Buffalo gnats, along with their partners in crime—no-see-ums (skilled infiltrators), black flies and a few others—are occasionally pests in the Rockies, but rarely do they get bad enough to be memorable. Deal with them in the same way you deal with mosquitoes (mental adjustment being the best coping mechanism of all), with only one exception. No-see-ums are not hindered by normal mosquito mesh. More and more tents are equipped with special tighter mesh, and this is a worthwhile feature to look for. Some people claim that ordinary skin lotions are effective repellents for no-see-ums.

Ticks can be a nuisance, mostly between March and July in places where large animals are common. This means ranchland as well as meadows frequented by mountain sheep, elk or deer. There's really no way to avoid them, but it's not hard to defeat their efforts. Ticks cling with incomprehensible patience to the ends of grass stalks and the branches of shrubbery, just waiting for a passing warm body onto which they can leap, find a tender spot and drill their ugly little mouthparts into in search of blood. Repellant works fairly well, sprayed on pant legs tucked securely into high socks. Ticks seem to be intellectually unequipped to think of crawling down; up is the only direction they go. If you keep things tucked in, and check your collar line and scalp every so often, you're likely to get them before they get you.

To remove an embedded tick, pull it gently, trying not to leave the mouthparts in your skin. If that happens, go after them as you would a splinter, then apply an antiseptic. Ticks do on occasion carry Rocky Mountain Spotted Fever (although this illness is far more common in East Coast suburbs than in the Rockies), and if a moderately severe illness resembling influenza occurs within several weeks of exposure to ticks, a doctor should be consulted.

Poisonous Plants

Poison ivy occurs sporadically along river and creek bottoms in warmer parts of the Rockies, growing as a shrub or a climbing vine. The oils contained in its leaves and stems—even its smoke if burned—are highly irritating to the skin of most people, but rarely a health hazard. Certain wild plants are poisonous if eaten—various mushrooms, baneberries, nightshade berries (both distasteful and therefore unlikely to be a problem) and tubers.

Inanimate Concerns

Mountaineers refer to the dangers of mountain travel as "objective hazards," meaning such things as rockfall, hidden crevasses on glaciers, avalanches, flash floods and suddenly changing weather. The degree to which one is exposed to these dangers is proportional to one's ambitions. Prudent people, regardless of experience, who stay on marked routes and listen to the advice of rangers and wardens rarely get into trouble. Problems arise when they exceed their abilities, experience or equipment, and suddenly find themselves in danger. The mountain traveler should not risk such hazards without the knowledge of how to cope with them. That means knowing when a snowfield is safe to cross and how to cross it in a safe manner. It means knowing how to use an ice axe to stop a fall; when and how to use a rope; how to recognize a dangerous situation; how to find an easier route; how to deal with a mountain emergency; and much more. A knowledge of rocks, their relative strength and stability, is essential for anyone who leaves the maintained trail. No one should try rock climbing without training and proper equipment. It is beyond the scope of this book to cover these topics, and it would be irresponsible to try in the small space available. This is one of those areas in which a little knowledge is truly a dangerous thing. Experience is as important as training, so novices should expect to progress slowly. The mountains hold plenty of thrills without travelers having to seek the extreme.

Hypothermia

This is a deadly condition resulting from the body's core temperature falling below normal. What makes it particularly dangerous is that by the time a person is actually hypothermic, he is no longer able to recognize the condition. His thinking is muddled; he has gone beyond feeling chilled to a point where he feels little at all; and he is unable to function. He stumbles, talks incoherently, wanders aimlessly and doesn't think of putting on warm clothing or having something to eat. Eventually his body loses the ability to recover on its own. At that point, only the actions of companions who recognize the gravity of the situation can save him. Hypothermia is most common in wet conditions, when moderate cold and moisture combine to cause rapid cooling: a sudden rainstorm soaking hikers far from shelter, or a boater falling into cold water, or a backpacker who decides he can stay warm in a light mist simply by walking faster. Keeping dry is the best prevention. If shivering begins, take it as a sign and have something to eat, put on warmer clothing or get out of the cold. The only first aid for hypothermia is warmth.

Sunlight

Sunlight at high elevations has a greater proportion of ultraviolet light than at sea level, making it harder on the eyes and skin. Especially when on snow, be careful to wear goggles or *dark* sunglasses. Snow blindness and blistered skin are the penalties for carelessness.

Altitude Sickness

Altitude sickness is caused by a lack of oxygen. Almost anyone who comes from a low altitude to the mountains will experience this to some degree, perhaps only a slight feeling of nausea when hiking uphill, or a shortness of breath, or less hunger than he might expect. This is normal and to be expected. The dangerous condition is acute altitude sickness, or pulmonary edema. This life threatening disorder can strike even hardened mountaineers and is cured only by hasty removal to lower elevations where increased air pressure will reverse the accumulation of liquid in the lungs. Going slowly to encourage acclimation is the best prevention. Of greater concern to the general mountain traveler is that thin air can aggravate heart ailments and cause dizziness or sleepiness while driving.

Crossing Streams and Rivers

Mountain hiking often involves crossing streams and rivers without benefit of bridges. Rocks are slippery and apt to roll, while the water is cold and fast. Several techniques minimize danger and discomfort. Often a stout stick, used as a third leg *upstream*, not downstream, is sufficient extra support. Several hikers can link arms and form a line parallel to the current. A rope helps, if used properly; the person on the bank should have a firm support, such as a tree trunk, and the wader should not be tied to the other end. If he falls, the rope can be used to pull him to safety, but he should have the option of letting go if pulled under by the dragging effect of the rope. Generally, if a moving stream is more than knee-deep, it might be too deep to cross.

Lightning

Lightning storms are common in the Rockies during summer. The usual pattern in thunderstorm season is for clouds to begin building around midday, coalescing into impressive anvilled thunderheads within hours, then dissipating by early evening. These storms are wonderful to watch—and to hear—as long as you find a safe place to sit them out.

What makes a place dangerous? Anyone knows to avoid exposed ridgetops and mountain peaks. Other risky places are on open water, under prominent trees, near farm machinery and on open fields (golf courses are notorious for lightning accidents). Of these categories, the most fatalities occur to people who have taken shelter from a storm under a tree. On the other hand, buildings and metal vehicles are among the safest places to be, which is of little consolation to the backcountry hiker who sees the afternoon storm brewing. Following are some rules for people caught in the outdoors:

- Do not stand under a prominent tree. If in a forest, look for a low-lying area, or a place where the trees are relatively small.

- Stay away from open water.

- If in the open, avoid being the highest object. Find a broad hollow. The middle of a ridge is safer than either end. Better yet, get off the ridge entirely. It used to be that people caught in an open field were advised to lie down, preferably in a ditch. This advice has been discredited by experts who point out that water may collect there and conduct electricity. Better, they say, to find a relatively dry place and crouch in a kneeling position, which minimizes body contact with the earth. For the same reason, do not squeeze into a rock crevice. On a smooth, wet rock face, current will probably flow through the thin sheet of water; better to crouch away from the face on a ledge than to hug the rock.

- Most mountaineers can tell tales of having their hair stand on end during an electrical storm. It happens to them because they get caught in exposed positions unable to move away quickly. This is a dangerous sign. If you feel the electricity in the air, crouch or kneel down, preferably on a climbing rope or a pack to provide insulation. Getting under overhangs and ledges is a good idea if you can avoid proximity to the roof or the walls—meaning the protected space should be large. Remember that in a lightning strike, electrons are flowing, seeking paths of conductance. You don't want your body to become a transmission line. This goes against natural instinct, which makes it all the more important to point out. Naturally, we seek cover. We snug ourselves into a hollow, or squeeze into a crevice, partly to avoid the rain and wind, but also because we want to feel less exposed. This is a healthy desire in most places, but it must be ignored when trapped on highly exposed ridges or cliff faces.

- Groups caught in exposed places should spread out instead of bunching together, so that if lightning hits, not all members are affected.

- Roughly two-thirds of lightning accident victims survive the experience, probably because they were not directly hit. Instead, they suffer from induced current in the vicinity of a strike. Some recover on their own; others need help. Mountain hikers should know how to use mouth-to-mouth resuscitation and C.P.R.

A Final Word on Mountain Dangers

One of the chief joys of the mountains is the sense of freedom and self-sufficiency that comes from understanding the alpine world. A skilled mountaineer goes virtually anywhere he wants, and does so safely. In this context, knowledge of objective hazards becomes a source of comfort rather than fear; it makes it easier to do things, not harder; it serves to break barriers rather than establish limits. Most of all, the more one learns about what dreadful things can befall the unwary traveler, the less one should worry. It's rather like walking through a railroad tunnel. If you have the train schedule and plan accordingly, there's nothing to fear; however, without a schedule, and only the general knowledge that tracks, tunnels and trains often coincide, such a walk could be an exercise in terror. Mountains are not dangerous; careless people are.

EQUIPMENT

With Just His Knife

Perhaps the most succinct statement ever made about outdoor equipment was spoken by Hugh Glass, a man with unusual expertise even among his mountain men friends. His statement came after having been robbed by Aricara Indians in the late summer of 1823 of almost everything he owned. His companions in that incident, less lucky than he, or maybe less able to hide themselves, had been killed. He was alone on the Great Plains, surrounded by enemies, with no means of transportation save his feet. Of all his equipment, he had only his knife and a flint. For most people even back then it would have been the end, but for Glass, situations like this were just another day, another dollar.

Glass was the man to know about such situations. Only a few months before that, he had been traveling across what is now South Dakota with about eighty other men. They were the first employees of the Rocky Mountain Fur Company, men who had answered the famous advertisement, published in a St. Louis newspaper in 1822 by General William Ashley, asking for a hundred "enterprising young men … to ascend the Missouri to its source," there to make their fortunes (or at least Ashley's fortune) on the beaver streams of the Rocky Mountains. Among Glass's companions were men who in the next few decades would carve themselves permanent places in the history of the West: Jedediah Smith, Jim Bridger, Tom Fitzpatrick, Jim Beckwourth, Etienne Provost, William Sublette and others whose exploits in the fur trade have given them an almost mythical stature. Yet among all their stories, their feats of endurance and their hairbreadth escapes, the story of Hugh Glass stands tall.

They were traveling overland, nervously on the watch for Aricara Indians, with whom they had fought an indecisive battle a few days earlier. Glass, because he was a good hunter, had gone ahead along the river bottom in search of game. In dense brush, he surprised a grizzly sow, who attacked and brutally mauled him before help arrived. The party halted there and argued about what to do. Clearly Glass could not travel. He was horribly mangled; the bear had torn off a buttock and shredded his back. Yet it was dangerous to linger any longer than necessary in Aricara country, and the party was divided on whether to stay or go. Eventually a solution was agreed upon. Two men, one of them apparently the young Jim Bridger, and an older man named Fitzgerald, would stay with Glass until he died, which was obviously only a matter of time. The rest would chip in a dollar each as a reward for the two who remained.

For several days, Bridger and Fitzgerald waited for Glass to die, but the gristly old hunter hung on, delirious and babbling, until their nerves got the best of them. Surely, even if he lacked the grace to die and get it over with, the old man was doomed, and staying simply put all three of them at risk—or so one guesses they might have reasoned. In any case, the two men left Glass alone, and because they could never hope to explain why they had left a dead man with his belongings, they took his rifle, his knife and everything else of value.

Yet Glass did not die. In fact, his anger at having been stripped and deserted by his friends may have provided him with the strength to do what followed. For days he stayed along the river, eating berries and whatever else he could find, until at last he dragged himself out onto the prairie determined to crawl on his elbows to Fort Kiowa, some hundred miles away on the Missouri River. It was the act of a man who knew he had no choice but to try the impossible, and Glass was rewarded by fate. Worming his way along one day he came upon a pack of wolves just as they killed a buffalo calf. Somehow he wiggled in and beat the wolves from the carcass. As historian Hiram Chittenden describes it, "Without knife or fire, it was not an easy thing to turn to account his good fortune, but hunger is not fastidious and Glass most likely took counsel of the wolves as to ways and means of devouring what he required. Taking what he could with him, he pursued his way, with inconceivable hardship and distress, and at last reached Fort Kiowa."

The story goes on and on in melodramatic fashion as he pursues the men who abandoned him, too long a story for this book. More than once, Glass escapes death by the narrowest of margins while those around him lose their lives. Eventually, his travels take him to an Aricara village whose residents feign friendship long enough to lure Glass and his companions into the chief's lodge. When the mountain men discover the trap, they run for their lives. Glass escapes by hiding himself until the Indians give up the search; his friends are murdered. Alone, he sets off once more toward the same Fort Kiowa he had struggled toward months earlier, but this time walking instead of crawling, and equipped with a knife and flint.

That first trip on his elbows, he admitted, had been rough going. He was missing a buttock, not to mention a knife. Compared to the state in which his comrades Bridger and Fitzgerald had left him, the Aricara had been downright generous. "Although I had lost my rifle and all my plunder," quotes an 1825 article in the *Missouri Intelligencer*, "I felt quite rich when I found my knife and steel in my shot pouch. These little fixens make a man feel right peart when he is three or four hundred miles away from anybody or anywhere—all alone among the painters [mountain lions] and wild varmints."

The mountain men were, by necessity, adept at getting along with nearly nothing, and the Indians they met were all too happy to give them chances to practice their skills. The first mountain man, John Colter, met a group of Blackfeet in Montana while he and his companion, named Potts, were setting traps from a dugout canoe. They heard a rumbling, Colter reported, and before they realized the cause of it, the high bank of the stream was suddenly crowded by several hundred Blackfeet on horseback. Colter and Potts had no choice but to obey the command that they paddle to shore, but Potts, as Colter stepped from the canoe, pushed back from shore. An arrow was fired. Potts fired back, killing an Indian, and was instantly, in Colter's words, "made a riddle of."

Colter, with a keener sense of survival, kept his head and convinced the Blackfeet to give him a sporting chance—a footrace. They liked that idea, so they stripped him naked, gave him a few hundred yards head start and came roaring after him. But Colter was fast on his feet, and fear gave him added incentive. It was six miles to the Jefferson River, across a flat covered with sage and prickly pear cactus. At one point, he turned to see that he had outdistanced all of his pursuers except for one man, who carried a spear and who was steadily gaining on him. At the last moment, Colter stopped and turned, and so startled the other man that he stumbled and fell, giving Colter a chance to grab the spear, stab the man with it and escape to the river before anyone else caught up. He hid all that day in the water beneath a log jam, praying that the Blackfeet, who he could see clambering about on the surface, would not decide to set the wood on fire to flush him out. Finally, in the dark of night, he slipped into the current and let it carry him away.

So what had he gained? There he was, naked, in the middle of the Montana plains, with nothing but cactus spines for shoes. At least he wasted no time weighing options; there were none. He had to make it hundreds of miles back to the Bighorn River, where the trader Manuel Lisa had a fort. With characteristic determination, gnawing on the roots of the blue camas as he walked, Colter made the journey in seven days.

No one would suggest that modern travelers should try to live like mountain men. For one thing, the mountains are too crowded, too heavily used; people just can't go around shooting animals whenever they feel hungry, or hacking apart groves of trees for temporary shelter, much less striking off across Montana in the altogether. There are rules against such behavior. The best reason for using modern techniques, however, is modern equipment. Jim Bridger would likely have given a good horse in trade for a set of polypropylene underwear, and another one for a pile jacket. In wet conditions, no natural fiber, not even wool, comes close to the warmth of synthetic pile. And consider other bits of modern gear: nylon tents, lightweight boots, sleeping bags, gas stoves, aluminum pots, flashlights, plastic bags, zippers, Velcro, sunglasses, even the simple, astonishingly reliable propane lighter.

It makes for an enjoyable anachronistic image: down from the mountains rides a hoary, scarred old fur trapper, followed by a string of packhorses loaded with bundles of beaver pelts. Across his saddle he carries a rifle, but as you get a closer look, the buckskin and buffalo grease image begins to break down. Behind his saddle is a down sleeping bag in a nylon stuff sack. Tent poles protrude from another nylon cylinder. He wears a Gore-tex parka over his pile jacket, and loose pants made of bunting. On his feet, he still chooses smooth-soled moccasins (you don't ride a horse with lug-soled boots), but inside are polypro socks and covering the legs of the moccasins are gaiters reaching well over his knees. Somewhere back on a packhorse is a pair of waterproof, nylon chest waders for setting traps. Around his waist, or slung beside the saddle, is a fanny-pack of waterproof cordura cloth, containing rifle cartridges, several propane lighters, a tiny flashlight with an argon bulb, extra lithium batteries and even some mosquito repellant. If he's inclined toward record keeping, he has a tiny, automatic, weatherproof 35mm camera. He comes into sight of an Arapahoe Indian encampment and gives a whoop to announce his arrival. The Arapahoes pile out of their dome tents dressed in brightly colored polypro underwear, and they party all night long, gorging themselves on freeze-dried ice cream and chicken tetrazzini.

The scene is only partly fanciful. With slight alterations, it happens all over the Rockies even today. Trappers and hunting guides still work on horseback, and quite a few of them have gone enthusiastically for the best in modern lightweight equipment. I report this from my usually conservative attitude toward equipment, an attitude that automatically distrusts the so-called new and improved in favor of the old and tested. Nonetheless, I have to admit that, if we exclude highly experimental designs and materials, new equipment is generally a step up from the old.

If money were no object, you could walk into any reputable outdoor shop and emerge two hours later with a complete, competent outfit for any mountain activity, including the food. Of course, for most of us money is quite a large object. We collect our gear over a period of years, making do, repairing and replacing one item at a time only when necessary. Remember the words of Hugh Glass. Somewhere between his knife and the complete multi-thousand-dollar outfit that the outdoor catalogs would like you to purchase is a compromise which fits each person's needs. Regardless of how good the new triple-ratchet whammy might be, you can still get by with the old manual version. I made my first backpack trip with a canvas duffel—not a pack at all—and an old rectangular sleeping bag, the kind with a flannel lining and pictures of ducks on it. I worked hard to get where I was going, and I didn't go far. But I had a wonderful trip. I remember it with a clarity undiminished by nearly thirty intervening years.

Now, considerably better equipped, I wince when I pass, along a steep trail, a party of kids carrying Coleman lanterns and cast-iron fry pans. But I don't laugh. Poor equipment is the last thing that should keep people with adventurous spirits from seeking the outdoors. Even in the Rockies there are gentle trails through sheltered areas which grandmothers could negotiate in high heels carrying their gear in cardboard boxes. If they were really determined, they could derive some pleasure from the exercise, in addition to some memorable lessons.

On the other hand, the Rockies are not the kindest of teachers. Poorly equipped people can die in situations that come up suddenly (shifts of weather can be major hazards), and in situations they get into because of inexperience (for example, trying to descend a steep snowfield without an ice axe or knowledge of its use). The mountains are not to be taken lightly. If you camp on a high pass and a sleet storm comes up in the night, you simply must have a tent. If you wish to go rock climbing, and you want to get more than five feet off the ground, you must have a rope—a real climbing rope, not just a length of clothesline. It is true that knowledge and skill can go a long way in making up for shortfalls in equipment, but it is equally true that the very people most lacking in skill are those also lacking in equipment.

The point to be made here is this: a certain minimum of equipment is necessary for any given situation. If you need a tent, it can be something less than the latest $800 marvel, yet it must stand up to whatever the weather might offer. The only way you will know whether a bargain is a bargain and not a disaster, is through experience and the advice of others. Unfortunately, advice is unreliable, and experience may be bitter. Even a big budget is no guarantee. A vastly experienced friend of mine recently bought a fancy new tent built by a famous tentmaker for a summer in the mountains. He spent $600 for it, assured by the salesperson that this was the best in the shop, and of course it was windproof—thanks to its precision aerodynamic shape. He took it up a high range in Alaska, where in the middle of the night he was awakened by a heavy freezing rainstorm and gale-force winds. In less time than it took him to wake up, the tent popped its poles, the fly came loose, and the whole rig came down around his ears. The rest of the night was what he calls an adventure.

Suggested Equipment List

Clothing

FOOTWEAR: Boots, of light or medium weight, are needed for rough trails and cross-country travel; running shoes are fine for day-hiking on trails and are used by many people for backpacking as well.

SOCKS: Polypropylene or wool.

UNDERWEAR: Long underwear is not needed for most of the summer, but it's nice at high altitude. Polypro and blends have generally replaced pure wool.

PANTS: Loose-fitting long pants (not jeans) of synthetic mixes; whipcord or cotton are best. They should breathe and dry quickly. Shorts are pleasant in summer months.

SHIRTS: T-shirts are a standby. Wool overshirts, light sweaters, flannel shirts and almost anything else is appropriate. The mountains are a good place to use up old dress shirts.

JACKETS: Mountain parkas, with their big pockets, are one of the best inventions ever. Take a down vest for warmth (or a down sweater) in combination with the parka. The need here is for protection from both wind and cold, together or separately.

GLOVES: A light pair of gloves or mittens, especially early and late in the season.

RAINGEAR: Should you use Gore-tex, which is supposedly waterproof yet breathable? Some say it is a wonderful material, others disagree. It is certainly expensive. I find waterproof, coated nylon garments suitable for conditions in the Rockies, which are not so wet as some other ranges. Whatever material you choose, you need a hood, and chaps or pants, although I rarely carry more than a parka. Often as not, I rely on a poncho, or even my tent fly, wrapped around me and my pack and held in place with my arms. It has the advantage of being easily adjustable, but no, it isn't ideal. What is?

HAT: A hat with a brim; a wool cap in colder weather.

Shelter

TENT: I've gone out many times with no tent, or with only a tarp, on short trips when the weather was stable and insects were no concern. It's very nice to go so light, but perhaps risky. While a tent is a luxury at times, at others it can save your life. Options include little tubes, bivvy sacks, spacious domes, and so forth. Whatever you choose, keep it light, and if you need to economize, then match your camping goals to your equipment. A simpler tent can be sufficient in a stand of big trees well below the ridgetops, or near your car, while a true mountain tent is a necessity in exposed sites.

For car-camping, the possibilities for shelter are endless, from vans to motorhomes to mountain tents and canvas wall tents. This is purely a matter of personal preference. For the most part, almost anything will do, although obviously a $20 drugstore tent will have its failings.

SLEEPING BAG: Should you choose down, artificial fiber or what? The controversy rages. Talk to a competent salesman, and remember that in New York, people who are not remarkably tough spend whole winters in cardboard boxes.

SLEEPING MAT: It is a nasty fact of geology that the ground has gotten harder over the past 30 years. When I first began camping in the mountains, I slept with nothing but the bottom of my sleeping bag between me and the sometimes frozen ground. Not anymore; the earth has hardened up. I can't explain why this is so, but it seems to be an ongoing phenomenon. My grandfather agrees that the ground is harder than when he was a boy, and no doubt the process will continue.

Whatever the cause, some sort of sleeping pad has become, for me, a necessity. The cheapest option is a closed-cell pad, which you can use as it comes. Open-cell foam absorbs water and needs a waterproof cover to avoid getting wet from rain or even condensation of body moisture. A fairly recent addition to the field is the inflatable mat, which has a foam pad inside it—expensive but wonderful.

Packs

DAYPACKS: These are necessary for everyone, backpacker or not, who plans to carry something for more than a hundred yards at one stretch.

BACKPACKS: Again you are faced with a choice. Should it have a frame or not? I have both types, and either one does the job. I like my frame pack better, but this seems to be another matter for personal choice. One thing I can say for certain, the pack must have shoulder straps.

Cooking

STOVES: Stoves are more and more important, as fires become less acceptable. You also need a *cooking pot* or two. Making life easier are these items: *nylon washpad, pot pliers, cup and spoon, matches or propane lighter.*

Odds and Ends List, Many Optional

Camera and film
Binoculars
Books
Maps
Notebook and pen
Compass
Flashlight
Lighter
First-Aid and emergency kit: moleskin, firestarter, signal mirror, whistle, bouillon or tea, several coins for phones
Water purifying equipment
Bandanna
Moccasins
Gloves to double for cooking use
Bear bell
Pocket knife with can opener
Sunglasses
Insect repellant
Sun screen
Toilet paper
Tiny utility kit: wire, safety pins, nylon string, tape, rivets, needle and thread, candle stub, plastic bags
Boot waterproofing, silicon-based
Head net
Rope for hanging packs
Personal kit: toothbrush, dental floss, etc.
Lip salve
Swimsuit
Fishing gear
Watch

Clothing for Cities and Towns

Happily for the traveler, mountain towns as a rule are informal places. Except for certain events in larger cities, casual clothing is acceptable everywhere. Even in fancy restaurants (with the occasional exception in places like Aspen and Sun Valley), men will feel at home with open collars and walking shoes. Women might wish for a simple skirt and top with sandals or light shoes. But even that could make you feel overdressed in most places. The uniform of mountain towns, for men and women, is a pair of jeans, light boots or running shoes, T-shirts, wool shirts—really any shirt— and some sort of hat if you want sun protection. Only two sorts of dress will make you stand out: a suit with a tie and polished shoes, or a glaring tourist rig (polyester leisure suit, souvenir hat, cameras and so forth).

If you visit Indian reservations, especially for festivals or religious ceremonies (which I highly recommend), keep in mind that standards of modesty and social manners are more strict here than off the reservations. Women should wear skirts and loose-fitting tops. Men should never go shirtless, and no matter what the temperature, shorts are not acceptable. In some cases, you'll be asked to leave if people find your clothing immodest. Other times, you'll just not be treated with the friendliness that is commonly shown to visitors who demonstrate sensitivity to the cultural values of others. While it may be true that some dances and other events are held off the reservations for the benefit of tourists, and are performed for pay, it is well to regard anything happening on Indian land as a religious event, and not as entertainment. Non-Indians are invited in the same spirit that prompts most religions to keep the doors of their churches open. Visitors must behave appropriately.

Car Camping Extras

If you have some sort of camper, then your basic needs are met by the vehicle. But if you travel in an ordinary auto, there are items you can include, along with your stripped-down backpacking equipment, that make camping a lot easier:

- portable sun shower
- plastic wash basins
- clothesline
- folding grate for the fire
- lantern (to be used with sensitivity)
- camp chairs
- "occupied" sign

- 5-gallon water jug
- cast-iron skillet, maybe a wok
- cutting board
- plastic tablecloth
- wooden or plastic crates for storage
- short-handled spade
- tarp with ropes and stakes
- axe
- saw
- cooler.

Tips on River Running Gear

I assume that private river runners know what is needed on mountain streams. Suffice it to say that proper equipment is essential to survival, and that almost nowhere in the Rockies can you float a whitewater river without some experience. The water, being snow-melt, is cold throughout the summer, while weather can change with such speed and ferocity that even mirror-smooth mountain lakes become death traps in a matter of moments. Wet suits are required where there is any white water.

If you decide to take a commercial trip with a guided party (highly recommended; see page 30), whatever you need by way of specialized gear should be provided, and if not, then you should consider going with a different company. This equipment includes wet suit, life jacket, waterproof bags for clothing and sleeping bag, and ammo cans for cameras and small miscellaneous items. These companies usually rent, optionally, anything else you may need.

Photo Equipment

The choice of a camera for the mountains is fairly straightforward. Anyone at all serious about photography will want to carry a camera that uses film no smaller than 35mm. And unless you're willing to carry the extra weight, and have some reason to desire a larger format, you don't want anything bigger than 35mm either. The standard piece of equipment, for professionals along with most other people, is a single-lens-reflex camera with interchangeable lenses. The new breed of ultra-light, compact SLRs, which come loaded with automatic features, will please most users most of the time. However, these compromise lightness for durability. Some parts are plastic where they should be metal, while electronics are more sensitive to damage, dust and moisture than the simple spring-driven levers found in heavy, non-automatic models.

I use both electronic and manual cameras; each has its place. The automatic features are convenient when photographing wildlife or fast-moving activities like skiing and kayaking. The lightness of the compact cameras make them easier to carry, and of course any camera around your neck takes better photos than one left at home because of its weight. On the other hand, when reliability is essential, when I must come home with photos, I always take a heavy, no-nonsense working machine (Canon and Nikon F-Series cameras fit this class). Another approach is used by a friend of mine who makes his living doing adventure photography using nothing but lightweight cameras. He has them checked regularly for accuracy and tosses a spare body or two into his pack as he would a couple of candy bars. He's never had three of them fail on one trip.

One other sort of camera is worth mentioning. Several companies put out tiny 35mm jobs hardly bigger than two rolls of film. Their lenses fold inward to make a flat unit that fits happily in a shirt pocket. The better models are serious cameras. They may not have changeable lenses, but the ones they do have are good, slight wide-angles, the best choice for a lens if you're limited to just one. These have the great advantage of being simple and ultimately portable.

As for lens selection, your decision will hinge on budget and method of travel. Obviously, what you can carry in the car is quite different from what you'll be willing to take in a backpack. My stripped-down hiking kit includes a moderate telephoto zoom with macro focusing and a 28mm wide-angle—just two lenses and a camera body.

Other items worth having in a simplified kit include skylight and polarizing filters (high-altitude air is thick with bluish ultraviolet haze), a cable release, a lightweight tripod (to me a necessity because the low-intensity light early and late in the day is the best for pictures) and a lens-cleaning brush. Be sure to have some means for keeping the camera dry in wet weather—a heavy-duty plastic bag at least.

For film, remember that low-speed film gives a sharper, generally more satisfying image, but only if not blurred by camera motion. During the day, there's usually no problem using fast shutter speeds, but toward dawn and dusk, you begin to need a tripod or a high-speed film. I prefer to carry the tripod wherever I go. Many others—even some professionals—rely on fast film.

WATER FOR DRINKING

There has been considerable attention paid lately to a micro-organism found in mountain water which causes intestinal distress. Its name is *Giardia lamblia*, and it causes an illness called giardiasis. The symptoms are intestinal bloating, diarrhea, nausea, cramps and loss of appetite. Without treatment, dehydration can result in serious trouble. This is apparently one of those maladies that lingers until you purge yourself with a drug like Flagyl, also used against amoebic dysentery. People who have suffered from giardiasis report that it leaves a powerful impression—definitely, they say, something to avoid.

Giardia is a relatively new concern. Ten years ago, no one mentioned it as a pollutant of mountain water. Now, every bulletin board in the Rockies has a posted warning against what is popularly called beaver fever, referring to one of the animals that acts as a carrier. Rumors say it came from Asia in the digestive tracts of traveling mountaineers, who infected the mountains of North America through uncareful toilet habits. But Giardia is not new, exotic, nor is it limited to mountain areas. This protozoan has been with us for centuries and commonly occurs in the general population of the United States and Canada. Incidence rates are as high as ten percent, although only about half the people who have it ever suffer from symptoms. Contamination to other people occurs through oral-fecal contact, which results simply from not washing one's hands before preparing food. The way it gets into mountain streams and ponds is through badly located latrines. Once in the water, Giardia forms cysts, which can survive for two months; the colder the water, the longer they survive.

Besides humans, the only known carriers of the infectious strain of Giardia are beavers and domestic dogs. Beavers can be a problem because they live in the water, although research done recently in Canada shows an infection rate of only four percent. The equivalent figure for dogs is 22 percent. Although not aquatic animals, the toilet habits of dogs are certainly casual, and in the company of backpackers they are likely to cover more ground, and higher ground, than beavers. Hikers who insist on taking their pets into the backcountry with them might keep this in mind.

How do you know if you have it? Symptoms show up anywhere from a few days to a few weeks after ingestion. Without treatment, they may disappear, only to recur periodically after that. The illness can also be serious enough, if dehydration occurs, to require hospitalization. Treatment is simple, once diagnosed. If you develop symptoms as much as six weeks after drinking untreated water (or poorly treated water; see below), you should suspect giardiasis and inform your doctor.

Although Giardia is the main worry, other microbial meanies, carried by sheep, cattle, wild animals and, of course, humans, can be found in mountain waters. Fortunately, hepatitis and cholera are not concerns in North American mountains as they are in say, the Himalaya. In any case, proper water treatment will kill whatever might ail you. The questions are when to treat, and how.

A totally prudent answer to the first question is always. If you follow that advice, you'll never get giardiasis from mountain streams. However, if the results of the Canadian study mentioned above are any indication, the chances of finding it in untreated water are far lower than the warnings would have us believe. Of 51 mountain ponds tested, only 2 were infected. Looking at those figures, I am willing to accept a certain amount of risk. When I find water at the base of a snowfield, I drink. I also drink from streams well above timberline, and in places little traveled by other hikers or their dogs. But when in doubt, I use one of several treatment methods.

The first is boiling. Five minutes of rolling boil takes care of the problem and is no trouble when preparing breakfast or supper. It is, however, an inefficient way to deal with water for your canteen or water you need for the middle of the day. Boiling takes time and requires a fire; if you use a stove, much more fuel must be carried. Besides, boiled water is flat-tasting and unpleasant. You need a way of dealing with cold water.

A thorough discussion of backcountry water treatment by Frederick Kahn and Barbara Visscher was published in the *Western Journal of Medicine*. What prompted them to do their research was that, while on a hike in the California Sierra Range, they drank the icy, clear water of a mountain stream, and both came down with giardiasis. Their article is a valuable contribution to the whole question of water purity for outdoorspeople.

First they reviewed the most common purifying method used by hikers—Halazone tablets. Actually a chlorination technique, Halazone works adequately when water is not badly polluted, but it does not kill amoebic cysts and certain viruses. In addition, if the water has nitrogen compounds, or if the water is alkaline—common in the Rockies—Halazone quickly reacts to form other chemicals which have little or no purifying power. This means the recommended dose might not do the job. Consider also that Halazone has a limited shelf life, which is shortened by moderate heat or exposure to air. It's hard to know if that bottle is still potent or not.

Kahn and Visscher recommend iodine as an alternative for treating water. Iodine, at very low concentrations, apparently kills anything objectionable: amoebic cysts, Giardia cysts and all. Except for people with hyperthyroid conditions or iodine sensitivity, they say iodine is perfectly safe. Tincture of iodine can be used (eight drops of two percent tincture per quart; and let it sit 20 minutes), but this noticeably flavors

the water. Another form of iodine—actually tetroglycine hydroperio-
dide—is pills. The trouble is, like Halazone, these tablets lose effectiveness
with exposure to air. Many hikers carry water pumps with microscopic filters. These work well under most conditions, but they vary in quality.
Some combine active ingredients with filtering action for better results. But
they can fail mechanically, and it's a good idea to have a backup system.

My choice is that described by Kahn and Visscher. It is very simple,
very cheap, easy, lightweight, foolproof and affects the water flavor the
least of all. You need elemental iodine crystals, about eight grams of
them, usually obtainable at a pharmacy. Buy the kind that look like rock
salt, not like powder or flakes. The pharmacist might have to be convinced that you want them for treating water. It's possible to make an
extremely unstable explosive from elemental iodine. The first time I
tried to get some I was 14 and I had just that intention—a big bang. The
pharmacist saw through me and refused. I suppose I should be grateful.

While at the pharmacy, ask for a one-ounce clear glass medicine bottle, the kind with the hard, black plastic cap. The crystals go in there.
Now you have an iodine source capable of treating as much as 250 gal-
lons of disgustingly polluted water. To use it, fill the bottle with water
and shake it for 30 to 60 seconds to saturate the solution. A saturated
solution is one that will dissolve no more iodine from the crystals. There
is no fear of getting too strong a solution. Then let the crystals settle to
the bottom. Important! You want the solution, not the crystals. This is
why you asked the pharmacist for chunks of iodine, not flakes, which
can float. Iodine in too great a quantity is a poison; according to Kahn
and Visscher, no fatalities have been reported from ingestion of less than
15 grams of the stuff, which is one reason for putting only 8 grams in
your bottle. Supposedly, you could accidentally swallow it all and survive. Please don't try.

Using the cap as a measure (the standard black medicine bottle cap
holds 2.5 cc), pour the right amount of iodine solution into your filled
canteen. The amount varies with the temperature of your iodine supply
bottle, because warmer water will contain more iodine. At 37°F, you need
20 cc to purify a liter of water; at 68°F, 13 cc; at 104°F, 10 cc. This
assumes a wait of 20 minutes following treatment. If you can wait 40
minutes, you can get the same results by cutting the iodine dosage in half.
On the other hand, for very badly polluted water, you might want to
double the iodine dosage. Another thing—immediately after treating the
water, loosen the cap of your canteen and hold it upside down, washing
the top with the iodined solution. It would be ironic to treat the contents
and be infected by a beastie clinging to the threads of the canteen lid.

MAPS

Canada

The most useful maps for hikers are the 1:50,000 series (2 cm. equals 1 km.). For reference, Map Index #2 covers the Canadian West. In addition to the following address, many park offices, bookstores and sporting goods stores carry maps applicable to their locales. To order by mail, contact: **Canada Map Office**, Department of Energy, Mines and Resources, 615 Booth St., Ottawa, ON K1A 0E9 (tel: 613-998-9900; 800-465-6277).

British Columbia publishes a series of maps showing locations of provincial parks and campgrounds. These are also useful as highway maps, because the detail is better than a general road map. One large map, "British Columbia Road Map and Parks Guide," covers the province. Regional maps are available for smaller areas, including the Kootenay Region, Cariboo-Shuswap-Okanagan Region, Northern B.C., and Lower Mainland and Vancouver Island Region. These maps are free, along with good descriptive brochures for individual provincial parks, from these offices: **B.C. Parks**, 2nd floor, 800 Johnson St., Victoria, BC V8V 1X4 (tel: 604-387-5002).

B.C. Parks has 13 district offices. They include: **Cariboo District**, 181 First Ave. N., Williams Lake, BC V2G 1Y8 (tel: 604-398-4414); **East Kootenay District**, Box 118, 20 miles north of Cranbrook on Wasa Lake Dr., Wasa, BC V0B 2K0 (tel: 604-422-3212); **West Kootenay District**, R.R. #3, Site 8, Comp 5, 4750 Hwy. 3A, Nelson, BC V1L 5P6 (tel: 604-825-3500).

Alberta publishes a free map titled "Alberta Forest Service Recreation Areas," which covers the entire province and includes, in addition to Forest Service facilities, campgrounds maintained by the Provincial Parks Service. A variety of other maps of many scales is available through retail map sellers. For information, contact: Environmental Protection, Natural Resources Service, Recreation and Protected Areas Division, Outdoor Recreation and Operation Systems Branch, 8th Floor, 10405 Jasper Ave., Edmonton, AB T5J 3N4 (tel: 403-427-7009).

United States

Topographic maps are needed for any backcountry travel, and are sporadically available in local outdoor shops and bookstores, or by mail from the following address for $4 each: Distribution Branch, **U.S.**

Geological Survey, Box 25286, Denver Federal Center, Denver, CO 80225. Index charts, which show the coverage of topographic maps, are free on request; index charts are often published on national forest visitor's maps also.

Each national forest publishes a detailed visitor's map, which shows roads and highways, trails, water features, buildings, land ownership and more. These maps are essential for anyone who wishes to strike off on backroads, as most highway maps are of too large a scale to include this sort of detail. Some Forest Service maps include surrounding jurisdictions as well as their own; these become indispensable for navigating on county roads, finding fishing access sites, boat launch sites, isolated patches of public land and so on. The cost is $3 each, with most forests covered by a single map.

Forest Service offices often have other, specialized maps. Travel plans, free of charge, indicate vehicle restrictions, areas closed to hunting and seasons of closure. Wilderness maps, increasingly available, have contour lines and more up-to-date trail information than older topographic maps. These are usually sufficient for hiking use and have the advantage of covering the entire wilderness area in a single, inexpensive sheet. This book mentions these maps for wilderness areas where they are available.

METRIC–IMPERIAL MEASUREMENT CONVERSION

To convert degrees Celsius to degrees Fahrenheit, multiply degrees Celsius by 1.8, then add 32:

10 Celsius × 1.8 = 18
18 + 32 = 40 Fahrenheit.

To convert degrees Fahrenheit to degrees Celsius, subtract 32 and divide by 1.8:

70 Fahrenheit − 32 = 38
38 divided by 1.8 = 21 Celsius.

Or remember these rough descriptions:

CELSIUS		FAHRENHEIT
40	Sweltering	104
30	Hot enough to seek shade	86
20	Room temperature	68
10	Pleasant autumn day	50
0	Freezing point	32
−10	Pleasant winter day	14
−20	Distinctly cold, sharp air	−4
−30	Exposed skin freezes quickly	−22
−40	Clear January nights	−40
−50	Photograph the thermometer	−58
−56.6	A new record for the Rockies; call the papers and take several photos.	−70

To convert meters to feet, multiply meters by 3.28 (305 meters equals 1,000 feet). Converting feet to meters is the opposite—divide feet by 3.28.

To convert miles to kilometers, multiply miles by 1.6. Converting kilometers to miles is the opposite—divide kilometers by 1.6. Or just think of 6 miles being roughly 10 kilometers.

CHAPTER TWO

The Colorado Region

COLORADO, FOR ALL its apparently jumbled landscape, has a simple geography. There are three provinces: the plateaus, the mountains and the plains. Taking these in reverse order, the plains rise gently, all the way from the Mississippi Valley to the base of the mountains. There is no question about where one ends and the other begins. You can draw an almost straight line separating the eastern third of Colorado from the rest of the state and there you have it—the plains.

The mountains take up most of what is left. One range crowds against the next, over the Continental Divide and beyond. Where they fade out, they meet the high desert plateaus of the western slope, a country of wide, flat-topped mesas and deep river canyons, which look off into the red rock distance of Utah. This western boundary of the mountain province is less well defined than its eastern edge; the ranges form no distinct rampart shining above the desert. Even so, you can tell you've left the mountains behind by the bright colors of the rocks, by the heat on a summer day and by the parched look of the land.

Three distinct provinces. Now add to your mental picture a series of high, broad mountain valleys strung in a north-south direction just east of the Divide, each valley enclosed by mountains. Finally, imagine a chain of mountains running southward out of the state, actually two parallel chains on either side of one of the valleys mentioned above, and you have the whole picture. Or rather, you have an image of the skeleton of the Rockies from their beginnings at Santa Fe, New Mexico, to the Wyoming border.

In adding flesh to the bare bones, you find a huge diversity in land-forms. Mountains are dominant, but their long shadows encompass the broad open areas of North, Middle and South parks, the sweep of New Mexico's high grasslands, the edge of redrock desert on the west, the dune-filled wilderness of Great Sand Dunes National Monument, the rich fossil beds of Florissant and Dinosaur national monuments, and lush fruit-growing valleys of the western slope.

In New Mexico, a sweep of sage-covered valleys washes over the mountains. The peaks are rugged but are surrounded by lavish expans-es of empty land, which are matched in their atmosphere of spacious-ness only by the high desert sky. Crossing into Colorado, the sense of openness continues for some distance if you stay in the San Luis Valley, but if you turn west and follow the Continental Divide along the crest of the San Juan Range, you find yourself plunged into the most precip-itous, ragged, closed-in terrain in the state. Spectacular country to be sure, but what a contrast to New Mexico. There, you can see summer thunderstorms coming for a hundred miles, flickering along on lightning legs, sending gusts of air, scented by water and dust, ahead of them as they cruise along. Thunder rolls in from the distance, indistinct and muf-fled. But in the San Juans, a blue sky is suddenly obliterated by black-ness as a thunderhead peers over the mountain rim. Lightning shatters against the mountainsides; sharp blasts of thunder rattle the cliffs; the air roars through the passes. Wonderful stuff, every minute of it.

From the San Juans, the Divide cuts back to the east and climbs onto the crest of the Sawatch Range. Here is the backbone of the Rockies, a region of big, broad-shouldered mountains covered by mile after mile of open tundra, with deep glaciated valleys separating one range from the next. And in addition to the Sawatch, there are other impressive ranges in the neighborhood, all competing for space. As in the San Juans, there is little flat ground to be had. Mount Elbert, summit of the Sawatch at 14,433 feet, is the highest point in Colorado, and in the Rockies. Within 30 miles of it are numbers two and three, Mount Massive (14,421 feet) and Mount Harvard (14,420 feet). All told, Colorado has 54 peaks over 14,000 feet, called affectionately by Coloradans "Fourteeners." Residents of the state feel chauvinistic about those 54 summits because in all the rest of the Rockies there isn't another mountain peak above 14,000 feet high.

Where the Sawatch Range ends, the Divide takes a further jaunt east-ward, to follow the high peaks of the Front Range above Denver, past the scene of the first big Rocky Mountain gold discoveries and the state's major population center. The Divide enters Rocky Mountain National Park, its easternmost point, before turning back west and finally following the Park Range into Wyoming.

This tangled upheaval of rock is the headwaters of six important rivers. The Colorado and Gunnison flow westward. The North Platte, route of westward settlement, pushes north into Wyoming before starting its long journey across Nebraska. The South Platte and the Arkansas run eastward, down the broad slope of the plains to the Mississippi Valley. Flowing south is the Rio Grande, the river of the U.S.-Mexico border, which ends its travels in the Gulf of Mexico in south Texas. In addition are smaller rivers of interest to boaters: the Yampa and the Dolores, to name two.

The human landscape shows as much variety as the physical landscape. Northern New Mexico is a land of adobe homes, old mission churches, Spanish language sprinkled with idioms dating to the time of Cervantes, the oldest continually occupied public building in the United States and the even more ancient villages of Pueblo Indians—the land of *poco tiempo*. The pace of life there remains slow, especially compared with the booming Front Range in Colorado. Dominated by the cities of Denver, Colorado Springs and Pueblo, this narrow band of foothills country is by far the most populated part of the state. Beyond commuting distance, tucked in the valleys of interior mountainous regions, dozens of small towns go about the business of Colorado. Some are ranching towns, serving as administrative and supply centers. Others remain from the days of the gold rush. Mining has mostly disappeared as a way of life, but the towns that have survived retain some of their early flavor from Victorian times. Of these mining towns, Aspen, Breckenridge, Crested Butte and Telluride have become well-known ski resorts. Others, such as Cripple Creek, Central City and Silverton, rely on ghosts and relics from their boom days to draw tourists.

In these communities, large and small, still bustling or gone to ghosts, lies the story of Colorado, and in a larger sense, the story of the entire Rocky Mountain region. The chief builder of the region was mining and the supplying of mines. After the placer fever came hard rock mining and more permanent towns. Between 1880 and 1890, the state population doubled to over four hundred thousand. Growth like that encouraged the dreams of speculators and entrepreneurs, who poured money and effort into projects which matched the scale of the mountains. Cities grew up far from supply lines. Roads and railroads were not far behind. Dams were built, and tunnels bored under the Continental Divide to carry irrigation water. Some dreams were failures on a grand scale (witness the Colorado, South Park and Pacific Railway, which was intended one day to provide a route all the way from Denver to the West Coast, but was so expensive to operate that freight charges from Denver to Leadville were greater than from New York to San Francisco via Cape Horn); however, even those were no more than bumps on the fast-rising curve of history.

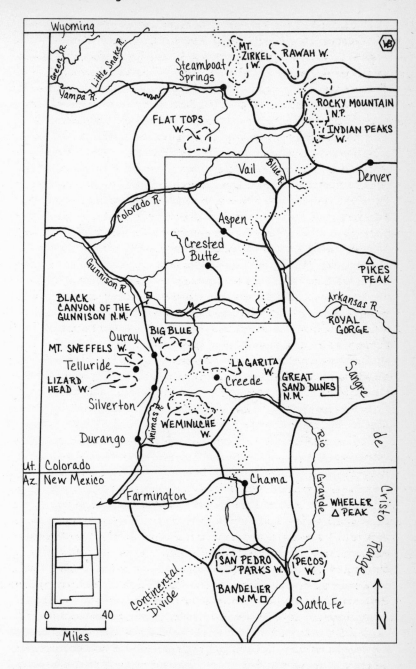

Wyoming

Green R.

Little Snake R.

Yampa R.

MT. ZIRKEL W.

RAWAH W.

Steamboat Springs

ROCKY MOUNTAIN N.P.

FLAT TOPS W.

INDIAN PEAKS W.

Vail

Blue R.

Denver

Colorado R.

Aspen

Crested Butte

PIKES PEAK

Gunnison R.

BLACK CANYON OF THE GUNNISON N.M.

Arkansas R.

ROYAL GORGE

BIG BLUE W.

Ouray

MT. SNEFFELS W.

Telluride

LA GARITA W.

Creede

GREAT SAND DUNES N.M.

Sangre

LIZARD HEAD W.

Silverton

Animas R.

WEMINUCHE W.

Durango

Rio

de

Ut. Colorado

Az. New Mexico

Chama

Grande

WHEELER △ PEAK

Cristo

Farmington

Range

Continental Divide

SAN PEDRO PARKS W.

PECOS W.

BANDELIER N.M.

Santa Fe

0   40

Miles

N

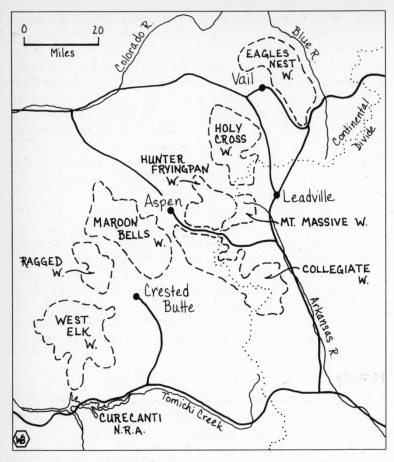

Useful Names and Addresses

General travel information is available through the **Colorado Travel and Tourism Authority**, P.O. Box 3524, Englewood, CO 80155 (tel: 303-296-3384). For the **State Patrol recording of road and pass conditions** around Colorado, call 303-639-1111.

NEW MEXICO

Northern New Mexico is a region of high, expansive landscapes, where the air is dry and clear and fragrant with the scent of juniper and pinyon pine. The tones of the earth are subtle in midday, but in the evening they glow in the warm light, their colors matching the sky as if both were of the same material. The buildings, some of them centuries old,

literally are of the same material. The adobe gives them the appearance
of having been attached to the landscape for so long that homes, garden
walls, roads and trails have all become a part of it. This is best felt in the
evening after a hot summer day with the mountain skyline glowing red
and the air absolutely silent as only desert air can be. Then the old adobe
seems most like the ancient mountains.

In summer, great thunderstorms are visible a hundred miles away,
flickering in the night sky. If you are caught by one in the mountains,
there is no color but black. The air turns suddenly cold and the rain
comes in quarter-teaspoon drops. It drains off fast in runnels the color
of the ground, leaving behind an inch of mud. You can almost sense the
plants expanding in the presence of the new moisture.

D.H. Lawrence called the skyline above Taos the most beautiful in
the world. Many others have agreed with him, including renowned
artists who have chosen this place, which seems at first glance so aus-
tere, as their homes. Willa Cather, Georgia O'Keeffe, Edward Weston,
Ansel Adams, Robert Henri and E.A. Robinson are among those who
found inspiration here. People claim that this land weaves a spell which,
once sensed, cannot be put out of mind; that it has something to do with
the high desert air and the light which inhabits it. This is no idle boast;
it takes some time, and some adaptation, to feel it. But it is there.

History

In New Mexico, the human landscape is very different from other parts
of the Rocky Mountains. Few Americans or Canadians realize that the
oldest communities in either country are not on the Atlantic Coast, but
here in the desert highlands of northern New Mexico and Arizona.
People have lived here, in permanent dwellings, for many centuries.
While cities and towns elsewhere in the range celebrate their centenni-
als, communities along the Rio Grande lay claim to some seven hundred
years of occupancy. A Wyoming rancher proudly describes himself as a
fourth generation resident: "My great-grand-pappy settled this land."
Ask the same question of a Taos Indian, and he'll have to estimate the
number of generations of his family who have raised children and corn
in the same valley.

When the Spanish conquistador Coronado arrived from Mexico in
1540, he found ancient cities inhabited by people with a rich culture
well adapted to life in an arid land of extreme climatic fluctuations.
They were Tanoan people, believed to be descendants of the Anasazi,
who built the famous cliff-dwellings at Mesa Verde and other places. At
the end of the 13th century, the cliff-dwellers abandoned their canyons.

Some of them apparently moved east to the Rio Grande Valley, where they lived for a time in canyons, then moved up onto the plains. At the time of Coronado, they numbered an estimated 30,000 people, farmers who irrigated nearly 25,000 acres. They made high-quality pottery, wore clothing made of cotton from their fields, and lived in multistoried dwellings like those seen in the area today.

The encounter between the two cultures was a violent one. The Spanish thought of themselves as pioneers and conquerors who had the right, and even the responsibility to force their style of government, their taxes and their religion on the Pueblo people. It began with Coronado, who ordered the residents of a Pueblo village out so that his men could move in. He also confiscated winter food supplies from a number of pueblos, and tortured two chiefs so that they would tell him about the gold he was certain they had. The Indians revolted, and the Spanish put them down with appalling violence. Hundreds of Indians were killed, some by the cherished Spanish method of burning people alive. That set the pattern for centuries of Spanish-Indian relations. The most famous revolt occurred in 1680, when the Pueblos rose in a carefully synchronized attempt to exterminate all the Spanish in northern New Mexico. The revolt succeeded in causing the Spanish to abandon the territory for 12 years. When they came back, it was in force and with traditionally bloody results.

With time, accommodations were worked out. The desert demanded equally of both cultures and forced the Spanish, so far removed from other Mexican cities, to live in peace, if not friendship, with the Indians. Their ways of life converged somewhat as they learned from each other and faced common challenges. One challenge came from the Apache and Comanche tribes, who lived an aggressive, nomadic existence in the Sangre de Cristos and neighboring plains. They raided the Rio Grande not only for horses but slaves as well, and did so with impunity. There are reports of Spanish captives being offered for ransom by Comanches at the annual Taos summer trade fair.

Another challenge came in 1847, when the American Army under General Stephen Kearney invaded New Mexico during the Mexican-American War. This time it was the Spanish and the Indians against the Americans. When the time seemed ripe, they revolted together. The Americans put them down in a manner that Coronado would have approved. In following decades, the U.S. government proceeded to dismantle, override or simply ignore many aspects of Spanish law and culture, just as the Spanish had done centuries earlier. Resentment still boils to the surface over these questions, one of which, applicable to this book, is the matter of national forest ownership of old communal Spanish grazing lands. Users of the forests should be aware of these local feelings. In general, as had happened before, a peace of sorts was made. Over the years, the three groups have settled in together, continuing to borrow from one another, living parallel but mostly separate lives. The modern culture of the Rio Grande is a fascinating blend of elements from all three. To an "Anglo" visitor, which means anyone not Indian or Hispanic, the towns of northern New Mexico feel both foreign and familiar. This is the United States, but it is two older nations as well, each of which has kept its language and many of its traditions.

For a mountain traveler, it means that a visit to the Sangre de Cristo or Jemez ranges is a cultural experience as well as a natural one. The Pueblo villages give visitors a warm welcome, at the same time requiring that certain rules of conduct be met. If you can time your visit to coincide with one of the Pueblo dances or ceremonies by all means do so. More can be learned in two hours of watching one of these ancient activities than in a week of reading anthropology books. Also, throughout the year, other festivals are held. Some go back to traditions of Old Spain, while others have been invented locally. All are a unique blend of cultures; the best example might be the Fourth of July—the most solidly Anglo of all holidays, but celebrated in Santa Fe with enthusiasm by everyone.

Sangre de Cristo Range

Two New Mexican mountain chains stand at the south end of the Rockies—the Jemez and the Sangre de Cristo ranges. Separating them is the Rio Grande Rift, a major geologic feature caused by the pulling apart of the two neighboring mountain blocks. The rift extends from southern New Mexico all the way to the San Luis Valley in Colorado, providing a channel for the Rio Grande. The Jemez are built of volcanic material which erupted along fault lines on the west side of the rift. The great Jemez volcano actually surmounts one of the sinking blocks, while its neighboring subrange, the Sierra Nacimiento, achieved its position on one that rose. If you drive along the west flank of the Sierra Nacimiento on Highway 44, you can see the straight rampart which betrays its fault-block origins.

The Sangre de Cristos came into existence by the same mechanism, rising on a massive chunk of pre-Cambrian basement rocks, which rose on the east side of the rift. Three-hundred-million-year-old sediments overlie much of the range, but on higher peaks and at the bottom of deeply cut drainages, the ancient granitic core has been exposed by erosion. The name, Sangre de Cristo, means "Blood of Christ." The first

Spanish were apparently unimpressed by the mountains and called them simply Sierra Madre or Sierra Nevada. The new name appeared later. According to legend, a Franciscan priest, Padre Juan, lay dying from wounds suffered in the 1680 Pueblo Revolt. He asked God for a sign, whereupon the peaks were lit red in the sunset, and Padre Juan uttered his last words, "Sangre de Cristo!" The legend fails to say who reported what he said.

From the San Luis Valley, where they abut the Sawatch Range, the Sangre de Cristos parallel the rift valley for 200 miles to Sante Fe, where they fade into foothills. At their northern end, they form a single, dramatic crest; upon entering New Mexico, they subdivide into a broader range. Two main chains, the Taos Mountains and the Cimarron Range, embrace the interior valleys of Moreno and Costilla creeks, which have a lively mining history. South of there, the Santa Fe Mountains rise above the city of the same name.

The Cimarron Range is privately owned, while the Taos Range is contained by Carson National Forest and the Taos Indian Reservation. Access to private land is by permission only, which can be hard to get. National Forest lands are of course open to the public, but trailheads are frequently on private land, requiring that hikers get permission from the owner to park there or to be dropped off and to park cars elsewhere. Public lands in the Taos Mountains include two small wilderness areas: the Wheeler Peak, with the state's highest mountain, and the Latir Peak Wilderness areas. The former is adjacent to the Taos Ski Valley resort, from which access is straightforward. The Santa Fe Mountains are largely covered by the Pecos Wilderness, one of the older and more famous wilderness areas in the country. Access varies with approach and is discussed below. Vandalism is a serious concern for people leaving their cars unattended; read the cautions in the Pecos Wilderness discussion.

Latir Peak Wilderness

This small wilderness area occupies the drainage of the Lake Fork of Cabresto Creek. A central high ridge dominates the basin with several 12,000-foot peaks. Latir Peak (12,708 feet) stands at the head of the basin near the wilderness boundary. All of these can be climbed from Cabresto Lake, either by following Lake Fork Creek to its headwaters at Heart Lake (Trail 82), or by branching off to the north after two miles and following Bull Creek (Trail 85). The two trails come together again near Heart Lake. Also in the Heart Lake area, Trail 81 goes east to Baldy Mountain, continuing on the divide until it drops to rejoin the access road on Cabresto Creek. To get there, drive to Questa on Highway

522 north of Taos. In Questa, turn east on New Mexico 38, go about a quarter-mile, then turn north on State Road 563, which becomes Forest Road 134, to the trailheads. 134A branches to Cabresto Lake Trailhead, but is not suitable for passenger cars.

Wheeler Peak Wilderness

Adjoining the Taos Indian Reservation on the south and Taos Ski Valley to the north, the Wheeler Peak Wilderness includes the highest point in the state, 13,161-foot Wheeler Peak. Also on its eastern boundary is Taos Peak, one of the more famous mountains in the Southwest. Both mountains are popular hikers' climbs, usually done as day-hikes. To reach the Wheeler trailhead, drive to the ski resort by turning off Highway 522 onto Highway 150 several miles north of Taos. The road enters Rio Hondo Canyon and passes frequent Forest Service campgrounds on its way to Taos Ski Valley. Trail 62 from the base of Taos Ski Valley goes to Williams Lake; the peak can be reached from there on steep slopes, or on trails 90 and 91 from a trailhead farther up Lake Fork Valley.

Taos Peak is close by, but the trailhead is not. To get there, you take Highway 38 from Questa to Red River, where a right fork (F.S. 58) takes you on up the Red River Valley to the East Fork Red River (F.S. 58A) and the Ditch Cabin trailhead. Take the trail up Sawmill Creek for three miles to Sawmill Park, and climb east to the summit.

On the north side of the Rio Hondo, outside the wilderness, a number of trails are worth considering. One suggested circuit is to go up Manzanita Canyon on Trail 58 (one mile downstream from Italianos Campground) to Lobo Peak, traverse from there on Trail 57 to Gold Hill, then back via Trail 64 to Bull-of-the-Woods pasture near the ski area.

Useful Names and Addresses

For a forest map ($3) and other information, contact the **Carson National Forest**, 208 Cruz Alta Rd., Taos, NM 87571 (tel: 505-758-6200). District offices in the area are in Questa and Taos.

Pecos Wilderness

The Pecos Wilderness covers 224,000 acres in the heights overlooking Santa Fe. It is basically one large basin surrounding the headwaters of the Pecos River. On its ridgeline are several striking summits, most notably the Truchas Peaks, four summits of approximately 13,000 feet in elevation with South Truchas (13,103 feet) being the highest. On both sides of the basin, the mountains drop steeply to the valleys below, and the wilderness includes the upper parts of these outer slopes. If you wish to avoid crowds, head for those areas: on the northeast, the Rincon Bonito, and on the northwest, the Sierra Mosca. The terrain is very rugged, ranging from 8,400 to over 13,000 feet, and largely covered by dense forests dominated by Engelmann spruce. Ridgelines rise above the forest and surround a small number of glacial lakes. These lakes are so few, so fragile and so popular, that camping is not allowed in their immediate areas. Wildlife includes mule deer, elk, bighorn sheep and black bear.

Most hikers access the wilderness through the Pecos River drainage, because it is centrally located, there are several Forest Service campgrounds at the trailheads, parking is permitted on public land, and the trails start high. To get there, drive to Pecos, New Mexico, east on Interstate 25. From Pecos, Highway 63 follows the Pecos River to the wilderness area. The choices for trails here are many.

The other common access is at the Santa Fe Ski Basin, reached directly from Santa Fe on the Hyde Park Road (State Route 475). Forest Service campgrounds are located along the road, and parking for either of two trails is at the ski area.

Several other trailheads exist in all directions from the wilderness area, with a wide variety of trails and options. However, a warning is in order. Vandalism and theft has happened frequently enough in this area that people try not to leave their cars unattended. Some places are worse than others. The local procedure is to have someone drop you off and pick you up at the end of your trip; or to arrange parking with someone living near the trailhead who is willing to have the car in his driveway. The warning extends to campsites as well. Don't go off for a day-hike leaving an expensive set of equipment, complete with packs for carrying it, in plain view.

A complete list of trailheads, with access information, is on the back of the Pecos Wilderness Map, available through the addresses given below. Detailed information on each trailhead should be obtained from the appropriate Forest Service office before you embark on your trip.

Useful Names and Addresses

The map mentioned above is large scale, with 80-foot contour lines; it and a forest map covering the entire area are available at the following addresses for $4 and $3 respectively. A wilderness permit is not required, but users are limited to 15 per party and 14 days in one campsite. East side: **Las Vegas Office**, 1926 7th St., Las Vegas, NM 87552 (tel: 505-425-3534). South side, including Pecos River: **Pecos Ranger Station**, P.O. Drawer 429, Pecos, NM 87552 (tel: 505-757-6121). North side: **Camino Real Ranger District**, P.O. Box 68, Penasco, NM 87553 (tel: 505-587-2255). West: **Espanola Ranger District**, P.O. Box R, Espanola, NM 87532 (tel: 505-753-7331). For general information, contact the Forest Supervisor, P.O. Box 1689, Santa Fe, NM 87501 (tel: 505-988-6940).

Cimarron

Cimarron—with various spellings—means "wild animal" or "fugitive slave." In the case of this frontier town, it refers specifically to bighorn sheep which inhabited the nearby mountains. The town, on the old Santa Fe Trail east of the Taos Mountains, began as headquarters for the ranch of Lucien Maxwell, one-time mountain man, who settled here in 1849 on a Spanish land grant he inherited from his father-in-law. After a variety of disputes, the grant was eventually determined to cover 1.7 million acres. His property was a western kingdom with mountains, rivers, forests, quantities of gold, silver and coal, and vast areas of grazing land. Maxwell ruled from Cimarron, his house a famous location for wild times and famous guests. Among them was Buffalo Bill Cody, who started his Wild West Show here. Gold was discovered in the Moreno Valley in 1866, leading to a gold rush and the establishment of Virginia City and Elizabethtown. Maxwell sold the grant in 1869, which was probably good for his health. He escaped having to deal with the Colfax County War, fought over ownership of the grant and its boundaries. Prospectors and settlers had swarmed into the grant, and when informed that this was private property, said that that was hogwash— no one in these free United States could have that much land. Battles erupted. Outlaws were attracted like flies to meat. At one time, the owners hired none other than Bat Masterson and 35 of his colleagues to enforce their claim.

A story is told of Clay Allison, a notorious gunman. One day a man by the name of Pancho Griego, in a gambling dispute, shot two soldiers and stabbed another, killing all three. Apparently emboldened by his prowess, he decided he was ready to test the great Allison. In the showdown that followed, he thought he might trick the gunman by holding his sombrero across his gun holster to hide the motion of pulling the gun out. Allison was not taken in and shot Griego twice in the head.

During that period, the *Las Vegas (NM) Gazette* once noted: "Everything is quiet in Cimarron. Nobody has been killed for three days." It was bad enough that Henri Lambert, owner of the St. James Hotel, where 26 killings are said to have taken place, posted a sign: "Gents Will Please Leave Their Six-Guns Behind The Bar While In

Town. This Will Lessen The Customary Collections For Burials." The hotel has been carefully restored, preserving the 29 bullet holes in the saloon ceiling, and is operated now as a museum. Besides the hotel, there is a museum in the Old Mill, containing all sorts of regional memorabilia; also a stone jail, a cemetery and other old buildings. Order came to Cimarron eventually, although it took until the 1890s, and the grant was sold into smaller but still huge corporate cattle ranches.

Taos

When you speak of Taos, you must specify which one you mean. There are three: Taos Pueblo, the town of Taos and Ranchos de Taos (Ranches of Taos). The Pueblo, the ancient home of Tiwa Indians, is located three miles north of the town of Taos and is probably the most visited, most photographed pueblo. Founded in 900 A.D., it has been continuously occupied ever since. Two multistoried complexes stand facing each other across a central plaza, a multipurpose area used for important dances, stabling livestock, parking cars and socializing. Beside the plaza stands an adobe church, the chapel of San Geronimo de Taos, built to replace an earlier church destroyed during the 1847 revolt. Other smaller, detached buildings are clustered in the neighborhood. Through the middle of the plaza flows the Pueblo de Taos River, reduced to a creek by irrigation ditches which water the fields you pass on your way in. The river originates on the slopes of Taos Peak to the northeast, draining the sacred Blue Lake, and it is still the drinking water source for people living in the two building blocks, which are being maintained as traditional dwellings without running water. The darkness of the outer rooms has been relieved, however, by windows and doors. In Coronado's time, ladders through hatches in the roofs were the only way in.

As you drive to the plaza, signs provide directions. A booth at the edge of the plaza sells permits for photography or painting. A parking fee of $5 is levied, along with entry fees of $1 per person. Visitors should keep in mind that this is not a museum. Taos Pueblo is a working town of some two thousand people, only a few of whom produce things for sale. Its residents have learned that by charging fees they can maintain some control over tourists, some of whom can be astonishingly rude and insensitive. The fees go toward community projects in the Pueblo. The plaza is a lively place much of the year. The two main buildings are occupied by people going about their daily business. Some of the ground floor "apartments" are shops, which sell everything from fresh bread, baked in the adobe beehive ovens still in use around the plaza, to drums made from hollowed sections of tree trunks with hide stretched across the openings. The methods of curing the wood to prevent cracking are carefully guarded secrets of the drum makers. These drums are famous and are sold in galleries all across the United States. The shops, whatever they sell, are informal places. You are likely to find yourself in someone's living room looking at pots or paintings and talking about politics. This is a most pleasant way for visitors to gain some perspective on Pueblo life. Mind you, it will be a partial understanding at best. These people know the value of privacy.

The town of Taos is nearby and has almost as long a history as the Pueblo. It was founded in 1615, and in the traditional Spanish style, grew up around a town square, or plaza. The buildings faced inward, presenting their backsides as walls of a fort, while narrow entrance lanes could be closed by gates or wagons if the need arose. This is the best place to begin seeing the city. Park on a side street and walk to it unless you arrive early in the morning or in the off-season; this is a crowded place in summer and on festival weekends. The plaza itself is not the original; it was rebuilt in the early 1700s, having been destroyed by the 1680 revolt and its aftermath. From here, walk the side streets. You might go first to the Taos Visitors Center on Paseo del Pueblo Sur, 2 miles south of the plaza, where you can get maps, walking tour information, a schedule of Pueblo dances and answers to questions. Taos is a city of artists, which becomes immediately apparent from the number of galleries here. Among the historic highlights in Taos are the Kit Carson Home and Museum, the Governor Bent House and Museum, and the Blumenschein Memorial Home.

The third Taos is the village of Ranchos de Taos, four miles south of the city. It is best known for its Church of Saint Francis de Assisi, built in the 1770s and a classic among adobe churches. As lovely as its front courtyard and entrance may be, it is the back of the church, with its buttressed sanctuary, which is the reason for its fame.

Some Useful Information About Taos

CAMPGROUNDS: Capulin and Las Petacas are two Carson National Forest campgrounds east of Taos on U.S. Highway 64. South of the town of Taos, on U.S. Highway 68 and State Highway 570, is Orilla Verde Recreation Area (BLM). North of the city, on Highway 522 and west on Highway 378, is Wild Rivers Recreation Area.

USEFUL NAMES AND ADDRESSES: **Taos Tribal Offices,** P.O. Box 1846, Taos Pueblo, NM 87571 (tel: 505-758-3873). **Taos County Chamber of Commerce,** P.O. Drawer 1, Taos, NM 87571 (tel: 800-732-8267). **Carson National Forest,** 208 Cruz Alta Rd., Taos, NM 87571 (tel: 505-758-6200).

The High Road to Taos

While most traffic between Santa Fe and Taos goes by way of Highway 68, a beautiful alternate exists, called locally the High Road to Taos. It winds through canyons and foothills past small villages, historic churches and Pueblo towns. Heading north, turn off to Nambe Pueblo on Highway 4. It joins Highway 76 and continues through the hamlets of Chimayo (famous for weavers), Cordova (famous for woodcarvers), Penasco and others, much of the road affording fine views of the Sangre de Cristo Range.

Santa Fe

Santa Fe, the capital of New Mexico, is a city of around 62,000 people. Currently a building boom is going on, as its fame grows and people discover it as a place to retire or to have a second home. Although the city is doing an admirable job of zoning and setting architectural standards, the inevitable sprawl clutches at Santa Fe from all sides. As with Taos, the best way to see the city is to pass by the outskirts and go directly to the plaza, preferably via the Old Pecos Trail road (one of the freeway exits), which winds its way through the old section of town. From the plaza, a good beginning is the Governor's Palace, the oldest continually occupied public building in the United States, having been built in 1610 and used to this day. Presently, it is a museum with an excellent regional bookstore. Outside, under the portico, local craftspeople display jewelry and other wares. Among the most instructive exhibits in the museum is a series of photographs showing the building at various times in its long history. The changes in the structure, and in the plaza which you see in some pictures, show Santa Fe as the distant outpost it was. In the courtyard stands an ancient oxcart with huge, solid wooden wheels carved from what looks like a cottonwood trunk. Carts like this provided Santa Fe's link with the Spanish cities of Mexico; it took three months to haul a train of these the long way north from Chihauhau City. Compared to this cart, the wagons of pioneers on the Oregon Trail look like marvels of modern technology.

On the west side of the plaza is a tourist information office open in summer, which can supply maps, historic walking tour descriptions and other material. The main office is two blocks northwest at the corner of Sheridan and Marcy streets. Follow a walking tour route, or simply wander the side streets of the plaza. Early morning is a good time, but summer evenings are the best. A characteristic of Mexican architecture, which comes as a surprise when you aren't expecting it, is the interior garden courtyards, which open through gateways to the street. From outside you see a narrow road with adobe walls crowding the curbs; it doesn't look particularly homey. Then as you walk past openings in the walls, you glimpse, maybe at the end of a short corridor, gardens rich in greenery, with a fountain perhaps, and trees arching overall. In the downtown area, some of these interior courtyards are now commercial establishments. One of the nicest is the Sena Building on East Palace Avenue.

From the plaza, you have dozens of possibilities too numerous to include in this book. Some highlights include the Chapel of Our Lady of Light, with its marvelous (some say miraculous) spiral stairway, on Old Santa Fe Trail. Facing the plaza in the east is Saint Francis Cathedral, a Romanesque church built in the 1870s by Bishop Lamy, the central character of Willa Cather's novel, *Death Comes for the Archbishop*. On Palace Avenue is the Fine Arts Museum, with galleries and a concert hall designed in the form of a traditional Spanish church. Also in the plaza vicinity are several fine historic homes: the Pinckney Tully House, the A.M. Bergere House, the Delgado House, and on De Vargas Street, the oldest house in Santa Fe, claimed by some (probably not true) to be the oldest non-Indian house in the United States. On the same street stands San Miguel Mission Church, one of the oldest in the Rio Grande area. It has a fine wooden altarpiece and a number of historic artworks.

Some Useful Information About the Santa Fe Area

HOW TO GET THERE: Santa Fe uses the Albuquerque airport, an hour's drive to the south. An airport shuttle runs between the two cities seven times daily (**Shuttlejack Inc.,** 505-982-4311); **Greyhound** and **Trailways** bus lines run twice daily. **Amtrak** stops in Lamy, 14 miles from Santa Fe, which requires making arrangements to get from the depot to town.

CAMPGROUNDS: Several Forest Service campgrounds are found northwest of Santa Fe along State Highway 475 (F.S. 101) toward Santa Fe Ski Basin. Facilities vary and few have drinking water available.

USEFUL NAMES AND ADDRESSES: Local bookstores carry excellent guides to Santa Fe, Taos and the surrounding area. One worth special mention is Robert L. Casey's *Journey to the High Southwest* (Pacific Search Press, Seattle, 1985); it includes detailed walking tours, driving tours, annotated lodging and restaurant lists, and insightful comments on the area. General information can be had from the **Santa Fe Convention and Visitors Bureau,** P.O. Box 909, Santa Fe, NM 87504 (toll-free tel: 800-777-2489).

Jemez Mountains

The Jemez Mountains, like the Sangre de Cristos which rise on the other side of the Rio Grande, originated in connection with movement along the Rio Grande Rift. However, while the Sangres are fault block mountains, meaning they were pushed upward by underlying forces, the Jemez are capped by layer upon layer of ejecta from a huge volcano, which eventually collapsed to form a caldera 15 miles in diameter. The rim of the caldera makes up the crest of the Jemez. One of its last acts occurred some five million years ago, when the volcano spewed out a mass of low density ash which covered 400 square miles to a depth of 1,000 feet— the Pajarito Plateau. The ash has eroded into a complex landscape of canyons and mesas.

Since the collapse of the original volcano, numerous smaller eruptions have built low hills and mountains in the caldera, making it impossible to see the entire feature from any one point. However, in the magnificent Valle Grande, you can get an idea of the size of the caldera. Only about a fifth of the total area, this high valley stretches in a grand sweep down from the highway, across a network of meandering streams and up along the base of hills on the other side, the whole grassy expanse dotted with cattle and reminiscent of the days when some western ranches were the size of small European nations.

Most of the caldera is private land with restricted access, but it is surrounded by the Santa Fe National Forest. State Highway 4, between Los Alamos and La Cueva, is a good place to start on an exploration of the area. The road climbs steeply from Los Alamos to the rim of the caldera and follows it past the Valle Grande through moist country of forest and meadow. The East Fork of the Jemez River begins in the Valle Grande; where it enters public land, it is popular among trout fishermen. The Forest Service has built several campgrounds along the highway, and several unpaved roads head off southward, eventually dropping off the mesas, into canyons, and emerging at the base of the Jemez.

At La Cueva, you have a choice of route, which might be dictated by weather. State Highway 126 continues across the high Jemez to Fenton Lake, where the pavement ends and, if it's been raining recently, the mud begins. A sign at La Cueva warns that the road is impassable in inclement weather. This is no exaggeration. Summer thunderstorms are common, and one determined cloudburst can turn a solid roadbed into a quagmire. Forest Service maps clearly distinguish between dirt (dry weather) roads and ones that can be driven in the rain. Those who doubt the warning have obviously not experienced

New Mexico mud, a substance that is so slippery that snow tires spin even on level stretches of road, and stationary vehicles are in danger of sliding sideways on the slightest grade. Wheels quickly become great useless gobs of fine mud. If you have the misfortune of getting stuck in it, you step out ankle-deep into material the consistency of tar, which is not only difficult to stand up in, but which also sticks to your feet as well as your shovel. The challenge of getting unstuck provides an experience that you will long remember and hopefully never repeat. A word of advice from one who knows: putting chains on at this point is next to useless.

If the road is passable beyond Fenton Lake, you can follow it north and west through high, rugged, forested country, coming close to the San Pedro Parks Wilderness (San Gregorio Reservoir is popular with fishermen), and then dropping into the valley of the Rio Puerco to the town of Cuba, where limited services are available. The distance from La Cueva to Cuba is 49 miles. San Pedro Parks Wilderness is a high plateau, averaging about 10,000 feet in elevation, and crowned by San Pedro Peaks; access is from Forest Road 103, which leaves Highway 96 east of Gallina headed for Rio Puerco Campground.

At La Cueva, the alternative to Fenton Lake is to continue down high-walled Jemez Canyon, past several small hot springs to the town of Jemez Springs. This quiet little community contains the ruins of an early mission, the ambitiously large fortress church of San Diego, built in 1617 and destroyed during the rebellion of 1680. Adjacent to the massive remains of the church are the ruins of the Guisewa Pueblo, abandoned by its Jemez residents when the Spanish re-conquered the territory. Continuing downstream past the modern pueblo of Jemez, the canyon cuts through the dark Jemez volcanics into brilliant red rock, which forms the cliffs on either side of the valley. In the spring, as you come down from the high alpine meadows of the caldera, where the aspens haven't yet leafed out, the warm air of the lower Jemez River, along with the red rock and the electric green of new cottonwood leaves, makes you feel solidly in the Southwest desert. In fact, this is the eastern boundary of the Colorado Plateau, a distinct geologic region extending all the way to southwest Utah and containing most of the big desert canyons of the Colorado River drainage. It might be fair to say that here is the Southwestern corner of the Rocky Mountains. Looking upstream from Jemez Pueblo, you see a classic cross-section of the southern Rockies, from red sedimentary rocks and traditional Southwestern dwellings to high peaks covered with snow, alpine plants and—quite often—thunderheads.

Bandelier National Monument

One of the great mysteries of archaeology is the disappearance of the Anasazi, the ancient inhabitants of the canyons and mesas of the Southwest. The Anasazi (a Navajo word which means "the ancient ones," or "the ancient enemy") built the famous cliff-dwellings at Mesa Verde, Betatakin, Chaco Canyon and many other locations throughout the region—elaborate cities, some with irrigation systems, multistoried buildings and thousands of inhabitants. Everywhere you travel in northern Arizona and southern Utah, you are reminded by ruins and relics that this land was the home of an energetic and numerous people who for some reason utterly abandoned their homes. The disappearance seems to have happened in a short period of time at the end of the 13th century. In some cases, villages appear to have been left with intentions of returning—corn was left in storage bins, pottery and other artifacts were left sitting beside fireplaces. Some cliff-dwellings had only just been built. Betatakin, for example, in Tsegi Canyon near Kayenta, Arizona, is a fairly large ruin, which archaeologists say was built and abandoned in the space of about fifty years. Possible explanations for the exodus include a severe drought, which occurred in the latter half of the 1200s, depletion of natural resources, disease, rivalry with hostile neighbors, the loss of contact with declining civilizations in Mexico, or perhaps a combination of factors. No one really knows the reason, but clearly the Anasazi did leave, and their homes, empty today, are excellent places for the contemplation of history.

The second half of the mystery—where did they go when they left?—is less of a puzzle. Modern Hopis, who live in northeast Arizona, recognize the Anasazi as their ancestors, and indeed there is much similarity between the centuries-old Hopi pueblos and the mysterious ruins. Some Anasazi may have moved out of the canyons and onto the Hopi mesas. However, archaeologists believe that the bulk of the migration was to the Rio Grande Valley, to places like Frijoles Canyon in what is now Bandelier National Monument.

Judging from tree-ring data, the first settlers in Frijoles Canyon arrived during the 12th century. What they found was a sheltered area with permanent water, deciduous trees and sheer-walled cliffs—familiar country for people who had come from canyons of the Colorado River. But Bandelier had an important difference. Instead of sandstone, the canyon walls were made of soft volcanic tuff, a material so soft that even a fingernail can gouge it. Natural erosion had created thousands of small caves, from a few inches to six or eight feet in diameter. It was a simple matter for homebuilders using stone tools to carve out whatever shape or size room was needed, adding homey touches like storage alcoves and smoke holes, then plastering and perhaps even painting the walls. Often one or more rooms would be added outside the cave, built in a more traditional style, while on the canyon floor, other builders constructed full-scale pueblos. Tyuonyi (tchoo-OHN-yee), a ring of low stone foundations today, was once a single building of about four hundred rooms, two stories high, built in a rough circle with only one entrance leading into the plaza. This may have been for defensive reasons. Just above the pueblo, set in and against the canyon wall, were Talus House and Long House, where traditional walled structures abutted enlarged cave rooms. Other pueblos were scattered throughout the neighborhood, notably Tsankawi, a structure similar to Tyuonyi but on an exposed mesa a half day's walk to the north (you can drive there now).

These people were farmers and hunters. They grew corn, beans and squash, the three staple foods of the region. They made pottery and wove cotton cloth on looms, although because of the climate, they probably traded with people from warmer places for the cotton itself. Then, in about 1550, shortly after Coronado's expedition and for perhaps the same reasons that made them leave their cliff-homes centuries earlier, they abandoned these pueblos, too, and moved to present-day Rio Grande communities.

Bandelier National Monument protects these ruins and many others in a 50-square-mile area. It was named for Adolph Bandelier, a Swiss-American scholar who surveyed ruins in the Santa Fe area during the 1880s. He wrote a historic novel, *The Delight Makers*, set in prehistoric Frijoles Canyon. The monument visitor center and administration buildings are located in the canyon, south of Los Alamos on State Highway 4. A short self-guided walk takes you through the ruins, where you have a chance to climb into several cave-homes and a restored kiva, a ceremonial room. The caves are remarkable things, reminiscent of similarly carved homes found in Turkey and Egypt. At Tsankawi, where the cliffs are less vertical than at Frijoles Canyon, erosion has carved rounded shapes, which residents hollowed out like so many stacked igloos. You walk through them on trails worn deep into the tuff by centuries of sandals and bare feet; in places the grooves are knee-deep. Where a ladder might be needed if the rock were harder, you find comfortable steps, deeply worn, following the natural curve of the slope. It must have been quite a sight at dusk 500 years ago, as fires were lit in the hundreds of chambers, the cliff face glowed with internal light, and silhouetted human figures moved across the openings.

Trails

Most of Bandelier is designated wilderness, accessible only by a 60-mile system of foot trails. The terrain is canyon and mesa, quite rugged and mostly forested. On the edge of the monument, the San Miguel Range (Boundary Peak, 8,182 feet) provides overviews of the region. Archaeological sites make hiking in Bandelier more than a wilderness experience. The Painted Cave is a high alcove covered with colorful drawings. San Miguel and Yapashi are unexcavated ruins, which you can visit without the distraction of other people; in addition, something about having walked so far to get to these ruins, just as the Anasazi themselves traveled, enhances the contemplative aspects of a visit. Because Bandelier is at a lower elevation than much of the surrounding country, hiking is possible when snow closes the high trails.

Sample destinations and round trip distances from Frijoles Canyon: Painted Cave, 20 miles; Yapashi, 10 miles; Ceremonial Cave, 2 miles.

Some Useful Information About Bandelier National Monument

HOW TO GET THERE: To get there, turn off U.S. 85/284 fifteen miles north of Santa Fe onto State Highway 502, signposted for Los Alamos and Bandelier. Drive through Los Alamos by continuing on 502 to 501 to 4, or skip the town by turning onto 4 directly from 502.

GENERAL INFORMATION: The visitor center has a small, well-designed museum and bookstore. During summer, rangers give guided walks through the ruins and present evening talks at the campground, located on the rim of Frijoles Canyon. A shaded picnic area is on the canyon bottom; also a snack bar and store with crafts and limited supplies. Lodging is found in neighboring towns.

USEFUL NAMES AND ADDRESSES: Write to **Bandelier National Monument**, HCR 1, Box 1, Ste 15, Los Alamos, NM 87544 (tel: 505-672-3861; 24-hour information recording: 505-672-0343).

GREAT SAND DUNES NATIONAL MONUMENT

They strike most travelers as an unlikely sight to find in the heart of the Rockies: sand dunes, a vast field of them, hundreds of feet high, rippling across the surface of the flat San Luis Valley in the shadow of the Sangre de Cristo Mountains. They look as if they belong in the Sahara Desert, or along the eastern shore of Lake Michigan—certainly not in Colorado, where one expects to find mountain streams, groves of aspen trees, wildflower meadows and hayfields. But here they are, like some alien presence, a visitation from a distant climatic zone.

In fact, while sand dunes are indeed an unusual feature of the alpine landscape, these fields in Colorado are by no means unique. Comparable dunes exist in mountainous areas all over the world—in Tibet, the high Andes, Canada's Yukon and other places. The explanation for them is fairly simple, arising from a combination of erosion and local climate. In Colorado, ever since the rise of the Sangre de Cristo and San Juan mountains, erosive forces have been filling the San Luis Valley with debris—rocks, gravel, dirt, dust and sand. The same thing has happened throughout the Rockies, of course, but elsewhere differences in climate have affected the eroded materials differently.

The first factor causing the great sand dunes is aridity. The San Luis Valley is Colorado's driest corner. Less than ten inches of rain fall each year, and that in sporadic fashion. The plants are what one expects to find in desert regions—rabbitbrush, sage, greasewood, blue grama grass, Indian ricegrass and prickly pear cactus on the valley floor, with thin forests of pinyon and juniper trees in the foothills. These plants grow sparsely, leaving patches of ground exposed to the wind, unanchored by the mat of vegetation which covers and stabilizes regions with more moisture.

The second factor is wind, and no gentle zephyr, either. Especially during the spring, but all year long, strong westerlies sweep across the high San Juans and pour into the San Luis Valley. As the air comes off the San Juans, it picks up speed in the same way that water falling over the lip of a cascade does. It might seem logical that a mountain range would provide some protection from wind, but in fact the windiest places in the Rockies are along their eastern slope. Residents of Boulder, Colorado, who on occasion find themselves suddenly roofless, know this to be true.

The San Luis Valley wind beats across the dry, desert soils and drives any loose material—dust, bits of vegetation, sand—to the east and north, where several passes provide wind channels through the rampart of the Sangre de Cristos. The passes, like broken sections of a great wall, are sought out by the wind in its hurried journey toward the plains. As it blows through these natural weaknesses, the wind still must climb high above the valley floor, and in doing so, it spends enough energy that the heavy sand grains are left behind. Dust and organic material, however, are light enough that the wind carries them over the mountains. In effect, the wind sorts the sand from lighter materials and leaves it in great heaps at the foot of the mountains almost like travelers dropping excess weight from their loads as they start up a long, exhausting grade.

It's not just the mountains and the prevailing westerlies that trap the

Great Sand Dunes National Monument. The sand, carried by westerly winds, is trapped at the foot of the Sangre de Cristo Mountains.

sand here, however. Winds from the opposite direction—storm winds—periodically roar in from the plains, beating the sand back toward the valley. Thus the mountain barrier is reinforced, preventing the dunes from making what would otherwise be an inevitable upward creep. It seems that the dunes survive as a result of a delicate balance between topography and climate, a balance of which could tilt fairly easily with a subtle change in weather.

This strange, evocative landscape has encouraged stories of myth and mystery. Tales tell us that herds of wild webfooted horses can be seen racing through the soft sands just before dawn or on moonlit nights. They gallop over the unknown graves of sheepherders and their flocks which vanished in the shifting sands. One of the strangest stories of all recounts the fate of a wagon train which camped one night near the River of the Dunes. It was spring, and the river was flowing. The mule-skinners unhitched their teams and hobbled the animals to graze, as they did every night. Nothing seemed unusual or out of the ordinary, but in the morning, not a mule, nor a wagon nor a set of tracks could be found. Some claim that quicksand swallowed them all, but that hardly seems possible. Quicksand, a much over-rated danger, doesn't behave th.. way; it has no suction properties. Animals become mired in it easily enough, but usually not above their bellies, and they make a lot of noise about it too. As for wagons, they would float unless loaded with pig iron or something of similar weight. Surely the explanation is more prosaic than mysterious, but it's the nature of a dunescape to encourage fantasy and outlandish notions.

Another example was the Mystery Family of the Dunes, a man and his wife who lived with their son near the edge of the sand in the early years of white settlement. They stayed apart, choosing to have little contact with their neighbors, an action which by itself made them the subject of stories and speculation. The true extent of the Mystery Family's oddity was proven one day when the boy, showing signs of shock, staggered into a nearby farm. People went to check on his parents and found them both dead from an unknown cause. They buried the couple, and a local sheep rancher gave the boy a foster home, but things were never right. Finally, one day in a dust storm he disappeared into the dunes with a flock of sheep and was never seen again. Why? Well, of course, the dunes.

Some Useful Information About Great Sand Dunes National Monument

CAMPING: **Pinyon Flats Campground** is open year-round. Collecting of firewood is not permitted; if you want a campfire, bring wood from outside the monument, or purchase it at the campground. No fires are permitted in the backcountry, so carry a stove and obtain a permit. In some areas, backcountry sites are designated. Just to the south, at **Great Sand Dunes Oasis**, is a motel and private campground with utility hookups, gasoline, general store, restaurant and laundromat; they also offer tours. The nearest town of any size is Alamosa, 35 miles away to the southeast.

USEFUL NAMES AND ADDRESSES: **Great Sand Dunes National Monument**, 11999 Hwy 150 Mosca, CO 81146 (tel: 719-378-2312); **Great Sand Dunes Oasis**, 5400 Hwy 150 N., Mosca, CO 81146 (tel: 719-378-2222); **Alamosa-Monte Vista National Wildlife Refuge**, 9383 El Rancho Lane, Alamosa, CO 81101 (tel: 719-589-4021).

Other Area Ideas

The Alamosa-Monte Vista National Wildlife Refuge, comprising several units, protects a variety of birds including whooping cranes. A self-guided drive winds through both the Monte Vista Unit, south of Monte Vista, and the Alamosa Unit, southeast of Alamosa.

MOUNTAINS

...er, author of the excellent book *The Rockies*, a history of ... section of the Rocky Mountains, grew up in Telluride, an ... uan mining town. In the book, he describes this range as a "sea of pinnacles split into subranges by giant gorges." The traveler cannot know how accurate that description is until he or she has driven or walked through these amazing mountains. The San Juans, and here I include the various subranges in the vicinity, are a superbly rugged range, deeply gouged, pouring with water, some of its peaks brilliantly colored and streaked by minerals, others gun-metal gray.

They stand on the edge of the desert provinces of the Southwest. Here rise the San Juan, the Dolores and the Rio Grande, all of them desert rivers which begin their lives as clear, icy mountain streams. They soon leave the mountains behind, falling through ever-drier, ever-lower country, leaving behind the volcanics of the San Juan Mountains and entering the old, undisturbed layers of sandstone and shale which characterize the Colorado Plateau. This vast land of mesas and canyons stretches all the way to the other side of Utah and halfway across Arizona and New Mexico. As the rivers cut into these softer stone layers, they pick up heavy loads of silt and red-brown sand. The Rio Grande flows vigorously southward through the great Rio Grande Rift to the Mexican border, where it turns east to the Gulf of Mexico. The San Juan and the Dolores go in the opposite direction, west and northeast, to join the Colorado River on its way to the Gulf of California.

The valleys of the western San Juan Range are deeper and less spacious than their neighbors in the Sawatch. Drive from Silverton to Ouray over 11,018-foot Red Mountain Pass to get a good sense of the region's character. The route climbs steeply out of Silverton, which at 9,318 feet is one of the highest towns in Colorado. It barely hesitates at the pass before plunging down the gorge past the Idarado Mine to Ouray. The descent is so steep that a truck which lost a wheel and careened off the road ended up crushing the roof of a building in Ouray. The road itself, U.S. Highway 550, is called in this stretch the Million Dollar Highway. As the story goes, the name comes not from the cost of construction but from the gold-bearing fill unwittingly used beneath the pavement. Beyond Ouray, drive north to the town of Ridgway, then west and south over Dallas Pass. The Uncompahgre Plateau stands to the north, while to the south is the stunning rampart of the Mount Sneffels area. Twenty-four miles from Ridgway, the highway drops into the valley leading to Telluride, another old mining town turned ski resort in a cul-de-sac valley of astonishing beauty, scarcely ten miles from Ouray as the crow flies. There's a jeep road between the two towns—all up one way, all down the other.

Farther south, near Lizard Head Pass, the mountains stack up rank on rank in some of the grandest scenery anywhere, but the view is especially fine in the fall when the aspens are yellow. They cover vast areas. If you get there during the warm days of Indian summer after an early storm has turned the peaks white, you see it in its prime. Life doesn't get any better than a day like that.

If the highways from one town to another seem like a roundabout way to go, consider the detour taken by the Continental Divide on its way north. As it enters Colorado from New Mexico, it takes a sharp turn to the west, runs over to Silverton, then all the way back again before hitting the Sawatch Range and finding a more northerly route. This loop contains the headwaters of the Rio Grande and a superb mountain valley. The valley is broad, not precipitous like the mountains at Telluride, and reminiscent of the area around South Park. This is cattle country: high open range, streams wandering through flat-bottomed valleys, groves of aspen and distant snow-topped mountains. Peaks in the immediate vicinity tend to be massive, square-jawed affairs sitting heavily above the road. Few people live here, and most of them live in Lake City and Creede, both one-time mining towns, which survive now on a mixture of tourism and resourcefulness. Most traffic between Silverton and Lake City follows the long way around, either through Pagosa Springs and Durango, or through Montrose. There is, however, a jeep road that goes more directly, emerging on pavement a few miles south of Ouray. This country is like that: complex, difficult, spectacular, but full of hidden routes and surprises.

Silverton

Silverton is the seat of San Juan County, which derives some distinction from having not one acre of tillable soil for its population of 833 non-farmers, of whom all but 39 live in Silverton. San Juan County, established in 1874, once occupied a huge area, virtually the entire southwest corner of Colorado, but as other towns appeared, they set up their own counties and cut San Juan down to its current size.

The town is best known now as the terminus of the Durango & Silverton Narrow Gauge Railroad, a remnant of the once extensive system of the Denver & Rio Grande Railroad. The tracks arrived in Silverton in 1882, giving impetus to otherwise marginal mining operations. By the turn of the century, 5,000 people lived in San Juan County. From that high point, the population declined slowly as the mines

Silverton, Colorado, seat of San Juan County. Because of its high altitude and rugged terrain, this country has no arable land.

played out and shut down. The last big mine, the Sunnyside, closed in 1985, apparently leaving it up to tourism to keep the town alive and inhabited. The train still carries some freight, but its main function today is as a living museum of early steam-driven railroading. The line follows the course of El Rio de las Animas Perdidas, The River of Lost Souls, for 45 miles through the San Juan Range. (According to one story, the river gets its name from a battle between Navajo Indians and a local tribe; the victorious Navajo pitched the enemy bodies into the river, where they became fish.) The train ride is a worthwhile trip through spectacular country, although tiring by the end of the day. One option worth considering, if you're not a committed railroading fanatic, is to ride the bus one way and take the train the other way. Backpackers headed into the San Juans can arrange to be dropped off and picked up by the train.

Some Useful Information About Silverton

CAMPGROUNDS: **Forest Service campgrounds** are at South Mineral Creek west of town and East Lime Creek near Molas Pass to the south. THE DURANGO & SILVERTON NARROW GAUGE RAILROAD: The railroad makes four daily round trip runs during summer, leaving Durango early in the morning, arriving back in the late afternoon. Fares are $42.70 for adults and $21.45 for children. From Nov. 27 to late

April, a winter train goes to Cascade Canyon and back. Fc
tions, write to the Railroad office at 479 Main Ave., Dura
81301 (tel: 970-247-2733).
GENERAL INFORMATION: Several backroads through mining c an-
try are suitable for ordinary cars; go out the north end of Silverton and
follow either Cement Creek to Gladstone or the Animas River to Eureka.
USEFUL NAMES AND ADDRESSES: The **Silverton Chamber of
Commerce**, P.O. Box 565, Silverton, CO 81433 (tel: 970-387-5654).
Services include lodging, restaurants, several fine restored saloons, jeep
rentals and tours.

Ouray

Ouray, named for the great Ute chief, sits in a deep pocket in the
Uncompahgre Range. The town, which has an elevation of 7,800 feet,
is surrounded by Whitehouse Mountain (13,493 feet), Hayden
Mountain (13,100 feet) and Cascade Mountain (12,100 feet), which so
dominate the atmosphere in town that it has taken to calling itself
Switzerland of America. The mountain slopes are riddled with mine-
shafts. By one estimate roughly 10,000 shafts and tunnels can be found
within ten miles of town. The first of these was started by Gus Begole
and John Eckles, who came over the pass from Silverton in 1875 to
claim the Mineral Farm Mine, named because nuggets lay around like
potatoes; all one needed to get at them was a shovel. Soon other miners
had staked placer claims all around the Ouray Basin. They also named
the town for Chief Ouray, which seems somehow ingenuous since, in
fact, they were trespassing on Ute land at the time.

In 1882, the rich strike was made on Red Mountain Pass. There is a
clear view of this wonderfully colorful mountain from the Silverton
Highway. Deposits in the mountain kept the town going until the
Denver & Rio Grande Railroad arrived in 1887, making it profitable at
last to mine lower-grade ores. Until then, all shipments had gone out by
mule train and horse-drawn wagons. While much of Colorado mining
collapsed in 1893, Ouray kept alive on its gold production, the largest
share of which came from the famous Camp Bird Mine in Yankee Boy
Basin. Hundreds of miles of tunnels riddle the mountains in all directions. If you happened to be so inclined (unlikely), and could get permission (even less likely), you could cross the mountains to Telluride
underground. A more popular route is to go by four-wheel drive vehicle
over Imogene Pass above the Camp Bird Mine. Normal cars can make
the drive to the mine, but above that the road gets quite rough.

Ouray is proud of its network of mining roads, to the point of billing itself as the "Jeep Capital of the World." Truly, the number and complexity of old, barely negotiable tracks is bewildering. Not just Telluride, but Lake City and Silverton can be reached by a choice of several high altitude backcountry routes. Anyone keen on seeing relics of mining days will find this a rewarding place. Jeep rentals and guided tours are available in Ouray (Switzerland of America Jeep Rentals and Tours, P.O. Box 780, Ouray, CO 81427, tel: 800-432-5337; San Juan Scenic Jeep Tours, P.O. Box 732, tel: 800-325-4385).

Perched above Ouray to the east is a shallow basin called the Amphitheater, in which the Forest Service maintains an unusually scenic campground. A thermal swimming pool at the north end of town is open seven days a week in the summer.

Trails

Hiking in this country is steep and strenuous but worthwhile. Trails near Ouray include the Portland Trail, which begins at the Amphitheater Campground and climbs 700 feet to the alpine basin above. A branch of this trail goes north to the Chief Ouray Mine, 1,600 feet and three miles above the trailhead. Longer and very scenic is the Horsethief Trail; the roadhead is at the end of the Dexter Creek Road (F.S. 871), three miles north of Ouray. The Horsethief connects with the Bear Creek Trail, which starts on the highway south of Ouray, making it a nearly complete loop—hard to do in a single day. West of Ouray, near the Camp Bird Mine, a trail climbs Blue Lake Pass and then descends dramatically 5,000 feet to the trailhead on the East Fork of Dallas Creek.

Useful Names and Addresses

Ouray County Chamber of Commerce, P.O. Box 145, Ouray, CO 81427 (tel: 303-325-4746; or **Chamber Resort Association** at 800-228-1876).

Telluride

If Ouray and Silverton are sister cities, then Telluride is a cousin, kept from its relations not by distance but by an imposing mountain wall. The town takes its name from an unusual ore found in the vicinity, a combination of gold, silver and tellurium. In the days of passenger trains, railroad conductors played with the name when announcing their destination. "To Hell You Ride!" they would sing out, but anyone who sees the place has to agree that this valley is closer to heaven than hell.

The comparison with Aspen is unavoidable. Telluride sits at the end of a steep-sided valley, almost a canyon, with splendid mountains rising on all three sides and a sizeable snowmelt stream flowing through town. The buildings are of the same era; Victorian homes line quiet tree-lined streets. Mining relics are everywhere. A challenging ski mountain overlooks Main Street, its lifts beginning within walking distance of the old town. But so far, Telluride is quiet, relatively unknown to celebrities and their followers. Some would call it undercapitalized. You can still find a restaurant in the downtown area with unmatched tables and make-do decor. It's a charming, relaxing atmosphere, where you can feel comfortable even if you didn't happen to put on your gold Rolex Chronograph that day.

Telluride, at least part of Telluride, would like to shake that image. Developers eagerly promote their town as an awakening giant—"This is Aspen before the boom," crow the realtors. "Fabulous opportunities! Get in on the ground floor." But if you spend a little time perusing their offerings, you find that the entry is at least a few stories above the ground. You'd need a $90,000 ladder just to get to the first step.

Promotion fever hasn't struck everyone, and people are happy to stand on a street corner and shoot the breeze. Like people in all western mining towns, they love their history, whatever its color, and you'll quickly hear that Butch Cassidy robbed the Bank of San Miguel in 1889. Not that a simple robbery is much of a distinction; Cassidy and his gang seem to have done the same favor for most other towns of the era. Their former banks and hideouts are to the West what George Washington's bedrooms are to the East. What makes the Telluride robbery special, you hear, is that this was his first. Telluride got him started, gave him his stake, so to speak. However, a far classier bank job was pulled by a less-renowned man named Charles Waggoner, who as president of the Bank of Telluride in 1929 foresaw disaster and devised a successful scheme to bilk a group of Denver and New York banks of $500,000. He used the money to cover his bank's debts and to protect the deposits of local people, and although he served 15 years in prison, he became a Telluride hero for his public-spirited thievery.

Trails

Hiking trails go off in all directions from Telluride. Popular destinations are Bridal Veil Falls, which overlooks the townsite, Bear Creek Canyon, Silver and Blue lakes, and a number of mine ruins. In an ordinary car, you can drive to Alta, a picturesque mining town abandoned in 1945. Follow Highway 145 six miles south of where it crosses the San Miguel River to Forest Road 632 on the left side of the highway. On your return, you can make it a loop by turning left when you get back to the highway. Drive another 1.5 miles south, then turn right on the Ilium Valley Road, which follows the South Fork of the San Miguel back to the main valley.

Some Useful Information About Telluride

CAMPGROUNDS: Limited camping is available in the town park. Several Forest Service campgrounds are fairly close. To reach **Sunshine Campground**, go south of town on Colorado Highway 145 toward Ophir. The campground is across the road from Cushman Lake. **Matterhorn Campground** is farther south on Highway 145 past Ophir and near Priest and Trout lakes.

ACTIVITIES, EQUIPMENT SALES AND RENTALS: River rafting is offered by **Telluride Whitewater** (970-728-3895). **Telluride Sports** (970-728-4477) and **Paragon Sports** (970-728-4525) sell and rent mountain equipment.

EVENTS: The summer festival calendar highlights are as follows. May: **Mountain Film**. June: **Wine Festival, Balloon Rally, Bluegrass Festival**. July: **Independence Day Fireworks**. August: **Jazz Celebration, Chamber Music Festival**. September: **Telluride Film Festival**, presented by the National Film Preserve, **Hang Gliding Festival, Fall Color** events, photography workshops.

USEFUL NAMES AND ADDRESSES: Write to the **Telluride Visitor Services** at P.O. Box 653, Telluride, CO 81435 (tel: 970-728-4431); for reservations call 800-525-3455 in the U.S., or 970-728-4431.

Big Blue Wilderness

The Big Blue Wilderness occupies an area of about ten miles by twenty miles between Ouray and Lake City. High, craggy peaks of the Uncompahgre Range dominate the wilderness: Uncompahgre Peak (14,309 feet), Wetterhorn Peak (14,015 feet), and Matterhorn Peak (13,590 feet). It is a fine hiking area. Despite its formidable appearance when seen from the south (a good view from Slumgullion Pass above Lake City), Uncompahgre is one of the easier of Colorado's big peaks to climb.

Access is from the south, via the Henson Creek Road (F.S. 3300) from Lake City; there is a road from Silverton over Engineer Pass, but it requires four-wheel drive. At Capitol City, a ghost town, take Forest Road 870 two miles along the North Fork of Henson Creek to a right turn up Matterhorn Creek. Where this road ends the trail begins. It leads to all three major peaks.

Mount Sneffels dominates the Mount Sneffels Wilderness in Colorado's San Juan Mountains.

Abandoned buildings like these in Creede, Colorado, are often the only remaining signs of once-booming gold and silver mines.

Lizard Head and Mount Sneffels Wildernesses

Two wilderness areas protect the high peaks west of the Million Dollar Highway. Lizard Head Wilderness, once called the Wilson Mountains Primitive Area, centers on the San Miguel Mountains, three of which are over 14,000 feet. Access is generally from the north, off Highway 145 between Placerville and Telluride. One road (F.S. 618) follows Fall Creek to the Woods Lake Picnic Area. A more direct trail begins at a barricade at the end of the Bear Creek Road (F.S. 622), which leaves the highway about three miles east of Sawpit.

Mount Sneffels tops the wilderness area of the same name. The wilderness includes the beautiful set of peaks you see on the drive over Dallas Pass west of Ridgway. To get closer, you can drive in on the north side, but the elevation gain on northside trails can be daunting. The option, certainly a pleasant one, is to drive past the Camp Bird Mine out of Ouray, parking in Yankee Boy Basin and hiking toward Blue Lakes Pass.

Creede

Creede was founded by Nicholas Creede, who in 1890 found color (flecks of placer gold in the sand) at a place where he stopped for lunch. He called his mine the Holy Moses, after what one suspects may have been his first words upon making the discovery. In what was by then typical fashion in the Rockies, other prospectors flooded into the area, pushing Creede's population to 8,000 by 1893. A man named Cy Warman edited one of the town's early newspapers, *The Creede Chronicle*, and wrote the famous poem "And There Is No Night in Creede":

> Here's a land where all are equal—
> Of high or lowly birth—
> A land where men make millions,
> Dug from the dreary earth.
> Here meek and mild-eyed burros
> On mineral mountains feed.
> It's day all day in the daytime,
> And there is no night in Creede.
> The cliffs are solid silver,
> With wond'rous wealth untold,
> And the beds of the running rivers
> Are lined with the purest gold.
> While the world is filled with sorrow,
> And hearts must break and bleed—
> It's day all day in the daytime,
> And there is no night in Creede.

Creede's glory played out quickly, not from shallow veins, but from
the repeal of the Sherman Silver Purchase Act in 1893, which dropped
the bottom out of the silver market and brought disaster to every silver
camp in the Rockies. Mining continued in Creede, however, on a small
scale, until the winter of 1985, when the last mine, operated by
Homestake Mining Company, shut its gates. The town would like to see
the mine reopen, of course, but meanwhile attention is directed at
tourism and the hopes that there remains room for another restored
mining community among the many already operating in Colorado. Of
particular interest might be the Fourth of July mining contest, with com-
petitions in hand drilling, machine drilling, mucking (a good word for
using a shovel to load ore) and more; also the Underground Mining
Museum and the Bachelor Tour, a self-guided 17-mile loop of Creede's
historic mining district.

Some Useful Information About Creede

CAMPGROUNDS: Write to the **Telluride Visitor Services** at P.O. Box
653, Telluride, CO 81435 (tel: 970-728-4431); for reservations call 800-
525-3455 in the U.S., or 970-728-4431.
USEFUL NAMES AND ADDRESSES: Rio Grande National Forest
District Office, P.O. Box 270, Creede, CO 81132. **Creede Chamber of
Commerce**, Creede, CO 81130 (tel: 800-327-2102). For a schedule of
major events in Creede write for a free summer guide to **Mineral
County Miner/South Fork Times**, Box 219, Creede, CO 81130 (tel:
719-658-2603).

Weminuche Wilderness

Where the Continental Divide takes its sharp westward detour on the
backs of the San Juan Range, it separates the headwaters of the two
great rivers, the San Juan and the Rio Grande, and forms the backbone
of the Weminuche (Wem-in-OOTCH) Wilderness Area. The wilderness,
463,700 acres large, was established in 1975 from the existing Upper
Rio Grande and San Juan primitive areas. Its name is taken from the
Weminuche Indians, who lived here when the first Europeans arrived—
Spanish explorers probing north from the pueblos of New Mexico. Don
Juan Maria de Rivera was the first, leading an expedition in 1765.
Eleven years later, Dominguez and Escalante, trying to find a feasible
land route between Santa Fe and the California missions, passed to the
south of the San Juans. Natural features in the area still bear the names
given them by these early Spanish travelers: Los Pinos River, Vallecito
Mountain, Cimarrona Creek, Rincon La Osa and others. Interestingly,
on the eastern side of the Divide, which is actually to the north, the

names are mostly English: Hope Creek, Starvation Gulch, Beautiful Mountain, Stair Steps and so on.

Over 290 miles of marked trails follow drainages and traverse the Divide. Of special note are the Needle Mountains on the west end of the wilderness, an area of crags and pinnacles, several over 14,000 feet, which stand above alpine lakes. Also, the trail to the head of Rincon La Osa provides a panoramic view. North a few miles along the Divide, Rio Grande Pyramid (13,081 feet) is an easily climbed area landmark. The shortest trail leaves the Thirty Mile Trailhead, crosses Weminuche Pass and goes up the southeast shoulder of the mountain.

Some Useful Information About Weminuche

HOW TO GET THERE: To get there from the north, follow Forest Road 520 west of Colorado 149 toward Rio Grande Reservoir; trailheads are at Lost Trail and Thirty Mile campgrounds. Another access is through the Ivy Creek Campground on Forest Road 526 (via F.S. 523), which leaves Highway 149 at Marshall Park Campground seven miles west of Creede; four-wheel drive may be necessary to get near the wilderness boundary. From the south, in the San Juan National Forest, the Vallecito and Pine River trailheads are near Vallecito Reservoir; several others are at the ends of Forest Roads north of Pagosa Springs.

USEFUL NAMES AND ADDRESSES: **Rio Grande National Forest,** 1803 West Highway 160, Monte Vista, CO 81144 (tel: 719-852-5941); there is a district office in Creede. **San Juan National Forest** headquarters are at 701 Camino del Rio, Durango, CO 81301 (tel: 970-247-4874) with district offices in Pagosa Springs (970-264-2268) and Bayfield (970-884-2512).

La Garita Wilderness

La garita is Spanish for "overlook," a name that seems fitting if you stand on the Continental Divide in the La Garita Mountains, far above timberline, looking south to the San Juans and northwest to Big Blue Wilderness, where Uncompahgre Peak stands imposingly beside the Matterhorn and the Wetterhorn.

The La Garita Wilderness, 130,000 acres to the north of the Divide, is very high, between 12,500 feet and 14,000 feet in elevation, and not much visited, perhaps because its peaks are broad and chunky in contrast to the rugged, steep-sided peaks around Silverton. Even so, trails follow most of the important drainages, and it is possible to traverse the wilderness along the Divide from one end to the other. San Luis Peak (14,014 feet) is the highest point in the area; you can climb it via the

Stewart Creek Trail, which starts at the end of the Gunnison National Forest Road 794. To get there, take Highway 114 south of Gunnison through Cochetopa Canyon to the Dome Reservoir Road (F.S. 3083). At the far end of Upper Dome Reservoir, turn right on F.S. 3086, which about five miles farther meets 794. Other roads beyond Dome Reservoir lead to Stone Cellar campground and trailheads; beyond are trails to Machin Lake. A four-wheel drive road follows the Middle Fork from Stone Cellar to the boundary; passenger cars can usually make it to the boundary on the South Fork by continuing on 787. These and other access routes are complicated and numerous enough that a Forest Recreation Map is nearly indispensable.

Also in the area, but on the south side of the Divide, is the Wheeler Geologic Area, one square mile protecting an intricate set of hoodoos, accessible only by foot or by a four-wheel drive road from the southeast. Adjoining La Garita to the northwest is the Powderhorn Primitive Area, administered by the Bureau of Land Management. It lacks any outstanding peaks, but lakes and timberline meadows make it a good place for hiking. Access via Indian Creek on the north (Forest Road 3033 off Highway 149 west of Powderhorn) or via the Cebolla Creek Road (F.S. 3036), which together with the Mill Creek Road (F.S. 788) runs between Slumgullion Pass and Powderhorn; five Forest Service campgrounds are maintained along these creeks. Right at Powderhorn, Forest Road 3034 goes south to Tenmile Springs Trailhead.

Useful Names and Addresses

Write to **Rio Grande National Forest,** 1803 West Highway 160, Monte Vista, CO 81144 (tel: 719-852-5941); district offices are in Saguache (719-655-2553), Creede (719-658-2556) and Del Norte (719-657-3321).

THE SAWATCH RANGE

The Sawatch Range is the roof of Colorado. In this chain rise the highest mountains in the state. On the east, the valley of the Arkansas River supports a climate warm enough that locals call it the banana belt. In the shadow of the Sawatch, and protected from easterly flows of air by the Mosquito Range on its other side, it gets less than ten inches of precipitation per year. Pinyon and juniper trees grow along the foothills, making the valley look more like one in Arizona than in Colorado—a strange feeling when you look up at the perpetual snows on the mountains. The valley also provides one of the best views of the range. From almost any other perspective, the mountains are too close together to get an impression of their general shape. But from Trout Creek Pass, as you drive east on U.S. Highway 24 to Buena Vista, you can see almost the entire eastern front of the Sawatch Range, from Marshall Pass at its south end to Mount of the Holy Cross near its north end, a distance of more than seventy-five miles.

Sixteen of these peaks are over 14,000 feet high. Carrying the Continental Divide across the center of Colorado are such peaks as Mount Elbert, the highest in the state, Mount Massive, Shavano Peak and a string of others, including the striking Collegiate Range. (For accuracy, I should point out that the Divide avoids the actual summits of many of these mountains. It is a curiosity of geography that the watershed of the continent runs on a ridge parallel to but just below the highest mountain chain in the range.) This high timberline country is some of the nicest in the Rockies; because the mountains are so well watered, they are green nearly to their summits. They are also exceptionally easy to access. Of places with equivalent altitude and ruggedness, only the San Juan country has so many roads. The reason for this is that the Colorado Mineral Belt cuts squarely across the Sawatch, from Leadville to Aspen. Mining activity began in the 1870s, but hit its peak in the '80s, when Leadville and Aspen boomed, along with many other, less well known mining camps. One was St. Elmo, above the modern town of Buena Vista, where the Mary Murphy gold mine gave up $60 million from 1875 to 1924. Strikes like that spurred miners to absurd efforts in developing claims on the highest mountains in the area. There was almost nowhere that a miner wouldn't try to build a road, or at least a mule track. If a mine showed promise, a railroad spur might even be built to it. Today many of the tracks and roads survive; some of the mines are still worked, or have been recently. As a result, large areas of alpine country are open to vehicles, especially those with four-wheel drive.

Among the more memorable drives are Independence Pass between Aspen and the Arkansas Valley, and Cottonwood Pass just to the south. West of Cottonwood Pass is Taylor Park and the Taylor Park Reservoir, a high, broad alpine valley with numerous Forest Service campgrounds and backroad routes to Aspen and Crested Butte. Above Taylor Park south of Cottonwood Pass is Tincup Pass, which at 12,154 feet is the highest (four-wheel drive) road pass on the Continental Divide. Numerous other roads penetrate mountain valleys throughout the range, many winding up steep-sided valleys to the ruins of abandoned mines. The state of these dirt tracks is unpredictable. Even with a four-wheel drive vehicle, you should ask about conditions on the more remote ones or be ready to turn around in sometimes tight quarters.

Despite all the roads, there's quite a bit of wilderness here: the

Collegiate Peaks, Mount Massive, Hunter-Fryingpan and Mount of the Holy Cross wilderness areas either adjoin one another or are separated by road corridors. And although not in the Sawatch Range proper, superb mountain wilderness areas are a short distance west in the Elk and West Elk mountains, including the famous Maroon Bells Wilderness bordering Aspen.

Aspen

In a state filled with ski towns and mountain resorts, Aspen remains the original and the classic. It sits in an alpine cul-de-sac, ringed by high mountains just below the Continental Divide, and watered by the many streams that pour off the high snowfields—certainly one of the loveliest natural settings in Colorado. The town suits its surroundings; almost without exception, Aspen's architecture is tasteful and expensive. Zoning laws control not only the design of buildings, but their location and height as well. You don't get the sense, as in some other ski towns, that the older part of town is separated from the mountains, walled off by an imposing barrier of high-rise condominiums. The lifts of Aspen Mountain, the original ski development, begin on the virtual doorsteps of impeccably restored Victorian miners' homes.

Aspen got its start in 1880 as a successful silver mining town. The initial boom lasted a little more than a decade, until silver was demonetized in 1893 and a long decline set in, with downvalley ranching being the main industry. Interest in skiing developed after World War II and grew rapidly. By the late '50s, Aspen Mountain (the locals call it Ajax after a mine on its slopes), Aspen Highlands and Buttermilk were operating. In 1968, Snowmass opened, completing the quartet. For many years, Highlands was separately owned. In 1994, Aspen Ski Corp. acquired it, and now operates all four mountains as one giant ski area and resort.

The original miners, even considering their affection for wealth and their unquenchable optimism about obtaining it, would be astonished by Aspen today. Aspen has the reputation of being a flashy town filled with celebrities, given to outrageous extremes and activities more appropriate to Hollywood Boulevard than to a peaceful mountain town. It certainly is a rich place. The streets are paved with antique brick and lined with shops where most of us could drop a year's salary on a single item we could carry out under one arm. People don't walk here, they strut, apparently enjoying the ambience of mystery: Who is that person? He could be anyone.

That part of being in Aspen is enjoyable. The town is a treat for the senses, with a great many worthwhile things to do. If you do nothing else on a summer visit, at least take the time for breakfast or lunch at a sidewalk cafe on one of the streets closed to automobiles. The food will be good, the air delicious and the passing promenade most entertaining. If you walk through the old residential streets, past meticulously restored Victorian homes in the shade of big arching trees, Aspen starts to feel like the perfect mountain town. It's only later that doubts begin to creep forward. You begin to wonder where the ordinary people are. Not the students living on restaurant salaries who are there for the fun of the place and who ask for nothing more than a room in a shared apartment, but people who work for a living at salaried jobs and who send their kids to public school. In other words, the middle class. How can they afford to live where studio condos start at $250,000? According to one disillusioned former Aspen resident, they can't. "It's a town of the very rich and the people who serve them," he claims. "No one in between." Others dispute this, saying that under the glitter is a town like any other in its most important aspects; that having made great efforts to provide employee housing, it remains a good place to live and raise a family.

Whichever description is correct (probably both), Aspen and its surroundings are a pleasant destination for the mountain traveler. Any choice of lodging is available, including Forest Service campgrounds a short distance from town. You don't need a car; Aspen has an excellent shuttle bus system, which serves not only the town but also outlying destinations. The town itself is small enough to walk anywhere. River rafting companies float the Roaring Fork, which comes through town. Bicyclists burn out their thighs on the formidable climb over Independence Pass, or the less steep climb to Maroon Lake. Aspen has a 20-mile county trail system for bicycles and walkers. Others take their mountain bikes on dirt roads and tracks through areas littered with relics from the days of silver mining. One route goes over the mountains west to the town of Crested Butte—barely 30 miles that way but a day's drive by car. Several wilderness areas are suitable for day-hikes and longer trips. In one, Maroon Bells, you can take the bus to the trailhead.

In the townsite, summer activities include the famous Aspen Music Festival, the Aspen Tennis Festival, the Snowmass Repertory Theatre, the Summer Dance Festival, the autumn rugby tournament and a variety of arts and educational programs.

Some Useful Information About Aspen

HOW TO GET THERE: Aspen is served by major airlines flying 757s and other jets, with many arrivals per day. For current information, call **Aspen Central Reservations** at 800-262-7736. Major airlines serve

Denver, which is five hours away by road, and Grand Junction, 2 1/2 hours away; both places are served by bus and car rental companies. **Amtrak** comes as close as Glenwood Springs, 40 miles from Aspen.

GETTING AROUND: **Shuttle bus:** free in Aspen town, according to a schedule usually at 15-minute intervals; outside town, a fare is charged. **Maroon Bells shuttle:** leaves from Aspen Highlands Ski Area, approximately 9:00 A.M. to 5:00 P.M.; the road to Maroon Lake is closed to private traffic for those hours.

LODGING: For lodging, call **Aspen Central Reservations** at 800-262-7736.

CAMPGROUNDS: Three tiny and very popular campgrounds are located up Maroon Creek. Reserve a site five days in advance by calling the Forest Service national information number (800-280-2267), or try for a cancellation by going there early in the day. The road is closed to private vehicles during the day, but if you tell the person at the gate that you want to camp, you can go through.

ACTIVITIES AND EQUIPMENT SALES AND RENTALS: The **Aspen Music Festival** runs for most of the summer with an impressive schedule, which includes chamber, choral and orchestral music and opera. Impromptu outdoor concerts by music students are not unusual. For a schedule of this and other festivals, call 970-925-9042.

Activities: **Colorado Riff Raft Inc.** (800-759-3939); **Blazing Adventures** (800-282-7238); **Unicorn Balloon Company** (970-925-5752). Outdoor equipment shops: throughout town; the **Ute Mountaineer** (970-925-2849) is a good source of hiking advice.

USEFUL NAMES AND ADDRESSES: For general information, contact the **Aspen Chamber Resort Association**, 425 Rio Grande Place, Aspen, CO 81611, or call 970-925-1940.

Maroon Bells-Snowmass Wilderness

Southwest of Aspen, the Maroon Bells-Snowmass Wilderness encompasses 174,000 acres of the Elk Mountains. Most famous among these are the Maroon Bells, a group of postcard peaks which rise above the alpine waters of Maroon Lake and which, to many visitors, symbolize the scale and character of central Colorado's mountains. This area is extremely high and rugged. Any bushwhacking is likely to involve climbing. The Maroon Lake area is popular and heavily used, to the extent that a Forest Service regulation forbids wedding receptions in Maroon Valley and limits weddings to two locations on a reservation basis. A bus runs between Aspen and the lake during July and August (see the information section on Aspen).

The Maroon Bells, near Aspen, Colorado, are landmarks of one of the state's most popular hiking areas.

One hundred miles of trails originate from a number of roadheads, with Maroon Bells being the most heavily used because of its proximity to Aspen. Day-hikers here include a two-mile trail to Crater Lake, where the path splits and goes to Buckskin Pass or West Maroon Pass. Another well-trod route (Trail 1975) heads for Trail Rider Pass near Snowmass Peak.

On the west side, Highway 133 goes south from Carbondale to Marble, where a network of old mine roads leads to several trailheads for both the Maroon Bells and the Raggeds Wilderness areas. It's possible but hazardous, with four-wheel drive, to continue over Schofield Pass to the town of Crested Butte and several more trailheads.

Useful Names and Addresses

White River National Forest, Box 948, Glenwood Springs, CO 81602 (tel: 970-945-2521); district offices in the Maroon Bells area are located in Aspen (806 W. Hallam St., CO 81611, tel: 970-925-3445) and at 620

Main St., Carbondale, CO 81623 (tel: 970-963-2266). **Gunnison National Forest** has a district office in Gunnison (216 N. Colorado, CO 81230, tel: 970-641-0471).

Mount Massive and Hunter-Fryingpan Wildernesses

Just east of Aspen, bordering each other on opposite sides of the Divide, these two areas form a complementary unit. Fryingpan is the larger of the two, but Mount Massive, although it isn't on the Divide, is the highest point at 14,421 feet. The Collegiate Peaks continue southward, and the Holy Cross area is north. Hunter-Fryingpan centers on the Williams Mountains. These are less spectacular than the Elk Mountains in the Maroon Bells area on the other side of Aspen, but they are easier wandering country with expansive views of surrounding ranges. Much of the Hunter-Fryingpan is tundra on peaks gentle enough for hikers to enjoy. You can see a goodly portion of the area on a drive over Independence Pass, which everyone should do whether they mean to hike or not. The road is spectacular and makes it easy to get into the country above timberline where cross-country travel is a matter of simply going in the direction that looks interesting.

There are also a number of maintained trails. Where Lost Man Creek crosses Highway 82 (14 miles east of Aspen), the Midway Trail climbs to Midway Pass. This trail gives access to Williams Mountains, a small group of summits to the north and east where you can wander above treeline. Just up the highway, at the hairpin turn, a gravel road goes about a hundred yards north to the Lost Man Creek Trail, which crosses the wilderness to the Fryingpan River drainage (the trail goes around the west side of the Lost Man Reservoir). A few miles farther east on the highway, at the next hairpin, yet another route, this one well above timberline, goes up to Independence Lake and beyond; you can connect with the Lost Man Creek Trail this way. From Independence Pass itself, tundra walking is pleasant in both directions.

Access from the north is along the Fryingpan River, past Ruedi Reservoir and the Norrie Ranger Station, where Forest Service roads branch out into three separate valleys, each road ending at a trail. Road 504 is the trailhead for the trail that comes over from Lost Man Creek.

Getting into the Mount Massive area is best done by driving up Halfmoon Creek on Forest Road 110 from Leadville to the Elbert Campground. From here, trails go north to Mount Massive and the lakes country north of it; another trail heads south to Casco Peak, which can be walked up (with some effort) for fine views. Mount Massive Wilderness is bordered on the north by the abandoned grade of the

Colorado Midland Railroad, which for 40 years between 1883 and 1921 struggled to make a profit carrying freight over Hagerman Pass. The decline of Aspen and other silver towns in the 1890s did little to help matters, but the pass itself was a formidable opponent. Two tunnels were bored during the railroad's life span, the Hagerman and the Carlton, now disused and not to be entered. The old right-of-way, however, is an interesting place to walk; depending on conditions, four-wheel drive vehicles can negotiate the pass.

Useful Names and Addresses

These areas are in the **White River National Forest**; the nearest district offices are in Aspen (see above) and in Minturn: 24747 U.S. Hwy 24, P.O. Box 190, CO 81645 (tel: 970-827-5715).

Mount of the Holy Cross Wilderness

Mount of the Holy Cross was named for the giant cross on its east face. The cross is formed by snow-filled gullies and is about 1,500 feet high— a striking feature and one which many have called miraculous. One story tells of Spanish priests who traveled to Colorado in the 1500s. Winter caught them in these high peaks, where they wandered around half frozen, nearly dead and without hope. Then, as they were about to give up, and with the blizzard at its most fierce, the clouds parted momentarily. The desperate priests turned their eyes skyward, and there beyond the howling storm appeared a cross of snow. Inspired to new effort, they made their way out of the mountains to safety.

William Jackson, the frontier photographer who became famous for making the first photos of Yellowstone National Park, went to some effort to find and photograph Mount of the Holy Cross. His son wrote a book about the trip. Thomas Moran, the artist and Jackson's companion in Yellowstone, painted a well-known landscape of the mountain, and even Henry Wadsworth Longfellow got into the act with his poem, "The Cross of Snow."

After World War I, the mountain became a popular destination for religious pilgrims seeking enlightenment and miracle cures. Many who couldn't make the trip in person sent handkerchiefs, which were carried to the vicinity of the mountain, blessed within sight of the cross, and returned to their owners, who reported miraculous results.

Mount of the Holy Cross is now the focus of the surrounding wilderness area, which takes up about 116,000 acres, and varies in elevation from around 8,000 feet to over 14,000 feet on the summit of the famous mountain. You can get a good view of the cross (most visible from mid-June to mid-July) from the saddle of the Notch Mountain. Drive south of Minturn 1.5 miles to Forest Road 707, which leads to Half Moon Campground and the trailhead. The round trip distance is 11 miles, with a 3,000 foot elevation gain.

The same trail, if you branch off to the left before starting the long climb to the saddle, goes up the Fall Creek valley to Lake Constantine and beyond, coming out through the abandoned Holy Cross City mining area to Gold Park Campground on Forest Road 703. Another trail runs more or less parallel to this but on the other side of Holy Cross Mountain. A 20-mile trip, it begins about two miles from U.S. Highway 24 on the Half Moon Campground Road (F. S. 707) at a sharp hairpin turn, and follows Cross Creek to Missouri Pass, Missouri Lakes and a dirt road up Sopris Creek near Gold Park Campground.

Useful Names and Addresses

Mount of the Holy Cross Wilderness is contained mostly in **White River National Forest**, which has a district office at 24747 U.S. Hwy 24, P.O. Box 190, Minturn, CO 81645 (tel: 970-827-5715).

Collegiate Peaks Wilderness

The Collegiate Peaks Wilderness sprawls along the Continental Divide between the two roads that cross Independence and Cottonwood passes. Its boundaries are unruly, detouring widely to exclude roads and mines and giving it the shape of a creative amoeba. At its heart is the Collegiate Range: Mounts Yale, Columbia, Oxford, Harvard and Missouri, all over 14,000 feet, all of them massive pyramids with easy walking routes to their summits. Mount Princeton stands just south of the wilderness boundary, having failed the wilderness entrance exam on the basis of the mines on its flanks (or was it that someone from the University of Missouri drew the boundaries?).

These peaks, because of the way they dominate the scenery for miles around, are the objectives for many hikers. As throughout Colorado's mineral belt, mining roads seem to go up virtually every feasible drainage. Trails continue up most of these, crisscrossing the Divide and making any number of day-hikes or backpack trips possible. Mine relics—old buildings, machinery, tunnels, tailings piles—are as common as Indian paintbrush. A San Isabel National Forest map is indispensable if only for its detailed indications of roads.

A major access road is the one over Cottonwood Pass, which has recently been widened and paved (closed in winter). Among others, the trail up the North Fork Denny Creek and the high trail from the pass to

Texas Creek Basin are worth considering. Outside the wilderness, the trail to Ptarmigan Lake is a nice day-hike to a popular and scenic fishing place. The trailhead is well marked, about five miles east of the pass on the south side of the road.

North of Buena Vista, Forest Road 120 leaves U.S. Highway 24 at Clear Creek Reservoir. A good trail follows Missouri Gulch from Vicksburg to Elkhead Pass, from which you can climb Mounts Oxford or Belford, both over 14,000 feet. The trail goes on to Missouri Basin and a scattering of small lakes. An alternate return route follows Pine Creek to the highway.

Useful Names and Addresses

Contact the **San Isabel National Forest Headquarters**, 1920 Valley Dr., Pueblo, CO 81008 (tel: 719-545-8737); **Leadville District Office**, 2015 North Poplar, Leadville, CO 80461 (tel: 719-486-0749).

CRESTED BUTTE

Topographical complexity is one of the chief joys of touring the Rockies. Suppose you are in Aspen, and you have a desire to see the town of Crested Butte. You look on the map and find that Crested Butte is a mere 30 miles away; but to drive there, if you travel a comfortable pace on paved roads, will take all day. It could take three or four if you wanted to stop off in some of the more interesting places en route. On the other hand, with a Jeep or a mountain bike, you could go directly to Crested Butte on old mining roads. With a little energy and ambition, you could even walk there, through the Maroon Bells Wilderness, in the time it took a companion to drive around and meet you at the opposite trailhead. That's not a bad idea.

Crested Butte is the flip side of Aspen in more ways than simple geography. Both towns began in the silver boom of the 1880s, but while Aspen's strength remained with precious metals, the backbone of Crested Butte's economy was much more prosaic—coal for the smelters. Both towns grew up in a similar manner, each community at the head of an isolated valley, the buildings Victorian, the winters hard, the pleasures and difficulties of mountain living much the same; and both declined at the same time. Their fates were interconnected. Crested Butte's coal was used to fire the smelters and drive the trains. When silver and gold mines shut down, so did the smelters, along with some of the trains. At least there were other markets for coal; through various economic fluctuations, the mines stayed open until 1952, preventing Crested Butte from decaying quite as much as Aspen. It never experienced the glitter of a big gold boom, but neither did it suffer from a complete crash. Even so, neither town did well until skiing attracted new money. Both places developed ski resorts, but while Aspen aimed its development at an international trade, Crested Butte retained its low profile. Despite recent developments on the mountain, and a stepped-up campaign for outside investment in condominiums and the like, Crested Butte holds on to its atmosphere of being out of the way, unhurried, fond of simpler pleasures and happy to stay that way. I hope it does. Aspen is nice right where it is.

Crested Butte is actually two towns. On the shoulder of the mountain, at the ski area, sits the new, modern cluster of condominiums and boutiques, which you grow to expect of a ski resort. Three miles back down the road lies the old town of Crested Butte, which is home to the majority of the 1,350 year-round locals. The upper town is dominated by visitors and short-term rentals. Together, the two communities sustain each other in what appears to be a happy, mutually beneficial relationship.

In summer, the big sport in Crested Butte is mountain bicycling. Everyone, it seems, owns one of these fat-tired, many geared, rugged machines. It seems only natural. The valley has only one paved road, Highway 135 to Gunnison, but hundreds of miles of gravel and dirt backroads, which go off in all directions—to ghost towns, uninhabited valleys, alpine passes and places where people still live, including Aspen. Throughout the summer, mountain bike races are held on these roads. In addition, hiking, river rafting, hang-gliding and the other pursuits of active Rocky Mountain towns are all possible here.

Places of interest around Crested Butte are: Gothic, seven miles north, an old silver mining camp; Irwin, at Lake Irwin, on the Kebler Pass Road, the original boom town in the valley, with a one-time population of 5,000; Ohio Pass and the road to Baldwin; Carbon Peak, which can be climbed from a trailhead several miles south of Ohio Pass.

Some Useful Information About Crested Butte

LODGING: For reservations call 800-215-2226.

CAMPGROUNDS: There is a Forest Service campground at Lake Irwin, eight miles west of Crested Butte up Kebler Pass. Gothic Campground, also run by the Forest Service, is north of town past the ski area, through Gothic and up F.S. 317. **Gothic Natural Area** is just past the two campgrounds.

ACTIVITIES, EQUIPMENT SALES AND RENTALS: **Flatiron Sporting Goods** (970-349-6656, or 800-821-4331) and **The Alpineer & Bicycles, Etc.** (970-349-5210) can both give information on trails for hiking and mountain biking.

EVENTS: Summer festival season highlights—All summer: **Mountain Theatre; Crested Butte Music Series.** July: **Wildflower Festival; Fat Tire Bike Week; Aerial Weekend** brings balloons, hang-gliders, sky divers, stunt planes; **Dansummer** is a three-week schedule of workshops and performances. August: **Festival of the Arts.** September: **Pearl Pass Bike Tour** (Crested Butte to Aspen).

USEFUL NAMES AND ADDRESSES: Crested Butte/Mt. **Crested Butte Chamber of Commerce (located at the four-way stop),** Box 1288, Crested Butte, CO 81224 (tel: 800-545-4505).

Ruby Range

Above Crested Butte on the west is the ridge of the Ruby Range, named for the reddish color of its intruded granite composition. On the town side are numerous mines, while on the west slope is the Raggeds Wilderness. For the most part, this wilderness is a large basin, drained by Middle Anthracite Creek through Dark Canyon and bounded by the Rubies and to the north, the Raggeds. Climbing the Ruby Mountains from Crested Butte is feasible for hikers. You can get a good view of Mount Owen from Lake Irwin, where the Forest Service maintains a campground; a mining road goes northwest from here, leading to open slopes and a route up the southeast ridge of Ruby Peak, which connects to Owen. To get into the Anthracite Basin by trail, drive up the Slate River Road (F.S. 734) to the trail over Angel Pass.

West Elk Range

The West Elk Range is hard to distinguish from the Elk Range, which in turn appears solidly connected to the Sawatch Range. The ranges here are too closely packed together for distinctions to make much sense. No significant valley separates the two mountain complexes, nor does a river flow between them. To consider them separately, especially from a traveler's point of view, is an arbitrary decision based partly on access. The Elk Mountains, which include the Maroon Bells and Snowmass Peak, are visited mostly from Aspen and the Roaring Fork Valley (see page 115). Between them and the West Elk Mountains is the Raggeds Wilderness (hardly visited at all, from any direction), considered to be a part of the Elk Range. Perhaps the most meaningful distinction is juris-dictional: almost the entire West Elk Range is a designated wilderness.

An improved gravel road runs through the narrow valley from Crested Butte to Paonia. This road gives access to the Beckwith Pass Trail at Lost Lake Campground. Another road, F.S. 709, extends a long way into the mountains, where an array of trails branch off into the area's characteristic ridge-and-canyon topography. Long backpack trips are possible here, but most hikers stick to the east side of the wilderness, where the Baldy string rises in a series of ever higher peaks to West Elk Peak, the highest in the area. To the north about two miles are The Castles, a cluster of vertical pinnacles and the landmark of the West Elks. The pinnacles are remnants of repeated lava flows, which originated a short distance to the west. The route to this area is from the east, up Mill Creek on Forest Road 727 from the Baldwin Road. Baldwin, by the way, was one of the larger coal mines in the Crested Butte area; it operated from 1897 until 1946, producing about two million tons of coal.

SUMMIT COUNTY

Summit County lies just across the Divide from Denver, and to westward travelers seems to consist of little more than a valley through which Interstate 70 hurries on its way from the Eisenhower Memorial Tunnel to Vail Pass. However, for its relatively small size, it offers a wide variety of mountain activities. In the heart of the valley, the Dillon Reservoir collects water from a network of alpine streams and sends much of it under the Continental Divide to Denver via the Harold Roberts Tunnel. What remains is allowed to drain as it always has down the Blue River northward to the Colorado River at Kremmling. The towns of Frisco, Dillon and Silverthorne cluster around the reservoir. Breckenridge, a mining town turned ski resort, is located a few miles south. Vail itself, the biggest single ski mountain in Colorado, is just over the pass to the west.

Years ago, the only way to reach Summit County from Denver was to cross Loveland Pass, which at 11,992 feet presented a serious barrier. Especially in winter, when storms or slides could close the highway with little notice, people were reluctant to cross it for the weekend for fear of not making it home on Sunday night. Construction of the Eisenhower Tunnel changed that, making it easy to zip up to Vail or Breckenridge for the day, and turning Summit County into a Denver playground.

It offers plenty to do. On its west side is the Gore Range, an unusually rugged chain protected now as the Eagles Nest Wilderness Area. South of there, at Breckenridge, is the Tenmile Range, with a more relaxed topography which is excellent for hiking and skiing. Breckenridge Ski Resort is built on four of these mountains. One benefit of this activity is seen north of town, where the gold dredges from the days of placer mining left their usual devastated landscape. Bulldozers are now busy flattening the dredge dunes, spreading topsoil and reclaiming the valley bottom.

The other Summit County ski resorts are Copper Mountain and Keystone, both expanding in a big way, and the venerable classic, the highest ski resort in North America, Arapaho Basin. Together with Vail, they create a resort atmosphere throughout the valley, which attracts large numbers of vacationers. Breckenridge holds an annual music festival in July. Footraces and bicycle races happen all summer, in addition to various workshops and art events, and other cultural activities.

Trails

A 40-mile, paved bicycle trail parallels the highway from Vail through Frisco to Breckenridge and Keystone. Short hiking trails include: Tenderfoot Mountain east of Dillon Reservoir, an easy hike to a viewpoint; Lenawee Mountain, up the Montezuma Road east of Dillon to Peru Creek (F.S. Road 214), then a mile to the trailhead on the north side of the road; Argentine Peak, with the trailhead located four miles farther up the Peru Creek Road.

Longer trails include: Miners Creek Trail, which crosses the Tenmile Range through high meadows, and starts in Frisco near Interstate 70, Exit 201; Wheeler National Recreation Trail crosses the Tenmile Range from Copper Mountain to Breckenridge in ten miles of hiking, which starts a mile south of the Copper Mountain interchange on Highway 91.

Some Useful Information About Summit County

HOW TO GET THERE: The area is served from Denver by: **Resort Express** airport shuttle (800-334-7433 outside Colorado, 970-468-7600 in-state) and **Airpost Shuttle** (800-222-2122; 970-668-5466).

ACTIVITIES AND EQUIPMENT RENTALS: **Dillon Reservoir** is open for boating and fishing; because it provides drinking water, sports involving body contact with the water are not permitted. **Blue River**, downstream from the reservoir, is a popular place for canoes, with a short stretch of kayak water (Class II and III) at Boulder Creek about eight highway miles north of Silverthorne. Then below the **Green Mountain Reservoir dam** is another four-mile, Class III and IV kayak stretch, ending at Spring Creek Road (F.S. 201). Bike rental: **Wilderness Sports** in Silverthorne (970-468-8519); **Mogul Mike's** in Dillon (970-468-5506).

USEFUL NAMES AND ADDRESSES: For general information, contact the **Breckenridge Resort Chamber**, P.O. Box 1909, Breckenridge, CO 80424 (tel: 970-453-6018; Central Reservations 800-221-1091); **Summit County Chamber of Commerce**, P.O. Box 214, Frisco, CO

80443 (tel: 800-530-3099); **Copper Mountain Resort Chamber** (tel: 970-968-6477).

EAGLES NEST WILDERNESS

The Eagles Nest Wilderness occupies 134,000 acres on the crest of the Gore Range between Dillon and Vail. The hiking here is rugged, more so than in surrounding ranges, and there are few trails to make it any easier. A good bit of the hiking here is on unmaintained primitive trails, or no trails at all. Important access points are the Cataract Creek Campground near Green Mountain Reservoir, with trails leading to Eaglesmere Lakes and the area at the base of Eagles Nest Peak; and Blue River Campground on Highway 9 a few miles south. Also, the Gore Creek Red Buffalo Pass Trail, which crosses the range, begins on the east side at the end of a short frontage road at Interstate 70, Exit 203.

Trails

DAY-HIKES: Gore Creek Campground (on Interstate 70 seven miles east of Vail) to Deluge Lake, or up Gore Creek over Red Buffalo Pass to Frisco; to Booth Lake via Booth Creek, take Exit 180 from Interstate 70 and follow the frontage road a mile west to the trailhead; Pitkin Creek to Pitkin Lake, trailhead at Exit 180, on the north side; Lost Lake and Wheeler Lakes, on Trail 37 from Interstate 70, Exit 195.

LONGER HIKES: From Piney Lake at the end of Forest Road 410 north of Vail, up Piney River, over the pass at its head to Booth Lake, and down Booth Creek (this is the approach for climbing Mount Powell from the south side).

Useful Names and Addresses

White River National Forest, Box 948, Glenwood Springs, CO 81602 (tel: 970-945-6582); the district office closest to Eagles Nest is at Hwy 9, Silverthorne, CO 80498 (tel: 970-468-5400).

Other Area Ideas

Across the valley from the Eagles Nest Wilderness is a basin formed by the Williams Fork Mountains and the Vasquez Mountains on the Continental Divide. The basin, closed to motor vehicles in the summer, has a 29-mile loop trail, which traverses high country at the heads of Bobtail Creek and the South Fork of the Williams Fork. The loop trailheads, at Sugarloaf and Southfork campgrounds, are scarcely a mile apart. To get there, follow Forest Road 132 across Ute Pass from Colorado

9 south of the Green Mountain Reservoir. Turn right where this road ends and follow the Williams Fork about five miles to the campgrounds.

PARK RANGE

After the Continental Divide finishes its spectacular northward traverse of the Front Range, past Longs Peak and others in Rocky Mountain National Park, it turns a sudden corner and strikes toward the west across a line of low forested ridges. It turns north again on the back of the Park Range, a little-known but worthy chain of mountains named for their commanding position above the high open expanse of North Park. These mountains continue the line of the Gore Range, which reaches its climax in the Eagles Nest Wilderness to the south near Vail. Above the ski resort town of Steamboat Springs, the Park Range is gentle, with rounded summits at or near timberline—excellent country for ski touring and mountain biking. A short distance north, however, the peaks rise higher and provide superb hiking in the Mount Zirkel Wilderness.

Steamboat Springs

Famous as a ski resort, but still a thriving ranch town, Steamboat Springs has a feeling of genuineness that is hard to find in places like Vail, which was built from the ground up as a resort town. In fact, Steamboat is two separate towns, one being the old ranching supply center in the broad valleys of the Elk and Yampa rivers, the other being the Chinese Wall of condominiums rising at the base of Mount Werner. If you ask how many people live here, you need to specify what month you're interested in. Like the other ski towns of Colorado, April and October are the "normal" months, while winter and summer populations swell with seasonal workers, not to mention visitors. So while Steamboat has a native (meaning October) population of 6,000 with 4,000 more in the surrounding area, it has a peak population (during the Christmas holidays) of about 23,000. That may sound like a radical fluctuation, but compared to some other Colorado towns, Steamboat is a rock of stability.

Settlement in the area had its beginnings with the gold rush of the 1860s, when Bugtown and Poverty Bar popped up about 30 miles north of where Steamboat Springs now stands. With names like that, it seems the miners were either terrible pessimists or they wanted to discourage competition. They needn't have bothered; the gold discovery never amounted to much. Steamboat was established in 1875 by ranchers, and

Bugtown eventually changed its name to Hahns Peak, after a symmetrical volcanic cone, which can be seen from Steamboat Lake.

The name Steamboat Springs, so the story goes, originated when a group of French fur trappers, following the Yampa River through unknown country in the 1850s, saw a puff of steam and heard a chugging sound, which they took to be a steam-powered riverboat. The springs are still there, beside the library on the west end of town, although they ceased their chugging many years ago. At the opposite end of Main Street is a thermal swimming pool and water slide operated by the town of Steamboat and open to the public. Fish Creek Falls are spectacular in the spring runoff, cascading 283 feet. A short hike leads from a parking area reached by driving north on 3rd Street and following signs.

Some Useful Information About Steamboat Springs

HOW TO GET THERE: Steamboat is served by Continental Express (303-879-2648). During the ski season, the Yampa Valley Regional Airport (about 20 miles out of Steamboat) is served by American Airlines (303-276-3020), United Airlines (303-398-4141), Continental (303-879-2648) and Northwest (800-225-2525).

CAR RENTAL: Adventure Rent-a-Car (303-879-6025) or Hertz (870-0880 or 800-654-3131).

LODGING: Lodging varies from rustic to expensive; information and reservations can be obtained through **Steamboat Central Reservations** at 800-922-2722.

CAMPGROUNDS: Numerous Forest Service campgrounds are located in surrounding areas, notably at Steamboat Lake and on the road over Rabbit Ears Pass east of town. Two commercial campgrounds are close to town: **Fish Creek Campground**, on Highway 40 between the ski area and the town (303-879-5476), and **Ski Town Campground**, two miles west of town on Highway 40 (303-879-0273).

ACTIVITIES, EQUIPMENT SALES AND RENTALS: Ballooning: **Aerosports Ltd.** (879-7433); **Balloons over Steamboat** (879-3298); **Eagle Balloon Tours** (879-8687); **Steamboat Activity Center** (879-2062); **Pegasus** (879-9191). Bike Rentals: **Awesome Cyclery** (879-2323); **Genessee Ski Shop** (879-9152); **Good Time Sports** (879-7818); **Inside Edge Sports** (879-1250); **Rebel Sports** (879-4125); **Ski Haus International** (879-0385); **Sore Saddle Cyclery** (879-1675); **Steamboat Ski & Resort Corp** (879-6111); **Steamboat Velo Bike Shop** (879-1495); **Telegraph Shack Cycles** (879-6254). White Water Rafting: **Adventures Wild** (879-8747); **Buggywhips Fish and Float Service** (879-8033); **Colorado River Runs** (653-4292). Numerous sporting goods shops throughout Steamboat offer information and equipment. The ski area gondola operates in summer every day through Labor Day weekend and weekends after that until the end of September with adult fares at $10, children 6-12 at $5 and children 5 and under free.

EVENTS: All summer: frequent rodeos, footraces, mountain bicycle races, fly fishing classes, treks for senior citizens, art classes and music concerts. July: **Cowboy Roundup Days** on the Fourth of July weekend (rodeo, barbecues, fireworks, etc.); **Hot Air Balloon Rodeo** later in the month.

USEFUL NAMES AND ADDRESSES: General information can be obtained from the **Steamboat Springs Chamber Resort Association**, P.O. Box 774408, Steamboat Springs, CO 80477 (tel: 970-879-0880).

Mount Zirkel Wilderness

The Mount Zirkel Wilderness occupies 160,648 acres on the crest of the Park Range, north of Steamboat Springs, dominated by Mount Zirkel (12,180 feet) and including 14 peaks over 12,000 feet and more than sixty-five lakes. Trails are good for hiking any time after the end of June, but especially in the fall, when aspens are gold on the lower slopes, and ice forms thin plates on tiny ponds in alpine cirques. This is easy terrain for cross-country travel and a satisfying place to get away from crowds.

You can access trails from either the east (North Park area) or the west, driving north from Steamboat Springs along the Elk River. By far the most popular trailhead leads into the Gilpin Lake area; this trail can be crowded to the point of overuse. You can avoid some of the crowds by using the east side of the wilderness, going in through North Park. The Rainbow Lake area is a nice choice; even if you continue across the Divide, you get into superb lakes country which is hard to reach from the west, and consequently less used than the Gilpin Lake area. Also consider trails from Big Creek Lakes Campground at the far northeast end of the wilderness. A traverse of the range is feasible, staying high the whole distance and going either north or south, with bushwhacking and cross-country travel necessary in some trailless sections. This route is called the Wyoming Trail: for 48 miles, it stays along the Divide with spectacular views to the east and west. Twenty miles of its length are within the wilderness, the rest following trails that are not always on the crest. During May or early June, cross-country skiers find the traverse a rewarding trip.

Useful Names and Addresses

Write to **Hahns Peak/Bears Ears Ranger District**, 57 10th St., P.O. Box 771212, Steamboat Springs, CO 80477 (tel: 970-879-1870). A district office for the east side approaches is at Walden in North Park (970-723-8204).

FRONT RANGE

Along Colorado's Front Range, the history of the Rockies is presented in microcosm. It begins with geology. The mountains rise abruptly from the plains, their hard granitic cores standing proudly more than 14,000 feet in elevation. The layers of sedimentary rock deposited by a series of ancient seas, which last receded about 90 million years ago, have long since been stripped from the heights by erosion. They still underlie the plains and are visible in the foothills and on the lower slopes of the mountains. In the northern part of the Front Range, glaciers still occupy positions on the highest peaks, showing on a diminished scale what things must have looked like during the Ice Age, which ended only 10,000 years ago.

The story proceeds through millennia of minor changes, when the people who lived in the area—wanderers like those whom archaeologists call Folsom Man, and later the modern tribes of Utes, Cheyennes and Arapahos—left behind only transient marks, a few relics and a knowledge of the landscape. The familiar assortment of trappers, explorers and travelers passed through in the first half of the 19th century, but none of them stayed until the gold rush of 1859. That discovery marked the beginning of the region's modern history. With it came virtually all the development we see today. Any watercourse holding a trace of color was torn apart by placer miners, and many of them remain torn apart today. Denver, Golden, Central City and other towns exploded into existence. Discoveries farther west prompted the building of roads, railroads and supply centers. As miners turned from the streambeds to deep hard-rock mines, they stripped the forests from the hills to make mine timbers and to power huge wood-fired stamp mills. The transcontinental railroad was built in the mid-1860s, bringing with it settlers interested in farming. To solve the problem of chronic water shortages in the rain shadow of the mountains, they engineered elaborate irrigation schemes, which actually brought water from the western slope to the eastern.

For a long time, the emphasis was on exploitation with no holds barred. One gold or silver strike followed another, and these mines—from Central City to Telluride—dominated the economy of the region as well as attitudes toward the land. Finally, as the mines played out, and those whose only interest was exploitation left the mountains or turned their attention to other things, there developed a growing interest in the more lasting aspects of mountains. Conservation became an issue at the same time that tourism became an industry. The two, it was discovered, go hand in hand; no one wanted to come to see devastated mountains. In addition, many of those who stayed to make Colorado their homes did so because they valued the natural setting.

The results are an interesting study in comparative attitudes. At the south end of the Front Range, the development of tourism has been a project of private individuals. A cog railway and toll road, both privately owned, climb to the summit of Pikes Peak. A private bridge spans the 1,200-foot-deep Royal Gorge of the Arkansas River, while a tram ride carries people into the gorge. A cliff-dwelling, similar to those at Mesa Verde National Park, looks out of place until you learn that it was built in 1905 to attract tourists. They hauled the stones all the way from the Mesa Verde area. The Cave of the Winds, one of the few limestone caves in the state, is private property. So is the nearby Seven Falls, a long cascade with ladders built alongside it and bright-colored lights at night. Near the toll road, at a place called North Pole, a man in a Santa suit tries to look cool and welcoming in the July sun; Santa never wears shorts. All these places charge admission, and some are quite worthy of a visit.

At the other end of the range, Rocky Mountain National Park stands as a contrast in method. Five dollars buys a week's entry permit, and while campground fees are collected, there isn't another toll charge or fee for access in the entire park. Both places, Rocky Mountain and Pikes Peak, are extremely popular.

These factors—gold mining, railroading, logging, farming, tourism, conservation—whether seen as beneficial or not, have all left their marks on the Front Range as they have on the entire Rocky Mountain chain. Denver, Colorado Springs, Boulder and a host of smaller cities now form a continuous metropolitan area on the edge of the mountains, growing at one of the fastest rates in the country, filled in part with people who came here for access to mountain recreation and what they saw as a more relaxed lifestyle—an increasingly elusive commodity in this area of new skyscrapers. In its eagerness to grow, Denver now looks little different from any large city, especially when, during inversions, the Front Range disappears behind a pall of polluted air. It is hard to think of Denver as a place in the mountains.

Even so, the mountains are close by. On weekends and holidays, the highways west of the cities are crowded with recreationists heading into the high country—to Rocky Mountain National Park or its surrounding wilderness areas, to the restored Victorian towns of the gold country, to ski areas in winter, to reservoirs, lakes and streams scattered throughout the region, or to less well known but equally attractive mountain areas along the Continental Divide. Despite the crowds, Colorado's Front Range remains a gorgeous place to visit, with all sorts of activities and recreational opportunities. You might just consider avoiding the place on weekends.

Rocky Mountain National Park

To get an idea of how Rocky Mountain National Park is shaped, take the drive across Trail Ridge Road. This was the route used by the Ute Indians as a way between the plains and the interior. Today it remains a thoroughfare, with motorhomes replacing Indian ponies. It also gives visitors a splendid opportunity to see the alpine landscape in intimate detail. For four miles, the road stays over 12,000 feet high, and stays above 11,000 feet for eleven miles, all of it above timberline on open tundra. The journey from the valley below to the crest of Trail Ridge is a cross-section of mountain ecosystems, from spruce-fir wetlands through several stages of subalpine forest to arctic tundra with its fascinating world of miniature vegetation. Plan to drive slowly, stopping often, for this is a route surrounded by extremes. Looking down at your feet, you see a 300-year-old tree no thicker than your thumb; looking up, you see for tens of miles in all directions some of the grandest scenery anywhere.

To the west, on the far side of the Kawuneeche Valley, are the Never Summer Mountains; the park boundary runs along their crest, while a small wilderness area protects their western slope. To the north is the Mummy Range, and to the south, for a long distance south, is the heart of the park, the Continental Divide and a mountain rampart running unbroken well south of the park itself. Separated from the road by the depths of Forest Canyon, these peaks present to your view a series of canyons, gorges, glaciers and icefields, which challenge climbers and invite backpackers. As it continues south, the range becomes even more rugged, with sheer valley walls and several imposing vertical faces. The most famous of these, the Diamond, you can see on the east aspect of the park's highest and best-known mountain, Longs Peak (14,255 feet).

Near the east end of Trail Ridge Road, the view opens on Estes Park. The word *park*, in this case, means a relatively flat open patch of ground surrounded by mountains. In Wyoming, they call the same topographical feature a hole; were Jackson's Hole in Colorado, it would be called Jackson Park. Estes is the largest of several holes, or parks, on the east slope of Rocky Mountain. The others include Moraine Park, Hollowell Park, Meeker Park and Allens Park. Parks are another feature of the higher mountains that were created by erosional debris torn loose by glaciers and deposited at the foot of the mountains. This whole process in all its stages from glacier to barren debris to revegetated landscape is perhaps easier seen from below, at the Moraine Park Visitor Center with its panoramic view of the Longs Peak area. But before descending, look to the north, where the east side of the Mummy Range forms a barrier

Odessa Lake in Rocky Mountain National Park is an easy walk along the loop trail beginning at the Bear Lake parking area.

only slightly less formidable than the mountains to the south. The Mummy Range, wild and scenic, is a fine hiking area, which many people overlook in their eagerness to get close to Longs Peak.

At the heart of Rocky Mountain lies Bear Lake, surrounded by high peaks, the focus of a network of trails, and served by the most heavily used road in the park. So much traffic competes for space here that the Park Service has set up a free shuttle bus to relieve congestion. The system works, but people seem to take the bus only when parking lots are full, and to be convinced of that many drive the road, only to return to the shuttle parking areas; better to board the bus in the first place.

Trails

Permits ($10 during peak season) are required for all overnight use of the Rocky Mountain backcountry. Campsites are designated and the number of hikers using each location is tightly controlled. So is the number of nights a hiker is allowed: a maximum of three nights in one site, and a total of seven in the park between June and September, and an additional fourteen during other months. In midsummer, demand far exceeds the number of permits issued, and hikers should be ready to consider alternate routes. Permits can be reserved, in person by filling out a form available at the park, or by mail. From October through May, the park takes phone reservations, although any request for the upcoming summer must be made after March 1. Reserved permits must be claimed by 10:00 A.M. on the day of the trip, or the entire permit will be canceled.

The second option is to get a permit for the areas that have been designated as cross-country zones. These have no maintained trails, no designated campsites and far fewer backpackers. Hikers are required to keep moving (only one night at a time in a given site and two nights per zone) and to make low-impact camps. Going this way provides a good bit more freedom, but quotas are in effect, and the zones are limited.

The third option is to get a special use permit, given for technical climbing bivouacs. These permits allow climbers to get started early—an important consideration in the season when afternoon thunderstorms are a daily occurrence. It also allows them to camp above timberline at a site of their choosing.

Avoiding the crowds in Rocky is not as hard as it may sound. The most popular hiking areas are on the east side of the park, along the Bear Lake Road, or in the Longs Peak area, or farther south in Wild Basin. Easy road access from the Denver metropolitan area explains why so many people head for these trails. There are plenty of other places to go—in the Mummy Range north of Trail Ridge Road and all along the west side of the park. Even there, you should expect to see people in summer. The Front Range is a popular place. Even the wilderness area which bounds Rocky to the south, Indian Peaks, imposes hiker quotas through a permit system—so far the only wilderness area in the Rockies to do this.

The heaviest trail use in Rocky occurs in the park's southeast corner, around Bear Lake, Longs Peak and Wild Basin. The Fern Lake Loop, taken from Bear Lake, climbs into one of the gorges visible from Trail Ridge Road and follows it past a series of alpine lakes, ending in Moraine Park. A branch of this trail climbs to the summit of Flattop Mountain. A third route goes from Bear Lake to Nymph, Dream and Emerald lakes. Less than a mile down the road, at the Glacier Gorge trailhead, another set of trails presents hikers with more choices. Hundreds of people each day walk the short distance to Alberta Falls, a thunderous and very beautiful cascade. Beyond there, the trail narrows on its way to Glacier Gorge and Mills Lake, where you get a backside view of Longs Peak. Optionally, bypass Glacier Gorge and continue to Loch Vale. Both valleys climb above timberline, taking hikers to high lakes and little patches of tundra clinging to the glacier-scoured rock slopes. Climbers and scramblers favor this area; with ice axe and crampons, a variety of high routes are feasible.

Longs Peak, despite its forbidding east face, is climbed by hundreds of hikers each year, most on the East Longs Peak Trail, which starts at the Longs Peak Ranger Station (through Estes Park townsite and south on Highway 7). The climb, 4,800 feet up, requires stamina, about 12 hours of steady effort, and some technical skill. In July and August, start the climb early enough to be off the summit before noon, when summer thunderstorms begin playing electrical roulette on exposed places. This means hitting the trail in the day's first gray light. From the same trailhead, and with less effort, you can hike to Chasm Lake at the base of the famous Diamond.

For less-used trails, consider Lawn Lake or Ypsilon Lake in the Mummy Range, or any of the west-side trails: Timber Lake Trail at the base of Trail Ridge Road, Tonahutu Creek Trail, which crosses the park to Bear Lake, or the East Inlet Trail.

Some Useful Information About Rocky Mountain

HOW TO GET THERE: You can get to Rocky Mountain from either the east or the west on good highways. The park is only 65 miles from Denver and is served from there by the **Charles Tour & Travel Service**, P.O. Box 4373, Estes Park, CO 80517 (tel: 970-586-5151 or 800-586-5009).

LODGING: Although the park has no overnight lodging, a full range of services exists just outside the park; information can be obtained from the Estes Park Chamber of Commerce, P.O. Box 3050, Estes Park, CO 80517 (tel: 800-443-7837).

CAMPGROUNDS: The park has five campgrounds, which fill early in the day during summer. Reservations can be made for **Moraine Park** and **Glacier Basin Campgrounds** (tel: 800-365-2267). **Longs Peak Campground** on Highway 7 south of Estes Park is for tents only, first come, first served. In addition, private campgrounds and Forest Service campgrounds circle the park. For **Forest Service campgrounds**, go south on Highway 7 to Meeker Park and Olive Ridge sites. If these are full, there are more along Highway 72 farther south. On the west side of the park, there are sites in the Arapaho National Recreation Area (two large lakes formed by the Granby and Shadow Mountain dams on the Colorado River). These can be crowded on weekends and virtually empty on Sunday nights. For information call 970-498-2770.

USEFUL NAMES AND ADDRESSES: The address for **Rocky Mountain Park Headquarters** is: Superintendent, Estes Park, CO 80517 (tel: 970-586-1206 or 627-3471 for the west unit office near Grand Lake). Backcountry permits are available at either office, but phone reservations must be made from March through May at 970-586-1242. Books include: *Rocky Mountain National Park Hiking Trails* by Kent and Donna Dannen and *Rocky Mountain National Park Road Guide* by Thomas Schmidt (FreeWheeling Guides, see p. 241).

Indian Peaks Wilderness

The Indian Peaks Wilderness adjoins Rocky Mountain on the south and continues protection of the lofty central chain of the Front Range. Not a large area (16 miles from its south boundary at Rollins Pass to its north limit at the park), it is nonetheless a spectacular one. The mountains, as in Rocky, are built of Precambrian granite and metamorphosed rocks with intrusions of quartz. In other words, these are hard, steep-sided mountains with deep valleys where glaciers did their carving—country similar to that in the Longs Peak area. The high valleys hold chains of lakes, while the lower ones, where they widen out, are lined by huge lateral moraines down to an elevation of about 8,000 feet. A few small glaciers remain, including Arapaho Glacier, the farthest south in the United States.

A relatively new wilderness, Indian Peaks was designated in 1978. It takes its name from the string of peaks named for Indian tribes: Ogalalla, Paiute, Pawnee, Shoshoni, Navajo, Apache and so on. Already it has the sort of regulations more common to national parks than wilderness areas. Quotas are set by both Arapaho and Roosevelt national forests for the various zones into which the area is divided. At some lakes, no camping is permitted, while in other places, no fires are allowed. Campsites are designated in high-use areas, but hikers may stay where they wish in other locations, as long as they observe proper backcountry low-impact manners. These regulations are prompted by heavy use: more than 2,000 overnight backcountry parties each year. Forest Service offices in Estes Park, Boulder, Granby and Fort Collins can give out permits ($5). Permits are limited between June 1 and September 15, with demand in high-use areas often greater than supply. Planning a few days ahead is recommended.

Some Useful Information About Indian Peaks

HOW TO GET THERE: Access is easy. From the east, on Highway 72, trailheads are in the Middle St. Vrain Creek drainage (a rough road past Camp Dick Campground), the South St. Vrain Creek drainage (a campground and picnic areas at Brainard Lake west of Ward), and in the area of Nederland. Just south of the Indian Peaks Wilderness you can drive almost to the Continental Divide on the historic Moffatt Road. Currently the road ends about a mile shy of the Divide because of a rock slide that closed Needle's Eye Tunnel, preventing onward travel. If the slide is cleared, it might be possible, as in the past, to continue along the abandoned grade of the Denver and Rio Grande Railroad to the pass and a trailhead at Corona Lake. The road continues down to U.S.

Highway 40 near Winter Park resort—a scenic drive even if you're not going hiking, but check on its condition before trying it.

On the western side, turn off Highway 34 on the south side of Lake Granby and follow the south shore road to Trailhead Campground on Monarch Lake. The other trailhead is at the end of Forest Road 129, which turns off U.S. 40 near Tabernash and goes to Meadow Creek Lake. Generally, distances to the Divide are longer from the west, but none of the trails here are long.

USEFUL NAMES AND ADDRESSES: Write to these **Forest Service** offices: Boulder District Office, 2995 Baseline, Boulder, CO 80303 (tel: 303-444-6600); Estes Park District Office, 161 2nd St., Estes Park, CO 80517 (tel: 970-586-3440); Granby District Office, P.O. Box 10, Granby, CO 80446 (tel: 970-887-4100); and Fort Collins District Office, 240 W. Prospect, Fort Collins, CO 80526 (tel: 970-498-1100). The *Indian Peaks Wilderness Area Hiking Guide*, by John Murray, is available at area bookstores or from Pruett Publishing, Boulder, CO.

Pikes Peak

Pikes Peak became the focus for gold-rushers of 1859, even though the actual strikes occurred roughly a hundred miles north in the mountains above Denver. "Pikes Peak or Bust" was the famous slogan, and while neither the highest nor the most scenic mountain in the Front Range, it is arguably the most famous.

Pikes Peak has been the subject of many stories and outrageous legends, but none surpass the tales of Sergeant John T. O'Keefe, a young man who lived with his wife at the Summit House during the winter of 1880. His job was to observe and report on weather; what he saw, with the apparent help of whiskey and imagination, was positively Hitchcockian. At the end of October, he reported to his superiors a volcanic eruption, which melted several feet of snow all around its crater. Then in November came reports of a series of eruptions rivaling Vesuvius in power—very interesting considering that no one at the base of the mountain saw anything and that O'Keefe had obviously survived the incident. Even more dangerous than volcanism was the attack of the killer rats.

O'Keefe, as quoted in *Colorado*, one of the Federal Writers Project books produced in the Great Depression, "described an army of ferocious pack rats that inhabited the rocky crevices of the peak. One evening, alarmed by screams, he rushed into the bedroom to find his wife besieged by rats. With rare presence of mind, he encased her in zinc roofing material, thrust his legs into joints of stovepipe, and with a heavy club proceeded to battle the ferocious carnivorous rodents.

Hundreds were slain, only to be replaced by reserves from outside. Meanwhile, the rats had devoured a quarter of beef hanging in the room, not to speak of the infant daughter of the couple. Finally, O'Keefe's wife, a mountain-bred girl and an expert with a lariat, threw a wire noose over her husband and attached it to a powerful storage battery. The heavy current electrocuted most of the rats busily nibbling on the sergeant and routed the survivors. O'Keefe's reports soon ceased—whether because the resourceful sergeant was removed to a less dangerous post or because the eruption checked the flow of 'strong waters' from Colorado City, is not clear."

Today, travelers drive to the top of Pikes Peak without fear of volcanic eruption or packs of pack rats. The road, built in 1915 as a business venture, begins at Cascade on Highway 24 west of Colorado Springs ($5 per adult, $2 for children 6 to 11), and is open from May until the middle of October, daylight hours only. The other way to the summit, aside from walking, is the Pikes Peak Cog Railway ($20.50 per adult, $9 for children 9 to 11; reservations required), which leaves from its terminal in Manitou Springs. An option for those who would rather not pay the road toll is to drive to the summit of Mount Evans (14,264 feet), which is actually higher than Pikes Peak and served by a public road from Idaho Springs on Interstate 70 west of Denver.

Other Area Ideas

The Garden of the Gods, in Colorado Springs, is a series of spectacular red sandstone fins, set on edge and sheltering a city park with hiking trails, a paved drive and a visitor center. Florissant Fossil Beds National Monument is worth the short detour off U.S. Highway 24; it is on the backroad to Cripple Creek, one of the Front Range's more colorful gold towns. Other places, such as Cave of the Winds, Cliff Dwelling Museum, Royal Gorge and the North Pole are adequately described and promoted in the vicinity.

FLAT TOPS WILDERNESS

The White River Plateau, bracketed on three sides by the Yampa and Colorado rivers, rolls across the Colorado sky at an average elevation of between 10,000 and 11,000 feet. Although local parlance calls it a mountain range, this uplift is actually a broad, flat volcanic plateau—the Flat Tops. The plateau has been deeply eroded in all directions, making it a landscape of rolling timberline meadows strewn with lakes and drained by streams, which fall off into steep-sided canyons on all sides.

A number of peaks rise above the plateau, although usually only about a thousand feet higher than the surrounding terrain. Among the highest are Trappers Peak (11,990 feet), Shingle Peak (11,996 feet), Turret Peak (11,470 feet) and Big Marvine Peak (11,879).

In the late '40s and '50s, nearly 400 square miles of timber were killed by spruce budworm, whose larvae eat the tender buds of new needles and kill the trees by defoliation. The dead forest still stands over much of the Flat Tops, gray and weathered, giving mountain slopes the look of an old silver tip grizzly. Like a grizzly, it might be better appreciated from a distance; even if you enjoy viewing the ecological process of recovery after forest fires, watch out for falling snags when the wind blows. Add to that the difficulty of making your way through areas littered with trees that have already toppled. They fall every which way, tangled up with new trees and boggy areas filled with mosquitoes. It may look like easy country to bushwhack through, but it's not. Adding to the difficulty of walking a straight line are heaps of large, angular talus at the base of mountain slopes.

Fortunately, trails wander all across the Flat Tops, with trailheads on every side. Trips of all lengths are possible, including loops and traverses, although car shuttles might be too long to bother with. There are three major access points. From the town of Yampa on the east, the Bear River road (it becomes Forest Service 900 as it enters Routt National Forest) ends at the Stillwater Reservoir. From here, Trail 1119 climbs above the canyon and crosses a place where erosion from both sides has nearly cut through the plateau, resulting in a feature called the Devils Causeway, a popular day-hiker's destination. Just to the west is a wide basin containing Trappers Lake. You could walk there from Stillwater Reservoir as fast as you could drive around to it—maybe faster. To get there, take county roads west from Phippsburg (just north of Yampa), south from Hayden on Highway 40, or east from Meeker. All routes converge on the North Fork of the White River (Forest Service Road 205), which begins at Trappers Lake. From there, hiking and fishing opportunities are many. The Chinese Wall encircles the basin; there are lakes and streams both above and below it, including Skinny Fish Lake, which is presumably a place for hikers and not anglers. If you want to avoid crowds, stay away from Wall Lake and its well-used trail.

The third main access point is also a fine scenic drive. Two miles north of Dotsero, where the Eagle River joins the Colorado (turn north off Interstate 70), Forest Service Road 600 climbs steeply onto the plateau. It passes Coffee Pot Spring Campground after about twelve miles of switchbacks, then continues to a group of small lakes in Supply

Basin (several more campgrounds). The road ends finally at a resort and
the wilderness boundary in the meadows of the South Fork White River.
As at the other roadheads, trails climb out of the canyon onto the
uplands—a rise of between one and two thousand feet. One trail, however, follows the South Fork through the narrows of its canyon to another trailhead supplied by a road from Buford. The opportunities for
undesignated camping are numerous around the Flat Tops.

Useful Names and Addresses

White River National Forest district offices are located in Meeker (317
E. Market St., CO 81641; tel; 970-878-4039), Rifle (0094 Country Rd.
244, CO 81650; tel: 970-625-2371) and Eagle (P.O. Box 720, CO
81631; tel: 970-328-6388). **Routt National Forest**, which contains only
a small portion of the wilderness, has a district office in Yampa (300
Roselawn, P.O. Box 7, CO 80483; tel: 970-638-4516).

THE HIGH UINTAS

The Uinta Range is well to the west of the main chain of the Rockies,
and I thought about leaving them out of this guide. Part of a system of
mountains in central Utah, they connect with ranges extending all the
way to the southwestern part of the state, clearly in the province of the
Southwest deserts and not the Rocky Mountains. Nonetheless, the
Uintas themselves are alpine mountains, not desert mountains, a characteristic that sets them apart from ranges in other parts of the state.
Snowfields and cirque lakes lie against steep-faced peaks, aspen forests
embrace moist wildflower meadows, and pikas, or coneys, shout warnings from their lookout rocks in the talus.

Besides that, the traveler headed from southern Colorado toward
Idaho or the Yellowstone area passes the Uintas, and it seems appropriate to include them.

The Uintas are the highest east-west trending range in North America,
except for the Brooks Range in Alaska. Named for the Ute, or Uintat,
Indians, they run at right angles to the Wasatch Range, which forms a
sort of spine down the center of Utah. The Uinta peaks cluster along a
divide, which averages around 11,000 feet. Their rock is Precambrian
sediments metamorphosed into hard, fine-grained quartzite and shale.
Characteristic banded cliffs stand above talus slopes and rolling
morainal basins, which because of the vertical walls and flat floors feel
a bit like immense open-air rooms. The wilderness area varies in elevation from 8,000 to over 13,000 feet, with much of it over timberline and

The High Uintas, made of metamorphosed sediments, are unusual because the crest trends east-west instead of north-south.

easy to wander across. From the central divide, ridges stretch to the north and south, embracing a series of high basins, almost all of which are dotted with small mountain lakes. Trails reach these basins via relatively direct, short routes from over a dozen main trailheads (in all, 23 trailheads on all sides). These trails and the fairly easy access to the lakes are the reasons for the area's popularity among fishermen and hikers. People tend to congregate at the lakes. For hikers, however, the high ridges are reasonable routes with only moderately difficult bushwhacking.

Trails

A high trail traverses the main divide (the Highline Trail). At one end, where Highway 150 crosses Bald Mountain and Hayden passes, the trail provides easy, almost level access to Naturalist Basin, Four Lakes Basin, Brinton Meadow and the Lightning Lake area, all heavily used in the summer season. Of course, as in any range, there are alternatives close by. Just on the other side of the highway, to the west and outside the designated wilderness, numerous trails traverse less well known lakes country around imposing Mount Watson and Notch Mountain. Also from Hayden Pass, those willing to bushwhack can find a way up over the ridge between Mounts Agassiz and Hayden into Middle Basin, an area otherwise accessible only by a fairly long trail from Christmas Meadows Trailhead located farther north.

Continuing on past the first ten miles, the Highline Trail reaches less heavily used country, although because so many trailheads make access easy, you need to exercise imagination if you seek real solitude. At the east end of the wilderness stands Kings Peak, the highest point in Utah (13,528 feet). The Highline Trail crosses Anderson Pass only about a mile away and 700 feet lower.

Other access: of the dozen or so main trailheads, most have Forest Service campgrounds at or near the end of the roads. The most direct access on the south side is through Yellowstone Creek, Moon Lake and Rock Creek trailheads. From the north, East Fork of Blacks Fork, Christmas Meadows, Henrys Fork and China Meadows trailheads have campgrounds and are accessible by normal cars.

Useful Names and Addresses

The single most useful thing to get from the Forest Service is the **High Uintas Wilderness Area Map**, a large-scale map with 200-foot contours sufficient for most hiking needs; it costs $3. For more detailed information, write to **Wasatch National Forest**, 8103 Federal Bldg., 125 State St., Salt Lake City, UT 84138, or to the following district offices for specific questions. For the Naturalist Basin area, **Kamas Ranger District**, 50 E. Center St., Kamas, UT 84036 (tel: 801-783-4338); for the northeast approach to Blacks Fork area, **Evanston Ranger District**, 1565 Hwy 150, Ste A., Evanston, WY 82931-1880 (tel: 307-789-3194); for the northwest corner, **Mountain View Ranger District**, Lone Tree Rd., Mountain View, NW 82939. **Ashley National Forest** also has a piece of the Uintas. Its main office is at 355 N. Vernal Ave., Vernal, UT 84078 (tel: 801-789-1181), with district offices in Duchesne and Roosevelt.

CHAPTER THREE

Yellowstone Country

Yellowstone National Park is the sizeable heart of an even larger area of wild country. In the region are more than ten designated wilderness areas, six national forests, nearly a dozen distinct mountain ranges and several major river systems, all of them centered on the world's first national park. Yellowstone itself, 3,400 square miles averaging seven to eight thousand feet in elevation, is a rolling volcanic plateau covered with trees and dotted with lakes. Its gentle landscape belies a history of staggering violence; it remains one of the most geologically active spots on earth.

On all sides, mountain ranges rise higher than the park before dropping decisively to a region of surrounding plains. Some of these mountains, the Absarokas being noteworthy, are of volcanic origin like the park. Others—the Tetons, the Winds, the Beartooths—are built of Precambrian metamorphics, the so-called basement rocks of the continent, very old and very hard. They were heaved up in blocks along deep fault lines to form magnificent ramparts and then carved by glaciers to their current shapes.

The vegetation reflects a relatively dry climate. Lodgepole pine is far and away the dominant forest tree. Builders of log houses appreciate its straight, untapered shape and low-density wood. But because it rarely grows to more than about a foot in diameter, loggers have little use for it. As you travel the region, you'll see many log houses and few sawmills. In parts of the Rockies with more moisture, or better soil than

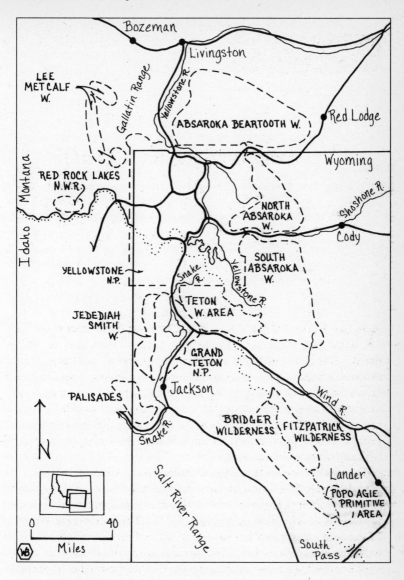

the Yellowstone volcanics, lodgepole is an intermediate forest type. It quickly establishes itself in burned areas but is replaced eventually by spruce and fir, which crowd out the lodgepole and form the mature forest. This forest, which biologists call the climax forest, will then sustain itself until a fire or some other disaster occurs. In the Yellowstone environs, however, where the porous soil is poor in minerals, lodgepole forms the climax forest. Spruce and fir survive only in wetter areas where the soil is not volcanic.

At higher elevations, blasted by storms, wind and heavy snowloads, limber pine and white pine grow twisted and picturesque. Cottonwoods and willows, because they need much water, grow along riverbanks and streambeds. Pinyon and juniper, the classic forest partnership of the Southwest, are found on warm, well-drained slopes at lower elevations—Yellowstone's northern range, for example, or the canyon of the Snake River south of the Tetons.

From this amalgamation of high plateau, mountain range, meadow and forest flow some of the world's more famous rivers: the Yellowstone, the Missouri, the Snake, the Green, the Bighorn, the North Platte. The names of these and their tributaries—the Wind, the Sweetwater, the Popo Agie, the Madison and many others—reverberate through the history of westward exploration and settlement.

Following is a regional inventory: against Yellowstone's south and east borders lie three national forests (Targhee, Bridger-Teton and Shoshone), three wilderness areas (North Absaroka, Washakie and Teton), in addition to Grand Teton National Park, Jedediah Smith Wilderness and the Teton National Elk Refuge. These run essentially contiguous with the Gros Ventre (gro-VAHNT) Mountains near Jackson, and, in the Wind River Range, the Bridger and Fitzpatrick wilderness areas and the Whiskey Mountain and Popo Agie (po-PO-zha) primitive areas. It sounds like a large piece of country to get hold of in your mind, and it certainly is.

Farther east from Yellowstone, visible from the park's higher points, the Bighorn Mountains rise on the other side of the Bighorn River. The Cloud Peak Wilderness encompasses the wildest part of that range. Looking to the north and west of Yellowstone, we find two more national forests (Custer and Gallatin), two wildernesses (Absaroka-Beartooth and Metcalf, the high, forested expanse of the Madison Plateau, and a crowd of smaller ranges standing shoulder-to-shoulder all the way across southwest Montana.

A party of hikers could start on the Continental Divide at South Pass in west-central Wyoming and follow high mountains all the way to Livingston, Montana, a distance of almost two hundred fifty crow-flying miles, and at least three times that by wilderness trails. In that distance, they would have to cross only three roads. The trip would take them through some of the highest, wildest, most spectacularly scenic country in the West. Unlike the massive, canyon-riddled complexity of Idaho, much of the journey would be above or near timberline on well-defined mountain crests. Unlike the great rounded bulk of Colorado's high country, these mountains are more sharply cut. In many places, narrow glaciated ridges rise above relatively flat meadows, which support a huge population of wildlife: elk, deer, sheep, goat, black bear, and, north of the Wind River Range, grizzly.

Having completed their journey, the hiking party would by no means have covered the territory. Just south of Livingston, they could walk across the highway (and the Yellowstone River) and continue south on the crest of the Gallatin Range, connecting in the weeks to come with other high crests all the way to the Grand Tetons. Although they would have seen one big rugged hunk of country, they still would have missed the bulk of Yellowstone National Park.

History

Indian interest in the Yellowstone region centered mostly on its surrounding plains, where game was plentiful and traveling was easy. Blackfoot, Crow, Cheyenne, Shoshone, Sioux and others hunted and traveled throughout the region. No doubt they also knew and used the mountains. In many cases, their trails have become the routes of paved highways, while their campsites are locations for both cities and hamlets. But because so much of the region has stayed wild, you can still follow their old trails through wilderness areas just as they did, by foot or horseback. You can camp in the same places, and for the same reasons—for wind shelter, access to drinking water, or just the view.

Sometimes the sense of commonality with ancient travelers is uncanny. For example, an old Indian trail crosses the Wind River Range in the area of Fremont Peak. If you walk this trail, and consider the best locations for rest stops or campsites, you can find evidence that people thought the same way hundreds of years ago. A friend of mine and I once found such a place along that trail. It was above timberline in a meadow studded with boulders. One was a particularly good seat, and all around it were flakes of obsidian and chert. We could picture generations of stone tool makers perched on that boulder, chipping away. Among the flakes we found a broken arrowhead, nearly finished. Somehow we guessed that it had fractured in the maker's hand when it was almost done. What would our reaction have been in the same circumstance? Frustration, naturally. My friend sat on the rock with a stone the size of an arrowhead, and imitating disgust, he hurled it against the vertical face of a larger boulder nearby. We started looking in the fine gravel where his stone had landed, and sure enough, found the other half of the nearly completed arrowhead.

The first white known to have penetrated the area was John Colter, once a member of the Lewis and Clark expedition, who stayed in the mountains as a fur trapper. In the winter of 1807-08, he crossed the Absarokas, visited Jackson Hole and probably saw sections of Yellowstone on a long foot journey. In the years that followed, the mountain men frequented the area from Yellowstone south, although they avoided the country around three forks of the Missouri, controlled by hostile Blackfoot Indians. The Wind River Range and valleys on both sides of the Tetons were their favorite haunts.

Wider knowledge of the area came, as it did throughout the Rockies, with the gold rush. Gold was discovered in southwest Montana in the early 1860s, giving rise to the state's first towns, Bannack and Virginia City. Thousands of miners poured in, overflowed and spread across the countryside in hopes of finding new lodes. Some succeeded, and communities of all sizes grew up across southwest Montana. As Virginia City played out, activity shifted toward Helena, destined to become the state capital, and to Butte, where deep copper mining would build fortunes and sustain a large population for nearly a century.

With the miners came all the ancillary benefits and disasters of gold fever. Virginia City was witness to one of the more notorious examples of vigilante law, when its sheriff turned out to be the leader of a gang of highwaymen and murderers, and the community responded with a lynch mob. Butte was to become the focus of bloody battles between labor unions and mine owners, battles that presaged the rise of unions in general many years later. At the same time, finding a foothold were the industries that would remain after the miners had packed up and gone home: ranching, agriculture, transport, railroads and logging. These are the backbone of the western economy even today.

Meanwhile, in northwest Wyoming, things were relatively quiet—no gold mines to speak of, no railroads, no great development schemes. Ranchers moved into the valleys and there they have stayed. Scattered supply towns—Lander, Pinedale, Dubois, Cody, Jackson—grew up to serve the ranches and provide local government. This remains their major function, although tourism, recreation, land speculation, logging and other enterprises grow in importance.

WIND RIVER RANGE

The Wind River Range, a backpacker's gem, carries the Continental Divide southwest from the Yellowstone area into central Wyoming. Where it comes to an end, the Divide bifurcates around the Great Divide Basin, an area roughly one hundred miles in diameter with no outlet for its sparse moisture. The primarily granite mount   range are the result of block faulting, which lifted th   allowed erosion to strip off the overlying sediments. H   and sheer above rounded glacial valleys dotted with m   hundred lakes. The walking is easy in the high country   soil remains after the Pleistocene glaciation. Today, se   largest glaciers in the lower 48 states hang on the crest of   ,,inds." For a walker, it is hard to imagine a lovelier, more enticing landscape. Backpackers can virtually strike off in any direction and find a route through some of the finest alpine scenery anywhere.

Most of this range is protected from development. The Jim Bridger Wilderness (392,000 acres) occupies nearly sixty airline miles along the west side of the Divide. Adjoining on the east slope are the Fitzpatrick Wilderness Area (191,000 acres) and Popo (pronounced po-Po-zha) and Whiskey Mountain primitive areas, which, although they are not contiguous, are joined by the Wind River Roadless Area.

Several places, all on the Continental Divide, attract the attention of hikers. Near the south end of the range, the Cirque of the Towers, dominated by a striking symmetrical tower called Pingora Peak, encircles Lonesome Lake. On the other side of the Divide, Shadow Lake occupies a nearly twin cirque. Both lakes and both cirques are highly, deservedly popular.

Northward along the Divide, past a maze of lakes and rounded granite knobs, is Titcomb Valley, five miles of classic glacial carving, holding the two large Titcomb Lakes, which drain into the painfully beautiful Island Lake. Anyone who arrives late in the day at the low saddle overlooking Island Lake and sits for a while to take in the view will feel extravagantly rewarded for the effort expended in getting there. Forming a wall on the eastern side of the valley is the sheer mass of Fremont Peak, the third highest mountain in Wyoming. The sharp buttresses of Mount Sacajawea Peak stand out distinctly to the north, near Mount Woodrow Wilson, which supposedly got its name from its 14 skyline pinnacles and the connection with President Wilson's Fourteen Point Peace Plan. Over the pass at the head of the valley stands Gannett Peak, which at 13,804 feet is the highest in Wyoming (the Grand Teton is number two). Although the valley bottoms are clear of ice, the peaks themselves are weighted down with glaciers, especially on eastern and northern exposures where they catch less of the summer sun.

From the top of Gannett one can see a great deal of country, including the third popular part of the Wind River Range, the Green River Lakes area. With Square Top Mountain looming distinctively above their blue waters, these lakes are a common postcard view of the range,

The striking granite pinnacle of the Pingora rises in the center of the Cirque of the Towers in the Wind River Range.

Titcomb Valley in Wyoming's Wind River Range lies entirely above the timberline.

and the headwaters of one of the major drainages in the West. Looking east from Gannett, out across the expansive Gannett and Dinwoody glaciers, are the steep-sided valleys and high plateaus of the adjoining Fitzpatrick Wilderness (once the Glacier Primitive Area). The name is appropriate. Jim Bridger and Tom Fitzpatrick were friends and business partners for most of their time as mountain men, and both of them thought of the Winds as home turf. These mountains, with the ranges to the west on the Utah border, were the richest beaver country in the Rockies; they probably knew every stream and willow flat in the region.

The popular areas of the Wind River Range, plus several other small zones, have special restrictions regarding their use between July 1 and September 10. Group size is limited to ten persons and twenty horses. Campfires are prohibited, as is camping in a spot visible from a lakeshore, if tents are within 200 feet of the shore. These are as reasonable as rules ever get; careful campers would do well to follow them even outside the special areas.

Trails throughout the range are numerous and convenient. They interconnect over passes and through alpine valleys to provide a variety of routes. Most hikers make loops from trailheads, but with shuttle arrangements it's quite feasible to walk the entire length of the range, crossing and re-crossing the Divide according more to whim than necessity. Even nonhikers or those interested only in short walks from the roads will find it rewarding to drive to any of the trailheads. Beginning from the southwest, the first access point is the Sweetwater Ranger Station, located over eight thousand feet high and about ten miles down the range from the very popular trailhead at Big Sandy Campground, which serves as the shortest route to the Cirque of the Towers. The Big Sandy road is well marked, about twenty-four miles south of Pinedale on U.S. Highway 191.

Twelve miles south of Pinedale, at Boulder, another road—State Route 353 for about three miles, then Forest Road 114—leads to the Boulder Lake Campground and trailhead. The Boulder Creek Trail leads to an area best known for its myriad lakes. North another ten miles or so is the Elkhart Park trailhead and Trail's End Campground. Located high above Fremont Lake, which looks as if it has been transplanted, complete with sheer cliffs, from Norway's fjord country, Elkhart Park is the most accessible and perhaps most popular and heavily used trailhead in the Winds. The road is paved all the way from Pinedale; even the parking lot is paved. The volume of traffic here is due partly to the proximity of Island Lake and the glaciers above it, but also because of its elevation. The view is tremendous—worth anyone's time even for a short drive off the highway—and the walking is essentially level. If you crave solitude, avoid August days on this trail, but don't forget about September or even October.

Beyond Pinedale, heading north, another road turns off to the north through the town of Cora toward Green River Lakes. Past Cora, Forest Road 109 ends at Willow Creek Ranger Station and another trailhead, not heavily used, which accesses the lakes country west of Gannett Peak. A little farther on the Green River Lakes road, Forest Road 107 turns off to New Fork Lakes and a developed campground, with trails that also lead to the lakes country. And finally, as it closely follows the meandering Green River, the road leads to Green River Lakes, the third of the three major west slope trailheads.

Access from the east is less easy, in part because the bulk of the east slope is in the Wind River Indian Reservation and thus privately owned by the Eastern Shoshone and Northern Arapahoe tribes. Access roads exist, but they are subject to fees or closures. Trailheads and campgrounds on public lands are as follows. About five miles east of Dubois (pronounced DOO-boys), turn south to Torrey Lake, where there are several campgrounds. At the end of the road is the Trail Lake trailhead to the base of Gannett Peak and the glaciers on the Divide. The trail, 27 miles each way and heavily used, passes through extremely rugged and scenic country dotted with lakes. The Dickinson Park trailhead and campground are reached by a reservation road from Fort Washakie, which may be subject to closures (check with the Bureau of Indian Affairs in Fort Washakie; address below). The road leaves U.S. Highway 287 sixteen miles from Lander at Hines General Store, turns to gravel after about four miles, and climbs 3,000 feet in fifteen miles to Dickinson Park. From here, the High Meadow Trail is the shortest east-side route to the Cirque of the Towers. The other way in is through Lander on the Sinks Canyon Road (Wyoming 131) to the Middle Fork Trail. This trail is longer than trails from either Big Sandy or Dickinson Park, but it's a pleasant way in.

Scenic Drives

Wyoming 131 from Lander to Atlantic City climbs through the Sinks Canyon, where the Popo Agie River disappears into a cavern, only to reappear a few hundred yards later. The road turns to gravel and climbs into the little Popo Agie Basin, past mountain lakes, Sinks Canyon State Park and numerous Forest Service campgrounds, ending at Atlantic City near South Pass.

U.S. Highway 191, on the west side of the range, is a lovely drive in the spring or fall. Optionally, take the Big Sandy Road (Wyoming 353) from Boulder to Farson; gravel most of the way and a close view of Wyoming ranching country along the foothills. North of Pinedale, along the Green River, old Fort Bonneville was built in 1832 and soon abandoned. This site was also the location of the famous Green River Rendezvous of 1835, an event commemorated each year in Pinedale during the second weekend in July. A plaque on an overlook along U.S. 191 north of Pinedale marks the spot.

On the east side of the valley stand the snowy-topped mountains of the Wyoming and Salt River ranges. A forest road runs along Greys River between the ranges, starting at either LaBarge or Alpine Junction. Half a dozen Forest Service campgrounds are located at the north end of the road; various short trails can be walked to gentle summits.

Pinedale

This ranching town, growing into a summer resort, has most services, including a specialty outdoor shop, general sporting goods stores and a medical clinic (the nearest hospital is in Jackson, 77 miles north). Several outfitters and guest ranches operate from Pinedale. Events include: Winter Carnival, last weekend of February; Chuckwagon Days (in Big Piney) with rodeo, fireworks and free barbecue, July 4; Green River Rendezvous, with mountain man contests and other activities commemorating the annual rendezvous of the Rocky Mountain fur trade, second weekend in July. Write to Chamber of Commerce, Box 176, Pinedale, WY 82941.

South Pass

At the south end of the Wind River Range lies South Pass (elevation 7,550 feet). This wide plain, which looks very much like other sage-covered regions of Wyoming, played a critical role in the settlement of the West. At no other point along the Continental Divide, from Santa Fe all the way to northern British Columbia, is there a pass that could be so easily crossed by horses and wagons. The route had two critical advantages: the climb was gentle, suitable for wagons weighing up to four thousand pounds fully loaded; and the trail followed water and forage all the way, coming first along the North Platte and the Sweetwater rivers, then Pacific and Sandy creeks to the Green River Crossing. South Pass was destined to become the key to westward expansion, the chosen path for the Oregon Trail, the California Trail, the Mormon Trail, the Overland Stage Route and the Original Pony Express.

The first non-Indians known to come this way were the Astorians, returning from the mouth of the Columbia River in 1812. The mountain

The wagon tracks of westward bound immigrants on the Oregon Trail are visible today at South Pass.

men were familiar with it and used it often during the 1820s and 1830s. The missionary Marcus Whitman came this way with his wife, Narcissa, and a party bound for Oregon in 1836. The Mormons under Brigham Young used the pass in 1847 to reach the Great Salt Lake, following faint wheel marks left the year before by the ill-fated, California-bound Donner Party. The Mormons profited indirectly from the California gold rush. During the summer of 1849, tens of thousands of weary travelers pulled into the infant city of Salt Lake, where Mormon merchants and farmers eagerly sold them food, livestock and other supplies.

Despite the huge volume of traffic, the journey on the wagon roads was terribly difficult, demanding good equipment and careful planning. A delay of only a few weeks could be fatal. In the fall of 1856, 202 Mormon members of "Willie's Company," most of them European immigrant converts, met disaster in an early winter storm; pulling meager belongings on handcarts, exhausted by their long walk across the plains, the entire party died on South Pass. Most travelers, however, hundreds of thousands of them, made the journey safely. It must have been a stirring moment to crest the pass and to realize that the long upward pull was over, that they were now officially entering Oregon Territory and that all the waters they would encounter from then on flowed to the Pacific.

With the construction of the transcontinental railroad, South Pass lost importance. Trains were less dependent on local water supplies than teams of oxen, and they certainly had no use for grass. Surveyors for the Union Pacific chose the shorter route across the barren Red Desert through Laramie and Rock Springs.

A brief gold rush in the area of South Pass in the late 1860s gave rise to a handful of settlements with a population of about two thousand— South Pass City, Atlantic City, Lewiston and Miners Delight. These are now ghost towns with numerous mining relics and a few functioning businesses, located on a side road away from the highway. A visitor center and museum give information. The best museum of all, however, is the pass itself, where you can still see the wagon ruts of pioneers heading bravely across the vast sage-covered expanse of southwest Wyoming. Of all the historic remnants in the West, be they mining towns, battle sites, old trading posts or Indian rock writing, few are so evocative and poignant as those purposeful, century-old wheel ruts.

Some Useful Information About Wind River Range

HOW TO GET THERE: Pinedale is reached by the Jackson-Rock Springs Stage, a bus that runs between Rock Springs and Jackson.
GENERAL INFORMATION: Books: *Wind River Trails*, by Finis Mitchell, is both a good guide and a historical document by one of the earliest Wind River backpacking pioneers. For trail and climbing information, look for the *Field Guide to the Wind River Range*, by Orrin H. and Lorraine Bonney, or *Climbing and Hiking in the Wind River Range*, by Joe Kelsey, a Sierra Club Totebook.
USEFUL NAMES AND ADDRESSES: For information on the Bridger Wilderness, contact the **Pinedale Ranger District**, Bridger-Teton National Forest, P.O. Box 220, Pinedale, WY 82941 (tel: 307-367-4326). A Forest Service map of the Bridger Wilderness is available for $1. For the Fitzpatrick and Popo Agie wildernesses, write to (respectively) **Wind River Ranger District**, Box 186, Dubois, WY 82513, and the **Lander Ranger District**, Box FF, Lander, WY 82520. Wilderness maps cost $1 each. For information about the Wind River Indian Reservation—Pow-wow schedule, camping and road access—contact the **Bureau of Indian Affairs Programs Office**, Fort Washakie, WY 82514 (tel: 307-322-7810), or **Tribal Fish and Game** (307-332-7207).

TETON RANGE

If somewhere deep in the human psyche there is a model, imprinted in the pattern of synapses and transmitted from one generation to the next, of how mountains *should* look, that model must resemble the Tetons. They rise without introduction or warning from a flat plain for a giddy 7,000 vertical feet. The angle of slope is the same from base to summit: unrelentingly steep. The peaks themselves come to sharp points, while somehow retaining the sense of massive strength which separates mountains from pinnacles. The rock is hard granite, clean and blue-gray in color. Snowfields and glaciers perch like hawks on what appear from a distance to be vertical cliffs. From up close, they look, if anything, steeper.

At the base of the mountains are a string of lakes—Jenny, Leigh, Bradley, Taggart—each one perfect in its design. Beyond them spreads the broad valley called Jackson Hole, most of it open sage flats, with neatly spaced groves of aspens, cottonwoods and conifers. Elk, mule deer and pronghorn (or antelope) favor these flats, especially in the fall during the rutting season. Through Jackson Hole, the Snake River meanders along, having grown to size in Yellowstone Park and in no particular hurry to leave the Tetons. On either side of the river, willow flats and ponds support all manner of wildlife, including trumpeter swans, osprey, bald eagles, beaver and moose.

Although the Tetons consist of very old rock, they are relatively young mountains, only about ten million years old. They were heaved up along the Teton Fault like some massive trapdoor being opened from underneath. As they tipped up, Jackson Hole tipped down, accentuating the appearance of dynamic uplift and explaining the lack of foothills. Jackson Hole actually tips toward the mountains, not away from them. So far, the combined rise and fall of the two adjacent blocks totals about thirty thousand feet of movement. Were it not for erosion busily at work tearing material off the summits and piling it into the valley, these mountains would be far higher, but no more impressive. That would be impossible.

The motion has not stopped. Measurements indicate that the mountains rise perhaps one foot in 500 years, while the valley falls about a foot every century. But measurements are relative things at best. The entire region seems to be lifting at the same time, making it difficult to find reliable reference points.

From the western side, in Idaho, the Tetons present a different aspect. Because the range dips in that direction, the mountain slopes are less abrupt. The high peaks—the three Tetons, Mount Owen, Teewinot Mountain and Mount Moran—stand just as sharp and naked as on their eastern slopes, but the valleys approaching them are longer, and the surrounding country is less steep. They even have foothills on this side, which are made of Paleozoic sediments, which once overlay the entire range.

Grand Teton National Park

Grand Teton National Park's 485 square miles include most of Jackson Hole, some of the hills to the east, Jackson Lake and the Teton Range to its crest. Looking from the east, you might assume that the crest follows the line of high peaks, but in fact it runs behind them to the west. The park was established over strong local opposition in 1929, and included then only the peaks and a few of the small lakes at their base. Political wrangling continued to prevent enlargement for many years, until 1943, when President Franklin Roosevelt declared parts of Jackson Hole a National Monument, and made it possible for the nation to accept a gift of some thirty-three thousand acres from the Rockefeller family. The monument was added to the park in 1950.

To see the park, you have a choice of two main roads. U.S. Highway 89 goes from Jackson to Moran, where it meets U.S. 287 from Dubois. Together, they continue north to Yellowstone. This way is usually chosen by people in a hurry, which is not to say you can't drive it slowly. Numerous pull-outs allow for stopping. Look for antelope and coyote here, and in the fall, elk. If you come by on an early autumn morning or evening, be sure to walk away from the car a little distance and listen for elk bugling. That eerie, passionate sound, coupled with the sharp bite of autumn air, is one of the Rockies' most powerful and lasting experiences.

The option to U.S. 89 is the Teton Park Road, which begins at Moose, where there is a visitor center and mountain man museum, and runs closer to the base of the mountains, past Jenny Lake and part of Jackson Lake to a junction with U.S. 89 and 287. From this second road, you access most of the mountain trailheads and a number of small lakes. At every turn, you see another angle of the range, each one a classic. North of Jenny Lake, a narrow one-way road (two-way for bicycles) cuts back south to the Cascade Canyon trailhead and the shore of Jenny Lake, rejoining the main road there. These roads get heavy use in summer, and one glimpse of the surrounding country explains why. Jenny Lake is the center of attention, with several trails branching out from its shores. Other highlights along the road include Signal Mountain, rising in the middle of Jackson Hole; a paved drive takes you to the summit and a panoramic view of the area. Just past the Moose entrance, visit Menors Ferry, a historic site.

Turning south at Moose, a road which few visitors ever notice leads through aspen forest, glorious in the fall, to Teton Village, Jackson Hole ski resort, and the town of Wilson. Death Canyon, Phelps Lake and Open Canyon are all reached along this road. All the way on the other side of the valley is one more park road, which goes to the Gros Ventre

The Snake River flows out of Yellowstone Park and winds through Jackson Hole at the base of the Grand Teton Range.

Campground, Kelly and Slide Lake. Slide Lake is the scene of the Gros Ventre Slide, which happened in dramatic fashion in June of 1925. A cowboy named Huff was herding cattle down the valley when he noticed the mountain sliding toward him, trees, rocks and all. He lost several cattle, but he managed to escape himself. Behind him, the slide built a dam 225 feet high with a growing lake rising behind the debris. It took two years for the lake to breach the dam; when it did, a wall of water swept down the canyon, taking Kelly with it, and into the Snake River, where it did serious damage to the town of Wilson.

Boating

The Snake River between the Jackson Lake Dam and Moose makes a good one-day float. Several companies offer raft trips here. It is not a whitewater run, but the current moves right along, wildlife is seen, and views of the mountains are superb. Canoeists accustomed to quick-flowing streams will enjoy this stretch. Another pleasant canoeing area is Leigh Lake, which can be reached via String Lake and two short portages. There are several backcountry lakeshore campsites on Leigh Lake; nothing else you can do in Teton Park will get you so quickly and easily into the peace of a wilderness setting. Motorboats (maximum 7.5 horsepower) are permitted on Jackson, Jenny and Phelps lakes. Boat permits are required by the park and cost $5 for hand-propelled craft, $10 for motorboats.

Trails

Teton Park operates on a permit system using a combination of specifically designated campsites and backcountry zones. The zones limit the number of groups in an area, but allow hikers to choose their own sites as long as they abide by common sense regulations of sanitation and backcountry use ethics. Permits are free and obtainable at ranger stations.

Trail use in the Tetons centers, quite naturally, on the area around the central Teton group. You have the option of walking along the flat valley bottom past exquisite lakes with mountains soaring from their opposite shores, or of heading into the mountains themselves. As grand a landscape as this one is, it is remarkably accessible.

Easy lakeshore walking trails include the ever-popular circuit of Jenny Lake, which can be shortened with a boat ride one way. It connects with another trail, which passes String Lake and wanders along the east shore of Leigh Lake, with spectacular views of Mount Moran and Leigh Canyon. South of Jenny Lake, Bradley and Taggart lakes lie cupped in forested basins with high peaks fully exposed above them. These are the most popular lakes, but you might consider hiking around lakes on the other side of Jackson Hole for a different sort of trip. Two Ocean and Emma Matilda lakes stand out as wildlife viewing areas; the moose may even outnumber the people.

Most of the mountain hiking in Teton Park is along trails in several main valleys, called canyons for their precipitous sides. Cascade Canyon, at the bottom of which lies Jenny Lake, is a hanging valley, meaning that it was not carved as deeply by glaciers as the main valley, and is now marked by a steep drop at its lower end. The trail climbs steeply up this drop for a short distance to an overlook and from there rises more gradually. From open areas, you can see the dividing line on the canyon wall between smooth glaciated rock and the more angular, broken surface which was never reached by the ice. About three hours of hiking will take you to the backside of the central Teton group, where the trail forks. Heading south, the Teton Crest Trail circles the peaks by way of spectacular Alaska Basin, which is actually part of the Jedediah Smith Wilderness, and returns to Jackson Hole by way of Death Canyon. Either of these canyons are good for day-hiking; go up until you feel like turning around.

Turning north at the head of Cascade Canyon, the trail continues on to Lake Solitude, with its unforgettable view of the Grand's north and west exposures. Above the lake, the trail climbs across the barren heights of Paintbrush Divide and returns to Jenny Lake having made a circuit of Mount St. John. On the east flank of the Grand, a steep trail to Amphitheater Lake also sees heavy use. It ends at the base of Disappointment Peak, so named because from below, climbers take it to be the actual summit.

Unless you walk these trails in the fall, you'll be sharing them with quite a few other hikers, and you may have trouble getting a backcountry permit for camping. Far less well known is the northern section of the park. Access is more difficult and the trails are poorly maintained, if at all, but the country is wonderfully scenic. In the drainages west of Jackson Lake, you end up bushwhacking up steep slopes and thrashing around in willow tangles along stream bottoms—explorer's country. Trails do exist in Webb Canyon and along Owl Creek. Access is either by boat or by a long, little-used trail originating on the Grassy Lake Road north of the park.

Some Useful Information About Grand Teton

CAMPGROUNDS: The park has six campgrounds. One, Jenny Lake, is limited to tents only. All of them fill early in the day during summer, with Gros Ventre, at the south end of the park, filling last. Camping fees are $8 per site.

GENERAL INFORMATION: As you enter Teton Park, you'll receive a copy of *The Teewinot*, the park newspaper, which lists interpretive programs, park facilities and commercial concessions, in addition to other seasonal material. Lodging and meals are available at a number of private facilities, including Flagg Ranch Village north of the park, Colter Bay, Jenny Lake Lodge, Jackson Lake Lodge, Moose and Signal Mountain. Gas, groceries and other supplies can be obtained at Colter Bay, Flagg Ranch, Kelly and Jackson. Visitor centers are at Moose and Colter Bay, while ranger stations are located throughout the park.

USEFUL NAMES AND ADDRESSES: Grand Teton National Park, P.O. Drawer 170, Moose, WY 83012 (tel: 307-739-3300).

Teton Wilderness

Surrounded on three sides by Grand Teton National Park, Yellowstone National Park and Washakie Wilderness, the Teton Wilderness occupies 557,000 acres on the Continental Divide. The western part is gentle country, with rolling timbered ridges and large grassy meadows. The Divide itself is relatively low at this point, having abandoned the most rugged mountains to follow a meandering route across the Yellowstone Plateau. At one point south of the Park on Two Ocean Plateau, the Divide is so lacking in definition that two streams come together, only to split again, each one going toward a different ocean. These streams are named North and South Two Ocean creeks. They meet in the marsy Two Ocean Pass, where together they spawn Atlantic and Pacific creeks. The highest peaks in the area rise east of the Divide, across the Yellowstone River on the Absaroka crest, where elevations top 12,000 feet. Between those peaks and the Continental Divide is the broad valley of the Yellowstone River headwaters, an expansive wildlife sanctuary and one of the most remote parts of the greater Yellowstone region. Because of the distances involved, and the relatively gentle terrain, horse trips are by far the most popular way of travel here.

Some very long trips are possible, crossing both the Teton and the Washakie wilderness areas, by going up Pacific Creek over the Divide to the Yellowstone River and following its meanders over Marston Pass into the Washakie, thence down the South Fork of the Shoshone to the trailhead. As in most wilderness areas, private horse trips are permitted with the normal restrictions: maximum group size of 20, with combined stock and pack animals numbering no more than 35; some grazing restrictions in sensitive areas; no hay or straw to be carried; and other commonsense rules.

This is not to recommend that hikers stay away; only that the distances are long and rewards are more subtle than in some areas. One major consideration is the chance to be utterly remote and on one's own (although solitary travel should be avoided in this grizzly-populated country). In the fall, a large number of elk move south through this area on their way to the National Elk Refuge, and this is an electric time to be there. However, because of the number of hunters working the elk migration, nonhunters might be wise to walk north of the park boundary, where they can enjoy the excitement of the rut without worrying for their own safety.

Useful Names and Addresses

Bridger-Teton National Forest, 350 N. Cache, P.O. Box 1888, Jackson, WY 83001 (tel: 307-739-5500); **Buffalo Ranger District**, Blackrock Ranger Station, Box 278, Moran, WY 83013 (tel: 307-543-2386).

Jedediah Smith Wilderness

Located on the west slope of the Teton Range, the Jedediah Smith Wilderness takes up where the park leaves off. In one sense, this is the flip side of the Tetons, the side less traveled and less known. Most of the reasons that draw people to the east side of the Tetons pertain to the west side as well, although because access is less easy, and because this is off the beaten Yellowstone route, solitude remains part of the experience in most of the wilderness.

The wilderness itself is bounded on the east by the Teton Divide; all its streams flow west into Idaho. This is a young landscape showing the recent tracks of glaciers and prehistoric lakes, which drained as the ice melted. Dense forest covers the lower slopes, owing in part to the high annual snowfall; Grand Targhee Resort, above Driggs, Idaho, claims over five hundred inches of snow each year. In addition, the Tetons generate thunderstorms almost every day in midsummer, a spectacular feature of an already spectacular place. This relative lushness supports a large animal population including elk, moose, bighorn sheep, beaver, bobcat, red fox, black bear, and in the north Tetons, grizzly. Superb wildflower meadows buzz with bees and their feathered imitators, hummingbirds.

Hiking distances between the 11 trailheads and high country are short, owing to the shape of the wilderness—about fifty miles long and five miles wide, lying up against the mountain crest. All access, except by hikers coming from Teton National Park, is from Idaho. Near three of the trailheads—Teton Canyon, Trail Creek and Mike Harris—Targhee National Forest maintains campgrounds.

Trails

Although access routes are short, 287 miles of interconnecting trails make it possible to traverse the range in a north-south direction. Directly behind the three Tetons themselves is Alaska Basin, a popular and crowded backcountry campsite often used by hikers beginning their trips from the east. Other areas of the wilderness are much less used and equally spectacular. In general, the farther north you go, as in Teton Park, the fewer people you will encounter.

Useful Names and Addresses

Forest Supervisor, **Targhee National Forest**, 420 North Bridge St., P.O. Box 208, St. Anthony, ID 83445 (tel: 208-624-3151); **Teton Basin Ranger District**, Driggs, ID 83422 (tel: 208-354-2312).

Palisades

The Palisades lie to the southwest of Teton Park in the Snake River Range, an area of rugged peaks and deep, narrow canyons ranging in elevation from over ten thousand to around five thousand feet. Its name reflects the steep cliff faces which are common in the area. The ground is not terribly stable. Landslides have been an important feature of the topography. The floor of Blowout Canyon is covered with debris from a single slide, which occurred at its head end, and Palisades Reservoir itself is retained by a dam of landslide debris, which the outlet stream flows underneath instead of over.

A variety of wildlife live in the area, most notably a healthy population of mountain goats, which favor the cliff ledges above Palisades and Big Elk creeks. The goats are commonly seen in winter by cross-country skiers.

Because the canyon bottoms are relatively low in elevation, snow melts early and trails become passable by late May or early June, although the high country stays snow-covered much longer, and stream crossings can be hazardous. The warmest canyons are those with south and west exposures, a characteristic that explains the predominance of cottonwoods, aspens and willows here, in contrast to the Engelmann spruce, Douglas fir, limber pine and other conifers on the north and east.

Trails

Most trails work their way up creekbeds draining to the southwest toward the Snake River and the Palisades Reservoir, paralleled by U.S. Highways 26 and 89. Some trails take off from the highway, while others begin at the end of one forest road or another. The most heavily used of these is the Palisades Creek Trail, leading to the Palisades Lakes and a series of side canyons. Fewer people use the Big Elk Creek Trail, the Indian Creek Trail, and others to the east. On the north side of the area, two paved roads provide access over Pine Creek Pass and Teton Pass. Several trails begin along these roads, but the most popular are the trailheads in Mike Spencer Canyon and the North Fork of Rainey Creek, leading to high exposed ridges with views of surrounding mountain ranges.

Some Useful Information About the Palisades

USEFUL NAMES AND ADDRESSES: For a Palisades map, contact **Palisades Ranger District**, P.O. Box 398B, Route 1, Idaho Falls, ID 83401 (tel: 208-523-1412). **Campgrounds:** Eleven developed **Forest Service campgrounds** surround the Palisades, eight of them along Highways 26 and 89; the remaining three are on the north and are somewhat more isolated.

Other Area Ideas

The National Elk Refuge was established by the U.S. Fish and Wildlife Service in 1912 to compensate for the loss, due to ranching and settlement, of traditional migratory routes and wintering range south of Jackson. Essentially empty during the summer, it fills in late fall with about 7,500 elk, most of which come from southern Yellowstone and the country between that park and the refuge. On the same property, the Fish and Wildlife Service operates a fish hatchery, where visitors can see cutthroat and lake trout being raised for release in area waters.

Jackson

Jackson began as a ranching town, and despite its "gussying up" for tourists, it retains the feel of a working, western community. The town landmark is the central square, a shady park with entrance arches made from piles of elk antlers. Almost as significant a landmark is the Cowboy Bar on the west side of the square, where saddles serve as barstools; if you have too much to drink, people say, those darn things will buck you right off onto the floor and out the door. During the summer, Jackson serves as a border town to Teton Park; roughly three million people pass through between Memorial Day and Labor Day. Most people come for the mountains: to climb, hike or simply to picnic somewhere within view of the peaks. In addition, whitewater rafting on the Snake River is popular, and the Jackson Hole Music Festival is a highly regarded series of concerts and workshops based at the scenic ski resort. Winter attention is focused on skiing, either cross-country or alpine. Rendezvous Mountain has one of the highest vertical rises of any North American ski area. Cross-country terrain is unlimited, with gentle, rolling tracks in every direction; several highways climb above Jackson, notably the road to Teton Pass, allowing skinny-skiers to start high and spend the day leisurely cruising downhill.

Some Useful Information About Jackson

HOW TO GET THERE: American, Delta, Horizon and United Express airlines serve the Jackson Hole Airport; car rental agencies include Avis, National, Hertz, Budget, Alamo and others.

GETTING AROUND: Shuttle bus service within Teton Park, operated by **Grand Teton Lodge Company** (tel: 307-543-2811).

GENERAL INFORMATION: Jackson has good mountain equipment shops. One of the best-known climbing schools in the country operates in the park: **Exum School of American Mountaineering**, P.O. Box 56, Moose, WY 83012 (tel: 307-733-2297). **Jackson Hole Mountain Guides**, P.O. Box 7477, Jackson, WY 83002 (307-733-4979).

USEFUL NAMES AND ADDRESSES: For general information and a booklet with a list of outfitters, guide services, lodging, dude ranches and so forth, contact the **Jackson Hole Chamber of Commerce**, P.O. Box E, Jackson, WY 83001 (tel: 307-733-3316).

YELLOWSTONE NATIONAL PARK

Yellowstone defies characterization. It could be many parks, not just one. It was originally meant to protect the world's largest concentration of geysers, hot springs and related features. In 1872, those were the true marvels; the West, indeed the whole country, was filled with wildlife, forests, clear rivers and pristine landscapes. The national occupation was the subduing of wilderness, not its preservation. Furthermore, the original intent behind Yellowstone had less to do with natural preservation than with public access. If homesteaders were kept out, the park's wonders could be developed as a world class tourist destination, creating traffic for the railroads and commerce for local companies. That much came true. But as a matter of good fortune, Yellowstone's boundaries today protect far more than thermal features. The park is the richest wildlife preserve in the United States outside of Alaska. It contains snowy mountain peaks, several magnificent high-altitude lakes, numerous rivers and streams renowned for trout fishing, a vibrantly colored canyon which nearly dwarfs two major waterfalls, one of the most significant volcanic calderas in the world, layer upon layer of buried petrified forest, and much more.

But superlatives aside, what Yellowstone offers a traveler, perhaps more than any other place in the Rockies, are subtle things, not the biggest nor the most spectacular. This is the cause of occasional disappointment. To some visitors, the whole show—for that is what they expect of national parks—is somehow lacking in pizazz. Most of the land is forested, rank on rank of uniform-sized lodgepole pine. The topography, high as it may be, is for the most part gentler than the area immediately outside the park boundaries. Yellowstone's central mountain, Washburn, is a rounded hump, which pales in comparison to the Tetons, visible from its summit barely one hundred miles south. It's not uncommon for people seeing Old Faithful for the first time (or the first time since childhood) to say "Is that all?" as if the geyser's notoriety should somehow make it more than it is.

The lesson of Yellowstone is this: that the greatest wonders are personal matters, to be found inside each one of us, in the way we respond to our surroundings, no matter what they are. Yellowstone—indeed the whole of the Rockies—is no circus, no performance designed to delight us. It is simply there, wonderful and available. It is up to us to respond. Having lived in the literal shadow of Old Faithful for a number of years, I can report its effect on me. When I first saw it, I was jaded. A puff of steam and hot water, who cares? But after years of living within sight, smell and hearing of it, I regard it now with a deep-rooted sense of awe, a feeling that extends to the smallest feature in the park, and in a fundamental manner, to the smallest feature of myself. Without wanting to dig too deep here, let me say that in all the Rocky Mountains, I know of nowhere more conducive to introspection than Yellowstone.

Getting to Yellowstone

Yellowstone has five highway entrances, all of them located on natural routes through the surrounding mountains. From the north, U.S. Highway 89 follows the Yellowstone River through aptly named Paradise Valley to the north entrance at the town of Gardiner. In the northeast corner is the Beartooth Highway, one of the finest high-altitude roads in the Rockies. The highway climbs steeply up from the town of Red Lodge, Montana, tops the pass at 10,940 feet, and descends gentle slopes past alpine lakes and lush forest to Cooke City, an old mining town. The park entrance is several miles west at Silver Gate, deep in the Absaroka Range.

If you left your car at this point and walked along the crest of the Absarokas south from Silver Gate, you would follow the park boundary most of the way, eventually reaching the east entrance at Sylvan Pass (8,541 feet). The highway here climbs up from Cody, Wyoming, along the North Fork of the Shoshone River. Once over the pass, it winds down through forest and meadow to the shores of Yellowstone Lake. To the south we find U.S. Highway 89 once again, heading up from Jackson and Grand Teton National Park. The road cuts around the north shore of Jackson Lake, climbs through mature lodgepole forest and enters the park in a meadow at the junction of the Lewis and the Snake rivers. It then follows the Lewis along its canyon, past Lewis Lake, over the Continental Divide to the shore of West Thumb on Yellowstone Lake.

The fifth entrance is at West Yellowstone, Montana. Two highways come together at this point, one reaching north from Rexburg, Idaho, the other traveling south from Bozeman, Montana. The Bozeman road follows the beautiful Gallatin River Canyon most of the way south, and spends a fair amount of time actually in the park before ducking out for a few miles to carry traffic through the astonishing visual contrast of West Yellowstone. In one corner of town, just past the liquor store and an old railroad car garishly painted with ferocious animals, you will find the park entrance building, designed to look like a multilane customs station on an international border. With the town in one's rear view mirror, the sense of entering another country is strangely appropriate.

Once in the park, you are on a 142-mile figure-8 loop road. It follows river valleys for the most part, with an occasional pass. The highlights are

Yellowstone Lake, the canyon with its falls, Dunraven Pass over Mount Washburn, Mammoth Hot Springs, Norris Geyser Basin and the Old Faithful area.

Geysers and Hot Springs

It doesn't require a geological discussion to tell that the ground in Yellowstone is hot, but it helps to know why. As mentioned above, the plateau was built by volcanoes, but not all at once. The Absaroka Range, on the east of the park, is the result of a series of eruptions which began around fifty to fifty-five million years ago, after the Rocky Mountains in general came into being, and continued through cycles of activity for another twenty million years. The following period of relative quiet was marked by such events as the uplift of the Tetons starting some ten million years ago. The volcanic activity picked up again two or three million years ago, with massive flows building, among others, the Madison Plateau; the west entrance road passes the cliffs of these lavas. Meanwhile, the Snake River Plain in Idaho was also a hotbed of volcanism, leaving behind immense areas of chunky lava such as you find at Craters of the Moon National Monument. Yellowstone's rocks, because of weathering and differences in eruption, look older, but are in fact younger.

One event surpasses all, the great Yellowstone caldera. It happened roughly 600,000 years ago. Pressure from underground magma released itself in a cataclysmic explosion, a sudden burst similar to that of Mount St. Helens in 1980, or the infamous eruption of Krakatoa. It was said that the Krakatoa explosion was heard several thousand miles away; dust from that volcano rose so high and was so plentiful that it colored sunsets around the world for three years afterward. People in London spoke of Krakatoa sunsets. By comparison, the Yellowstone explosion was far, far greater. Windrows of its airborne ash have been found in Kansas and other parts of the Midwest. The caldera formed after the eruption, when what material remained fell back into the empty space, creating a crater which measured 30 by 50 miles across and several thousand feet deep.

Subsequent eruptions, this time not explosive, have filled in parts of the caldera and obscured its once distinct walls. You can see remnants of the rim on Mount Washburn and can look out over most of the caldera's expanse from points along the Dunraven Pass road. As a footnote to the story, geologists tell us that the caldera was not a singular event. There is evidence of two earlier eruptions, and one theory suggests that there have been more than that. They seem to be trending toward the northeast, each explosion partially wiping out the caldera of the previous one, and they seem to occur at intervals of roughly 600,000 years. Furthermore, the Yellowstone area is rising at a rate faster than the surrounding plains. Give or take a few millennia, we're about due.

What this means in respect to thermal features is that the ground is hot because of volcanism. Molten magma may be only a few thousand feet beneath the surface. When water flows through cracks in the rock, it heats to the boiling point and comes rushing back up. Where an abundant supply of water can flow freely, there are hot springs. Where pressure builds up, because of constrictions or simply the weight of water pushing on itself, that pressure sometimes releases itself in periodic outbursts, or geyser eruptions.

Most of Yellowstone's thermal features are centered along the Firehole River, which rises on the Continental Divide above Old Faithful. Strung along the Firehole is a series of geyser basins, called the Upper, Middle and Lower, containing the world's largest concentration of such features. The road takes you through this area, with numerous pull-outs and marked trails. No one should visit Yellowstone without spending a day in the Upper Geyser Basin. Besides Old Faithful (which is faithful only in its unpredictability; it is neither hourly nor regular), there are currently five other major geysers erupting frequently: Castle, Grand, Beehive, Riverside and Daisy. In the same area, geysers such as Giant, Giantess, Fan and Mortar are more sporadic but superb sights. Dozens of smaller geysers erupt on all sides, in the company of steaming pools, large and small. A network of boardwalks and trails makes for easy walking. If you plan it right, by stopping at the visitor center for a list of predicted eruption times, you can catch most of the eruptions in a period of several hours. Early morning is a particularly rewarding time to be out, as is late on a moonlit night.

Noteworthy farther down the Firehole is the Grand Prismatic Hot Spring, more than 300 feet across and brilliantly colored. Its neighbor, Excelsior Geyser, last erupted in 1888. Apparently the force of its 300-foot eruptions was too much for its plumbing. A boardwalk leads past both of these pools through dense clouds of steam for a close look. To really appreciate their size and color, you can climb the bluff on the opposite side of the road.

On the Firehole Lake Loop Drive, Great Fountain Geyser performs in a manner that lives up to its name, while at Fountain Paint Pots several large boiling mud cauldrons simmer like immense kettles of viscous sauce. Twenty-two road miles farther north is Norris Geyser Basin, the hottest, least stable ground in Yellowstone. Steamboat, the world's largest active geyser, has been known to hit 400 feet with a thunderous roar; it makes irregular, widely spaced appearances. Quite a few other smaller geysers, notably Echinus, Africa, Little Whirligig and Hurricane Vent, erupt fre-

Upper Geyser Basin of Yellowstone National Park is a spectacular display of hot springs, geysers and steam vents.

quently or even continuously, making the basin a noisy, active place. The third major thermal area, Mammoth Hot Springs, overlooks old Fort Yellowstone, a collection of fine stone buildings left from the days when the park was administered by the U.S. Army. Here are the famous hot spring terraces: no geysers, but hundreds of alkaline springs varying from trickles to small rivers, which build gleaming white terraces, tier on tier, brightly colored by algae and minerals. The springs are constantly changing, shifting their vents, building one month on this side, the next month on the other. You can see that change happens quickly, from the stands of trees being swallowed by fresh calcium carbonate deposits, and by the young vegetation growing up where the waters have temporarily ceased flowing.

Trails

The trails of Yellowstone cover a huge variety of possibilities, beginning with short walks near the road to longer backcountry trips. Permits, available free at ranger stations and visitor centers, are required for any overnight camping. Campsites are designated; at most of them, fires are permitted. Yellowstone is grizzly country, and all precautions should be taken (see page 46). You might find that certain areas are closed to all backcountry use for reasons involving bears, or that parties must include four or more hikers. Two good trail guides are available in area bookstores and visitor centers: *Yellowstone Trails* by Mark Marschall,

Yellowstone Library and Museum Association, and *Hiking the Yellowstone Backcountry* by Orville Bach Jr., a Sierra Club Totebook.

If you'd like to have a look at backcountry thermal features, Yellowstone has approximately ten thousand individual springs, geysers and fumaroles (steam vents). While the major concentrations are not in the backcountry, thousands of features are scattered throughout the park. Heart Lake and Shoshone Lake are two good places, as is the whole southwest corner of the park. Day-hikers will find any number of springs and fumaroles in the hills surrounding the geyser basins, many of them on short trails. Use great care in approaching backcountry thermal ground; it can give way and scald your feet, or more.

For wildlife viewing, there's no place like Yellowstone. Rather than looking for specific locales, learn to recognize the habitats for different animals. Moist open areas like Gibbon Meadows, Elk Park and Swan Lake Flats are home to elk. Moose are seen in wet bottomlands such as Pelican Creek and Lewis River. Bison favor Hayden Valley and the geyser basins. Antelope and more bison are scattered across the rolling open lands of the northern part of the park. For hikers as well as drivers, wildlife is most easily seen before mid-June and after mid-September.

Trails along the Yellowstone River pass through canyons and sage country; some years these are free of snow by April. Alpine areas, which clear in July, include the mountainous east boundary, where there are few trails, and the northern section. Parts of the Gallatin Range may be closed to hikers, but the trail up Mount Holmes and trails in the far northwest corner (along Highway 191) are usually free of restrictions. To get a sense of Yellowstone's size and remoteness, there's no better place than Thorofare, the southeast corner. Trails getting there are long, and once you reach it, it's even farther out the other side. Those looking for truly long, remote trips should consider tying in with one of the adjacent wilderness areas.

Good day-hikes include any of the thermal basins. Even the Upper Geyser Basin, subject to midday madness, can be deserted at 7:00 A.M., which happens to be its most beautiful time. In the north, visit the petrified trees of Specimen Ridge, or hike up one of the other bare mountain slopes in the Lamar Valley. From Dunraven Pass, you can climb Mount Washburn to a fire lookout and a panoramic view all the way to the Tetons. At the foot of Washburn is the Canyon of the Yellowstone River. Between the standard overlooks, pleasant shaded trails follow both rims. In the lake area, a morning beach stroll rewards you with the pelicans, gulls, jumping cutthroat trout and evaporating mists. From there, you might head to the east entrance, where a trail leads to the summit of Avalanche Park. In general, the outlying parts of Yellowstone are least crowded in summer, while the geyser basins represent the opposite extreme.

Some Useful Information About Yellowstone Park

CAMPGROUNDS: Eleven NPS campgrounds are located around the park. In summer, they fill by midday or earlier, so it is important to plan ahead. Try to arrive early and stake out a site before embarking on a day of touring. The only campground in the park that offers hookups is a concession-run RV park at Fishing Bridge. Smaller campgrounds are Lewis Lake, Indian Creek, Slough Creek and Pebble Creek.

FISHING: Fishing is permitted in many park waters, under a rather complex set of regulations. Some waters are for fly fishing only, others have minimum or maximum size limits. Much of the park is catch-and-release fishing. A free license is required.

BOATING: Boating is allowed only on certain lakes, with motor restrictions. Boat permits are required and available at ranger stations. Private companies run whitewater raft trips outside the park on the Shoshone, Yellowstone and Snake rivers.

GENERAL INFORMATION: Lodging, meals, bus tours and similar services are made available by **TW Services Inc.**, Yellowstone National Park, WY 82190 (tel: 303-297-2757). Gas, groceries and other supplies are conveniently available throughout the park during the summer. In spring and fall, locations are less convenient but available. In addition, full services are supplied by the surrounding communities of West Yellowstone, Gardiner and Cooke City. Some park services are open in winter, notably a lodge at Old Faithful and transportation around the park. For information contact TW Services. Independent guide services operate from West Yellowstone (Chamber of Commerce, West Yellowstone, MT 59758) in the winter. **Yellowstone Expeditions** (800-728-9333) maintains a comfortable ski camp at Canyon Village. FreeWheeling Travel Guides publishes a useful road guide to Yellowstone and Grand Teton ($6.45 post paid from P.O. Box 7494, Jackson, WY 83002).

USEFUL NAMES AND ADDRESSES: Any park information can be obtained by contacting the Superintendent, P.O. Box 168, **Yellowstone National Park**, WY 82190 (tel: 307-344-7381).

Other Area Ideas

Tobacco Root Mountains

This range, east of Twin Bridges, Montana, has lovely alpine lakes and snowfields beneath steep, mineral-laden peaks. The mountains are not designated wilderness, perhaps because there have been too many incursions by mining activities. Even so, most of this stopped long ago, leaving a delightful, little-known high country for backpackers and day-hikers.

Numerous rough roads climb steeply into side canyons. A four-wheel drive vehicle is useful for some. Abandoned mining roads are common once you get up into the forest, and bushwhacking, though steep, is easy in the open trees and meadows. Be careful of mine shafts; the range is riddled with them.

At the headwaters of the Ruby River south of Alder, Montana, is a high scenic trail, which runs along the ridge of the Snowcrest Range for 27 miles. Getting there is a fairly long drive on gravel and dirt roads, which explains why almost no one ever walks this trail. However, the road itself is well worth driving. It follows the scenic Ruby River Valley from Alder, and, among other options, continues through the spectacular Centennial Valley and the Red Rock Lakes National Wildlife Refuge, hitting pavement again near West Yellowstone.

Red Rock Lakes National Wildlife Refuge

The little-known Centennial Valley, location of the Red Rock Lakes National Wildlife Refuge, lies hidden on the north side of a spectacular little range of mountains which carry the same name. It's well worth a visit and can be used as an alternate route to Yellowstone if you come in from the west. For a brief time in the late 1800s, before tracks were laid to West Yellowstone, this valley served as the western gateway to the park. Disembarking from the train at Monida, tourists rode in stage coaches up the Red Rock River to the west entrance. Now a gravel road, which can be difficult in wet times of the year, discourages most travelers from going this way. It's their loss to miss such a fine place, but it's probably good for the wildlife to be so far off the beaten path.

The refuge, established in 1935, was primarily intended to protect trumpeter swans, which have since returned from the brink of extinction. At times, hundreds are present. The same birds fly back and forth from here to Yellowstone's rivers, many of them never bothering to migrate south. Other waterfowl are common, along with wading birds such as avocets and sandhill cranes. Look for bald and golden eagles, northern harriers and osprey. Moose, elk and pronghorn antelope are also seen.

To get there from the west, turn off Interstate 15 at Monida and head 28 miles east to the refuge headquarters at Lakeview, where there is an information center. From the east, drive to Henrys Lake on Highway 87. Forest Road 055 goes west along the north shore of the lake, crosses Red Rock Pass and continues to Lakeview (26 miles). A small campground is located at Upper Red Rock Lake. Canoeing is permitted in late summer, with dates subject to change. The idea behind restrictions is to protect nesting birds from disturbance, so observe signs or ask the refuge manager.

USEFUL NAMES AND ADDRESSES: The address is **Red Rock Lakes National Wildlife Refuge**, Monida Star Route, Box 15, Lima, MT 59739 (tel: 406-276-3536).

Virginia City

Virginia City grew up around the richest placer creek in North America, a stretch of 17 miles that turned up around $35 million in gold. During its first summer, 1863, the gravels gave up $10 million. For a short time, it was the territorial capital, stealing it away from Bannack, where gold was first found in Montana, and then losing it to Helena. Its biggest claim to fame, however, seems to be the legacy of Henry Plummer, a sweet-tongued man who had a way with the ladies. He took at least two away from their husbands, killing one of the aggrieved gents in the process, not that a simple murder would bother Henry Plummer. He left bodies and broken hearts in his wake from New England to California to Idaho to Montana, where he joined up with a gang of highwaymen, fell in love again, and true to form, shot and killed his rival. That led to trouble with the sheriff, whom he intimidated into resignation, where-upon he was elected sheriff not only of Bannack but Virginia City as well. This was too much for the old fox to resist, being in charge of two henhouses. Over the next two years, Plummer and his gang perpetrated all manner of robbery and mayhem. No one will ever know just how much; the matter never came to trial. Instead, when things reached the breaking point, the Montana Vigilantes were organized. In short order, they took care of Plummer, his gang and a few others they simply didn't care for, and then went back to mining.

Virginia City never died; it survived the years as the seat of Madison County. In recent years, many of its buildings have been restored in a pleasing manner which retains a sense of its age and history. You can spend time poking around in craft shops, antique stores, saloons, a small museum and so forth. The Virginia City Opera House puts on summer melodrama and serious plays. The Gilbert Brewery presents a follies.

A few miles north is Nevada City, a museum really, made up of build-ings hauled in from the surrounding area and stocked with a wonderful collection of relics from the gold rush years. The film *Little Big Man* was made here, but this is no movie set. The band organ hall is sheer joy. Band organs were the original jukeboxes, super calliopes operated by air pumps. The bigger ones would occupy a small house; they include horns, drums, whistles, pipe organs, cymbals and reed instruments, all operat-ed by a mechanism like the one in a player piano but infinitely more complicated. These have been restored and set up to operate on coins. As soon as one finishes its rousing tune, someone starts up another.

People wander from one to the next, big childlike grins plastered to their faces. You can stand and stare at these self-propelled music machines for longer than you'd care to admit. Other buildings contain an astonishing collection of antique tools, furniture and oddities. Some structures were acquired complete with all their inventory after the owners died or abandoned their businesses. Others are compilations. Nevada City deserves more attention and more money for preservation (it gets no government funding). Across the highway is the other half of the museum, a collection of railroad cars, engines and other memorabilia.

In both Virginia City and Nevada City, you can find lodging in historic buildings. The atmosphere is authentic, but at last report the two-story outhouses were no longer available for use.

Useful Names and Addresses

Virginia City Chamber of Commerce, P.O. Box 218, Virginia City, MT 59755 (tel: 406-843-5419); **Nevada City Hotel and Cabins**, Nevada City, MT 59755.

Hebgen Lake

Seismographs in the Yellowstone area detect earthquakes every day; occasionally swarms occur, with more than one hundred in a 24-hour period. Few of these are strong enough to be felt by park visitors, but the numbers illustrate the instability of the earth in this highly active region. Every so often, a more powerful quake occurs. The largest of these in recent times was the Hebgen Lake Earthquake. It happened in the middle of an August night in 1959, centered west of Yellowstone in the Madison Valley. In places, the resulting subsidence of the ground measured 20 feet, forming scarps still visible in the area. The highway sank under Hebgen Lake, and buildings on the fault zone were split apart or shattered. More than that, the night is remembered for the landslide, which dropped the side of a mountain into the valley, burying a campground and a number of campers, and damming the Madison River just below Hebgen Lake to create Quake Lake. The scars of destruction are still raw and impressive to see. A visitor center stands opposite the landslide, and markers along Highway 287 point out details such as the scarp and the submerged road.

ABSAROKA RANGE

The Absaroka Mountains (ab-SOR-kee or ab-SOR-kah by local pronunciation) form the eastern boundary of Yellowstone Park, and continue for many miles to the north and south. Of volcanic origin, the range was built 50 to 60 million years ago by a combination of lava flows and erupted chunks, which give these mountains their distinctive look. Ledges built by flows alternate with what is essentially volcanic garbage forming disordered rubble-covered slopes. The volcanic period lasted for a long time; between eruptions, forests repeatedly pioneered the slopes, only to be buried in succession and then petrified. Stream deposits eroded from the Absarokas are littered with petrified wood for miles to the east and the north.

With few lakes owing to the porous nature of its soil, the Absaroka Range has ample rugged high country, some magnificent peaks, many high ridges and a sense of remoteness which is increasingly hard to find elsewhere. Campgrounds and forest roads are less used here than on the main approaches to Yellowstone, while backcountry trails are long, sometimes primitive and relatively unknown. Over a million acres are taken up by the North Absaroka and Washakie wilderness areas (the latter made by combining the old Stratified Primitive Area and the South Absaroka Wilderness into a 694,000-acre parcel), with another 920,000 acres in the combined Absaroka-Beartooth Wilderness. The Absarokas are a big range, essentially contiguous with all of Yellowstone, the Tetons, the Gallatins, the Wind River Mountains and others that lie between.

On their south end flows the storied Wind River, through whose valley U.S. Highway 26 travels to Teton National Park from Riverton, Wyoming. The Wind River turns north at Riverton, cuts its way through spectacular Wind River Canyon, where the strata are tilted in a way that makes the water appear to be flowing uphill, and breaks out into the broad Bighorn Basin. Here it becomes the Bighorn River and picks up two more important drainages on its way north, the Greybull and the Shoshone, which flow down from the Absaroka crest to meet it. Meanwhile, the Yellowstone, which shares headwaters with the Shoshone, has cut its course on the west side of the Absarokas, through Yellowstone National Park and the Paradise Valley to Livingston, Montana. There it turns east, swallows the Bighorn and runs on to its meeting with the great Missouri.

In all its extent, only two highways cross the Absaroka Range. U.S. Highway 14-16-20 (all three routes running together at this point) follows the North Fork of the Shoshone from Cody, Wyoming, over Sylvan Pass into Yellowstone Park. U.S. 212 climbs from Red Lodge, Montana, over Beartooth Pass to the valley of the Clarks Fork and into Yellowstone from the northeast. In addition, a number of access roads follow drainages deep into the mountains on the south, east and north, climbing into lush, well-watered basins with trout-filled streams, many Forest Service campgrounds and a network of foot trails, which extend as far as anyone cares to walk. If you plan to stay overnight in the Yellowstone backcountry, a permit is needed from the park, which means driving to a ranger station. The nearest ones are at the east and northeast entrances.

Washakie Wilderness Trails

From the South Fork of the Shoshone Trailhead (45 miles southwest of Cody on Forest Road 479) to the Horse Creek Campground 12 miles north of Dubois, an 80-mile trail traverses a goodly portion of the wilderness from north to south. The trip is strenuous but rewarding, as the trail crosses four major mountain passes through prime wildlife habitat. From the same trailhead, a second trail goes up Deer Creek over the Absaroka Divide and into the remote Thorofare country southeast of Yellowstone, then back via Pass Creek to the Ishawooa Trailhead just five miles from the start of the trip, a total of 50 miles with excellent mountain scenery and wildlife viewing opportunities.

From Double Cabin Trailhead 27 miles north of Dubois (continue past Horse Creek Campground on Forest Road 508), a 60-mile loop goes up Wiggins Fork to the Absaroka Trail, down the East Fork of the Wind River and back to Double Cabin via Tepee and Bug creeks. Few people but many elk; good bear habitat, some timberline hiking.

North Absaroka Wilderness Trails

From the Big Creek Trailhead (20 miles west of Cody on the road to Yellowstone), a 25-mile trail follows Big Creek, then traverses high country on the Trout Peak Trail and down Dead Indian Creek to Dead Indian Trailhead on Clarks Fork of the Yellowstone (State Route 296, the Sunlight Basin Road). This is a popular trail, partly because of the high traverse; it can be done either direction. From the South Crandall Trailhead west of Crandall Ranger Station (also on the Sunlight Basin Road) and back, a little-used 45-mile loop follows Crandall Creek to Papoose Ridge, crosses into Yellowstone at Bootjack Gap, leaving the park about ten miles farther at Canoe Lake, and following Timber Creek back to the original trailhead. There's good cutthroat trout fishing in Timber Creek; elk and bison range along the divide.

Scenic Drives

Wyoming 291 (F.S. 479) follows the South Fork of the Shoshone River from Cody to the end of the road (45 miles); no campground. Wyoming 296, the Sunlight Basin Road, runs from the Beartooth Highway east of

Cooke City, following Clarks Fork of the Yellowstone, then climbing steeply over Dead Indian Pass to Wyoming 120 north of Cody. Numerous campgrounds are strung along the road, and a variety of side trips lead to stream valleys and occasional mining ruins. This road is an alternate route to Yellowstone from the east.

Useful Names and Addresses

Shoshone National Forest, 808 Meadow Lane, P.O. Box 2140, Cody, WY 82414. Visitor's maps, North Half and South Half, cost $3 each.

ABSAROKA-BEARTOOTH WILDERNESS

The Absaroka-Beartooth Wilderness occupies 943,000 acres of the Gallatin, Custer and Shosone national forests north of Yellowstone, including the north end of the loose, volcanic Absaroka Mountains and essentially all of the granitic Beartooths. Only one dead-end gravel road penetrates the area, dividing the two ranges along the Boulder River south of Boulder, Montana. The word *absaroka*, which locals pronounce ab-SOR-kee, is the Crow Indian word for themselves—that is, "Crow." The name Beartooth comes from sharp-topped Beartooth Butte near the head of the Clarks Fork.

Except for their wildness and inclusion in a single wilderness area, the two ranges have little in common. The Beartooths are ancient, made of Precambrian granite as much as 2.7 billion years old, which was heaved up from the north like an immense hinged trapdoor, causing all the sediments piled on top of it to slide off toward the south. Remnants of these Cretaceous sedimentary rocks can be seen on the perimeter of the range, but the Beartooths themselves are proud, hard, naked granite, smooth and rolling when seen from the south slope, abrupt and towering from the north. High plateaus, covered with small lakes, drop abruptly many thousands of feet to canyon bottoms. The cliffs rival those in Yosemite Valley.

By contrast, their young neighbors the Absarokas are mere striplings, built by volcanic eruptions in the last 60 million years. The rock is softer, in some places even rubbly. Erosion happens more rapidly, hence the deeper soil, richer forests and steep rocky ridges—snowcapped and spectacular but somehow less formidable in appearance than the Beartooths. More animals live in the Absarokas; spring comes a few weeks earlier and summer lasts a little longer. In the higher Beartooths, it is accurate to say that winter never really leaves; it just turns its back for brief spells.

The Beartooths present an intriguing mixture of landforms. On the south side, gradual slopes climb gently up past timberline, where stands of weather-beaten conifers mix with domes of glacially smoothed granite, the entire area dotted with hundreds of lakes and shallow streams. Trails here are superfluous. The country is so easy to wander in, and the wandering is so enticing, that cross-country rambling is sheer joy. Names of lakes describe themselves: Froze-to-Death, Fossil, Cairn, Big Park. The north exposure is entirely different. Suddenly the land turns precipitous. Vast cliffs plunge thousands of feet to dark, shadowed lakes in narrow canyons. From the rim, which is an appropriate word here, to the lakes below is as much as five thousand vertical feet. Traveling is hard on this side, and glaciers are numerous. At the base of Granite Peak, 12,799 feet and the highest point in Montana, lies a rock glacier, surely one of the strangest places in the mountains, and a phenomenon found almost nowhere else. The rocks move continually, flowing under the pressure of their own weight just as ice does and creating a bizarre landscape, which makes for slow, difficult walking.

Granite Peak dominates a cluster of impressive peaks. No trivial mountain, it lacks a hiker's route to the summit. Although the first attempt was made in 1899, it was only in 1923, after continued attempts by local men, that a party finally reached the summit via the northeast ridge. Even today, it's a long walk in.

Scenic Drives

For those less interested in wilderness trails, the Beartooth Highway provides an excellent opportunity for exploring a superb alpine region without having to walk more than a few hundred yards from a vehicle. From the town of Red Lodge, U.S. Highway 212 climbs by steep switchbacks to Beartooth Pass at 10,947 feet, then descends gradually through rolling meadows of wildflowers, heather, small lakes and groves of hardy timberline trees. The road rivals Trail Ridge Road in Rocky Mountain National Park for its sense of high exposure. From numerous points along the highway, trails strike off, both east and west, toward distant lakes and meadows. To the south rise the Absarokas, with Pilot Peak and Index Peak conspicuous.

Road access is convenient from all sides. U.S. 212, the Beartooth Highway, bounds the range on the south and east. The Forest Service maintains campgrounds all along this road, with one, Island Lake, near timberline. An assortment of secondary roads penetrate to the base of the impressive north face of the range. These are all reached from Montana 78, which runs between the towns of Columbus and Red

Lodge. They include: East Rosebud Lake, at the end of Forest Road 177 and the trailhead for the main trail across the range; Emerald Lake (turn off 78 onto Montana 419 south of Absarokee, then turn left four miles later onto the West Rosebud Creek Road) with short trails leading to fjord-like Island and Mystic lakes surrounded by a ring of magnificent peaks; and Woodbine, the most remote of these (follow Montana 419 or 420 until they join and become Forest Road 400, which ends at Woodbine Campground) with trails leading up the Stillwater River to remote lakes.

Trails

Several hiking routes cross the range. Going from north to south requires more climbing, while going the other way might be harder on the knees. Routes to Granite Peak lead from three trailheads: from West Rosebud up Huckleberry Creek, or up Phantom Creek to Froze-to-Death Plateau and Tempest Mountain; from either East Rosebud or the Clarks Fork Trailhead to Fossil Lake on the divide, and from there through the Sky Top Lakes area. The least difficult route up the mountain is the northeast ridge, but even there a rope is recommended.

To reach the Absaroka section of the wilderness, choices are more limited. Roads following the Boulder River Valley penetrate to the center of the range. Take Montana 298 south from Big Timber (on the interstate west of Livingston) to the forest boundary, where it turns to gravel and becomes Forest Road 6639. Paralleling the river all the way, the road ends at Independence, an abandoned mining community. Five campgrounds and numerous trailheads are strung out along the road. Of most interest to hikers is the country to the east, called Lake Plateau, reached by a trail that climbs 3,000 feet up East Rainbow Creek (trailhead two miles south of Hicks Park Campground).

Driving along the Yellowstone River in Paradise Valley, there are clear views of the northern Absaroka peaks, which rise steeply and impressively from the valley bottom. These are, for the most part, trailless and exceptionally wild. At the north end of the valley, you can turn off onto Montana 540, a scenic alternate to the main highway; it goes to Yellowstone on the east side of the river and provides access to two Forest Service campgrounds—Pine Creek (turn on Forest Road 202) and Snowbank (F.S. 486). From Pine Creek Campground, a steep trail goes up like the space shuttle to Pine Creek Lake in the heart of the high peaks. From Snowbank Campground, surrounded by a busy network of trails and logging roads on the edge of the wilderness, you can choose routes in any direction. If ambitious, head north toward Mill Creek Pass.

Some Useful Information About Absaroka-Beartooth

HOW TO GET THERE: Major airlines and buses serve Bozeman and Billings. Bus service to Yellowstone is convenient from both places, through TW Services, the Yellowstone Concessionaire, but you still need a way to get to the trailheads and campgrounds.

USEFUL NAMES AND ADDRESSES: **Gallatin National Forest**, P.O. Box 130, Bozeman, MT 59715 (tel: 406-587-5271); **Custer National Forest**, P.O. Box 2556, Billings, MT 59103 (tel: 406-657-6364).

BIGHORN RANGE

The Bighorn Range stands on the other side of the Bighorn Basin from Yellowstone and the Absaroka Range, more or less isolated from the larger mountain chains to the west. Although the range extends across the Wyoming border into Montana, the center of interest is the high chain of peaks, glaciers and lakes dominated by 13,175-foot Cloud Peak and the Cloud Peak Wilderness Area. A major highway, U.S. 16, crosses the mountains over Powder River Pass, giving access to the south end of the wilderness. The drive itself is spectacular, staying for miles above timberline. On the east side of the divide, coming from Buffalo, Wyoming, it climbs 4,400 feet, crossing numerous small drainages, breaking into high parkland with small streams and groves of conifers— a surprisingly gentle landscape considering its altitude and nearness to the rugged Cloud Peak Massif. The road continues through high meadows for a few miles west of the 9,677-foot pass, and then drops into the narrow, limestone Tensleep Canyon, descending 5,200 feet to the town of Tensleep.

All along the highway, or a short distance from it, the Forest Service maintains more than a dozen campgrounds and a number of other facilities. You can drive to a lookout on Sheep Mountain, and another at High Park on the east and west sides of the pass, respectively. Meadowlark Lake, about a square mile in extent, is a popular fishing spot along the highway. A mile west of the lake, where the road joins Tensleep Creek at the head of the canyon, a Forest Service road turns upstream to the West Tensleep Lake Campground. The trailhead at this campground is one of the two most popular in the area, giving access to Mistymoon Lake and Florence Pass. If you went over the pass and continued down the trail to the east, you would arrive at the Hunter Corrals trailhead, the other popular wilderness entrance point. To get there by highway, turn off U.S. 16 at the North Fork Picnic Ground.

More campgrounds and access from the north can be reached off

U.S. 14 between Sheridan and Greybull. At Owen Creek Campground, about six miles south of the junction of U.S. 14 and Alternate 14, turn east toward Big Goose Ranger Station; in that area a number of trails branch into the wilderness area.

Buffalo

The city of Buffalo, in the basin east of the Bighorns, is the seat of Johnson County. Some say the name comes from the numbers of bison that lived in the area when the city was founded in 1884 on a cattle trail; that seems more appropriate than the other story that this was meant to be the sister city of Buffalo, New York. To the north, past Lake DeSmet, is the site of Fort Phil Kearney, built to protect travelers on the Bozeman Trail. The fort, as well as the trail, violated a treaty with the Sioux, who in turn waged bitter war on the fort. The most famous incident occurred on December 21, 1866, when Brevet Lieutenant Colonel William Fetterman set out from the fort to rescue a wagon train. He and 81 men rode into an ambush sprung by the Sioux; none of the whites survived. The site is marked with a stone monument on U.S. Highway 87 north of Buffalo. The Indians, under Chief Red Cloud, kept up the pressure, insisting that the treaty be upheld, until at last, in 1868, the beleaguered outpost was abandoned. The Sioux allowed the soldiers to leave and burned the fort to the ground. The taste of victory lasted only a few years, however. In 1876, Fort McKinney was built during the campaign following Custer's defeat on the Little Big Horn and used until 1894 when Wyoming took it over as a home for state war veterans.

The Buffalo area saw another of the West's more notorious incidents, the Johnson County Cattle War. It was a classic confrontation between big business and the little man, between cattle barons and homesteaders. The cattlemen claimed that their livestock was being rustled by the homesteaders, who in turn accused the cattlemen of trying to drive them out of the country with strong-arm tactics. The situation reached a climax when a gang of gunmen—The Regulators—hired by the big ranchers rode north toward Buffalo. South of town, they murdered two supposed rustlers in a ranch house. Word of this reached town and galvanized the citizenry. A hastily formed army galloped off southward and caught The Regulators at the T-A ranch house, where a shoot-out ensued. No one died, because the U.S. Cavalry came riding in and took The Regulators off to jail.

Buffalo has just under 7,000 people, 15 motels, 3 RV parks and the usual assortment of town services. The Jim Gatchell Museum, downtown, has a pioneer collection; free admission.

Some Useful Information About Bighorn Mountains

USEFUL NAMES AND ADDRESSES: The address for **Bighorn National Forest** is 1969 S. Sheridan Ave., Sheridan, WY 82801; a visitor's map costs $3.

GENERAL INFORMATION: A trail guide to the Cloud Peak Wilderness Area, *Cloud Peak Primitive Area*, is available for $11.95 from Tensleep Publications, P.O. Box 925, Aberdeen, SD 57401; *Guide to Wyoming Mountains and Wilderness Areas*, by Orrin and Lorraine Bonney, published by Swallow Press, Inc. ($24.95 from Ohio University Press at 800-621-2736), covers the whole state in 700 pages, or is available split into separate guides to individual mountain ranges.

LEE METCALF WILDERNESS

There are four separate units of the Lee Metcalf Wilderness, all in the Madison Range to the northwest of Yellowstone. The Bear Trap Canyon unit is 6,000 acres of Bureau of Land Management land on either side of the Madison River, below the Madison Dam north of Ennis. A fisherman's trail follows the river through the canyon. Access is by the trailhead on the north; drive seven miles east from Norris, turn south for three miles on the east side of the river.

The Spanish Peaks unit takes up 78,000 acres of high country above the Gallatin River near Big Sky Resort. Gallatin Peak is the high point at 11,015 feet, surrounded by a number of slightly lower peaks and glacial cirque basins with small lakes. Three trailheads are commonly used. Providing the most options for hikers is Creek Campground on the north; turn west on Spanish Creek off U.S. Highway 191 at the north end of Gallatin Canyon. Another is five miles south on U.S. 191 at Beckman Flat. The third is on the same highway, about four miles north of the Big Sky Resort turnoff.

The largest of the four sections is the Taylor-Hilgard unit, 140,000 acres on the crest of the range. The area is easily seen from the west along U.S. Highway 287. Mountains like Sphinx Peak rise stunningly above the valley floor. Access for hikers is somewhat confounded by private land along the base of the range, but there are access points. One is the Bear Creek Forest Service Station at the base of Sphinx Peak (turn east at Cameron 11 miles south of Ennis). Another is Indian Creek Trailhead. Turn east 19 miles south of Ennis, then follow the county road to the trailhead. Papoose Creek Trailhead is 32 miles south of Ennis. Turn east a quarter mile south of the west fork (Lyons Bridge) Highway rest stop. The area around Echo Peak at the south end of the wilderness can be reached from the Beaver Creek Forest Service Station on Forest Road 985 a mile below Hebgen Dam. From here, Trail 222 climbs to Blue Danube Lake, and Trail 202 climbs Sentinel Creek to the Hilgard Basin, which is dotted with high lakes.

The fourth unit of the wilderness is 34,000-acre Monument Mountain. Small but exceptional as wildlife range, it abuts Yellowstone on its northwest corner. It is part of a larger roadless area, which joins the Taylor-Hilgard unit through Cabin Creek Wildlife Management Area. A trail leaves U.S. 191 at Bacon Rind Creek in the park and climbs 3,000 feet to the summits of Snowslide and Monument mountains.

Other Area Ideas

Not in the wilderness but nonetheless a fine place for hiking and camping is Hyalite Ridge, a tight cluster of mountain summits, streams, waterfalls and lakes in the Gallatin Range south of Bozeman. Finding the road is a little tricky, as it starts in town. Coming into Bozeman from the west on U.S. Highway 191, follow signs for Montana State University (the highway angles left, and M.S.U. is straight). In six-tenths of a mile from the fork, turn right and drive straight south. After five miles, the route goes west to Hyalite Creek, which it then follows to Hyalite Reservoir on Forest Road 62; numerous campsites are scattered along the road, and the Hyalite Ridge trailhead is at Palace Butte Campground.

Useful Names and Addresses

Contact these offices for the unit under their jurisdiction: Bear Trap Canyon—**Dillon Resource Area**, BLM, 1005 Selway Dr., Dillon, MT 59725 (tel: 406-683-2337); Spanish Peaks—**Bozeman Ranger District**, Gallatin National Forest, 601 Nikles, P.O. Box 130, Bozeman, MT 59715 (tel: 406-587-5271, ext. 4261); Taylor-Hilgard—**Madison Ranger District**, Beaverhead National Forest, 5 Forest Service Rd., Route 2, Box 5, Ennis, MT 59729 (tel: 406-682-4253); Monument Mountain—**Hebgen Ranger District**, Gallatin National Forest, P.O. Box 520, West Yellowstone, MT 59758 (tel: 406-646-7369).

CHAPTER FOUR

Salmon River Country

Centered on the Salmon River and its bewildering variety of tributaries, or forks, all but a small portion of this area lies west of the Continental Divide. The topography is exquisitely complex and is better defined in terms of its watercourses than its mountain ranges. That's not to say that drainage patterns make any real sense; they run every which way, doubling back on themselves, forever changing their minds about which way they are supposed to run. The names of these streams alone are nearly as confusing as the rugged country through which they flow.

For example, most watercourses in Idaho, by local custom of nomenclature, lack independent names. Instead, rivers and streams are categorized according to their relationship to one another. Thus we have the Payette River and, tributary to it, the South Fork of the Payette. While that may seem eminently sensible at first glance, in practice it gets complicated and confusing. The higher you get in a drainage, the longer the names become; one map soberly labels the "East Fork of the Lake Fork of the North Fork of the Payette River." Adding to the confusion is the tendency of rivers to wander across the region with a total lack of discipline. As an example, the South Fork of the Salmon rises to the north of the headwaters of both the Main Fork and the Middle Fork, while the East Fork (not to be confused with the East Fork of the South Fork) is the most southerly of all the forks. Wait a minute; don't bother to re-read that, it makes no better sense the second time through.

If that tidbit of geography seems a little hard to grasp, consider that local people rarely use a stream's full family name. "Yeah, out there on the Norfork ... Which Norfork? Hell, there ain't but one. No, not the Salmon, the Clearwater, what else?"

What else includes seven river systems: the Salmon, the Payette, the Boise, the Selway, the Clearwater, the Lochsa and the Bitterroot. These streams, all on the west side of the Divide, drain ten national forests, seven designated wilderness areas, two national recreation areas, thousands of snowy peaks, alpine meadows, deep canyons, rolling cultivated ranchlands and all the varied terrain that lies between. The heart of the region is the heavily dissected canyon country on either side of the Salmon River. Where the Salmon flows through its formidable gorge, a distance of some one hundred thirty turbulent miles, it has become famous under its romantic-sounding name, The River of No Return. For decades after the first visit by Lewis and Clark in 1805, the Salmon defied exploration. Even today the gorge remains roadless, which is unusual considering that in most of the Rockies, river courses provide the most feasible routes for highways and railroads. To find a highway crossing Idaho, travelers must detour far to either side of The River of No Return.

Bordered to the south and west by the broad curve of the Snake River, to the east by the Continental Divide, and to the north by the Lochsa River Valley, the region is dominated by a great mass of igneous rock, the Idaho Batholith. The Batholith formed between 60 and 90 million years ago when the main uplift of the Rockies was taking place. While the region was still covered by layers of sedimentary rocks from Paleozoic times, an immense quantity of molten rock squeezed its way between layers without breaking the surface, forming a great bulge to make room for itself, and then hardened in place.

Subsequent erosion of the overlying sedimentary strata has exposed the Batholith to view and carved it into the wonderful shapes we see in the Sawtooth Range north of Sun Valley, the Bighorn Crags in The River of No Return Wilderness, and other formations throughout the region. The Batholith defines and explains the topography of central Idaho. Covering a total area of approximately fourteen thousand square miles, it runs 250 miles north-south and 90 miles east-west, shading into Montana where it forms part of the Anaconda-Pintler Wilderness Area.

Central Idaho is much drier than country immediately to the north, receiving as little as seven inches of precipitation annually, with the average closer to fifteen inches in valley bottoms. Near desert conditions prevail on slopes with southern and western exposures. High-country areas, however, collect generous snow; drifts commonly restrict travel on backroads and trails until early to mid-July. Some hiking can be done in June after dry winters or at low elevations along river valleys; as a rule, how-

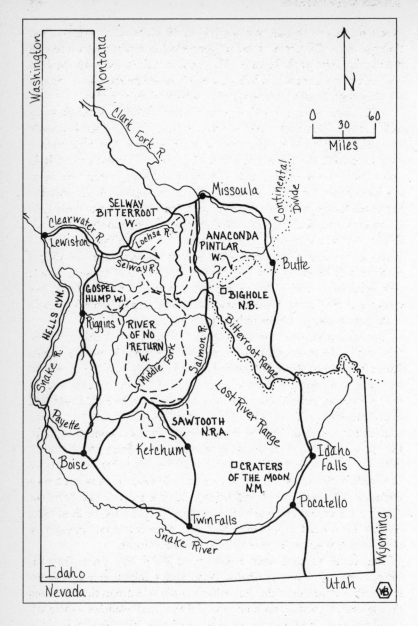

ever, backpackers should wait for July or be prepared to walk on and through snow. Winters in Idaho are generally less severe than winters on the eastern slope of the Rockies. The interior is sheltered from the deep cold of arctic air masses, which commonly inundate the central part of the continent. Sunny, warm days often follow subzero nights.

This region is not particularly easy to drive through, although every mile rewards the traveler with spectacular and changing scenery. Only one year-round road runs east-west across it, and that, U.S. Highway 12 over Lolo Pass, the Lewis and Clark Highway, was completed only in 1962. As for north-south traffic, U.S. 93 runs down the east side, making one sortie into the mountains through Stanley Basin and the Sawtooth Range, and State Highway 55 joins with U.S. 95 to carry traffic on the west side of the state. All three roads are extraordinarily scenic drives, but they give only a hint of what lies in the interior. Central Idaho is probably the wildest, least-known wilderness in the United States outside of Alaska. This may explain the number of eccentric people who settle here, from reclusive trappers and miners who prefer to live resourceful lives as far from contact with others as possible, to people with more pressing reasons to hide from public view.

One who achieved renown was Sylvan Hart, known as Buckskin Bill, "the last of the mountain men," who lived for many years at Fivemile Bar on the Salmon River. Following his death, family members converted his home to a small but fascinating museum. He came to Idaho during the Depression, judging that if there weren't jobs to be had, a man had to go where he could live off the land and on his wits. The Salmon River country met his needs. Despite trips "outside" for occasional jobs, or to Europe as a tourist, Hart always returned to the solitary life of a bushman. He was known for the exquisite craftsmanship that went into his handmade rifles, tools and accoutrements. However, he was not a misanthrope. Like many people still living in remote areas up and down the river, he welcomed company and enjoyed chewing the fat; he lived there because he wanted to live there and not, as is commonly thought of those who live alone, because of some maladjustment.

Hart comes to mind often as you travel Idaho. Far upriver from his cabin, a few miles north of Challis, an intriguing collection of cave-houses is built into the side of the canyon wall, easily seen across the river from the highway. Doorways open into the cliff-face, and windows—some salvaged from auto bodies—peer out from solid rock. The place looks like a combination of 20th-century junkyard sculpture and an ancient Ethiopian Koptic cave settlement. One fall day I decided to find out who lived there and why. Just upstream, an old iron bridge leads across the river to a gravel road. A sign, painted on a car hood with a stick for a brush, announces:

The Idaho Caveman

Ice caves
Ice is natural—But
Hand made

See my Ghost &
Primitive way of
Life Stories.
25 cts pr. Kids free under 12

Be sure you
dont miss my tunnel
    house

Take pictures $1.00
All you want

I drove down the road, feeling adequately welcomed, past a dozen or so doorways set against the cliff, each one a unique sculpture of museum-quality junk, weathered wood and auto body parts. Homey, but no one home. Only an old yellow dog, standing and stretching from where he slept in the sun, made any sign of greeting. I stayed there with him for a while, getting lazy in the sun, and then drove on toward Challis.

Other fugitives finding some degree of protection in the wilds of central Idaho include bighorn sheep, mountain goats, mountain lions, peregrine falcons, bald eagles, Swainson's hawks, ferruginous hawks, long-billed curlews, western yellow-billed cuckoos and quite a few game animals which, despite pressure from hunters, manage to hang on in the hinterlands. Continually, rumors of wolves make the rounds.

A great proportion of Idaho is national forest land. More than 75 percent of Idaho's timber is owned by the federal government, with almost a third of that Douglas fir, covering about 21 million acres. It's a bit of a surprise therefore to find that in the entire region there is no national park (although Craters of the Moon National Monument and the Nez Perce National Historic Park are included in the region, the first is on the southern fringe and the second is something quite different from other National Park Service areas).

History

Legend has it that the Shoshones and Nez Perce who lived near the Salmon originally named it The River of No Return, but history does not support that idea. Cort Conley and Johnny Carey, in their book *River of No Return*, write that the Nez Perce called it *Natsoh Koos*, or "Chinook-Salmon-Water," and the Shoshones called it *Tommanamah*,

"Big-Fish-Water." These Indians fished the streams of the Salmon drainage and hunted the meadows throughout central Idaho as early as 8,000 years ago. Rock paintings, campsites and the marks of old villages remain. But although they had canoes, and knew about rivers, they apparently did not float the Salmon gorge, which ranks as the second deepest river canyon (behind Hells Canyon of the Snake River) in the contiguous 48 states.

Lewis and Clark, with the members of their historic expedition to the Pacific, were the first Europeans in the area. They had dragged their canoes as far up the Beaverhead River as they felt was feasible, buried them in the riverbed for use on the return journey, and headed over the Divide at Lemhi Pass on foot, hoping to find a river that would carry them to the Pacific. More immediately, they needed food and directions, yet they had had no success in making contact with native Americans in the area. As luck would have it, they did finally meet up with a band of Shoshones in the Lemhi Valley on the west side of the Divide, whose leader was none other than Cameahwait, the brother of Sacajawea. Sacajawea had been kidnapped as a young girl by Minnetaree Indians and had been won from them in a gambling game by a French trader named Toussaint Charbonneau, who married her. Lewis and Clark, on their way up the Missouri, had encountered this pair and hired Charbonneau as an interpreter. Sacajawea, however, only about 16 years old and pregnant, was the more important addition to the expedition. Already the captains knew of the Shoshone Indians who lived on the Divide and raised horses, which would be needed as pack animals. Sacajawea could serve as interpreter to the Shoshones; but more importantly, they would be taking her back to her own people, thereby making a powerful gesture of good will and peaceful intent.

Sacajawea's role as a guide has been overstated. She had not seen her homeland for many years, and then only as a young child. Even so, she recognized certain landmarks, such as Beaverhead Rock, which stands above the Beaverhead River a few miles north of Dillon, Montana. And most importantly, she recognized her brother, Cameahwait.

The reunion was joyous, particularly between Sacajawea and a woman who had been captured at the same time as she, but who had escaped back to her people. More than anything, Lewis and Clark wanted directions, and asked if the Salmon River flowed to the ocean. Yes, said Cameahwait, it did, but the waters were too rough for canoes, and the canyon was impassable. Better, he said, to proceed north over Lost Trail Pass and up the Bitterroot Valley to Lolo Pass, where they could follow the ancient trail between the buffalo plains and Nez Perce country. Being told they would have to go overland was hard for rivermen to accept, for it would necessitate many pack animals and hard travel. Only after a scouting trip partway down the river canyon did Lewis and Clark reluctantly agree that the Salmon was impassable, and set about trying to buy horses from Cameahwait's people. For his part, Cameahwait saw in the white men an opportunity to obtain rifles, which their enemies the Blackfeet and Minnetarees had acquired some years earlier. Lewis replied that they had no guns to trade. But (and one can imagine his salesman demeanor slipping into gear) as a result of their exploration, many other whites would follow, with not only guns, but all sorts of wonderful things besides.

The Shoshones, not a rich tribe in the first place, had had a hard year and were not easily persuaded by what the captains did have to offer. After considerable haggling, the whites managed to buy 29 horses, far fewer than they reckoned were needed, and set off on what proved to be the hardest, most demanding leg of their journey.

For a time after that, the fur trade was busy, although it remains unclear how much time trappers spent in the area of central Idaho, as compared to the Snake River plain and the mountains of northeastern Utah, which was exceptionally rich beaver country. The first sizeable influx of whites came in concert with the Colorado gold rush of 1859, which sent miners scurrying like mad ants in every direction, including Idaho. Oregon-bound settlers had for a number of years already been using the trail over Mullan Pass well to the north, but they rarely wandered away from the main route, in part because it was illegal to enter the lands of the Nez Perce without an official reason to do so. At that time, the Nez Perce held legal title to almost all of what is now central Idaho.

Goldrushers coming from Washington territory were the first to probe streams for color. A few small deposits turned up, and then rich paydirt was found at Orofino ("Pure Gold"). Another gold rush was on, first at Orofino, then south at Florence and Elk City (Florence is a ghost town now, and Elk City, which once had a population of 20,000, is down to 450), and many other lesser places throughout the region. Miners trying to make their way from Colorado to Idaho via the Salmon River were stopped by its rugged gorge, and just like Lewis and Clark before them, were forced to detour. In turning aside, one group ended up discovering the gold fields of southwestern Montana at Bannock and Virginia City.

Mining of all sorts continues to be a major source of revenue for Idahoans, although the general trend is one of decline. Most of what a traveler sees now are relics: ghost towns, rusted machinery, tailings piles, dredge dunes, collapsing stamp mills and gaping mine tunnels. Idaho makes its living now through agriculture, logging, tourism and a scattering of other industries.

CRATERS OF THE MOON NATIONAL MONUMENT

Craters of the Moon National Monument, in south-central Idaho, is part of the Snake River Volcanic Plain, a 200,000-square-mile lava field which angles northeastward from southern Idaho to Yellowstone Park. Geologists theorize that volcanic activity has for millions of years crept toward the northeast (because the continent has been moving in the opposite direction over a stationary plume of magma) and that by studying the progression, we can see a record, a sort of time-lapse display, of what has been and what is yet to come. Craters of the Moon, they suggest, may have once been similar to Yellowstone. In the same way, Yellowstone may some day be a dry, barren volcanic landscape such as we see today here on the Idaho plains.

The monument is 83 square miles in extent. The bulk of it, lying to the south of the visitor center and campground, is designated wilderness, and an entirely different backpacking experience from anywhere else in the Rockies. The park is covered by 2,000-year-old lava flows, many of which have a jagged surface like a mass of fused coal clinkers. This surface is called by its Hawaiian name, *aa*, which translates to "hard on the feet." *Aa* is a two syllable word which anyone, regardless of nationality, is likely to pronounce correctly—and very loudly—the first time he steps on it with bare feet.

At first sight, this landscape is forbidding and monotonous, but a visitor quickly learns about the variety of lava forms and the story each formation tells. Before long it is not at all hard to picture the heat and bluster of the eruptions, which occurred such a short time ago, and which are likely to happen again some time in the future. Fields of *aa* lie interspersed with contrasting patches of pahoehoe (pah-HOY-hoy), a ropy, smooth-surfaced, more friendly material to walk on. Pahoehoe still looks semiliquid. Various interesting formations, such as spatter cones and pressure ridges, alternate with huge black cinder cones. There are numerous spatter cones, the names of which explain quite adequately how they came to be. Lava tubes, less easy to visualize, were built when a crust formed over a molten river, and the still-liquid center drained out before it hardened, leaving the perimeter of the tube rigidly in place. Indian Tunnel, the most visited one at Craters of the Moon, is 800 feet long and 40 feet high. In places, these subterranean caverns are so well insulated from the summer sun that ice remains in them year-around. With a flashlight and a reasonable amount of care to avoid dagger-like icicles of lava hanging from the roof, one can explore the tunnels.

Craters of the Moon National Monument encompasses a large, recent lava flow.

Despite what appears to be a total lack of soil, and precious little water, quite a few plants survive in the park. Big sagebrush, antelope bitterbrush and rubber rabbitbrush (try to say that several times quickly) are scattered as if in a garden, each framed by its private circle of empty space, a phenomenon explained by lack of water. During spring, wildflowers bloom in profligate disregard of the moonscape around them. More fitting to the mood of things are the limber pines, stout, gnarly trees given to bizarre shapes and the appearance of having been tortured most of their lives. Animals live here as well, and they seem quite happy with their lot. Some diligent soul has counted over 2,000 species of insects, 140 birds, 42 mammals—including mule deer, chipmunks and ground squirrels—7 reptiles and a single species of amphibian, the western toad. Craters of the Moon is a stark and forbidding landscape, yes, and a tough place to travel without a trail or road, but beautiful in its visual simplicity.

If backpacking here appeals to you, as it does to perhaps one person in ten thousand, I heartily recommend it, although I can't imagine what sort of incentive could draw me out there during the heat of midsummer. Spring and fall are best, when the sun is less intense and there is a chance of finding water in the form of ice. Even so, you'll be wise to carry what water you will need. The other idea is to go in winter, when snow takes this strange landscape and makes it even stranger. Free backcountry permits are required. Backcountry destinations include Echo Crater, the Bridge of Tears and Vermilion Chasm.

The park has a campground open from May to October. Evening programs and guided walks are conducted throughout the summer season. Short trails take off from a seven-mile loop road, which provides access to the variety of volcanic formations. The loop road, not plowed in winter, is a good ski trail. The visitor center remains open all year excepting winter holidays. Arco is the nearest town, 18 miles east. Carey is 24 miles west.

Useful Names and Addresses

WRITE: Superintendent, **Craters of the Moon N.M.**, Arco, ID 83213 (tel: 208-527-3257).

SAWTOOTH NATIONAL RECREATION AREA

The Sawtooth National Recreation Area, administered by the Forest Service, occupies the headwaters of the Main Salmon River. Its name comes from the toothsome peaks on the west side of the river, which rise picturesquely above the sage and grasslands of the Sawtooth Valley and Stanley Basin. East of the river stand two other ranges, the White Clouds and the Boulder Mountains. State Highway 75 enters the N.R.A. a few miles north of Ketchum, crosses Galena Summit, and from then on parallels the ever-broader Salmon River. At the town of Stanley—until recently a pleasant collection of unimposing log buildings, but suddenly exploding in a flurry of precut log tourist facilities—Idaho 21 comes in from the west, providing the only east-west route across the state between the Snake River Plain and the Lochsa River Valley far to the north.

Sawtooth Wilderness

The Sawtooth Wilderness, with its sharp-edged granite mountains, takes up 216,000 acres of the National Recreation Area. This is prime backpacking country. The ruggedness of the mountains makes for an intricate, intimate landscape with small meadows and lakes, numerous streams, a maze of ragged ridges and crenelated mountain peaks. The Sawtooth Range rewards cross-country hikers willing to do some bushwhacking in a way which larger-scale landscapes cannot. Walking just a few miles brings you to an entirely new scene, a new lake, or to an apparently unknown, postage-stamp meadow tucked high in the crags and lush with wildflowers.

This is a lucky thing, for the Sawtooth's popularity grows every year. Even with nearly three hundred miles of maintained and marked trails, solitude is a scarce commodity on the best-known routes between mid-July and September. However, several of the high cirques and basins have been intentionally left trailless, and these are less often visited. The most popular trailheads are all on the east and north sides, with easy road access from the Stanley Basin. They include Iron Creek, Redfish Lake (where a motorboat ride will cut off about four miles of hiking), Grandjean, Hellroaring Creek and Pettit Lake. More than 1,500 hikers per season register at each of these trailheads. Considering that most of this use occurs in the six weeks following July 15, hikers with a keen desire for solitude might do well to choose a different route or come at a different time of the year. Forest roads provide alternate access from the west through Atlanta (41 miles on Forest Road 384; alternately from U.S. Highway 20 on Forest Roads 163 and 156 through Featherville and Rocky Bar), where you can pick up the Boise River Trail into lakes country. Immediately west of there, and reached by the same roads, is the Queens River Trail. These roads are passable in ordinary cars during the summer season. They traverse an interesting and historic mining district, which can be coupled with visits to towns in the Idaho City area for an interesting auto tour.

Mule deer and elk live throughout the Sawtooth area. Mountain goats are relatively common at high elevations. Bighorn sheep, once considered abundant and easy to kill, are reduced now to a small band in the White Cloud Peaks. Black bears remain in small numbers, rarely seen; grizzlies are long gone. Rarely seen, but still resident, are mountain lion, bobcat, Canadian lynx and wolverine. Small rodents are everywhere.

Neither bears nor poisonous snakes are a problem in the Sawtooth. Small animals, however, especially wily nocturnal mice, can make a mess of backpacks left standing overnight against a tree. The major nuisances here are insects: mosquitoes, horse flies and deer flies. Those who lack repellant in July will rue the oversight. For climbers, the rock of the Sawtooth Range is entirely granite, but its quality varies from clean, monolithic texture all the way to garbagey rubble, often on the same peak.

Permits are not required for groups of fewer than ten persons; twenty in a party is the legal maximum. Winter trips and the use of horses require permits, which are free. Permits and other information are available at area ranger stations.

White Cloud Mountains

On the other side of the Stanley Basin rise the White Cloud-Boulder Mountains, also contained by the Sawtooth National Recreation Area, but lacking wilderness protection. In contrast to the igneous Sawtooths, the White Clouds, dominated by 11,815-foot Castle Peak, are built of light-colored sedimentary limestone resembling, some say, white clouds on the horizon. About one hundred twenty-five lakes cluster along the Divide in a compact, spectacular area well suited for wandering on foot and quite popular for just that reason.

The Boulder Mountains lie just to the south. A more massive, less dissected landscape, the Boulders have almost no lakes and consequently few visitors. This is a place for long, high ridge walks with broad views and wide exposure. Take note, however, that because the White Cloud-Boulder area is not a designated wilderness, you may find yourself sharing trails with motorcycles. The Sawtooth National Forest publishes what they call a travel plan indicating which places are open to vehicles, and it makes good sense to check this before deciding on a trail. For the most part, higher elevations are closed to motor vehicles, although at least two approved routes cross the range east to west. During the winter, snowmobiles have access to designated areas that exclude low-lying wildlife wintering range.

The most popular access to the White Clouds is via the northeast, following gravel roads up the East Fork of the Salmon River, then walking along Big or Little Boulder creeks, which lead in short distances to the lake country. The Boulder Mountains are also reached from the East Fork of the Salmon, which heads up on the Boulder Divide.

Other Area Ideas

Ghost towns from the days of gold mining surround the Sawtooths. On Highway 21, 40 miles from Boise, is the partially reconstructed Idaho City; a secondary road leads a few miles northwest to Placerville and New Centerville. Close to the south boundary of the wilderness area, Atlanta and Rocky Bar slowly crumble to the ground. North of the Sawtooths, along an alternate gravel route from Sunbeam to Challis, Custer has a museum of the gold rush, among other relics. Stanley is the junction for three designated Scenic Byways: Salmon River, Sawtooth and Ponderosa.

Some Useful Information About Sawtooth

CAMPGROUNDS: The 36 campgrounds in the area provide hundreds of sites at most of the popular trailheads and locations, including Redfish Lake; also along Highways 21 and 75 west and east of the Stanley junction.
SCENIC DRIVES: Highway 75 from Challis to Hailey; Highway 21 from Stanley to Boise, including side trips to Grandjean and to ghost

towns around Idaho City: Centerville, Pioneerville and Placerville; the road between Lowman and Banks follows the South Fork of the Payette, staying high above the river through its magnificent gorge.

GENERAL INFORMATION: Book: *Trails of the Sawtooth and White Cloud Mountains* by Margaret Fuller (revised 1996, Signpost Books, 8912 192nd S.W., Edmonds, WA 98026). Stanley provides basic services—restaurant, gas, groceries, lodging, guide services and an emergency clinic. The nearest hospital is in Sun Valley.

USEFUL NAMES AND ADDRESSES: **Stanley Ranger Station,** Stanley, ID 83278 (tel: 208-774-3000); **Lowman Ranger Station,** Lowman, ID 83637 (summer only); and **Sawtooth National Recreation Area Headquarters,** Star Route, Ketchum, ID 83340 (tel: 208-727-5000). Their building is seven miles north of town. Stop here to pick up a cassette (to be returned at the Stanley Ranger Station), which gives a mile-by-mile tour of the highway.

SUN VALLEY

Sun Valley was a fabrication, and a good one. It began when Averill Harriman, Chairman of the Board of the Union Pacific Railroad, had the idea that a western ski resort similar to the ones he had seen in Europe might draw passengers onto his trains. Interest in winter sports had recently received a boost in North America by the 1932 Lake Placid Winter Olympics. Accordingly, Harriman hired an Austrian, Count Felix Schaffgotsch, to find a suitable location; what he came up with was a small, flat-bottomed valley near Ketchum, Idaho, surrounded by rolling treeless hills with high peaks rising just behind them. For a reported $39,000, Harriman's men bought the 3,400-acre Earnest Brass Ranch and set about building their resort. They built the Sun Valley Lodge of poured concrete made to look like wood, with 220 rooms, enclosed swimming pools, ice rinks, and of course the ski area on Dollar Mountain. From out of the thin mountain air (and the need to reassure people that Rocky Mountain winters were not as dreadful as most easterners then believed) a Union Pacific promoter came up with the name, Sun Valley. This was more than ten years before Aspen began looking at the profit potential of steep snow and people's desire to ski on it.

The name wasn't the only invention. The first chairlift in the world was built here in 1936, invented by a Union Pacific engineer named James Curran, who had watched fruit being loaded onto ships in Central America. A cable with a line of hooks carried bananas bunch by bunch from the warehouse to the waiting ships. Somehow he made the connection between skiers and bananas, and replaced the hooks with seats. The original chair, reconstructed on a new location but not operating, is now a Sun Valley landmark.

Since then, Harriman's resort has grown into a posh international destination. For a time, it developed a reputation as a hot gambling spot, until new laws in the late '40s closed the casinos. Skiers soon outgrew Dollar Mountain, where the first runs were laid out, and development shifted to the other side of Ketchum, where Bald Mountain is now the center of ski attention. Sun Valley itself continued to grow, staying aloof from the older town, and ornamented with the lavish vacation homes of the wealthy and famous. One of the houses most often pointed out (but hardly noticeable otherwise) is the home of Ernest Hemingway, who was probably Sun Valley's most famous resident. The house stands back from the highway, across Wood River north of Ketchum. East of the original Sun Valley Lodge, on the Sun Valley Road, a sign points the way to a bust and a memorial plaque:

> Best of all he loved the fall
> The leaves yellow on the cottonwoods
> Leaves floating on the trout streams
> And above the hills, the high blue windless skies
> Now he will be a part of them forever.

The real town here, however, is Ketchum, a one-time mining community with its origins still evident in the modesty of its buildings and its unassuming demeanor. It grew up during the silver-lead boom of the 1880s, which also saw the founding of Hailey and Bellevue to the south. Hailey got the county seat; Ketchum got the smelter, and fortunately for its future, a railhead. When the boom died, it became, like so many Rocky Mountain mining towns, a center for ranching supply. It became the biggest shipping point for sheep in all of the United States. That may have been a source of some pride for residents, but it made for a seasonal business with higher peaks and lower lows than even those in the ski business. When Harriman's Union Pacific developers descended on the little valley up Trail Creek in 1936, they might as well have dropped in from heaven with trumpets blaring, so warmly were they received. It was certainly the turning point of Ketchum's fortunes.

Ketchum is a delightful town, filled with outdoor lovers and athletes of all ages. No wonder. Every mountain sport ever contrived is available at its best in the immediate area. During winter, skiing, of course, in all its myriad and expanding forms. During summer, the skis get stashed in closets and out come bicycles (road bikes, racing bikes, mountain bikes, even racing mountain bikes), kayaks, rafts, climbing hardware, backpacks, running shoes (recently, running mountain trails has become quite the thing in Ketchum), sailboards, hang-gliders and even, yes, skis on wheels. Ketchum is an excellent place to meet people, to get advice and to plan a trip. The Elephant's Perch, a competent outdoor shop named for a Sawtooth rock-climbing area, is located in the center of Ketchum. The shop publishes a quarterly newspaper of mountain sports events and advice on equipment and techniques.

To the north is the Sawtooth National Recreation Area. Immediately above Ketchum stands the Pioneer Range. Its mountains rise to between 11,000 and 12,000 feet, to stand as Idaho's second loftiest range. Not included in a wilderness area, they are a prime example of the opportunities available to those who take the time to search out places without the accustomed labels of parks or other designations. We tend to assume that any really worthwhile mountain areas have been designated and inventoried and labeled as better than the average. Not so with the Pioneers. Get there by driving up the Trail Creek Road past Sun Valley. The road goes to Trail Creek Summit, a nice scenic drive. Hikers can turn off on the Coral Creek Road (F.S. 137) to a trailhead at Long Gulch.

USEFUL NAMES AND ADDRESSES: **Sun Valley-Ketchum Chamber of Commerce**, Box 2420, Sun Valley, ID 83353 (tel: 208-726-3423); **Sun Valley Visitors and Information Center** (tel: 800-634-3347); **Elephant's Perch** (outdoor equipment store, maps, advice and information), P.O. Box 178, Ketchum, ID 83340 (tel: 208-726-3497).

FRANK CHURCH RIVER OF NO RETURN WILDERNESS

Established in 1980, the Frank Church River of No Return Wilderness incorporated portions of the former Salmon River Breaks Primitive Area and the Idaho Primitive Area. With 2.36 million acres in six separate national forests, this is the largest designated wilderness in the lower 48 states, an area roughly the same size as Yellowstone National Park. It straddles the Salmon River for 97 miles, most of it on the south side. A province of canyon, high plateau and mountain peak, even today it contains sizeable valleys without so much as a trail.

The Salmon River, of course, is the dominant feature. It begins in Stanley Basin north of Ketchum and flows down the east side of the wilderness through Challis and Salmon until it reaches North Fork, where it turns abruptly west and roars through its deep, famous gorge all the way across Idaho. Other major drainages include both the Middle Fork and the South Fork of the Salmon. Almost the entire length of the

Middle Fork is within wilderness boundaries. The same is true of Big Creek and Chamberlain Creek, which qualify as small rivers in deep canyons of their own. The terrain is complex and deeply carved, with great expanses of forest. Open areas occur mostly on ridgetops and well-drained south-facing slopes. Those looking for spectacular scenery on the order of the Canadian Rockies, or the Tetons, might do well to reconsider before coming here. The strength of this wilderness is its size; it has the mystique you can feel only in big, big country, filled with secrets and unseen, unknown places. Hiking involves following wooded watercourses, or wandering across ridges and mountain slopes where meadows alternate with stands of trees; distances are almost always long.

If you look closely at a detailed map, you'll find oddities in the wilderness boundary. All sorts of roads penetrate the wilderness. Technically, they are not inside the boundaries, but that's only because the boundaries have been drawn up one side of each road and down the other. Forest managers call these cherry stems, because they often end at a piece of private property, giving the corridors the shape of cherries. In addition, nearly 2,500 acres of the wilderness are private property, and airstrips are scattered throughout the territory. Critics say these inclusions compromise the meaning of the wilderness designation; others claim that without the compromise, much of the included land would have been left out.

In any case, these roads, airstrips and cabins have been there for many decades. Some mark backcountry ranches, which are home to people who have lived there for three generations. Settlement began with the gold rush of the 1860s. Mining activities continue today but lack the fever of the last century. When the peak of the rush ended, things in central Idaho quieted down to a few ranchers, trappers and eccentrics leading remote, private lives. Mostly they lived along the Salmon and its major drainages supplied by riverboats or pack animals. The Forest Service, established in 1906, added a few developments in the form of lookout towers, roads, trails and ranger stations. Some of these have been abandoned now that the area has been declared a wilderness. But families still live in the backcountry; the airstrips and roads, along with radio telephones, are their links with the outer world. A few guest ranches accommodate visitors; a stop at one of these adds a different dimension to a backcountry trip.

In summer, the climate is mostly dry and warm. Daytime temperatures are mild, although in low-lying places the temperature can hit 100°F. Fully three-fourths of the annual precipitation, which varies with elevation from 15 to 50 inches, comes in the form of winter snow. The rest comes as rain in the spring and fall, or during afternoon thunderstorms in July and August.

Habitats include rivers and lakes, deep forest, dry steep canyon sides, and meadows interspersed with loose stands of ponderosa pine and Douglas fir. The wilderness is home to 190 recorded bird species and most of the animals we associate with the wildest parts of North America: elk, moose, mule deer, whitetail deer, bighorn sheep, mountain goats, mountain lions, wolverines, black bears, fisher, lynx, osprey, bald eagles and peregrine falcons. There is some reason to believe gray wolves still wander the forest here. In the waters live chinook salmon, steelhead trout, sturgeon, arctic grayling and smallmouth bass.

Access is from trailheads at the ends of long, primitive dirt roads, or by small planes chartered from McCall, Cascade, Salmon, Challis and other neighboring towns. You might choose to fly in to one airstrip and be picked up after walking to another; or you could drive to a trailhead that has an airstrip, walk to another trailhead in the wilderness, and be shuttled back to your car. Numerous options of this sort exist and may even be the cheapest way, considering the cost of running long-distance car shuttles on gravel roads. The cost of airplane charter is by the hour; roughly $110 to $120 per hour for a two-passenger plane, $140 to $150 for four persons with gear (1,000 pounds is the usual maximum pay-load). Average flying time from towns of origin near the wilderness boundary is about one hour return.

The hiking and camping season runs from mid-June to mid-September, with snow blocking higher roads and trails well into July. Main trails have bridges over major stream crossings, but be prepared to ford in any case. More remote trails get less maintenance and traffic, hence may be faint and overgrown. The hiking season begins somewhat earlier than in higher parts of the Rockies, with trails passable by the middle of June, although even here there is snow to cross on the passes, and some roads stay closed for the same reason. For example, the 115-mile primitive road between Elk City, Idaho, and the Bitterroot Valley in Montana is normally not passable until the middle of July.

From Payette National Forest, on the west side of the wilderness, the Big Creek Trail is a popular route to the Middle Fork of the Salmon—popular, that is, among people interested in walking the 50-mile distance. From this trailhead, hikers can also get to Chamberlain Basin, a 300,000-acre expanse of rolling hills, big trees and meadows, via Hand Creek. Getting to Big Creek is a long drive regardless of which route you choose (the roads form a loop), but a scenic one worth making even if you aren't going into the backcountry. With a distance of 170 miles to cover through country God designed specifically, and exclusively, it appears, for hawks and not cars, allow two days for the trip from pavement to pavement. The road leaves Cascade, Idaho, on Highway 55, and goes through Warm Lake to Yellow Pine (F.S. 413). There it turns right onto Forest Road 412, which if you follow it all the way to its end will put you in Stibnite, the location of a once-large mining community abandoned in 1952. The road to Big Creek (F.S. 340) turns off the Stibnite road about five miles east of Yellow Pine and continues all the way through Warren and Burgdorf to pavement and a return to Highway 55 at McCall. The whole trip is shown on the Payette National Forest Visitor's Map; there are several campgrounds en route, with any number of undesignated, unimproved sites to choose from as well.

On the opposite side of the wilderness, and the state, is Bighorn Crags, with numerous 10,000-foot peaks. The main access to this well-known place for hikers and campers is through the Crags Campground, reached from Challis or Salmon. From Salmon, drive six miles south on U.S. Highway 93 to Williams Creek Road (F.S. 021). Follow signs for Cobalt Ranger Station, about forty-two miles away. The road climbs over Williams Creek Summit, then drops into Panther Creek Canyon. Where the road meets Panther Creek, a right turn will take you to the Main Salmon River below the town of North Fork. Turn left toward Cobalt to reach the Crags. Cobalt is the company town for a sizeable cobalt mine, which closed its gates after the winter of 1985. The road was kept open during the winter while the mine was operating, but its future status is uncertain. Turn right on Forest Road 112 past the Cobalt Ranger Station and follow the signs for Quartzite Mountain to Forest Road 118 and the Crags Campground.

Coming from Challis, take Forest Road 055 up Morgan Creek about eight miles north of town on U.S. 93. The road climbs through beautiful canyon country to Morgan Creek Summit and Panther Creek, reaching Forest Road 112 about six miles before the Cobalt Ranger Station. The trip following Morgan Creek to Panther Creek to the Main Salmon is a slow, scenic alternative to U.S. 93 from Challis to North Fork.

In an area of steep-sided hills jammed together as if they were attending a Central American soccer match, and covered with timber to their crests, the Bighorn Crags stand out as landmarks from every vista for miles around. They are a popular destination, but long, steep, rough, tiring gravel roads protect them from all but determined travelers. This is not a place for motorhomes and trailers. Some of the peaks are indeed craggy, while others are high and steep-sided but not enough to keep walkers off them. Lakes are numerous, and the fishing, they say, is good. For real solitude, try the little-used trailless areas in the southern end of the Crags—rough country but empty of people.

Other access to the Crags is along the Panther Creek Road about four miles in the Main Salmon. Three trails branch out from a single trailhead, following roughly parallel courses. The Crags Trail climbs a long, gentle ridge through good elk country, but dry for summer hikers; carry sufficient water. The Clear Creek Trail follows the streambed below, and the Gant Ridge Trail goes along the wilderness boundary. The first two are recommended. Yet another trail climbs to the Crags from the Middle Fork of the Salmon. Used mostly by river runners, it climbs for 6,000 vertical feet along the course of Waterfall Creek. Long-distance backpackers get to Waterfall Creek either via the Big Creek Trail, descending to the Middle Fork from the west, or via the Loon Creek and Rapid River trails on the south. These join the Middle Fork Trail which parallels the river for many miles.

Challis

Challis began as a supply center for the miners at Custer, Bonanza, Bayhorse and Yellowjacket, located in the mountains west of the Salmon River Valley. Mining is mostly dead now, and the town has settled into being another quiet, relaxed ranch supply center of around eight hundred people. Challis National Forest Headquarters is located here, and travelers will find basic services: food, gas, lodging and several cafes. Main Street runs up the hill and becomes Forest Road 70 up Garden Creek over the pass to Yankee Fork. It was here that William Norton, in 1875, hit a rich vein on his Charles Dickens claim. The next year, other miners opened the General Custer. But although they made fortunes in these mines, it was several years before the big rush was on; the town of Bonanza sprang up in 1879, only to be destroyed by fires in 1889 and again in 1897. Now you see a ghost town of relics, aging buildings, an interesting cemetery, an abandoned gold dredge, and the usual scattered, unidentifiable rusted machinery parts. If you drive in from the Challis side, you come to Custer before Bonanza; this mine lasted a little longer than its neighbor, with the Sunbeam Mine closing in 1911. The Forest Service maintains a museum in the old Custer schoolhouse.

Salmon

Salmon, located at the junction of the Lemhi and Salmon rivers, is the largest community in the upper Salmon River Valley. Since its founding after the Civil War, it has been a ranching and mining supply center— and always a river town. Beginning in the 1890s, when Henry Guleke and his partner David Sanderland began running the whitewater in commercial supply barges, Salmon has been the jumping-off point for prospectors, miners and adventurers headed down The River of No Return. Although most river trips now put in well downstream at Corn Creek, Salmon is headquarters for several river outfitters.

There are two good mountain shops in Salmon: Blackadar Boating north of town, which specializes in river gear, and Salmon River Mountain Sports on Main Street downtown. Brooks Montgomery, who owns the latter, is happy to point out trails and give advice. Especially useful are his suggestions for day-trips in the high peaks of the Beaverhead Mountains just east of town. They gleam with snow high above Salmon, but there is little direction from the Forest Service and almost no recreational development, even though just the other side of the crest is the proposed Big Hole Wilderness Area.

Some Useful Information About the River of No Return Wilderness

FLYING CHARTERS: Small charter planes operate from many surrounding towns. A list of these, along with all outfitters in Idaho, is available from the **Idaho Outfitters and Guides Association**, P.O. Box 95, Boise, ID 83701 (tel: 208-342-1919). Prices and flying times given above are estimates from **McCall Air Taxi**, Box 771, McCall, ID 83638 (tel: 800-992-6559).

GENERAL INFORMATION: Books: *The Middle Fork and the Sheepeater War*, and *River of No Return*, books by Cort Conley and Johnny Carrey, filled with historic tidbits, are found in area bookstores, or can be ordered from **Backeddy Books**, Box 301, Cambridge, ID 83610.

USEFUL NAMES AND ADDRESSES: Four national forests have management duties in The River of No Return Wilderness. These forests are on all sides, and it's a good idea to contact the one nearest the part of the wilderness that interests you. Any of them will have wilderness maps available. There are two of these, one for the north half and one for the south; both are needed for any planning, and with 50-meter contours, are sufficient for most hiking needs. Each map costs $2. The forest addresses are: **Payette National Forest**, P.O. Box 1026, McCall, ID 83638 (tel: 208-634-2255); **Salmon National Forest**, Cobalt Ranger District, P.O. Box 729, Salmon, ID 83467 (tel: 756-2240); **Challis National Forest**, Middle Fork Ranger District, Box 750, Challis, ID 83226 (tel: 879-4321); and **Nez Perce National Forest**, Red River Ranger District, Elk City, ID 83525 (tel: 208-842-2255).

SELWAY-BITTERROOT WILDERNESS

Over 1.3 million acres administered by four national forests (the Bitterroot, Clearwater, Lolo and Nez Perce) make up the magnificent Selway-Bitterroot Wilderness Area. It lies mostly in Idaho, edging across

The Lochsa River provides rafters and kayakers with Class III and IV whitewater during early to mid summer.

the crest of the Bitterroot Mountains into Montana. The Bitterroots form a high barrier on the east, which is crossed by no roads and drained by dozens of little streams pouring from hundreds of jeweled alpine lakes into the Bitterroot River.

The bulk of the area, to the west of the Bitterroot Divide, is drained by the Lochsa and Selway rivers. Selway comes from a Nez Perce word, *selwah*, meaning "smooth water," but the river is anything but smooth (see page 222). Bitterroot is a translation of the Indian name for *Lewisia rediviva*, a pink-flowered herb, which grows in moist areas throughout the region and is the official state flower of Montana. Its root is bitter raw, but tasty when boiled, and may well have helped sustain members of the Lewis and Clark expedition. One variety of bitterroot, when boiled, gives off a strong scent of nicotine. Eating it is said to have the same effect as chewing raw tobacco, hence the name Tobacco Root, also applied to the mountain range several drainages to the east where the plant is common.

Forming a barrier almost as imposing as the Bitterroot Range is a long ridge which parallels the Lochsa River and Highway 12 on the north boundary. Yet behind it, and out of sight from the river, is another, even higher ridge. Both of them are dotted with lakes and pouring with water; the Selway is considerably wetter than country just to the south. Behind the second ridge is a huge basin filled with smaller ridges and

There are several scattered, remnant groves of western red cedar found in northern Idaho.

canyons, all draining into the Selway River. The southeast rim of this basin is bounded by another dividing ridge, which hides a second, smaller basin (all of about 200 square miles). The Selway River has cut the only breach in this ridge, so it drains both basins.

The only way into this wilderness without climbing over a divide is to walk up the Selway Valley itself, beginning at Selway Falls and ending, if followed all the way, at Paradise Guard Station. This, by the way, is the route of river runners, although unless powerfully confused, they go in the reverse direction, downstream.

Partly because of its great size, its lack of regularly maintained trails, and the long distances involved in reaching certain remote parts of this wilderness, the Selway-Bitterroot trails suffer little from crowds. Not even the Indians who lived here—the Shoshone and Nez Perce—made much use of the area. Their cross-country trails avoided the rugged high country of the Bitterroot divide, and hunting was better in the broad, rich grazing meadows of the big valley bottoms. The exception was the upper Selway, where they kept camps in the summer, to catch and dry the migrating chinook salmon.

To reach the lake country along the Bitterroot divide, follow forest roads from Highway 93 in the Bitterroot Valley. These are too numerous to list here, but major ones, all with campgrounds at the trailheads, are Bass Creek on F.S. 1136 north of Stevensville (Charles Waters Campground), Big Creek on F.S. 738 north of Victor (Big Creek Campground), Mill Creek on F.S. 438 north of Hamilton (Mill Creek Campground), Lost Horse Creek on F.S. 429 north of Darby (Schumaker Campground) and Boulder Creek on F.S. 5631 at West Fork (Boulder Creek Campground).

From the Idaho side, trailheads are all along the highway and the Lochsa River. Of all the rivers in the world, this has to be one of the most beautiful. Try to be there on cool summer mornings when mists hang above the water and drift through the ancient western red cedars, lit by sun pouring from a blue sky. This is the place for casual day-hikers to get a sense of the northern Idaho wilderness. Walk up any of the several trails following stream valleys. A quarter mile is enough, although once into the coolness and beauty of the forest, you're likely to keep going much farther than you had planned. One of the best is the Warm Springs Trail.

In the area south of the Powell Ranger Station, a cluster of roads climb steeply to high basins on the wilderness boundary, thus giving the easiest access to the high country. One goes to Tom Beal Peak, where a short climb takes you to Walton Lakes. Another goes to either Elk Summit, Kooskia Meadows or Colt Creek. Any of these is a good choice for day-hiking or sightseeing. Elk Summit has a small undeveloped campground at Hoodoo Lake.

To get to the lower end of the Selway River, turn off Highway 12 at Lowell; Selway Falls is at the end of the road, and several campgrounds are located along the way. Two miles from the end, Forest Road 319 climbs like a frightened squirrel over Fog Mountain to Big Fog Saddle, where Trail 3 leads to Selway Crags and a tiara of alpine lakes. The upper end of the Selway River, at Paradise Guard Station, can be reached through West Fork, way over in the Bitterroot Valley. Directions are in the Selway River discussion (page 222).

Other Area Ideas

In the Lochsa Valley, below Lolo Pass, stands one of the finest surviving groves of virgin western red cedar, dedicated to conservationist and western historian Bernard De Voto. The Lolo Trail, an ancient route between the buffalo plains and western Idaho, used by the Nez Perce Indians for centuries and traveled by Lewis and Clark, can be followed in part by auto. See a description of this trip on page 212. Other scenic drives include almost any road in this part of Idaho. Highway 13 from Grangeville to Kooskia begins on high rolling plains and drops spectacularly into the valley of the Clearwater River. Highway 14 to the old mining town of Elk City follows the Clearwater upstream.

Useful Names and Addresses

A wilderness map with contour lines is available for $3 from most area ranger stations, including **Bitterroot National Forest Headquarters**, 1801 North First St., Hamilton, MT 59840 (tel: 406-363-3131) and **Nez Perce National Forest**, Route 2, Box 475, Grangeville, ID 83530 (tel: 208-983-1950).

GOSPEL-HUMP WILDERNESS

The Gospel-Hump Wilderness adjoins The Frank Church River of No Return Wilderness along the western end of the Salmon River Gorge, and takes up a chunk of country measuring roughly seventeen by twenty miles on the north side of the river. It's likely that fewer people know about this wilderness than any other in Idaho. Rugged, timbered terrain characterizes its landscape, with primitive trails and few high peaks. Trails follow densely timbered creek bottoms, or they traverse ridges near or above timberline—classic central Idaho canyon country.

The area hasn't always had an obscure reputation. On either side of the wilderness are two of the more famous mining districts of the 1860s: Florence on the west and Elk City on the east, twin boom towns that produced great quantities of gold. Florence, despite earnings of maybe $10 million in a few short years, isn't even a ghost town now. It's just a memory on the wind, with its buildings gone and forest reclaiming the townsite. Elk City survived as a mining town for a while longer because of some hard-rock mining, and supplemented its economy by supplying ranchers and other settlers along the Salmon River. Now it has some four hundred fifty residents with an economy based on tourism, outfitting, winter snowmobiling, and the supplying of people who own summer cabins in the area.

The road, U.S. Highway 14, is paved all the way along the South Fork of the Clearwater River to Elk City, a distance of approximately fifty miles, and thirty miles beyond there to Dixie. If you have a four-wheel drive vehicle, you can grind your way on down from Dixie to Mackay Bar on the Salmon River (Forest Service Road 222). Also in the area is Red River Hot Springs, privately owned, with a swimming pool and related facilities open to the public. Backroads run in every direction from Elk City, taking you through country littered with mining relics: old dredges, tumbledown buildings, strip mines. The 62-mile Gold Rush Loop Tour can be made with the help of a Forest Service brochure available at Nez Perce National Forest offices. It begins at State Highway 14, a few miles west of Elk City, and follows Forest

...nd 222 to Orogrande, Dixie and Red River Ranger
...k to Elk City; driving time is about 3 hours. Several
...ampgrounds are found along the route.

...orthwhile driving trip is the Magruder Road corridor,
... Idaho to the Bitterroot Valley in Montana, more or less
follo... ...ie of the old Nez Perce Indian routes. The road is very
rough, more than a hundred miles between services, and passable only
in the heart of summer, between early July and some time in September.
Its eastern end is on the road to Paradise Guard Station and the put-in
for Selway River floaters, out of Darby, Montana. To follow it from the
west, take the Red River Road (F.S. 222) to Red River Ranger Station.
The Magruder Road (F.S. 468) turns off there and makes its rough way
between the Selway-Bitterroot Wilderness on the north and the Frank
Church River of No Return Wilderness on the south. The views from
points along the road are extraordinary. One of the highlights is the
achingly beautiful Selway River racing through the forest. A solid day is
needed for the drive, but it's best to take two or more days, camping in
Forest Service campgrounds along the way.

As for access to Gospel-Hump Wilderness, there are trailheads on the
east, north and west sides. Getting to the east side requires the most driving. One trailhead is near the Dixie Guard Station, at Halfway House
Campground. You can reach the Crooked Creek trail from here and follow it north to the end of Forest Service Road 233 (which comes through
Orogrande). This puts you in the area of Wildhorse Lake and more trails
which go to the north and west. There's no trouble finding Forest
Service campgrounds here on the east side; all of them are small and
primitive—nice places.

Closer to Elk City, but reached by rough road, the Tenmile Creek Trail
(415) connects with routes that cross the wilderness. The trailhead is on
Forest Road 492 (take F.S. 1110 near the Leggett Creek Campground to
its junction with F.S. 492). If the road is too rough, another trailhead is
along the highway downriver three miles east of Meadow Creek
Campground; the trail crosses the river on a pack bridge near Wickiup
Creek. On the west side, the Wind River Trail is a popular starting point.
The trailhead is along the Salmon River, 24 gravel miles from U.S.
Highway 95 on Forest Road 1614 (turnoff is at the south end of Riggins
at a bridge over the Little Salmon River). The drive takes you on a scenic
excursion up The River of No Return. Twelve miles from the highway,
Spring Bar Campground has 17 sites. If you walk north from the Wind
River trailhead, you come out near Rocky Bluff Campground. A road
there, F.S. 444, "cherry-stems" its way into the wilderness, ending at
Square Mountain viewpoint; this is a four-wheel drive route.

Useful Names and Addresses

Gospel-Hump Wilderness and the Elk City area are in **Nez Perce National Forest**; head office at Route 2, Box 475, Grangeville, ID 83530 (tel: 208-983-1950); there is a District Office in Elk City. At this time there is no wilderness map available, but the "Nez Perce Visitor's Map" has a topographic index.

ANACONDA-PINTLER WILDERNESS

The Anaconda-Pintler Wilderness Area occupies 158,000 acres along the Continental Divide, where it forms a crest between the Big Hole and Bitterroot river valleys in Montana. The name Pintler comes from Charles Pintler, a trapper and settler who lived for much of his life on Pintler Creek. The mountains here form a true sierra, a ragged range carved by glaciers to form a narrow, serrated ridge lined by cirques, snowfields and alpine lakes. The actual crest of the Divide is a granitic intrusion, the eastern edge of the Idaho Batholith. The northeast part of the wilderness area consists of sedimentary rock of various ages dating from Precambrian to recent—remnants of the sediments that once overlay all of the great Batholith. The highest mountain in the area is West Goat Peak, which at 10,793 feet is a popular hiker's destination, along with Rainbow, Warren and Pintler peaks, all of which embrace alpine lakes. Whether or not you see mountain goats on Goat Mountain, chances are good that you'll see them somewhere above timberline, often merely as white furry spots high on nearly vertical cliffs.

A 45-mile high line trail traverses the wilderness along the Divide, dropping occasionally to a mountain lake, then climbing once again to the crest of the range. To get to the southwest end of the trail, drive up the East Fork Road from Sula, Montana, to Forest Road 725, which meets F.S. 1137 near the Continental Divide. The highline trail runs along the east side of the Divide for several miles before reaching the wilderness area. A few miles farther on 1137, F.S. 1245 turns left to Bender Ranger Station for another access. From the Big Hole Valley, turn off Highway 43 onto Forest Road 1251 to other roads; best to avoid confusion by picking up a Forest Map or Travel Plan before trying to navigate this country. The north end of the trail is accessible from Seymour Lake on Forest Road 934, off State Highway 274.

In addition, numerous trailheads located at the ends of forest roads from both sides are reached from Highway 43 in the Big Hole Valley, from the town of Sula in the Bitterroot Valley, or from a network of forest roads originating near Georgetown Lake on U.S. 10A. A Forest Service visitor's map is needed to find your way around on these roads.

Cross-country travel in the Anaconda-Pintler is moderately difficult. The steep angle-of-repose talus slopes which characterize the range can be very tiring and maybe hazardous because the rocks keep shifting under a hiker's weight.

Anaconda, a short distance to the northeast, is the closest town with full services. Hamilton is the largest community in the Bitterroot Valley. Gas, limited supplies and lodging can be found in Wisdom and Wise River. There are Forest Service campgrounds on nearly every access road and camping is permitted in undeveloped sites on most national forest land. Because black bears are common in the area, food should be locked in your vehicle at night, or if in the backcountry, hung from a tree.

Other Area Ideas

Humbug Spires is a stand of pinnacles south of Butte on Interstate 15, popular among nesting hawks and a pleasant place for walking. Take the Moose Creek Exit between Melrose and Divide, go left on a gravel road about four miles to a barricade. A footpath continues along the creek into the spires.

State Route 38 cuts across the Sapphire Mountains between the Bitterroot Valley and U.S. Highway 10A south of Philipsburg and the town of Porters Corners. It is good gravel road reaching its summit at Skalkaho Pass (7,260 feet), with a Forest Service campground east of the summit; it's closed in winter. Also, the high crests of the East and West Pioneer Mountains, between Wisdom and Dillon, hold a number of high lakes and alpine cirques accessible by trails, many of which have motorized vehicle prohibitions. A secondary road between the two ranges passes the Elkhorn Hot Springs Resort and several Forest Service campgrounds, providing access on both sides.

To the west of the Pioneers sprawls the valley of the Big Hole River (a Montana blue ribbon trout stream, by the way). If you want to see Montana at its best, and understand why people love the state so passionately, drive the Big Hole Valley on a sunny day in July. Gleaming with snow above green hayfields rise the Bitterroot Mountains on the Montana-Idaho border. The Montana side of the range is being considered for inclusion in the Federal Wilderness System. It's one of those undiscovered places which local hikers are reluctant to promote. Extensive trails lead to chains of lakes hidden in cirques below the Continental Divide. Usual access to these is via Miner Lake Campground, ten miles on F.S. 182 from the turnoff at the south end of Jackson, Montana; and via Twin Lakes Campground (or roads branching from this area) located 22 miles on F.S. 183 from the turnoff south of Wisdom.

Useful Names and Addresses

A visitor's map covering this entire area, indicating road closures and use restrictions, and an excellent map of the Anaconda-Pintler Wilderness Area, complete with contour lines, are available at area ranger stations including the **Bitterroot National Forest Headquarters**, 1801 North First St., Hamilton, MT 59840 (tel: 406-363-3131) and **Beaverhead-Deerlodge National Forests**, 420 Barrett St., Dillon, MT 59725 (tel: 406-683-3900). District offices are found in Wise River, MT 59762 (tel: 406-839-2201); Wisdom, MT 59761 (tel: 689-3243); Philipsburg, MT 59858 (tel: 859-3211); and Sula, MT 59871 (tel: 821-3201).

BIG HOLE NATIONAL BATTLEFIELD

During the summer of 1877, in their long, epic flight from the U.S. Army, Chief Joseph and 800 Nez Perce crossed from Idaho into Montana over Lolo Pass. They were headed for the buffalo plains, far from white settlements, where they hoped the army would not follow, and where they might be welcomed by their old friends, the Crows. General Howard and his forces, whom they had fought indecisively on the Clearwater River, were far behind, held back by the difficulties of the Lolo Trail. Having crossed the Divide, the Nez Perce breathed easier. Idaho was behind them, and the new country appeared friendly. Settlers in the Bitterroot Valley were happy to sell food and supplies to them. Chief Looking Glass, their overall leader, slowed the pace of travel. When they arrived at the Big Hole Valley, on August 7, Looking Glass called a halt. Tipi poles were cut, camp was made, and the Nez Perce rested without so much as posting sentries, a mistake which can be explained only by their confidence that trouble was behind them.

In fact it was only a few miles away, and coming fast, in the person of Colonel John Gibbon in command of the 7th U.S. Infantry in western Montana, with 163 army regulars and 34 volunteers. Early in the morning of August 9, 1877, Gibbon and his men waded across the Big Hole River and launched a surprise attack. For a brief time, they held the initiative, indiscriminately shooting and clubbing, and trying to burn the tipis. Then a group of Nez Perce, rallied by Chief White Bird, counterattacked, and in concert with a firing line of warriors on the other flank, drove the soldiers back across the river.

The Nez Perce followed, harrying the soldiers as they retreated through the willow flats and up to a wooded bench where they grouped behind hastily dug trenches and tried to defend themselves. Meanwhile, Chief Joseph, in charge of logistics, not war, hurried the women, children and older men in breaking camp, and herding the livestock out of the valley. All day, and partway into the night, the Nez Perce kept their attackers pinned down, terrified and desperate for water. Finally, deciding that the main camp had had enough of a head start, the Indians withdrew.

Behind them they left 29 dead soldiers and 40 wounded. Three of the 17 officers were dead and four wounded. The Nez Perce, however, lost between 60 and 90, many of whom were women and children killed in the first minutes of battle when the soldiers were inside the encampment. After this battle the tribe fled eastward, hoping for refuge with the Crow tribe. But the Crow could not help, and their only hope was a race to Canada, which they were fated to lose.

The area is now a National Battlefield, with bare tipi frames to show where the Nez Perce were camped and an interpretive trail through the woods at the site of the siege. The trenches are still visible as shallow depressions. Walking to the edge of the woods, you can sit at a viewpoint on the soldiers' side of the river and look across at the tipis. Below, the Big Hole River purls gently through the willows. In spring, you can hear Wilson's snipe as they fly their aerial mating dance, and red-winged blackbirds singing out their territorial claims. Sometimes a moose comes by. This is a sad piece of ground.

Some Useful Information About Big Hole

CAMPING: There is no camping at the Battlefield, but **Forest Service campgrounds** are nearby (May Creek, 10 miles west on Highway 43).
GENERAL INFORMATION: A visitor center has exhibits and a slide show. Basic services—gas, food and lodging—are in Wisdom; nearest large towns are Butte, Hamilton and Dillon, each roughly an hour away.
USEFUL NAMES AND ADDRESSES: The Battlefield is located on Montana Highway 43 between Wisdom, Montana, and Lost Trail Pass on the Idaho border. For more information and a brochure with a map, contact the Superintendent, **Big Hole National Battlefield**, P.O. Box 237, Wisdom, MT 59761.

HELLS CANYON NATIONAL RECREATION AREA

Occupying over 650,000 acres on both sides of the Snake River near Riggins, Idaho, this recreation area includes Hells Canyon and its neighboring mountain country. Within its boundaries are several distinct units. The 215,000-acre Hells Canyon Wilderness straddles both sides of the Wild and Scenic Snake River Corridor. On the east side, the wilderness is dominated by craggy Seven Devils Mountains; on the west, a more gently rolling topography of meadow and forest leads to steep canyon rims overlooking the river.

Hells Canyon is the deepest, narrowest gorge on the continent, cut by the Snake River through rough igneous rock to produce a V-shaped canyon quite different from the stepped appearance of the Grand Canyon. The river flows from south to north here, marking the boundary between Idaho and Oregon. Its Wild and Scenic status gives it protection from most development, but less than wilderness designation would. Thus motorized boats are permitted on the river. Another Wild river in the N.R.A., the Rapid River, is entirely unnavigable. It drains the Seven Devils, cascading eastward to the Salmon River, and the only way to see it is by hiking. The main reason it was protected was to preserve its value as a chinook salmon hatchery.

Boating in Hells Canyon requires a permit year-round (the reservation and river information phone number is 509-758-1957 in Clarkston, Washington).

Hikers not accustomed to the river canyons of Idaho should keep in mind that rattlesnakes, poison ivy and dry creekbeds complicate matters somewhat. Stay alert and plan ahead.

Access to the Seven Devils area is by a 17-mile road, F.S. 517 just south of Riggins on Highway 95. The road climbs over 5,000 feet to Windy Saddle and Seven Devils Campground (tents only, four sites, no potable water). Two miles to the north is Heavens Gate, a lookout from which the rim of Hells Canyon and the Wallowa Range in Oregon are visible. Several trails leave from Windy Saddle, leading into the lakes and peaks of the Seven Devils. Someone had fun naming them: He Devil, She Devil, The Ogre, Devils Throne, The Goblin, The Imp, The Tower of Babel and so forth. The lakes carry more pleasant names, such as Horse Heaven, with the occasional underworld reference, such as Purgatory Lake. Maybe that's where the mosquitoes are most fierce.

The other way in is via the town of Council on Highway 95 south of New Meadows. From Council, Forest Road 002 goes 28 miles northwest to Bear. From there it's a rough road (F.S. 105 and 112, not for low-slung cars or trailers) 13 miles to Black Lake at the edge of the wilderness. Forest Road 002 turns west at Bear, connecting at Cuprum with roads leading into Kinney Point and Sheep Rock overlooks (F.S. 106), which provide superb panoramas of the canyon and surrounding country. In the opposite direction, Forest Road 050 drops 2,500 feet down the Kleinschmidt Grade to the Hells Canyon Reservoir and a highway leading back to Cambridge, Idaho; turning north down the reservoir, this road comes to an end at Hells Canyon launch site, one mile below the Hells Canyon Dam.

A 60-mile scenic loop road north of Riggins takes you to other good overlook points and can be driven in half a day. Turn off Highway 95 nine miles north of Riggins on Forest Road 242 to Cow Creek Saddle, one of the viewpoints. From there, F.S. 420 goes south to a junction with F.S. 2060, leading to Saw Pit Saddle, and farther along yet, Low Saddle. Each of these points overlooks the river canyon. Beyond Low Saddle, on F.S. 1819, there are good views of the Seven Devils. The loop ends via F.S. 9903 at Riggins.

Useful Names and Addresses

Contact **Hells Canyon N.R.A. Headquarters** at 88401 Hwy 82, Enterprise, OR 97828 (tel: 541-426-4978); or the N.R.A. offices at P.O. Box 699, Clarkston, WA 99403 (tel: 509-758-0616; or 758-1957 for river information and reservations) and P.O. Box 832, Riggins, ID 83549 (tel: 208-628-3916). There is an information station, open in summer, on Highway 95 just south of Riggins. The **Salmon River Chamber of Commerce** is also located in Riggins.

LOLO TRAIL

In 1805 when Lewis and Clark met Cameahwait, the brother of Sacajawea, he advised them that to float down the Salmon, as they had hoped to do, was impossible. After sending a scouting party for a look, they reluctantly agreed, and set off north, back over the Bitterroots, toward what is today Missoula, Montana. With poor horses purchased from the Shoshones, they turned west over Lolo Pass and followed an ancient Indian trail across Idaho—the Lolo Trail. This was a route used for centuries by intermountain Indians on hunting trips to the bison plains. But it was not an easy route. Lewis and Clark had some of the roughest going of their entire journey here, arriving in the Lochsa Valley in September, with insufficient food and low morale resulting from the disappointment of their long detour. They needed a break at this point, and what they got was a trail described by Clark as "excessively bad and thickly strowed with falling timber and pine Spruce fur Hackmatack and Tamerack, Steep and Stoney our men and horses much fatigued."

It was over this same trail that the Nez Perce with Chief Joseph fled in their brilliant but futile attempt to reach the safety of Canada after all efforts at coexisting with encroaching white settlers had gone for naught (see page 209).

Today, the trail is closely followed by one hundred miles of dirt road built in the 1930s by the Civilian Conservation Corps. Although negotiable by normal vehicles and well marked by Forest Service signs, it can be a slow trip. The road starts a few miles west of Lolo Pass at the Powell Ranger Station, where you can get a map and information on current conditions. Two days should be allowed. The road stays high with fine views for roughly one hundred miles until it rejoins Highway 12 east of Kooskia. To reverse directions, begin at Kamiah and take Forest Road 100 through Glenwood to Bradford Bridge, where the trail officially starts. You can get a Clearwater National Forest map at the District Ranger Station in Glenwood (or at Powell), which has many of the historic campsites marked on it.

A short section of the trail can be driven from the east end. Start at the Powell Ranger Station as above, but drop back to the Lochsa Valley by either F.S. 565 and 566, or farther west, down F.S. 107.

NEZ PERCE NATIONAL HISTORICAL PARK

Nez Perce National Historical Park is unique among American national parks, in that this one consists of 38 separate sites, scattered throughout what was historically all Nez Perce land. This huge area covers central Idaho, the northeast corner of Oregon and the southeast corner of Washington—a rough circle about two hundred fifty miles in diameter. This area had been the home of the Nez Perce for thousands of years. When Lewis and Clark stumbled down from the Divide after their toilsome crossing at Lolo Pass, the Nez Perce welcomed them, fed them and gave them directions to the Pacific coast. The Indians might have been less gracious had they known of the changes that Lewis and Clark's expedition presaged and facilitated.

In the 1840s came waves of Oregon-bound settlers. These people had little interest in Nez Perce lands, which lay to the south of their route. Developments nearer the coast, however, prompted the governor of Washington Territory, Isaac Stevens, to push for the establishment of formal reservations. This was done, and in 1855 the Nez Perce received official recognition of their claim to 7,500,000 acres, less than half of their original territory. Among the treaty's provisions was a clause making it illegal for any non-Indian without official business or specific permission to enter the reservation.

Then came the gold rush. Elias Davidson Pierce, a prospector who knew he was trespassing, discovered placer deposits near Orofino, Idaho, in 1860. That this was Nez Perce land meant nothing to the hordes of gold-seekers who followed (including the governor of Idaho Territory in 1864, Caleb Lyon, who promised the Nez Perce that he would uphold the current treaty while scheming to acquire their land for himself). Miners formed groups traveling together for strength, and pushed ever farther into central Idaho. For the most part, the Nez Perce reluctantly allowed them passage. In some cases, when they learned that miners would pay outrageous prices for food and the hauling of equipment, the Indians happily made money from the situation.

Yet on the larger political scene, there rose strong external pressure to reduce the size of the reservation and throw it open to white settlement. Accordingly, this was done. In 1863, a new treaty, forming a reservation one-tenth the size of the original, was signed by one group of Nez Perce but not by others. Those who did not sign included Old Joseph and his people who lived in the Wallowa Mountains of northeast Oregon—far away from the new reservation. Joseph's refusal to participate in the agreement meant little to the Americans, who for obvious reasons wanted to see the treaty as a legally binding document. But to Joseph and the others who refused to give up their homeland, the treaty had neither legal nor moral validity. No one but themselves, they argued, could sign away their land.

Nonetheless, in 1867, President Andrew Johnson signed the new treaty into law and ordered the U.S. Army to forcibly move all Nez Perce onto the diminished reservation to make room for white settlers clamoring for the Indian lands. Events moved inexorably toward the tragic year 1877. Young Chief Joseph, the son of Old Joseph, was now political leader of the Wallowa band. For years he had tried to find a way to keep even a portion of their homeland. It was no use. Joseph finally gave in to an army ultimatum that they be on the reservation by June 14 or face military action. Early that month, the Wallowa band moved across the Snake River toward the reservation. Before they reached it, three young men, bitter over the expulsion of the tribe and the murder by a white settler of one of their fathers, and mindful no doubt of the numerous previous killings of Nez Perce by whites who had gone unpunished, went on a dawn raid, killing four settlers.

And so began the war. The Nez Perce felt there was no longer any possibility of going to the reservation. The first battle was fought at White Bird Canyon on June 17, when a small group of Indians under warrior chiefs Too-Hool-Hool-Zute, White Bird, Five-Wounds and others, defeated a superior number of hastily organized soldiers. Several indecisive skirmishes followed in the next few weeks, until in mid-July the group of about seven hundred fifty Nez Perce decided to leave the area entirely, hoping to find support and peace among their old friends the Flatheads in Montana. They found neither. The Flatheads were trying to maintain a delicate peace themselves, and influenced by Jesuit missionaries, were less than welcoming. And although the Nez Perce did not know it at the time, the army, with more than two thousand soldiers and the popular support of Washington settlers, was hot on their heels.

The Nez Perce survived a surprise attack at Big Hole, Montana (now a National Battlefield; see page 209). They fled through Yellowstone Park, causing much excitement among early tourists and nearly killing one man. Turning north from the Beartooth Range, they tried to escape to Canada, and they almost made it. The story of their journey is a celebrated, epic feat of courage and cunning. More than once they defeated or turned back forces larger and better equipped than theirs. Some 210 made it to Canada. When the remainder gave up, ragged and starving in snow and bitter cold, it was in the Bear Paw Mountains of Montana, just 42 miles from the border. It was there that Chief Joseph made his famous speech to Generals Miles and Howard of the U.S. Army:

> I am tired of fighting. Our chiefs are killed. Looking Glass is dead. Toohoolhoolzote is dead. The old men are all dead. It is the young men who say yes or no. He who led the young men is dead. It is cold and we have no blankets. The little children are freezing to death. My people, some of them, have run away to the hills, and have no blankets, no food; no one knows where they are—perhaps freezing to death. I want to have time to look for my children and see how many I can find. Maybe I shall find them among the dead. Hear me, my chiefs. I am tired; my heart is sick and sad. From where the sun now stands, I will fight no more forever.

The Nez Perce surrender was not the end of their difficulties. Although General Miles promised to send Joseph's people back to the Idaho reservation, they were instead packed into boxcars and flatboats and shipped south to Oklahoma Indian Territory, a journey and exile that many did not survive. The Indians, however, had friends in the East, due in no small regard to the great respect engendered for them by their fighting retreat and Joseph's much-publicized words of surrender. In 1885, the remnants of the Wallowa band were moved to the Colville Indian Reservation in northern Washington, where Joseph died, still an exile from his home, in 1904. At least he was spared yet another insult to the Nez Perce homeland. The General Allotment Act of 1887, ostensibly intended to assimilate native Americans more rapidly by giving them the incentives of land ownership, allocated a certain acreage for each Indian, to which he would be given individual title. The Nez Perce were allowed 90 acres per person, and the remainder of the land was sold to the public. In this way, another 70 percent of Nez Perce land passed from their ownership.

Today, the park includes memorable places involved in the flight of Chief Joseph, in addition to other significant locales connected with Nez Perce history. Musselshell Meadow is a place where camas lily bulbs, a staple food, were dug. Weippe Prairie was a gathering place and council ground; here Lewis and Clark first met the Nez Perce. Canoe Camp, on the Clearwater, is where the explorers built their canoes for the remainder of their journey to the Pacific. At White Bird Battlefield, visitors can follow a self-guided tour in their autos.

Useful Names and Addresses

A visitor center and park headquarters are located at Spalding, east of Lewiston. For more information, write to the Superintendent, **Nez Perce National Historical Park**, P.O. Box 93, Spalding, ID 83551.

RIVER RUNNING IN IDAHO

The most famous rivers in Idaho are the Middle Fork and main Salmon rivers, the Selway River and the Snake as it passes through Hells Canyon. These are all superb runs with well-deserved reputations for challenging whitewater and wilderness values. The problem lies in their popularity. Far more people want to float these rivers than regulating agencies feel the rivers can handle. While it is relatively easy to purchase a trip with a commercial outfitter (not at all a bad way to go, but beyond the means of some people), it takes extraordinary luck to win a permit for a private trip. You could try for years and never be allowed to set paddle in the Salmon. Persistent people manage nonetheless, by hook or crook, sometimes decidedly crook. Yet no one, no matter what sort of water he is looking for, should feel slighted in Idaho. There are thousands of miles of navigable streams in the region, few of which are subject to any regulation beyond state boating rules.

Idaho is full of whitewater runs for experienced boaters—whitewater as hard as anyone cares to paddle. Hot runs include the Bruneau and the Jarbidge in the southwest corner of the state, the Salmon just above Riggins, and various parts of the Payette drainage. None of these are regulated by permit. Some are seasonal, dependent on spring runoff for their most exciting conditions. Others, such as the formidable Deadwood run west of the Sawtooth Wilderness, are controlled by releases from hydroelectric dams. With all of them, it goes without saying that boaters should inquire locally about water levels and conditions.

Roads parallel several of these runs, making it easy to scout rapids in advance and to choose the stretch you want to float. Others are the material for adventures. Consider a few phrases from a guidebook published by the Idaho Department of Parks and Recreation. Speaking about runs in the Payette drainage, the guide warns, "Logjams. Difficult rock, remoteness, cold water. Extremely dangerous river," and "Dangerous rock gardens, waves, reversals, hydraulics, continuous white water, deadfalls. Injury or loss of life possible." In reference to the Bruneau River system, the guide adds terrestrial hazards: "Access is poor, rapids are tough, and portages are difficult. Rattlesnakes are common."

Gentler waters are equally common, with many stretches pleasant for open canoeing. You can easily spend an entire day drifting along quiet waters, never having to choose between rattlesnakes and life-threatening hydraulics, although even on these waters the guide finds potential for disaster: "Be sure to put in below *Lower* Mesa Falls (not Upper Mesa Falls)...." Omigosh, Martha, I think we made a mistake! That booklet is no longer in print, but information is available from the Idaho Department of Parks and Recreation, P.O. Box 83720, Boise, ID 83720. Local Forest Service ranger stations may also have copies.

Salmon River

The Shoshone Indians called the Salmon River the Tom-Agit-Pah, the "Big Fish River." It lives up to its name. Chinook salmon average about twenty pounds in the Salmon drainage; the largest ever taken here was 126 pounds. Renowned for their courage and fighting strength, steelhead trout, smaller than their cousins but big fish nonetheless, also swim these waters. Both fish are anadromous, meaning they grow to maturity in saltwater, but return to spawn in the freshwater streams where they hatched. Chinook migrate 800 miles from the Pacific Ocean up the Columbia and Snake rivers to the Salmon from March through June, actually spawning in July and August. Steelhead follow the same route during the fall and winter, laying eggs on their redds, or riverbed nests, in the spring. To see these runs is an important reason for visiting the rivers of central Idaho.

The chinook run has diminished terribly over the years; the fish are now at a small fraction of their former population. A number of factors are responsible. Overfishing has occurred both in rivers and at sea. Large hydroelectric dams create physical barriers. In addition, the turbulence in their outwash increases the amount of dissolved nitrogen in the water, an imbalance that kills fish. Small dams might actually divert an entire stream—"dewatering the streambed" according to official euphemism. Perhaps worst of all, damage to upstream spawning and rearing habitat decreases the number of young salmon produced each year. The Payette

National Forest reports that a third of the forest's streams are permanently blocked to the spawning runs of chinook and steelhead. Other streams are heavily sedimented by erosion from poor logging practices. The hooves of livestock destroy the banks and the streambed. Drainage from mine tailings carries poisonous chemicals—selenium, arsenic, mercury—into the water. Taken together, these influences add up to a devastating war on the life of freshwater streams and rivers. While awareness of these problems has risen recently, and new forestry techniques are intended to halt the decline, it seems clear that the awesome salmon runs of a century ago have been relegated to history.

The Salmon River system drains 14,000 square miles of central and eastern Idaho, receiving snowmelt from the Lemhi, Sawtooth, Clearwater and Bitterroot mountains. The Gorge of the Main Salmon measures more than a mile deep for a length of 180 miles. The entire river flows for 425 miles, first north, then west through its famous canyon, then north again. During this journey, it drops from over 8,000 feet in elevation at its headwaters to 905 feet where it joins the Snake River on the Oregon state border.

In the canyon, the Salmon is known as The River of No Return, the infamous one-way route for prospectors trying to cross Idaho. It was one way to the gold fields or one way to oblivion; for some it didn't matter which. There was no coming back, at least not up the river. The country was too rugged, as Lewis and Clark learned in 1805. It was in 1832 that the first white men on record floated the river. Four employees of the Hudson's Bay Company set out to negotiate the canyon with a load of furs. Two men and the cargo were lost. The other two dragged themselves into Fort Nez Perce a month later, half dead. Again, in 1862, a small group of prospectors, discouraged by the mobs who had already staked out most of the placer claims around Florence, tried to follow the river upstream, and in that way reach the Colorado gold fields. Near the junction with the South Fork of the Salmon, they saw a log raft coming down toward them. Two nearly naked, starving men clung to the makeshift craft, entirely unimpressed at just having become the first persons on record ever to successfully raft the Salmon Gorge. Today, no one even knows who they were.

In the 1890s, Henry Guleke and his partner David Sanderland built reputations on their ability to run flatboats through the canyon, loaded with supplies for gold miners and settlers along the river. New boats were built, of planks, for each trip—scows over thirty-five feet in length with two long sweep oars, one mounted at each end. Two boatmen stood on a platform at the center of the scow, each man working a sweep, not rowing with or against the current but rather across it, maneuvering to stay in the fastest, deepest water. At the end of the trip, the boats were dismantled and sold to become miners' shacks and water flumes.

Even now, in country where major river valleys normally provide the easiest routes for highways and railroads, the canyon of the Salmon remains wild. It should stay that way, having been designated as a National Wild and Scenic River, and surrounded as it is by The River of No Return Wilderness.

Yet the Salmon is hardly an unknown river. Since the boom in the popularity of river running, which began in the 1970s, it has become one of the most popular whitewater wilderness runs in the country. The difficulties of running its rapids successfully have become almost negligible compared with the odds against winning permission to try. The wilderness run begins at Corn Creek Campground, 46 miles west of North Fork, Idaho, and ends 80 miles later at Vinegar Creek upstream of Riggins, Idaho. The trip takes four to six days. The river gradient averages twelve feet per mile with boulder-bed rapids alternating with calm stretches. Shuttle distance is 385 miles on paved and gravel roads. With no dams moderating the flow, water levels fluctuate a great deal, depending on snowfall and the rate of spring runoff. Conditions in June can be deadly. The permit season runs from June 20 until September 7, with applications accepted between December 1 and January 31 each year by the North Fork Ranger District, Salmon National Forest, P.O. Box 180, North Fork, ID 83466 (tel: 208-865-2383). After the lottery, dates are assigned and winners have until March 15 to confirm their intention of making the trip. After that, all non-confirmed or unfilled dates are given away on a first-come, first-served basis. Cancellation rates are high enough to make it worth trying.

Outside the peak season, no permits are required, but early in the year, high water can be prohibitive, while late in the season, days are short and cold. The only guaranteed way of getting on the river is by booking a space on a commercial trip run by professional guides. These companies are allotted a certain number of user days each season by the Forest Service and are therefore independent of the lottery system imposed on private boaters. However, they get the same number of launches per day as private boaters (four) and are allowed the same group size (30). To be sure, floating any wild river in your own boat with a group of selected friends, traveling at a pace dictated only by your whims, is a satisfying way to travel—to my way of thinking, the best way. On the other hand, commercial trips have their own advantages. With very few exceptions, the companies involved in this business are conscientious and highly competent. They run comfortable trips. The food is good, the boatmen are interesting people eager to share their love of their rivers, and they do all the work. A commercial trip is a holiday, while a private trip is an exercise in self-reliance.

Upper Salmon

The Upper Salmon, where it flows through the Sawtooth National Recreation Area, drops an average of 15 feet to the mile. An 18-mile stretch from the Highway 75 bridge to Basin Creek is a moderately challenging run. Just below is a tougher section of river with some Class IV water, which ends at Sunbeam Dam. Below the dam, 15 more miles of Class IV whitewater, to Torreys through Warm Springs Gorge, can be deadly in high flows. The water level at the Sunbeam Dam gauging station varies from 12 feet during spring flood to less than one foot in the fall. Anything above six feet is considered hazardous. Below Torreys, the river mellows into a Class II canoeing river for over one hundred miles to North Fork. Highway 75 parallels the entire stretch from Stanley. Below North Fork is more Class III and IV water, runnable without a permit as far as Corn Creek, where the parallel road ends.

Lower Salmon

Lower on the Salmon, from Spring Bar through Riggins and on to White Bird, the road follows the river. Some of this stretch is challenging whitewater, while other parts, especially at low water, is pleasant for canoes. No permits are required. A booklet with maps is available from B.L.M., Resource Area Headquarters, Route 3, Box 181, Cottonwood, ID 83522; cost is $5.

Middle Fork of the Salmon

The Middle Fork of the Salmon flows northeast for 104 miles from the confluence of Marsh and Bear Valley creeks to the Main Salmon, which it joins just upstream from Corn Creek. Like the Main Salmon, this is a pool and drop river, meaning calm stretches alternate with rapids roaring through boulder beds. Throughout its length, the Middle Fork is a wilderness river; jet boats are not allowed here, as they are on the Main Salmon. Its canyon is deep, beginning in the cool shade of a spruce-fir forest at 6,400-feet elevation, and dropping into dry, warm country supporting ponderosa pine, mountain mahogany, bitterbrush and other plants associated more with the mountains of Arizona than Idaho.

The first third of the trip is through deep timber, shady and cool, with many side streams and hot springs. The river drops rapidly through technical whitewater with much variety. To start things off, First Bend Rapids is very technical; wrapping a raft is a serious concern for boaters still stiff from long drives (*wrapping*, in boating parlance, results when a raft collides sideways with a rock and the current, filling the raft, wraps it tightly, sometimes permanently, against the upstream side of the boulder). With hardly a chance to get the feel of the oars, boatmen launch directly into a gnarly raft-eater. Powerhouse Rapids, named for an old generating station located on the banks, is a long rocky S-turn. Ramshorn is short and spectacular, the entire river piling into a rock wall. Tappen Falls is one of the more difficult sections, a matter of hitting a chute correctly—a tricky lineup because of complex eddies upstream. A sharp rock on the left, followed by a wrap rock below, provide penalties for failure and incentives for success.

The middle third of the river traverses drier country, rattlesnake country with sage and prickly pear cactus. Here the temperature can get hot, a welcome feeling on a trip that can be cold due to icy water and the deep, shady canyon. The last third is the gorge; few campsites and fast current, but not difficult whitewater. The Bighorn Crags stand high and out of sight to the east; some boaters stretch their legs on the steep trail to them via Waterfall Creek, 6,000 feet of vertical rise.

The list of animals seen in the canyon make up a compendium of Rocky Mountain wildlife: elk, mule deer, bighorn sheep, mountain goat, cougar and black bear are the large animals. Coyote, bobcat, lynx, marten, fox, porcupine, badger, beaver, mink, otter, weasel, skunk, muskrat and dozens of smaller mammals mix with a great variety of birds. In Forest Service lingo, rattlesnakes are "prominent," which should serve as a word of caution.

The river system itself is a critical fish habitat. Nearly a third of all the salmon entering the Salmon River from the Snake eventually find their way to spawning grounds in the Middle Fork drainage. This speaks volumes about the still-undamaged nature of the spawning streams, most of which lie protected from logging damage in The River of No Return Wilderness. Besides chinook, steelhead, Dolly Varden and rainbow trout can be found.

The permit system for the Middle Fork is similar to that used on the main Salmon. The heavy-use season runs from June 1 to September 3, with applications for each season due between December 1 and January 31 of the preceding winter. Starting August 1 permits are given out for the rest of the year on a first-come, first-serve basis. The most desired dates are the six weeks from July to mid-August, when the river is at its optimum for floating. During June, the river can be too high to run, or snow can block access roads, forcing boaters to charter a plane for access. In August, the reverse situation can prevail, with levels so low that it becomes necessary to fly beyond the Dagger Falls roadhead to where the river has sufficient flow. This is reflected in Forest Service figures for applications. Making an application is a bit like playing roulette. The odds of getting a permit for June 10 are better than for July 10, but this must be weighed against the possibility of early water flows being too high to make the trip at all. The Forest Service doesn't give out rainchecks.

Information, a river map ($4) and applications are available from the Middle Fork Ranger District, Challis National Forest, Challis, ID 83226. The river information phone number is 208-879-5204.

Selway River

The Selway ranks as one of the finest, most challenging wilderness rivers in America. Falling at a rate of 28 feet per mile, the clear, snowmelt waters cut a 47-mile path through the heart of the Selway-Bitterroot Wilderness. The run is practically a continuous boulder-bed rapid, with numerous stretches rated Class IV and V. Quiet stretches, because they are so rare, become climactic moments of the trip.

The launching point is the Paradise Guard Station on the border of the wilderness area, with take-out at Selway Falls on the opposite border. While most boaters take four days, there is no restriction on the length of a trip, making it possible to combine days on the river with some time hiking. Access to Paradise Falls is via 67 miles of gravel road from Darby, Montana, or from the west through Elk City, Idaho. Both roads are rough. Snow can keep the Darby route closed until mid-June, while the western road might not be passable until mid-July. At the other end, a 20-mile road from Lowell, Idaho, on U.S. Highway 12, ends at the take-out at Selway Falls. The shuttle distance between the two points is 245 miles each way, via Darby and Lolo Pass.

Permits are required for the Selway May 15 through July 31. Only one launch is permitted per day during the permit season. Sixteen dates are reserved for commercial outfitters, leaving 62 for private trips, each with a maximum of 16 persons. Private permits are given to winners of a random draw. Applications for the draw can be obtained starting October 1 from the West Fork Ranger Station, 6735 West Fork Rd., Darby, MT 59829 (tel: 406-821-3269). The District Ranger will accept completed applications, if accompanied by a $6 *nonrefundable* application fee, from December 1 through January 31, after which the draw will be made and the winners notified.

Lochsa River

The Lochsa, which is a Flathead Indian word for "rough water," rises along the Bitterroot Divide on the border between Montana and Idaho, and drains westward for about one hundred miles to its junction with the Selway at Lowell. Together, the two rivers form the Middle Fork of the Clearwater. U.S. Highway 12 parallels the entire Lochsa River, making it easy to scout and choose a section to run. This is a solid Class IV river edging to Class V with big drops and holes on long rapids with few eddies for respite—serious business at high water. Rapids have names that are often either physically or emotionally descriptive: Killer Fang, Bloody Mary, Grim Reaper, Triple Hole, Eye Opener, House Rock, Keep Moving, Pipeline, and (oh no) Termination. Runs begin at the Powell Ranger Station, with continuous whitewater beginning about twenty miles downstream at Highway 12 milepost 140. Of two popular runs, the upper one begins at milepost 136 and ends ten miles farther at 126; the lower one starts five miles downstream at milepost 121, taking out at 110.5. No permits are required. The boating season runs from May to early July, after which the water level drops too low for any boats but kayaks.

Some Lochsa boaters consider a water level of 14,000 cubic feet per second as the prudent maximum for some stretches. Other wahoos wouldn't recognize prudence if it hit them over the head with a paddle (see Payette section below). Four thousand c.f.s. is the minimum level for rafts. Water flow information and a Lochsa whitewater brochure is available from the Lochsa Ranger District, Clearwater National Forest, Kooskia, ID 83539 (tel: 208-926-4275).

Other Runs

North Fork of the Clearwater

The North Fork run puts in at Orogrande Creek and takes out after 30 miles at the Aquarius Campground. It can be done as a two-day run, or less, because the road parallels the river all the way. Rapids are rated Class IV, about the same as the Lochsa but slightly easier. Portages may be necessary at low water levels. The usual season is late June through July, with access via gravel roads from Pierce, Idaho.

Payette River—North, South and Middle

The Payette watershed lies to the north and east of Boise, Idaho, providing in its three main forks some of the hottest kayak runs in the country in sequence with quiet canoe waters. The North Fork flows through a long valley, past McCall and through the Cascade Reservoir. This is a pleasant, broad canoe river until it crosses under the Cabarton Bridge. Then for ten miles, to Smiths Ferry, it hurries along with Class III rapids and a blind waterfall. Below Smiths Ferry, it becomes a dangerous river.

Its 15 astonishing miles to the town of Banks are rated Class V and above. The river drops 1,700 feet in that distance, averaging more than 110 feet per mile in a continuous flume of white water moving at a scary speed through immense constriction waves and souse holes. During spring high water, if you didn't actually see kayakers in the water (look fast and have faith that the helmet you see is in fact attached to a person in a kayak somewhere in that spray), it would never occur to you that the river is navigable. Boating that water seems akin to a bicyclist challenging semi-trucks on the Ventura Freeway to a game of chicken. The view from the road, however, is excellent. Spectating here is one of the best bargains to be had in sport.

The Middle Fork, above Crouch, provides a 13-mile quiet water canoe run, which takes an easy day. The South Fork is another matter entirely. Coming out of the Sawtooth Wilderness, it has two stretches that can kill and have done so. From Deadwood Campground to the Alder Creek bridge is 21 miles of Class IV water in a gorgeous canyon, including Big Falls, blind from above and not to be run. When I saw it, an orange banner in a tree upriver warned that the falls were near, but don't rely on that. From the Alder Creek bridge to the Deer Creek bridge, the river mellows somewhat, but below there, to Banks, it again pushes Class V. All this can be scouted from the highway. Below Banks, on the Main Payette, 24 miles of Class III river is a popular training area.

Maps and Books

Maps for river runners are available from Leslie A. Jones, 3451 N. River Rd., Midway, UT 84049 (tel: 801-654-2156). His list includes both forks of the Salmon, the Snake through Hells Canyon, the Lochsa, the Clearwater and the Selway.

Recommended books: *Idaho—The Whitewater State: A Guidebook* by Grant Amaral, Watershed Books, Box 721, Boise, ID 83701; *Idaho Whitewater* by Greg Moore and Don McClaran, P.O. Box 1794, McCall, ID 83638.

CHAPTER FIVE

The International Border Region

FROM THE MIDDLE of Montana all the way to the northern part of Alberta, the Rocky Mountains present a magnificent, unified rampart facing the eastern plains. A traveler can drive north or south, parallel to this mountain wall, taking several comfortable days to do the trip. The roads roll along on foothills and prairie, crossing frequent rivers which drain the high, remote valleys. This is ranching country, a land of long views across undulant grasslands cut sharply by rivers; the land of Charles Russell paintings, of dry summers and windy winters; the high plains at their best. Settlements occur infrequently. Unlike the Front Range in Colorado, the base of the Northern Rockies has not yet given birth to a megalopolis. Narrow, lightly traveled roads drop into sheltered valleys occupied by small ranch supply towns, follow main streets for a few blocks in the shade of big cottonwood trees, and then climb back onto the plains. Always visible to the west, demanding attention, stand the mountains.

Nearly all of these eastward-draining river valleys are served by ranch or forest roads, which get narrower and bumpier and more interesting as they get higher. They finally end along small streams under fragrant conifers at trailheads leading to the glaciers and snowfields above. Fishing streams, little lakes, reservoirs, Forest Service campgrounds and informal sites make this an ideal country for people inclined to ramble through the mountains. But even though hordes of vacationers crowd the main highways from Yellowstone to Glacier via Great Falls, few stop

Kinnerly Peak is typical of Glacier National Park's layered sedimentary mountains.

to consider what lies between. The classic and only too common family vacation involves marathon drives from one high point to the next. People leave Yellowstone in the early light of dawn, stoked up for the drive with truck-stop coffee, their sleepy kids in the backseat, and pitch their camp that night in Glacier. Ah, the Rockies.

What they've driven so hurriedly past is a banquet of wild country, laced with roads and campgrounds, highlighted by large chunks of wilderness. From Helena looking north, strung on the Divide like the jewelry of a Persian queen, are the Scapegoat, the Bob Marshall and the

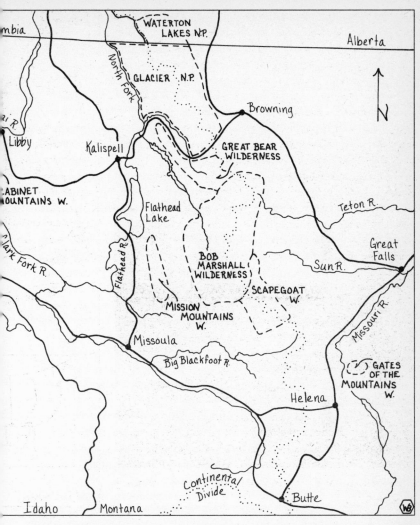

Great Bear wilderness areas, all of them huge, contiguous and for the most part intact. Not a single road crosses the range between Lincoln and Glacier Park, the south boundary of which is formed by U.S. Highway 2. The only other crossing, located inside the park, is the Going-to-the-Sun Highway, one of the world's loveliest alpine roads. Across the border, on the east side of the Continental Divide, lies Waterton Lakes National Park, but there is not another highway crossing for 50 miles north to Crowsnest Pass.

Nor is that all. Looking westward over the rampart, we see a major break in the mountains, the Flathead Valley with its sidekick the Swan Valley, both running north-south and embracing the extremely rugged Mission Range. Beyond the Flathead River extends mile upon mile of low, rolling mountain country, heavily timbered, well-watered, drained by big rivers and home to numerous small communities all the way to northwestern Idaho. Near Libby, Montana, the Cabinet Mountains rise well above timberline and support several glaciers. Otherwise, the western part of this region is less a place for mountaineers than for fishermen, campers, hikers and naturalists. Splendid country, all of it, loaded with hidden pleasures and untrampled corners.

Glaciers, more than any other single factor, explain the topography of the border region as we see it today. Everywhere, moving ice has left its mark. During the last ice age, which ended only 10,000 years ago, an immense continental ice cap, as much as 4,000 feet thick, pushed well into Montana, filling valleys, gouging at their sides and changing their shapes. At the same time, smaller alpine glaciers grew in the mountains and flowed down side valleys to join the great ice sheet. The glaciers created two very different sorts of landscapes. In the valleys, features were softened as the ice ground over them, removing or abrading sharp ridges and tight corners; the valleys themselves were left broadened in the characteristic glacial U-shape. In the surrounding mountains, however, instead of flowing over the crests, the ice moved away from the heights. So rather than smooth the landscape, these glaciers sharpened it, plucking rock from high basins, creating steep intervening walls and knife-edge ridges called arêtes.

Most of the ice has disappeared, due to the relatively warmer and drier modern climate. The remaining glaciers are in retreat, with significant shrinkage having occurred in just the last 50 years. It is worth pointing out that the word *retreat* is somewhat misleading when applied to glaciers. The ice does not actually move in reverse, like some great beast backing into its den. Even as it melts, it continues to flow downhill, but where the rate of melting is faster than the rate of flow, the bottom edge of the ice gradually moves uphill as the glacier shortens. Through all of this, material torn loose by the ice, anything from rock dust to immense boulders, is carried along and eventually deposited. These materials form a variety of post-glacial landforms. Large boulders left scattered across valley bottoms are called glacial erratics; nothing else can explain their presence. Drumlins, eskers and moraines are piles of rounded stones and gravel—glacial till—left by various patterns of melting. Potholes occur when a remnant chunk of ice buried in the till, a sort of terrestrial iceberg, melts and forms a hollow.

Of these landforms, mountain travelers owe most thanks to moraines and potholes, because both create lakes. The classic alpine lake lies impounded by a terminal moraine, a dam of gravel and rocks deposited at the foot of a glacier during a time when it was neither retreating nor expanding. The glacier carved steep walls on three sides and used the material for a dam on the fourth side. Sitting on the shore of such a lake as it sparkles in the summer sun beneath magnificent mountain peaks, it is sometimes hard to fathom such a degree of consideration for our aesthetic values on the part of a supposedly impersonal natural force.

The same process carved alpine cirques throughout the Rocky Mountains in the time of the ice age, but only in the north, within about a hundred miles of the border, were the mountain glaciers met by the larger ice sheet to create the broad intervening valleys so characteristic of the northern and Canadian Rockies.

Another factor travelers will quickly notice in this region is the relatively low elevation of both mountain peaks and valley bottoms. Compared to altitudes in Colorado, and even northern Wyoming, the highest peaks in Glacier National Park are not very high at all. In fact, if Going-to-the-Sun Mountain, one of Glacier's highest peaks, were located in the town of Silverton, Colorado, its summit would be scarcely 300 feet above the streets. Of course, this has no impact on the quality of the mountains. Altitude is a matter of relativity. The only figure that has any meaning is the relief of a range, or the distance from valley bottom to mountain summit, and in this regard the northern Rockies excel. Valley elevations along the border range in the neighborhood of 2,000 to 4,000 feet, while neighboring summits brush the sky at between 8,000 and 10,000 feet.

These low altitudes, coupled with the region's relative proximity to the Pacific coast, make for a milder, wetter climate than is found farther south. No high ranges block the flow of moist ocean air, which pours in most heavily during late fall, winter and spring. Accordingly, the dominant forest type is montane, similar to that of the Pacific Northwest. Dependent on generous rainfall, it occurs on western slopes and in areas open to the coastal weather. Western larch, hemlock, western red cedar, Douglas fir and western white pine grow to great size in these forests if permitted by nature and loggers to do so. Lower branches dip with hanging lichen, a favorite food of the woodland caribou which, although rare, still survive at the south end of the Purcell and Selkirk mountains. On the forest floor, vibrant green moss grows in luxuriant carpets around ferns and berry bushes.

These forests are a berry-picker's paradise. Huckleberries, strawberries, raspberries, service berries, thimbleberries, currants and holly grapes keep people, birds and bears busy in late summer and fall. The region has also developed a reputation as fertile ground for mushroom collecting. In particularly good years, residents claim to have gathered common mushrooms by the truckload, drying them and storing them in canning jars. For any mushroom collector, the hazard exists of picking a poisonous variety, and for that reason it's best to stick to the most easily identified types—the shaggy mane, true morels and coral mushrooms—and to ask advice of someone with experience.

The eastern slope of the Rockies, being in its own rain shadow, is much drier than most of the interior. Instead of rain forest, there are great expanses of quaking aspen trees reminiscent of Colorado's high country. In the dry Flathead Valley, sage brush and ponderosa pine thrive in the company of drought-resistant species. At higher elevations, alpine plants take over: mountain hemlock, alpine larch, white-bark pine, subalpine fir, alder, dwarf birch and a profusion of flowering herbs. Perhaps the best-known regional flower is bear-grass, a raceme of creamy white flowers on a slender stalk two or three feet tall—not limited to this area, but certainly characteristic of it.

History

Before the arrival of Europeans, the Kalispell, Flathead and Kootenai Indians lived south of the border and west of the Divide. Flatheads did not flatten the heads of their infants; perhaps this title refers to the shape of their heads being naturally less pointy than their neighbors' (in the neighbors' opinions at least). Lewis and Clark called them the Ootlashoots. More numerous were their friends, the Kootenais, who lived in what is now northern Idaho, northwestern Montana and southeastern British Columbia. The Kootenais were a powerful tribe, friends of the Flatheads but archrivals of the Blackfeet. They have long stirred the interest of anthropologists by the design of their bark canoes, a design closer to Siberian native craft than anything in North America. *Kootenai* comes from the Indian word for deer robes, a reference to their skill as tanners.

Lewis and Clark skirted the edge of this region without penetrating it, but their journey spurred the North West Company in Canada to send David Thompson on an exploration of the Columbia River system (see page 270), during which he canoed the rough passage down the Kootenay River into northern Montana and Idaho. Thompson was followed by missionaries (notably the Jesuit Father DeSmet, whose name appears all across the region), military men, Oregon-bound settlers, gold-seekers and loggers, but no developments of real size occurred before the arrival of the Great Northern Railroad in the 1890s. With it came the demand for lumber and transport for heavy machinery and mineral ores, and, of course, a wave of settlers. Logging became the biggest business, as timber kings who had depleted forests around the Great Lakes turned with hungry eyes toward the vast, well-watered stands of western white pine in the valleys west of the Continental Divide.

Logging practices in those years were pure exploitation with little regard for regeneration and other forest values. To make things worse, slash, left lying indiscriminately in the wake of the loggers, bred legendary fires which destroyed vast areas of forest. In 1910 alone, 700,000 acres went up in flames, killing at least 61 fire fighters.

By the time the Great Depression reached its nadir in the early '30s, the forests in the region had been depleted and burned, adding to the economic stagnation of both Canada and the United States. In the U.S., a Depression works program, the Civilian Conservation Corps, provided jobs and made the first headway toward replanting trees. It was during this time that many of the trails and roads which travelers use today were built. In the national parks of the United States, you can see their work in numerous visitor centers, bridges and interpretive displays. They specialized in heavy stone-and-timber construction, certainly some of the most appropriate public architecture ever conceived.

Butte

Butte, Montana, is an instructive place for those interested in history to spend half a day. Museums include the Copper King Mansion and Gallery at 219 W. Granite Street (drive downtown up the hill; Granite is a cross-street near the upper end) and the World Museum of Mining on West Park Street. From the immediate area have come more than 17 billion pounds of copper. The city boomed from the 1870s, reaching its peak in the 1920s with a population of well over 100,000. From that time on, it has witnessed a steady decline, as international competition and falling demand lowered the price of copper worldwide. The immense multihued Berkeley Pit stands silent now; most visitors do too, when they first see this man-made gulf, which seems to rival the Grand Canyon in size. Recently, the last smelter shut down its fires. Butte's population, now a bare 35,000, hangs on in the shadows of huge brick mansions and impressive granite municipal buildings, hoping for a rise in copper prices or for some other providence to halt the city's slide toward becoming a ghost town. Virtually everywhere one travels in the

Rockies, one sees small versions of Butte: towns and settlements with economies based on a single, primary resource which eventually played out, or lost its value.

Useful Names and Addresses

Butte Chamber of Commerce, 2950 Harrison Ave., Butte, MT 59701.

TRAVELING BETWEEN YELLOWSTONE AND GLACIER PARKS

The major route between these two extremely popular places is through Helena and Great Falls. From Yellowstone, drive north to Interstate 94, and follow it west to U.S. Highway 287 at Three Forks. At Helena, take Interstate 15 through Great Falls to Shelby, then turn west on U.S. 2 through Browning to Glacier Park. This can be done in a day, but I strongly recommend against it. It is fast because it follows broad valleys all the way, and although I think all of Montana is beautiful to drive through, some parts are nicer than others. Besides, I favor those routes which by their nature encourage a go-slow pace. At the very least, take two days for the trip, and choose one of these alternate routes.

Highway 89

U.S. Highway 89 is Yellowstone's north entrance road. From Livingston, it follows the lovely Shields River Valley past the Crazy Mountains (named for the meandering, confusing nature of their drainage patterns) and over the Little Belt Mountains south of Great Falls. The Little Belts, in the area of Kings Hill Pass (7,393 feet) are in Lewis and Clark National Forest. If you're looking for a camping spot halfway between the parks, this is the spot. Several Forest Service campgrounds are located along the highway, and numerous backroads provide access to undeveloped sites in the woods.

The next day, instead of joining Interstate 15 at Great Falls, stay on U.S. 89 through Choteau to Browning. It's a nice drive even without side trips; I've driven it at the height of summer and seen hardly anyone else on it. Options along the way include a variety of roads that climb into the mountains, dead-ending at lakes, trailheads and campgrounds. From Augusta, drive west past Nilan Reservoir; eventually the road becomes Forest Road 235. On the forest boundary it splits, the north branch (F.S. 233) heading to Gibson Reservoir on the Sun River and two

Swiftcurrent Lake lies at the base of Mount Wilbur in Glacier National Park.

campgrounds. The south branch (F.S. 235) follows Ford Creek over a low divide to Wood Creek Canyon, ending at an important Bob Marshall Wilderness trailhead; five campgrounds are in the area.

North of Choteau is another option. Five miles out of town, U.S. 89 turns sharply right; at that corner, a secondary road heads west along the Teton River past the Eureka Reservoir, headed for the Teton Pass Ski Area. In about twenty miles, where the pavement ends, F.S. 109 cuts off to the south, ending near a nice set of waterfalls and trailheads to the Bob Marshall. If you stay on F.S. 144 instead, you will reach Cave Mountain Campground in about five miles; a trail from the campground leads up the Middle Fork of the Teton River to "The Bob."

Finally, when you get to Browning, avoid the impulse to shoot straight on to Saint Mary at the heart of Glacier Park. Instead, drive to East Glacier and turn north on Montana 49 to the Two Medicine Lakes. In the days of train travel, East Glacier was one of the two main entry points for the park. No more. Now it's a relatively quiet corner with a fine old hotel. Two Medicine Lakes, certainly the scenic rival of anything in the northern Rockies, enjoys splendid isolation. Go here for quiet.

Highway 287 and Swan Valley

This route begins at Yellowstone's west entrance and follows the Madison River to Three Forks. From West Yellowstone, U.S. Highway 287 traces the shoreline of Hebgen Lake, past the great landslide of 1959 (see page 173) and through some of the finest ranch scenery in Montana. Side trips to Virginia City and Nevada City (described in the same section as the Hebgen earthquake) are well worth your time. U.S. 287 continues along the base of the Tobacco Root Mountains to the Jefferson River and from there to Three Forks; all of this, so far, a fine scenic drive. North of Townsend is the Canyon Ferry Lake, with numerous campgrounds and swimming for those hot days; most facilities are at the north end, along U.S. 284, 23 miles beyond Townsend.

At Helena, abandon U.S. 287 for U.S. 12 over MacDonald Pass; go to Avon, and turn on Montana 141. The road once again traverses isolated ranch country; you can see why people put up with a hard way of life to live in such a place. Montana 141 ends at Montana 200, where the route turns west for 24 miles to the Swan Valley Road (Montana 83). From here, almost all the way to Glacier, the road is surrounded by national forest lands. Campgrounds are frequent, as are side roads. Numerous opportunities exist for pitching a camp along the Swan River once you get north of Seeley Lake. Only a person driven by obsession could pass up the chance to stop and take at least a short walk through the forest along a lakeshore or on the river's gravel banks.

Montana 83 ends in the Flathead Valley near Kalispell. To get to Glacier Park at the west entrance, avoid Kalispell and follow signs for the park and Hungry Horse. If by this time you're keen to stay on backroads, and West Glacier seems a bit crowded, head directly up the North Fork of the Flathead toward Polebridge and beyond. This corner of the park is the isolation equivalent of Two Medicine Lakes on the other side: not deserted by any means, but not a circus either.

Useful Names and Addresses

The state of Montana publishes an information brochure on events and places of interest to travelers; a recreation map, which lists all government-operated campgrounds in the state, whatever the agency may be; and a Montana Accommodations Guide, including commercially operated campgrounds, motels and other lodging. Contact **Travel Montana**, Department of Commerce, P.O. Box 200533, Helena, MT 59620 (tel: 406-⸱⸱⸱-2654; outside Montana, 800-847-4868).

⸱⸱⸱al forest and national park addresses are listed at appropriate ⸱he text.

BORDER CROSSING INFORMATION

STATION SCHEDULES

CROSSING	HWY:	CANADA/U.S. HOURS	
ALBERTA:			
Wild Horse	41/232	8AM to 5PM	Oct. 1 to May 14
		8AM to 9PM	May 15 to Sept. 30
Sweetgrass/ Coutts	4/15	24 hours	all year
Del Bonita	62/483	9AM to 6PM	Sept. 16 to May 31
		8AM to 9PM	June 1 to Sept. 15
Piegan/ Carway	2/89	9AM to 6PM	Nov. 1 to May 15
		7AM to 11PM	May 16 to Oct. 31
Chief Mountain	6/17	9AM to 6PM	May 24 to May 31
		7AM to 10PM	June 1 to Sept. 15
		closed	Sept. 16 to May 14
BRITISH COLUMBIA:			
Flathead	West side of Glacier N.P.	9AM to 5PM	June 1 to Oct. 31
Roosville	93/93	24 hours	all year
Kingsgate	95/95	24 hours	all year
Rykerts	21/1	8AM to 12AM	Nov. 1 to Apr. 30
		7AM to 11PM	May 1 to Oct. 31
Nelway	6/31	8AM to 12AM	all year
Waneta	22A/251	9AM to 5PM	all year

Canadian and American citizens may cross the border without visas. Identification should be carried, in the form of a passport, driver's license, birth certificate, social security card or something of that nature. All other nationalities must have passports, and if required, visas. No special car licensing regulations are in effect, but if you drive a rental car, you must have a copy of the leasing contract; also, if the registered owner of the car is not present, you must have a letter stating that you are driving the car by permission. For more information, contact: **Revenue Canada**, Customs and Excise, 333 Dunsmuir St., Vancouver,

BC V6B 5R4 (tel: 604-666-0545); U.S. Customs Service, P.O. Box 118, Washington, D.C. 20004 (tel: 203-927-6724).

GLACIER AND WATERTON LAKES NATIONAL PARKS

Glacier National Park

Glacier National Park, 1,583 square miles of dramatic landscape on the Continental Divide is a scenic gem of brightly colored Precambrian rock, cut and polished by ice, decorated by more than two hundred lakes and home to a huge variety of plants and animals. Deep valleys rimmed by precipitous cliffs, hanging valleys, knife-edge arêtes and sharp peaks characterize its landscape. Lakes occupy many of the valleys, some of them filled with glacial meltwater the color of the finest turquoise. Nearly fifty small glaciers survive from the much larger icefields of the last ice age.

On the west side of the park, forests of immense western red cedar, Douglas fir and other moisture-loving species shelter a damp cool forest floor covered with lush, fragrant vegetation. On the east side, conditions are drier. Whole mountain slopes are covered with quaking aspen groves, which erupt in a blaze of color during the fall. Throughout the park, meadows come alive with wildflowers the like of which are never seen where the mountains are drier or the soil less rich.

Glacier provides a textbook example of what ice does when it flows through mountains. At every turn one sees the marks of its passing. Glaciers plucked the ancient stone from mountain heights, creating spacious cirque basins and the arêtes which stand between them. One of these arêtes, The Garden Wall, carries the Continental Divide through the center of the park. It is a remnant standing where two alpine glaciers, gnawing away from opposite sides, almost met. It is so narrow that in places, erosion has created windows in the wall. Below the mountain crests, ice scoured and deepened the valleys, and provided material for dams to retain water in the lakes. On a map of the park, these lakes look like so many blue fingers clutching the mountains. Among the larger of them are Lakes MacDonald, St. Mary, Sherburne, Waterton, Kintla and Bowman.

The rocks which have been the subject of all this carving were originally among the vast sediments deposited in Precambrian seas over a billion years ago. The layers of limestone, sandstone and mudstone, which now make up the cliffs of Glacier, tell their story clearly. Everywhere one sees evidence of how they were made. Ripple marks tell of shallow water stirred by the wind. Mud cracks reveal periods of dryness. Globular clusters the size of cabbages are the remains of algae colonies, which evidently filled the shallows before the time of hard-shelled animals.

These layers, some three to five miles in total thickness, were heaved up from their ancient horizontal position about 70 million years ago. This happened throughout the Rockies. But here, rather than simply rising in place, the slab underlying Glacier broke away from higher ground to the west, and like a stack of books on a sloping table, slid eastward nearly forty miles. The breakage created gaps in its wake—gaps that are now the Flathead and North Fork valleys immediately west of the mountains. As it slid eastward, the slab rode up on top of adjacent layers so that older rocks came to rest above younger rocks. Subsequent erosion removed the upper layers leaving a very strange anomaly indeed. Geologists call this feature the Lewis Overthrust; apparently the motion was lubricated by slippery Cretaceous mud, which happened to be the surface layer at the time.

After the Laramide Orogeny, or uplift, there came a long period of erosion in a climate much drier than that of today. The mountains were attacked by the forces of weather, but too little water flowed away from them to carry off the debris. Instead, the mountains were buried in their own decay, much like the desert ranges of the Southwest are today. Then about 10 million years ago, another uplift occurred, thrusting the mountains higher. The weather turned wet, and the forces of erosion became more vigorous, clearing out the accumulated gravels and digging the valleys deeper. In the interior valleys west and south of the park, the old gravels are a distinct part of the landscape, forming broad benches a thousand feet or more above big rivers which haven't yet been able to carry it all away.

History

In historic times, the Blackfeet ruled the northern plains, lording it over other tribes such as the Kalispell, Flathead and Kootenai, who lived west of the Divide and ventured onto the plains at the risk of their lives. The Blackfeet weren't always so powerful. Their position of dominance had been achieved with the help of weapons and other goods obtained from Canadian traders—a source of supply that they jealously guarded. To protect their hegemony, they fought to prevent traders, whether Canadian or American, from establishing posts farther west, and ruthlessly drove the other tribes back into the mountains. This explains why early fur traders along the Missouri River met with such wrathful opposition from the Blackfeet.

For their part, the Canadian traders were only too happy with the arrangement. Rivalries among tribes were good for business. It meant that everyone wanted to buy rifles and steel arrowheads; the more weapons one side obtained, the more their competition needed. So while the Canadians encouraged the Blackfeet in their war against the Missouri River fur traders, they themselves worked to establish their own lines of trade across the Rockies to the interior tribes. Furs were the object. They would sell anything to get them. Even whiskey. Even, unwitting an export as it may have been, disease. During the middle of the century, smallpox and illicit alcohol laid the Blackfeet low; they shrank back to the foot of the Rockies and sought to avoid contact. In this, they were only partially successful. Prospectors in the late 1800s found traces of minerals in the mountains and brought pressure to bear on the Blackfeet. In 1895, for $1.5 million, the tribe ceded all rights to their mountain lands east of the Continental Divide.

As it turned out, the miners found little of value in the area of Glacier Park, a development that no doubt disappointed many of them. The rest of us, however, should feel some gratitude for the region's mineral poverty; once it was realized that there was no gold to be had, objections to the establishment of a national park were swept aside. With support from the Northern Pacific Railroad, whose directors fully understood the gold mine to be found in the grandeur of western scenery, Congress established Glacier National Park in May of 1910.

Scenic Drives

Every visitor should drive the Going-to-the-Sun Highway at least once during his stay, but why does it seem that on any given day, everyone has decided to do just that? The crowds really can be thick here in the heart of the park. Even so, it's worth the trip. There's no faster way to get a sense of Glacier than by driving across Logan Pass, and of course by getting out of the car and hiking some of the trails along the way. This road is truly one of the most spectacular mountain drives in the world, traversing the park through all its diversity of climate and elevation.

From the west, the road follows the shoreline of Lake MacDonald to the valley of MacDonald Creek. One of the finest short trails in the park climbs to Avalanche Lake on the south side of the road; the route is moderate in difficulty, through beautiful big-boled forest to a gem of an alpine lake walled in by cliffs, which are wet from numerous waterfalls. Near the head of MacDonald Creek, the road begins to climb toward the pass. It was literally blasted into the cliff face and supported on bridgeworks a spider would admire. Pull-outs are frequent, but crowded; the wisest travelers go early in the morning, or wait until sunset.

Look up along the cliffs for mountain goats. They are quite numerous above the road.

On Logan Pass, the Hidden Lake Trail qualifies as the park's most popular single path. A three-mile round trip, beginning at the visitor center, leads to an overlook above a sparkling little lake. On the other side of the pass (north), the Highline Trail contours along The Garden Wall. It leads all the way to Goat Haunt at the south end of Waterton Lake, but a good day-hike takes you to Granite Park with its fine views of Heavens Peak. Standing on Logan Pass, it is easy to imagine glaciers filling the valleys in both directions, gnawing at the pass itself, but not quite eating it away. Another obvious result of glaciation is the hanging side valleys with their veil-like waterfalls. Descending to the east, the road clings only a little less precariously to the cliff edge, passing through several tunnels, sprayed by waterfalls and providing wonderful views of Going-to-the-Sun Mountain, Mount Reynolds and Mount Siyeh. It leaves the tundra behind, and then enters subalpine forest and ends in the drier, but still heavily timbered, forest of the valley bottom.

As superb a road as this is, it would be a mistake to drive over Logan Pass and feel you had seen the park. So many other places are worthy of attention. Many Glacier, site of the largest hotel in the park, along with other facilities, is discussed separately below, and I recommend it highly. However, if remoter areas are more to your liking, you should turn your nose toward either the southeast or northwest corners of the park. Here you will find the least-traveled roads and trails of Glacier; the 60-mile-per-hour tourists hardly give these places a glance, especially in the northwest, because of rough roads and long distances. Travelers with the foresight to have brought their own canoes are in luck at Bowman and Kintla lakes.

Trails

Glacier is primarily—quintessentially—a hiker's park. It has over seven hundred miles of trails. The mountain vistas rank with the best in the world, but distances are relatively short. Elevation gain and loss is enough to give the sensation of a grand landscape without being entirely overwhelming. Even in the forest, trails are pleasant and interesting. On the west side, they wander along clear streams in the shade of huge trees, past thickets of ferns and berry bushes. In places, the streams have cut deep pools in the red and green mudstones, resulting in exquisite shapes and frothy little waterfalls. More than one hiker has set off with ambitions of high alpine meadows, only to be waylaid by the restful banks of these trout-laden pools.

Permits are not required for day-hiking, but hikers planning overnights must have them. The permits specify campsite locations, meaning that itineraries must be followed. Glacier is the beleaguered home of grizzly and black bears. All advice given in Chapter 1 about keeping a clean camp and staying awake on the trail applies doubly in this park—for the well-being of both people and bears.

Among hiking areas, Many Glacier is surely the most popular, and for good reason (see below). But keep in mind that this is a crowded place, and alternatives are as numerous as candy-bar wrappers. Well, almost. The entire south half of the park sees less use than the north half. Try the trails at Two Medicine or Cut Bank. Also, consider the northeast corner; the trails here are longer, but rewarding. The classic park traverse begins (or ends) at Kintla Lake, going via Goat Haunt to Logan Pass. Another fine traverse begins on the Going-to-the-Sun Road and follows the St. Mary River to Gunsight Pass, where you will surely meet the resident group of friendly mountain goats and will almost as surely pause for a long time to gaze at Lake Ellen Wilson far below. The trail goes that way, when you are ready, past Sperry Chalets to Lake MacDonald.

Many Glacier

The Many Glacier area, on the shore of Swiftcurrent Lake and in the shadow of a great semicircle of peaks, is a hiker's paradise. Rarely in the Rockies is access to spectacular alpine country so easily found as here. Spectacular trails go off in a number of directions, past waterfalls, to alpine lakes and over the Divide to other valleys. Many day-hikes are possible, varying in length from several miles to 30 or more. A variety of paths leads through the valley bottom. Others climb to places like Grinnell Glacier, or Swiftcurrent Pass on The Garden Wall, connecting with the High Line Trail from Logan Pass. One of the best walks in the park is the trail south from Many Glacier under the imposing east face of Mount Gould, over Piegan Pass and down the shoulder of Mount Siyeh to the Logan Pass road: a superb day's walk if you can manage a car shuttle. Other of the Many Glacier area highlights include Iceberg Lake, Ptarmigan Tunnel on the trail to Elizabeth Lake, and the lesser-known trail around the east side of Mount Allen.

Some Useful Information About Glacier

HOW TO GET THERE: Scheduled airlines serve Great Falls and Kalispell; buses connect from major cities, with stations outside the park; **Amtrak**, as of this writing, stops at both East and West Glacier.
GETTING AROUND: Within the park, limited public transport from one hotel or lodge to another is provided on a space-available basis. Beginning in 1994, the higher part of Going-to-the-Sun Highway was

closed to vehicles wider than 7.5 feet (including mirrors) and longer than 20 feet, from June 15 to Labour Day. Restrictions on bicycles apply on certain narrow, shoulderless stretches of roadway.

CAMPGROUNDS: Auto campgrounds with paved roads and running water are located at Apgar, Avalanche Creek, Fish Creek, Swiftcurrent Lake, Rising Sun, St. Mary, Two Medicine and Sprague Creek. More primitive, less crowded and questionably suitable for trailers and motorhomes are the sites on the park's west side at Bowman Creek, Bowman Lake, Kintla Lake, Mud Creek, Logging Creek, Quartz Creek and River campgrounds; on the east side, Cut Bank Campground fits this category.

LODGING: Park hotels and lodges are located at East Glacier, West Glacier, Lake MacDonald, Rising Sun and Many Glacier. All lodges are well situated for hiking and other park activities, with Many Glacier being probably the first choice for anyone keen on walking. Glacier has two backcountry chalets, which provide beds and meals, one at Sperry Glacier and the other at Granite Park; accessible only by trail. Additional campgrounds, lodging, laundromats, groceries and other services are provided in surrounding communities, with complete municipal services on the west side in the Kalispell-Whitefish area.

SEASON: The summer season extends roughly from mid-May to mid-September, with specific areas and services closing or opening at different times. Logan Pass on the Going-to-the-Sun Highway can close briefly even in midsummer due to bad weather; this road is closed to vehicles in winter. Snowmobiles are not permitted in Glacier.

FISHING: No license is required to fish the park's streams and lakes. Species include rainbow, brook, cutthroat and Dolly Varden trout. Pick up regulations and other information at a ranger station.

BOATING: Motorboats are allowed only on some of the larger lakes, such as Two Medicine, St. Mary, Sherburne, Waterton, and Bowman. Nonmotorized boats are permitted on park rivers; the North Fork is a popular run, as is the Middle Fork (see page 266).

USEFUL NAMES AND ADDRESSES: For general park information, contact the Superintendent, **Glacier National Park**, West Glacier, MT 59936 (tel: 406-888-5441). For reservations and information relating to lodging, transport and other services, contact **Glacier Park Inc.**, Central Reservations Department, Dial Corp. Center, M.S. 0928, Phoenix, AZ 85077 (tel: 602-207-6000). For information on Sperry and Granite Park chalets, contact **Belton Chalets**, P.O. Box 188, West Glacier, MT 59936 (tel: 406-387-5654). **FreeWheeling Travel Guides** publishes a useful road guide to Glacier and Waterton ($6.45 postpaid from P.O. Box 7494, Jackson, WY 83002).

Waterton Lakes National Park

At the north end of Glacier National Park, one of the larger lakes in the area fills a long, glacial valley, which crosses the international border. Viewed from a boat traveling the length of that narrow, mountain-hemmed body of water, the only visible indication of the border is a straight cut made through the forest, glimpsed briefly when the boat is lined up just right, and invisible moments later. The obscurity of that line seems appropriate. From the standpoint of geography, geology, ecology and just plain common sense, the two parks standing on either side of the border are one land.

This is recognized by the designation of the two parks as the Waterton-Glacier International Peace Park, intended to symbolize the common interests and friendship of both nations. The designation was made official in 1932 by joint declarations of the U.S. Congress and the Canadian Parliament. It was more a formality than anything else, because both parks had existed previously. Canada had created Waterton Lakes National Park in 1895, making it the nation's fourth national park. Fifteen years later, the United States established Glacier.

Waterton's geology and natural history are essentially the same as that of Glacier, except that it ends at the Continental Divide and therefore lacks a western slope. Waterton is also a good bit smaller than Glacier, measuring only 518 km.² (200 sq. mi.). Its terrain is organized around three main valleys. One holds the chain of three Waterton Lakes, which begin in the rolling prairies at the edge of the mountains and extend deep into the American section of the range at Goat Haunt. Another, crowned by rock-walled Cameron Lake, drains through Cameron Creek to Waterton townsite, and can be driven along the Akamina Highway. The third, Blakiston Valley, can be reached by the Red Rock Canyon Drive.

Waterton has a superb trail system, well-maintained and offering great variety in a relatively small area. Day-hikers, especially, will find this area to their liking. Numerous short trails climb to sparkling lakes in glacial cirques, getting there by way of shady forest and alpine flower meadows. Crandell Lake can be reached in a half hour from the Akamina Highway, but most of the hikes range between 5 and 10 km. (3 and 6 mi.) one way, a distance which many hikers agree is ideal for a day's outing. Generally, trailheads are located along the park's main roads. One trail, however, to Crypt Lake, requires a short boat trip part way down Waterton Lake, a pleasure in itself.

Longer hikes are limited in this small park. The Tamarack Trail is an exception, measuring more than 32 km. (20 mi.) and following alpine

The Canadian Rockies near Waterton Lakes National Park rise abruptly from the rolling Alberta prairies.

country most of the distance; it begins at Rowe Creek on the Akamina Highway, climbs over the shoulder of Mount Lineham, and continues in the shadow of the Continental Divide to Bauerman Creek and eventually to the Red Rock Canyon Drive. Several options can be taken along the way. Another possibility is to combine trails of Waterton with those of Glacier. The Belly River, in the east section of the park, flows northward out of Glacier, and makes for a really fine trip to Stoney Indian Pass or to Many Glacier. And, of course, the trails from Goat Haunt at the south end of Waterton Lake are classics among mountain footpaths. Purists will choose to walk to Goat Haunt instead of taking the boat; the trail follows the lakeshore through forest, and although not a spectacular route, it is a pleasant enough way to go and an appropriate way of adjusting body and mind to the pace of wilderness travel. Permits are required for overnight use of backcountry in both parks, and this should be kept in mind when planning a trip that crosses the border.

Some Useful Information About Waterton Lakes

CAMPGROUNDS: Waterton has three campgrounds: **Belly River** (off Highway 6 toward Chief Mountain, $10), **Townsite** (in the town of Waterton, it offers trailer hookups and showers for $14 to $21) and

Crandell (on Red Rock Parkway, $13). In addition, private campgrounds are located just outside the park.

BOATING: Boats (canoes and rowboats) can be rented at Cameron Lake (no powerboats). The launches that operate between Waterton and Goat Haunt run frequently during the day. **Waterton Inter-Nation Shoreline Cruises** (403-859-2362).

GENERAL INFORMATION: A visitor center, where you can get information, maps, fishing licenses and backcountry permits, is located along the road into Waterton townsite, on the hill across from the Prince of Wales Hotel; summer hours are 8:00 A.M. to 8:00 P.M. (tel: 403-859-2445). The town of Waterton offers basic services, including lodging, meals, gas, groceries and camping supplies.

USEFUL NAMES AND ADDRESSES: For more information, contact the Superintendent, **Waterton Lakes National Park**, Waterton Park, AB ToK 2Mo (tel: 403-859-2224).

Other Area Ideas

Ten Lakes Scenic Area

This is a small 6,475 ha. (16,000 a.) scenic area just south of the border near Eureka, Montana, managed by Kootenai National Forest to preserve its natural condition. Dominated by a high curving ridge of the Whitefish Mountains, the area takes its name from the Ten Lakes Basin along the border. Other lakes lie tucked in high basins on either side of the mountain crest.

To get there, turn off 19 km. (12 mi.) south of Eureka on the Grave Creek road (F.S. 114). This road leads to a junction with F.S. 319, which continues in a wide curve to the Therriault Lakes and two campgrounds located at the center of the scenic area; it takes a bit more than a half hour to drive from U.S. Highway 93. From either campground, short trails access the ridgeline and connect with a series of trails, which follow the ridge its entire length. You can also get there from the valley of the North Fork, on Glacier Park's western boundary. To do this, drive up the west side of the river (cross the river at Polebridge); 10 km. (6 mi.) from the border, Forest Road 114 leads west past Tuchuck Campground to the junction with F.S. 319.

Museum of the Plains Indian

In Browning, Montana, on the Blackfeet Reservation, there is a fine collection of Blackfeet artifacts and historic exhibits covering 11 Plains Indian tribes.

THE BOB MARSHALL, GREAT BEAR
AND SCAPEGOAT WILDERNESS

Three large wilderness areas perch on the Continental Divide in the large roadless area south of Glacier National Park: the Bob Marshall Wilderness, the Great Bear Wilderness and the Scapegoat Wilderness. U.S. Highway 2 crosses Marias Pass at the north of this lineup, the only road, either paved or dirt, for almost one hundred straight-line miles to Montana Highway 200. On their eastern exposure, the mountains of these wilderness areas rise abruptly from the plains, standing covered with forest and snow above the dry grasslands around Augusta, Choteau and Dupuyer. Three important rivers, the Dearborn, the Sun and the Teton, along with numerous smaller streams, drain eastward from the Divide to the Missouri River, which angles off to the northeast. As they leave the mountains, they carve canyons which provide access for the roads and trails pushing up from U.S. Highways 89 and 287. Travelers lucky enough to drive these highways on a blustery day in June see a landscape of green prairie rolling to the shoulders of high snow covered mountains, rank upon rank of them. Yet for all that snow, this is the dry side of the Divide. The eastern slope receives a full third less rainfall than the Flathead drainage to the west, which is characterized by big-boled forests densely draped in lichen and moss.

That western slope lies more hidden than the bold eastern front. Although Montana Highway 83 runs through the wonderfully scenic Swan River Valley, a traveler catches only occasional glimpses of mountain heights through the trees and across occasional lakes. These western peaks—the Swan Range—are only the first of several ranges that lie beyond, each range surrounded by generously broad valleys, sizeable streams and rivers, and occasional lakes. The only access is by foot or horseback. Trails originate from roadheads and Forest Service campgrounds throughout the region. These are long trails covering long spectacular miles through country that is famous for its wildlife: elk, mule deer, white tail deer, the largest herd of bighorn sheep in the state, mountain goat, Shiras moose, coyote, both black and grizzly bears, lynx, cougar, wolverine and a shoestring population of Rocky Mountain wolves.

The last-mentioned of these species have long since disappeared from less wild places. Knowing that they still inhabit these mountains quickens the blood. Their presence proves that a higher degree of wilderness survives here—wilderness as a natural force, which can be sensed in certain large tracts of wilderness, and which, to those who have heard it, is

A young bighorn sheep looks out at Many Glacier Valley in Glacier National Park.

both powerful music and fragile entity. Many who have not heard it dismiss it as balderdash.

They probably always will. No scientific instrument can measure wildness. Lawyers could never call it to witness, or photograph it, or bring in plaster casts of its footprints. Wilderness is a quality, not a quantity, something we have to measure indirectly. The difference between a live body and a dead one is measured the same way, by a set of observable characteristics: warmth, motion, electrical signals in the brain, heart pumping, muscles contracting and so forth. These indicators tell us that life is here in this body, still surviving, still giving it meaning, still separating it from the insignificance of its component parts, just as the signs of wildness tell us that a specific wilderness area is more than so many acres with so many miles of trails, so many animals and views rated good to excellent by some government study.

Among these signs are the animals closely associated with land least altered by human activity: grizzlies, wolves, wolverines, cougars, eagles, peregrine falcons, bighorn sheep, condors and many more. When you find yourself face-to-face with what you know is the home of these animals, it feels almost as if you've arrived at the heart of an ancient crumbling empire, apparently doomed to extinction, but as yet harboring a few of the old noble breed. South of Montana, the feeling is hard to find anywhere but in desert areas. From the Bob Marshall Wilderness northward, it lives in many parts of the Rockies.

Bob Marshall Wilderness

Bob Marshall was a U.S. Forest Service employee in the '20s and '30s, a man from a wealthy eastern family who found himself passionately devoted to wild country. Renowned for his long walks (he once trekked 70 miles nonstop) and his detailed, carefully written records of even trivial events, he raised an early cry for wilderness protection at a time when such thinking was completely out of style. Working through his position in the Forest Service, and able to provide personal financing to promote his ideas, he had a significant impact on the nation's view of its wild lands. He founded the Wilderness Society in the 1930s and served for two years as the first director of the Forest Service Office of Recreation. During his short lifetime, he saw approximately 14 million acres of forest land designated to remain in a primitive state. These lands would become the nucleus of the nearly 100-million-acre U.S. wilderness system, given the status of federal law by the 1964 Wilderness Act. Marshall died of an apparent heart attack in 1939 at the age of 38. A year later, the Bob Marshall Wilderness was established.

"The Bob," as locals affectionately call it, is an area larger than the state of Rhode Island, over a million acres sprawled across 60 miles of the Continental Divide. The Bob is a big, generous landscape with several mountain ranges and plenty of space to roam. Trail mileages are long. Horses are popular here, and appropriate, although foot travel increases each season.

The central drainage is the South Fork of the Flathead and its three upper branches—White Creek, Danaher Creek and Big Salmon Creek. The river flows out of the wilderness and into Hungry Horse Reservoir. On the west, its basin is defined by the Swan Range. Its eastern boundary is the 12-mile-long Chinese Wall, a distinctive line of 1,000-foot-high limestone cliffs on the Continental Divide, which runs down the center of the wilderness. The eastern slope drainage is dominated by the north and south forks of the Sun River. Lastly, the Middle Fork of the Flathead rises in the northeast corner of the Bob before entering the Great Bear Wilderness, for which it serves as the major drainage.

To mountain hikers, this all adds up to a lot of walking, much of it along relatively level river valleys, through forest and meadow and foothills. Going over a pass does not mean leaving the wilderness, as it does in smaller areas. Marshall is reported to have said he wanted to see wilderness areas where a hiker could walk for two weeks and not cross his tracks. He would be pleased with the expanse of country that carries his name.

Trails

Trail access is primarily via the east along the Sun River, or the west, from the Swan River Valley. One popular trailhead provides access from the north. In addition, trails from the adjacent wilderness areas interconnect with those of the Bob. Of these options, the South Fork of the Flathead Trail is a major access to the Bob. Get there by driving down either side of Hungry Horse Reservoir (F.S. 38 or 895) to the Spotted Bear Ranger Station. Trail condition information can be obtained there; the trailhead is farther south. A trip starting here follows the river to various branching trails. Those leading west to the Swan Valley include: Big Salmon Creek Trail (Trail 110, connecting to the pass at Waldbillig Mountain and Holland Lake); Gordon Creek Trail (Trail 35, which makes a broad arc to meet Trail 110 below Waldbillig Mountain); and Youngs Creek Trail (Trail 141, connecting to Pyramid Pass). To reverse directions, the Holland Lake Trailhead is about eight miles south of Condon on U.S. Highway 83; turn east on F.S. 44 to Holland Lake. Pyramid Pass trailhead is reached by taking F.S. 477 east out of Seeley Lake, driving a long mile and turning north up Morrell Creek.

The classic traverse of the wilderness area begins (or ends) at Holland Lake, makes its way to the South Fork of the Flathead and follows the White River (Trail 112) to Larch Hill Pass in The Chinese Wall. From there, Trail 275/203 leads to the Sun River trailhead at Benchmark. To reach the Benchmark area, drive to Augusta on the east side of the mountain and head west of town past Nilan Reservoir to Lewis and Clark National Forest Road 235; just at the forest border the road forks, with F.S. 233 going north to the Gibson Reservoir; stay on 235, which passes a handful of campgrounds before ending at the trailhead.

Northern trails include: Gateway Pass Trail (Trail 105, over Gateway Pass to Gorge Creek and the headwaters of the Middle Fork of the Flathead); and Strawberry Creek Trail (Trail 161, connecting with the Gateway Trail and making a loop trip possible); both of these begin at Swift Dam, on F.S. 146 from Dupuyer on U.S. Highway 89.

Running the South Fork

This is a beautiful whitewater run, most of it within the Bob, which makes access a bit of a problem because boating gear must be hauled in on horseback, or carried. Fortunately for walkers, the river is easy enough to accept small lightweight inflatables. Just outside the wilderness boundary, Meadow Creek Gorge is five miles of steep-walled canyon in places as narrow as six feet wide, with three places that even skilled boaters portage. Most boaters put in at Cedar Creek on the Bunker Creek Road below the gorge for an easy float to Hungry Horse Reservoir.

Useful Names and Addresses

A good topo map of the wilderness complex is available for $3 from forest offices. On the west side: **Flathead National Forest**, 1935 Third Ave. E., Kalispell, MT 59901 (tel: 406-755-5401); **Hungry Horse Ranger District**, P.O. Box 190340, Hungry Horse, MT 59919 (tel: 406-387-2483); **Lolo National Forest**, Building 24, Fort Missoula, Missoula, MT 59801. On the east: **Lewis and Clark National Forest**, Box 869, Great Falls, MT 59403 (tel: 406-791-7700); **Rocky Mountain Ranger District**, P.O. Box 340, Choteau, MT 59422 (tel: 406-466-2237); **Helena National Forest**, 2880 Skyway Dr., Helena, MT 59601 (tel: 406-449-5201).

Great Bear Wilderness

The Great Bear Wilderness bridges the gap between the Bob Marshall and Glacier National Park. Its north boundary is U.S. Highway 2 just south of the park; its other boundaries are roadless except for trailheads. In shape, it loosely resembles a frying pan, with a long mountainous handle extending to the northwest along U.S. 2 and the North Fork of the Flathead River. One might say it even looks like the constellation *Ursa Major*, or Great Bear, but this is purely coincidental. It was named not for the shape of its boundaries, but for its dominant resident, the grizzly. Together with adjacent wilderness areas, it provides the great bears with one of their last refuges in the Lower 48.

Trails

U.S. Highway 2 provides access on the north and east. To the west, trails lead in from the Spotted Bear River and several points along the shore of Hungry Horse Reservoir. The heaviest use occurs in the area of Schafer Meadows, where small planes are permitted to land on a backcountry airstrip. This is the put-in point for boaters on the Middle Fork. Popular trails include: Schafer Creek Trail (Trail 327, trailhead on Spotted Bear River via Spotted Bear Ranger Station at the south end of Hungry Horse Reservoir); Granite Creek Trail (Trail 156, trailhead near the Challenge Guard Station on F.S. 569 off U.S. 2 just west of Marias Pass); Morrison Creek Trail (Trail 154, trailhead also near the Challenge Guard Station); and the Middle Fork Trail, which follows the river through the wilderness and on into the Bob Marshall (Trail 155, trailhead on U.S. 2 about five miles east of Walton).

Running the Middle Fork

This river provides a challenging whitewater run between mid-June and the end of July; boats must be packed in or flown to the airstrip at

Schafer Meadow, a distance of 22 miles by trail from U.S. Highway 2. For a description, see page 266.

Useful Names and Addresses

Contact **Flathead National Forest Supervisor**, 1935 Third Ave. E., Kalispell, MT 59901; or the **Hungry Horse Ranger District**, P.O. Box 190340, Hungry Horse, MT 59919 (tel: 406-387-5243).

Scapegoat Wilderness

The Scapegoat is the southernmost of the three contiguous wilderness areas. It occupies 240,000 acres of Lewis and Clark, Helena, and Lolo forests, straddling the Continental Divide. Its band of limestone cliffs, an extension of The Chinese Wall, is a dominant landscape feature. Mountain peaks, widely spaced by high timberline ridges, rise from piles of talus above well-watered glacial cirques, some with lakes. Like the country to the north, this is prime wildlife country, with grazing meadows punctuating the sweep of spruce, fir and lodgepole forest. And like the adjoining wilderness areas, the Scapegoat challenges strong backcountry travelers; it is not a place for one's first overnight with a pack.

Access can be had from all sides, even by foot from the Bob Marshall (the Danaher Creek Trail, Trail 126, connects directly with the northwest boundary). Road access points, beginning from the west side, include North Fork of the Blackfoot River Trail, a trail limited to hikers (Trail 32/17; drive west on Montana 200 from its junction with Montana 141 to Forest Road 500, which goes toward Coopers Lake; follow F.S. 500 to its end). The Meadow Creek Trail is nearby and goes to Meadow Lake (Trail 483, same directions as above, but turn off F.S. 500 onto F.S. 993 past Big Nelson Campground and beyond to a trailhead along Dry Creek). Also off Montana 200, seven miles east of Lincoln, Forest Road 330 leads north to Indian Meadows and a choice of several trails.

On the west side, Route 434, which is partially paved, runs between Augusta and Montana 200. From this road, two trailheads are reached. One is on the Dearborn River (turn onto Forest Road 577 at Bean Lake); ten minutes north of Bean Lake is Elk Creek (Forest Road 196). Trails from both places lead to the Dearborn headwaters and beyond. Finally, the Benchmark trailhead (see directions in Bob Marshall section) leads to the south fork of the Sun River.

Useful Names and Addresses

Contact the Supervisor, **Helena National Forest**, 2880 Skyway Drive, Helena, MT 59601 (tel: 406-449-5201); or either the Flathead or the

Lewis and Clark national forests, whose addresses are given on page 249. A wilderness map is available for $3; also a Lewis and Clark visitor's map for $3.

GATES OF THE MOUNTAINS WILDERNESS

When Lewis and Clark reached the area near modern Helena after their long journey across the plains, they could see mountains closing in on all sides. At river level, they were suddenly in a deep, craggy canyon, a change of topography which truly seemed to be a gateway into the Rockies. Unfortunately, it was no gateway at all. By entering the canyon and staying with the Missouri all the way to its source, they took the long way around and as a result suffered much hardship. Had they only known about the Indian trail which ran overland to the west, they might have spared themselves the arduous, ill-fed weeks of wandering which lay ahead on the Continental Divide between Montana and Idaho.

Returning homeward the next year, they knew the right way from their Nez Perce guides and decided to take separate routes eastward from Lolo Pass. Clark retraced their route through the Bitterroot Valley and continued via the Bighole Valley with the intention of exploring the Yellowstone River to its mouth. Lewis, it was decided, would have a go at the shorter, overland route, which they had previously missed. With good Nez Perce horses, he and his party made the journey up the Blackfoot River, over what is now called Lewis and Clark Pass (Montana 200 crosses the Divide south of it), and to Great Falls across the plains. The two captains met again at the mouth of the Yellowstone, so that both of them missed the Gates of the Mountains on their return.

The Gates of the Mountains Wilderness is 28,562 acres on the east side of the river, an area of limestone cliffs and weathered rock favored by resident mountain goats and bighorn sheep. Meadows fill with wildflowers in early summer, but generally water is scarce. The area is small enough to cross in a single day.

Access to the western border of the wilderness is by boat, across the Missouri River. Road access from the north is via Interstate 15 to Wolf Creek, then old U.S. Highway 91 north for a mile to the Holter Lake Road, which runs south to the Beartooth Game Management Area Headquarters. The road beyond there to the wilderness is primitive. The more straightforward access routes parallel the south boundary along Beaver Creek. The Beaver Creek Road (F.S. 138) is reached via Montana 280, on the north edge of the city; it leads to Hauser Lake and a bridge crossing to Forest Service land. From there, continue on F.S. 4021 to F.S. 224, which ends at

Beaver Creek and F.S. 138. None of these routes is straightforward; a map
of the forest roads is as useful as gasoline in the car's tank.

Useful Names and Addresses

A visitor's map showing all roads and a wilderness map are available for
$3 each from **Helena National Forest**, Drawer 10014, 2880 Skyway Dr.,
Helena, MT 59601 (tel: 406-449-5201).

MISSION MOUNTAINS WILDERNESS

On their west slope, above the Flathead Indian Reservation in Mission
Valley, these mountains form an impressive rampart thousands of feet
high. The base is a broad timbered slope. Higher, as side valleys open into
the range, trees disappear to be replaced by snow and talus and finally
the peaks themselves. To see this range in the warm light of a late summer evening when the grasses of the valley floor have turned gold and
thunderclouds climb into a darkening sky creates a permanent memory.

On the lower slopes of the Missions are the ancient, indelible marks
of a still more impressive natural phenomenon—glacial Missoula Lake,
which occupied this valley during the Pleistocene. The lake was formed
when the Purcell lobe of the continental ice sheet pushed south out of
British Columbia and dammed the Clark Fork River near where it now
joins Lake Pend Oreille in Idaho. The reservoir was enormous, as much
as 2,000 feet deep, which is apparent from the marks of its shorelines
high above the current valley bottom. Eventually, the impounded water
broke through the ice dam, which gave way catastrophically. Enough
water to fill half of Lake Michigan emptied in a matter of two or three
days toward the south and west, overrunning whatever watercourses
existed, flowing, if such a word applies here, at a speed of 45 miles per
hour and a volume of 9.5 cubic miles per hour roughly ten times the
flow of all the world's rivers, combined. This occurred not once but a
number of times as the glacier advanced only to be breached again and
again in the greatest floods for which geologists have evidence.

The old lakebed now hums with crickets on a summer evening. The
Flathead, still a powerful river, flows more gently now toward the Clark
Fork, which it joins at St. Regis. A Jesuit mission, St. Ignatius, was
founded here in 1854 to serve the Salish and Kootenai Indians, one year
before establishment of the reservation for Flathead, Pend d'Oreille
(from the French word meaning "earrings") and Kootenai tribes. The
Jesuit priests were joined in 1864 by four Sisters of Providence from
Montreal, Quebec, who taught school and ran a medical clinic.

A visit to the large brick mission church is an interesting side trip from the highway. It was built in 1891 to replace an older hand-sawn clapboard building. The original log chapel, built in 1854, stands on the church grounds beside the first home of the Sisters of Providence, now set up as a small museum with historic photos and other artifacts. The hospital and school activities of the mission were eventually taken over by nonclerical services, but the church remains a focus of the community.

While in the valley, consider stopping at the Ninepipe National Wildlife Refuge, 2,000 acres of open water and marsh surrounded by 3,000 acres managed by the Montana Department of Wildlife and Parks. This is the old lakebed, strewn with potholes and wet spots, a good place to see waterfowl and other birds. All access is closed during the hunting season; in nesting season, from March 1 to July 15, portions of the refuge are closed. A kiosk on U.S. Highway 93 at Allentown gives information. Two secondary roads about a half mile on either side of the kiosk provide auto access.

There are two adjacent Mission Mountain wilderness areas: 89,500 acres owned by the Flathead Tribe, and 73,877 acres of Forest Service land. The easiest access to the wilderness is from the Swan Valley side, but the best views of the peaks are from the Mission Valley. The Missions are unusually precipitous country, crossed by a scant 65 miles of steep, narrow trails better suited for hikers than horses. There are many lakes, glaciers and snowfields, but almost no flat country. The contour map is a solid mass of lines showing deep glacial pockets and high sharp ridges. The mountain peaks range between 8,000 and 10,000 feet, forming a sharp crest; in one place, the crest drops 2,000 near-vertical feet to form a striking, sinuous face called The Garden Wall. The imaginative names of features reflect the feelings this range engenders: The Angels Bathing Pool, Scenic Lakes, Picture Lake, Lake of the Stars, Sunset Crags, Pass of the Winds, Daughter of the Sun Mountain, Lake of the Clouds, Panoramic Peak.

The commonest access is from the east, along the Swan River Valley and Montana 83, one of the state's most scenic roads. On this side of the range, because much of the land is owned by the Forest Service, you will find the most convenient camping and recreation access. Trailheads include: Beaver Creek, on F.S. 906 just north of Summit Lake Overlook; Glacier Creek, on F.S. 561 about six miles farther north (no overnight camping on the shore of Glacier Lake because of overuse); Jim Lake and Cold Lakes, on F.S. 903, then 9568, about four miles north of Condon (no camping on the shore of Cold Lakes either); and Fatty Creek, on F.S. 888E, then 888F, then 10182, turning off at Cedar Creek about a twenty-minute drive north of Condon.

From the west, trails lead through the Flathead Reservation, requiring permits to go this way (you also need a permit to cross from Forest Service wilderness to tribal wilderness).

Useful Names and Addresses

For information and a contour map ($3), contact: **Flathead National Forest**, Swan Lake Ranger Station, Box 370, Bigfork, MT 59911 (tel: 406-837-5081); in summer, **Condon Work Center**, Condon, MT 59826 (tel: 406-754-2295); **Confederated Salish and Kootenai Tribes**, P.O. Box 278, Pablo, MT 59855 (tel: 406-675-2700).

Other Area Ideas

The Jewel Basin Hiking Area is at the north end of the Swan Range between Kalispell and the Hungry Horse Reservoir. Thirty-five miles of trails wander through 15,000 acres of alpine lakes, streams, snowfields and wildflower meadows, closed to all but hikers. The area is managed by Flathead National Forest. To get there, turn north off U.S. Highway 83 north of Bigfork, Montana, headed toward Echo Lake on Forest Road 5392; the trailhead is about nine miles from the highway. Other roads approach from the opposite side, along Hungry Horse Reservoir; from the Hungry Horse Dam, follow F.S. 895 on its sinuous course along the shore until you reach Graves Bay, then turn off on F.S. 897 for two miles to Handkerchief Lake, where there is another campground and a trailhead. For information, contact the District Ranger in Bigfork, whose address is given above.

NATIONAL BISON RANGE

Perhaps the most remarkable thing about the bison herds in places like Yellowstone and Wind Cave national parks is that they exist at all. Historians estimate that in the early 1800s, 50 million of these animals ranged across the continent from Pennsylvania to Oregon and from Mexico to the Great Slave Lake in northern Canada. Most bison lived east of the Rockies on the Great Plains, providing food, shelter, clothing and most other necessities of life for the Plains Indians.

From those vast herds, numbers plummeted by the turn of the century to a known wild population in the United States of around twenty animals; undoubtedly more survivors than that held on in isolated pockets, but without emergency measures and the foresight of several ranchers who had kept a few animals in captivity, it seems quite likely that bison would have disappeared as thoroughly and irrevocably as that other great continental wanderer, the passenger pigeon.

The National Bison Range was established in 1908 in a swell of eleventh hour public opinion generated primarily by the American Bison Society and supported wholeheartedly by President Theodore Roosevelt. The Society put up $10,000 for the acquisition of bison from private herds, and the President designated the necessary land. A year later, in October 1909, the first 41 bison were released on the range. This was not a new idea. Just seven years earlier, Congress had established the Yellowstone Park bison ranch, which augmented the park's tiny surviving herd with stock from private sources and was run on the same principles as a cattle ranch.

Both in Yellowstone and at Moiese, the bison prospered. In the 1950s the Yellowstone bison were released to survive as a wild herd, with current numbers of more than a thousand. Between 300 and 500 live on the 19,000 acres of the National Bison Range, along with a number of elk, mule deer, white tail deer, a band of bighorn sheep and pronghorn antelope. To keep these populations at desired levels, the U.S. Fish and Wildlife Service operates the reserve very much like a ranch, conducting annual roundups and selling animals alive for zoos, slaughter or breeding. The proceeds make the Bison Range partially self-supporting.

A 19-mile loop road is open to visitors. It begins at an information center at the Bison Range entrance, just off U.S. Highway 212 north of Dixon, Montana, and south of Charlo, in the Flathead River Valley. A good time to visit is in June, when newborn red-haired calves trot along behind their black mothers. After the lazy days of summer, activity picks up again in late August during mating season, when bulls and cows alike are in their annual prime, with heavy, rich winter fur.

Useful Names and Addresses

Contact the Range Manager, **National Bison Range**, 132 Bison Range Rd., Moiese, MT 59824 (tel: 406-644-2211).

NORTHWEST MONTANA

Cabinet Mountains Wilderness

The Cabinet Mountains form a rugged, high crest of glacially sharpened peaks and cirques lying southwest of Libby, Montana. The mountains are sedimentary, made from vast quantities of sand and carbonate deposited in a shallow sea more than half a billion years ago, then altered by heat and pressure into limestone, quartzite and argillite. Raised in the general uplift of the Rocky Mountain region around 60 million years ago, these layered rocks cracked and folded, allowing the intrusion of igneous material, which also hardened into granite and diorite.

By one story, their name comes from certain box-shaped openings found by French Canadian trappers in the canyon of the nearby Clark Fork River. According to another explanation, the mountains them- selves reminded the trappers of cabinets; if true, this says more about the trappers' states of mind or memories than the shape of the Cabinet Mountains. Perhaps these were the same fellows who gazed up from the floor of a Wyoming valley, and thinking wistfully of breasts, named the Grand Tetons.

It may be hard to picture French cabinetry on the skyline above Libby, Montana, but it's not difficult at all to envision the peaks buried in Pleistocene ice while the southernmost lobes of the continental ice sheet ground ponderously through the valleys below. Small alpine glac- iers plucked rock from the crest, giving the range its sharp-edged ridges and steep cirques.

Water still plays a major role in the landscape, although now it does its work primarily as a liquid. The Cabinets, like their neighbors the Selkirks and Purcells, are close enough to coastal weather patterns to be greatly influenced by the Pacific Ocean. The area immediately west of the Cabinets is the wettest part of the Rockies, receiving generous rain and snow during fall, winter and spring. Moisture-loving plants thrive here. In contrast to the dry valleys of the Salmon River country to the south, forests of red cedar, western hemlock, western larch and white pine (the last two reaching heights of 200 feet), protect a mossy forest floor where ferns com- pete for space with devils club and other coastal plants. Higher, where less vegetation serves to retain moisture, things are drier. Lodgepole pine (the common tree of the dry volcanic soils of the Yellowstone Plateau) and Engelmann spruce appear above 5,000 feet, along with a variety of decid- uous shrubs and small trees—maples, alders and mountain ash—inter- spersed with subalpine meadows of wildflowers, heath and bear grass.

Higher still, above 6,000 feet, annual precipitation commonly exceeds 100 inches, yet conditions are harsh, plant life stunted and soil thin. Most of the moisture hurries off the high slopes to the lush valleys below. Mountain hemlock, a sizeable tree at lower elevations, struggles to attain the status of a shrub in this zone. Of all trees in the Cabinets, the alpine larch is most tolerant of altitude, growing in pure stands above other trees; it seems to be climbing higher still as it pioneers the recently deposited moraines beneath the Snowshoe and Elephant Peak glaciers.

The Cabinet Mountains Wilderness Area takes up 94,000 acres of the Kaniksu and Kootenai national forests, riding the sharp, snowy crest of the Cabinet Range for about thirty-five miles, never more than about seven miles wide and usually less than that. A series of prominent peaks define the divide, the highest being Snowshoe Peak at 8,738 feet. Trails penetrate from both sides, climbing short distances along streams or ridges from numerous trailheads at the end of forest roads. This makes it a convenient area for day-hikers, with most lakes and peaks between two and five miles from the nearest road. Longer hikes are possible, of course, including a traverse of the range, which could take any number of days. While some technical climbing is possible, the Cabinets tend to be unstable and poorly suited for the rock climber.

The area's most popular trail ends at Leigh Lake at the base of Snowshoe Peak, all of 1.5 miles from the end of a road coming almost directly from the town of Libby, which might explain why so many people use it (about seven miles south of town on U.S. Highway 2, turn west on F.S. 278). Other trails originate on the outskirts of Libby, giving access to a series of high lakes along a loop with several options, most of which end up back in Libby. One follows Parmenter Creek (rough road, F.S. 280 climbs southwest above Libby to the trailhead); more popular, the Cedar Creek Trail goes to the same area, from a trailhead at the end of F.S. 402 (five miles west of Libby on U.S. 2).

At the southeast end of the wilderness is the Lake Creek Forest Service Campground, from which several trails scatter toward the mountains. To get to the campground, drive south of Libby approximately twenty-five miles to Forest Road 231. It turns off the highway just north of the Fisher River bridge and follows Fisher Creek to the campground. There is an optional route which forms a loop; F.S. 231 parallels the foot of the range north to Howard Lake, where there is another campground, and on down Libby Creek to U.S. 2.

On the west side, with access via State Route 56, trails follow the North and Middle forks of the Bull River, climbing to alpine basins below Snowshoe Peak and Vimy Ridge in the heart of the high lakes—a distance of about 3.5 miles. From the basin above the North Fork, it's possible to hike to the crest of the ridge; by going up Verdun Creek, you can cross over to a number of lakes and join a cross-country ridgetop route, which goes north to the lakes at the head of Cedar Creek.

Ross Creek Cedar Grove Scenic Area

A 100-acre grove of virgin western red cedars is preserved in the Ross Creek Cedar Grove Scenic Area west of the Cabinet Range. Some of these centuries-old trees measure 8 feet in diameter at breast height and are 175 feet tall. A short nature trail winds along in the deep shade of the forest floor, with signs describing the natural history of the grove. Great cedar forests once covered this part of the Rockies; this 100 acres is a tiny but precious remnant. Access: take Highway 56 to the turnoff at the south end of Bull Lake, then four miles west on F.S. 398 to the grove. Just beyond Bull Lake, as it climbs up the drainage, the road opens on a scenic overlook of the Cabinet Range. There is a picnic area on Ross Creek at the grove and Forest Service campgrounds at Bull Lake.

Other, less well known stands of old-growth cedar, hemlock and white pine grow on the East Fork of the Bull River, at the mouth of Spar Creek on Spar Lake (west of Bull Lake, on round-about backroads starting several miles north of Bull Lake) and along several Cabinet Wilderness trails, notably Deep Creek, Cedar Creek and Granite Creek.

Lake Koocanusa

North of Libby and extending into Canada, Lake Koocanusa, a 90-mile-long reservoir created by the immense Libby Dam, fills the old canyon of the Kootenai River. The Forest Service and the Army Corps of Engineers have made an effort to promote the lake as a recreation area, and it has become quite popular with fishermen. But because its water level fluctuates so, and because the road stays far above even the high water mark, the place is not conducive to lakeshore activities. There are, however, trails and scenic drives in the immediate area, which are worth pointing out (see below, National Recreation Trails).

Paved roads parallel both shores of the lake; the west shore drive (closed in winter) is a somewhat slower drive, but both roads wind along the hills with open views of the lake. If you approach from the south, you can get information at the Canoe Gulch Ranger Station on Montana Highway 37 below the dam. In addition, there is a visitor center at the dam.

On the east side, along Montana 37, two trails follow streams through deep forest; walking them just a short distance is rewarding. Driving north, you come first to Tenmile Creek; three miles of walking takes you to a waterfall. The second trail, McGuire Creek, is about ten miles farther.

If you drive all the way up the west side, you can cross the divide to the Yaak River Valley, a long, scenic approach to the very northwestern corner of Montana. The road, F.S. 596, which follows Sullivan Creek, turns off the paved road about five miles north of the Koocanusa bridge at the north end of the lake. About ten miles south of the bridge, a sometimes rough gravel road (F.S. 92) climbs the valley of Big Creek, over the shoulder of Baldy Mountain and down to Pipe Creek, where Forest Road 68 can be followed in either direction: north to the Yaak River and south to Libby. Generally speaking, forest roads penetrate this entire area. Many of them are suitable for passenger cars, and either follow creek bottoms or climb to ridgetops and high overlooks. This is ideal country for auto travelers armed with a forest map to set off on a wandering excursion.

Northwest Peaks Scenic Area

Northwest of Yaak, this is about as far off the beaten path as you can get in Montana. Two paved roads go to Yaak, which is little more than a crossroads. Route 508 follows the Yaak River from U.S. Highway 2 near the Idaho border, passing lovely Yaak Falls on its way upstream. Optionally, Forest Road 68 goes north from Libby, turning off just north of the Kootenai River bridge. About three miles downriver from Yaak, F.S. 338 heads off toward the Canadian border. Two miles short of the boundary it turns west, winds around some, then climbs to the base of Northwest Peak (7,705 feet). Trails continue to Hawkins Lakes and the Northwest Peak fire lookout.

Libby

Libby, Montana, has a population of about eleven thousand people. It began as a lumber town in 1892 when the Great Northern Railroad arrived with a need for ties and other lumber. In addition, the train carried mineshaft timbers to the copper mines in Butte and the silver mines of northern Idaho, whose demand for wood was insatiable. The wanton exploitation of the forests, no different in spirit than the events of the gold rush several decades earlier, was considered scandalous even then, leading to strong public reaction and the eventual formation of national forests and a federally regulated logging industry.

Some Useful Information About Libby

HOW TO GET THERE: Libby is served by Amtrak and scheduled bus from Kalispell, MT and Spokane, WA.

GENERAL INFORMATION: The town offers full municipal services, including a hospital.

USEFUL NAMES AND ADDRESSES: Forest Supervisor, **Kootenai National Forest**, 506 Hwy 2 West, Libby, MT 59923 (tel: 406-293-6211); **Libby District Ranger**, Libby, MT 59923 (tel: 406-293-8861); for Northwest Peak area—**Troy District Ranger**, Troy, MT 59935 (tel: 406-295-4693); **Trout Creek District Ranger**, Trout Creek, MT 59874 (tel: 406-487-2432); **Northern Region Headquarters**, P.O. Box 7669, Missoula, MT 59807 (tel: 406-329-3511).

NATIONAL RECREATION TRAILS

This designation applies to hiking trails which lie outside established wilderness areas, but which nonetheless have unique and worthwhile qualities. Depending on the trail and the reasons for designation, a variety of uses are permitted including jeeps, snowmobiles and trailbikes. Other trails are reserved for hikers only. Designations change; it is important to ask for information at a ranger station.

Kootenai National Forest contains five such trails, with more being studied, ranging from a five-minute to a several-day walk. The shortest is the Little North Fork Trail, which takes only a few minutes to reach a 50-foot-high waterfall in a deep, mossy canyon. The trailhead is halfway up the west side of Lake Koocanusa, a mile and a half off the paved highway on the Big Creek Road (F.S. 336), where it crosses the Little North Fork. Farther north along the lake, three miles beyond the Koocanusa bridge, Forest Road 337 climbs in a southerly direction to meet Boulder Creek. You can follow this road all the way over the Purcell Crest and down to the Yaak River Valley; hikers interested in a scenic walking route should turn south at the head of Boulder Creek on Forest Road 7183 to the trailhead for the 19-mile Vinal-Boulder Trail. It climbs Boulder Mountain past the Boulder Lakes, traverses the Purcell divide through subalpine country, climbs Mount Henry for fine views, and descends gradually along Vinal Creek through larch forest. This makes a nice day-hike from the west side.

The Skyline Trail, about twenty miles long, traverses a high ridge with several peaks, beginning on Quartz Creek just to the west of Libby and ending in the Yaak Valley. The other two trails are the Trout Creek Loop, near the town of Trout Creek, and the Pulpit Mountain Trail near Troy. Full details can be obtained at any of the area Ranger Offices.

IDAHO PANHANDLE

No particular feature stands out above others in northern Idaho, except perhaps the rivers and lakes. Generally, this is not spectacular country, with sheer mountains and sweeping vistas, but it is, nonetheless, picturesque and pleasurable for wandering. Anyone interested in boating, whether on whitewater, quiet rivers or lakes, will find plenty of variety. Fishing is moderately good throughout the region and excellent in a few places. With the exception of the Cabinet Mountains, the ranges found here—the Purcells and the Selkirks—are mere hints of their grandeur north of the border. Even so, opportunities for scenic hiking, cross-country skiing and camping either from a vehicle or in the backcountry are as broad as a person's imagination.

Selkirk Crest Special Management Area

The Selkirk Crest Special Management Area is a narrow, Y-shaped area, which follows a line of peaks for 26,000 acres of Kaniksu National

Forest and Idaho State Forest land located east of Bonners Ferry. More than twenty lakes lie tucked in cirques along the divide, many accessible by maintained trails, although cross-country travel is the only way to reach other areas.

Mountain, or woodland, caribou are indigenous to the Selkirks. Although numerous across the border, this part of Idaho is the only place on the U.S. side where caribou might be seen. Members of the deer family, mountain caribou (*Rangifer caribou*) stand slightly larger than mule deer but smaller than elk. A large bull weighs about six hundred pounds; cows are about half that. All males and most females carry distinctive semipalmate antlers, but the bull caribou have the larger and more ornate ones. They prefer moist subalpine country with boggy areas and open timber. Large, rounded hooves spread to support their weight on soft ground and snow, an adaptation which allows them to forage for their major winter food, Old Man's Beard, a lichen which drapes tree branches in mature subalpine spruce and fir forests. During the summer, caribou browse on a variety of plants. The woodland caribou is generally distinguished from its light-coated, smaller northern cousin (*Rangifer arcticus*), the barren ground caribou, famous for its awesome migrations across northern Alaska and Canada. The habits of these two animals are dissimilar in many regards and their ranges barely overlap, and then only during winter, but according to some biologists, both are in fact one species, *Rangifer tarandus*, or the Greenland caribou, which is the same animal as the domesticated Siberian reindeer. No one knows how many once lived in the Idaho Selkirks, but certainly there were more than the current remnant population of perhaps 20 to 25, which survive in the face of illegal hunting and other encroachments on their habitat. They are considered Threatened or Endangered in Idaho and are therefore protected.

Access to the Selkirk Crest is most reasonable from the east, via Forest Service roads originating near Bonners Ferry, almost all of them turning off Forest Road 417 which parallels the mountains on the west side of the Kootenai River Valley. The major highway in the valley is U.S. Highway 2/95 to Copeland, then State Route 1 north to the border at Porthill. To reach F.S. 417 at the south end, turn off U.S. 2/95 three miles south of Bonners Ferry, and follow it another three miles to the junction with 417.

In two miles, you reach the first access road, F.S. 2646A, which goes up Snow Creek past Snow Creek Falls. Three miles past that junction is one with F.S. 633 up Myrtle Creek, which forms a loop with the Snow Creek road; there are trails at the head of Myrtle Creek. Farther north, F.S. 417 passes the Kootenai National Wildlife Refuge and continues to F.S. 634, which ends at a trailhead for Pyramid Peak and several small lakes. Finally, just shy of the border, F.S. 281 cuts back to the south toward the Selkirk Crest along Smith Creek.

Useful Names and Addresses

There is a **District Ranger** at Route 1, P.O. Box 390, Bonners Ferry, ID 83805 (tel: 208-267-5561). The office is on the highway south of town. In Sandpoint, on Lake Pend Oreille, is a visitor center with travel information. For Forest Service campgrounds, go south of Sandpoint along the shore of the lake.

Kellogg and Wallace Mining District

Unlike most mining areas in the Rockies, which for a variety of reasons long ago ceased operations, the mines of Shoshone County, Idaho, continue to produce some of the richest lead and silver ore in the world. Northern Idaho mining began in earnest in 1881, when Andrew J. Pritchard, who had spent considerable time quietly surveying for the best site on a promising gold prospect, finally let the news out to his friends that they should hurry and join him. That news touched off a rush to the area, and although Pritchard's discovery was nowhere near as rich as he had hoped (Pritchard is now a ghost town), the influx of prospectors quickly uncovered lodes of silver and lead at Burke and Mullan. Even larger discoveries followed at Kellogg and Wallace, where mines still operate today. Since that first discovery, over $2.5 billion worth of metals have been mined in the district, and a great deal of history made, much of it bawdy and violent, colored by labor strife and the extravagance of boom towns, big money and big politics.

Geologically, this richness of minerals is the result of intrusions into extensive surface sediments. These layers of clay and silt, accumulating on the floor of the vast Precambrian sea, which covered much of the West more than a billion years ago, forced the sea floor to sink under their increasing weight, until the sediments were 50,000 feet thick, metamorphosed by pressure into rock. As the earth's crust adjusted to this weight, the rock was folded, warped and broken by faults, which provided zones of weakness into which flowed heavily mineralized igneous material. All this was eventually uplifted and eroded, exposing the veins of mineral, making it possible for people like Noah Kellogg and Colonel Wallace to come along and find silver lying on the ground. That particular fault, the Osburn Fault, runs across Idaho and probably well into Washington, meaning that a great deal of ore still remains in the rock.

Priest Lake Recreation Area

A variety of activities is possible at Priest Lake and Upper Priest Lake, the latter reached only by boat or on foot, and managed as an undeveloped scenic area. Priest Lake, by far the larger of the two, is lined with cottages and other developments, but much of the shore is national forest or state forest land. Public boat ramps are provided at Kalispell Bay, Coolin Creek and Indian Creek. Campgrounds, some on islands, are numerous. A National Recreation Trail follows the northwestern shore. This area is most attractive to boaters and fishermen who troll for mackinaw trout.

Cedar Groves

A number of western red cedar groves survive in isolated pockets of northern Idaho. Although red cedar is valuable wood today, early loggers were more interested in white pine and took cedar only where it was particularly easy to get at. After World War II, prices rose for cedar, and loggers came looking for what they had passed up decades earlier. By then there was some interest in preserving at least a few of the old trees, and these remnant groves are a result of that timely interest.

One of the best is the Settlers Grove of Ancient Cedars, above the Avery Creek Campground on the upper Coeur d'Alene River. Its 183 acres range along the West Fork of Eagle Creek close to the Montana border; a foot trail provides access. To get there, drive north from Wallace on the Ninemile Canyon Road (F.S. 456) to either Pritchard or Murray (the roads form a loop) and from there to Eagle. About a mile and a half up Eagle Creek, F.S. 805 turns off left to follow the west fork of the creek to the cedar grove.

Another worth a visit is the 16-acre Hanna Flats Cedar Grove, on Forest Road 313, which turns off U.S. Highway 57 a few miles south of Nordman, on the west side of Priest Lake. A nature trail wanders through the grove. There are other groves, without nature trails and more difficult to get to. They include the Roosevelt Grove of Ancient Cedars, on Forest Road 302 north of Nordman near Priest Lake; the Hobo Cedar Grove Botanical Area, near Hobo Pass on Forest Road 321, which runs from Clarkia (U.S. Highway 3) to the St. Joe River near Avery; the Upper Fishhook Research Natural Area at the head of Fishhook Creek on F.S. 301 (four miles east of Avery) near the Roundtop Guard Station.

Useful Names and Addresses

A single Forest Service map ($1) covers the entire panhandle, including private and state land as well as federal; write to the Forest Supervisor, **Idaho Panhandle National Forests**, 3815 Schreiber Lane, Coeur d'Alene, ID 83814 (tel: 208-765-7223; **Coeur d'Alene Chamber of Commerce**, P.O. Box 850, Coeur d'Alene, ID 83816. A booklet, *Official Idaho Travel Guide*, describes recreation possibilities and lists campgrounds, lodging, events, outfitters and more—available free from **The Idaho Travel Council**, P.O. Box 83720, Boise, ID 83720-0093 (tel: 800-635-7820 out of state: 208-334-2470 within Idaho).

RIVERS IN THE BORDER REGION

St. Joe Wild and Scenic River

The St. Joe River, said to be the highest navigable river in the world, drains the west slope of the Bitterroot Mountains and flows 132 miles across Idaho to Coeur d'Alene Lake. Sixty-six miles of this length is designated as part of the Wild and Scenic River System; from the North Fork of the St. Joe (a few miles east of Avery, Idaho) to Spruce Tree Campground, the designation is Recreational. Beyond Spruce Tree to the headwaters at St. Joe Lake, it is a Wild River. This upper portion runs through a deep roadless canyon; the 17 miles between Heller Creek Campground and Spruce Tree Campground make a challenging two-day run for whitewater boaters, with some Class V water, log jams, sharp bends and other delights. The trick here is timing; snow keeps the road closed until early in July, but water levels are too low after the middle of the month, giving kayakers a short season. Below Spruce Tree Campground, the river gets less gnarly (Class II and III) and stays that way until it reaches Gold Creek, where it enters a narrow sheer-walled canyon and decides to get serious. The next seven miles contain the toughest water on the river, with such enticements as Tumble Down Falls, preceded by 200 yards of Class IV nastiness.

Things quiet down somewhat for another 16 miles to the Turner Hats Campground, below which lies Skookum Canyon, another boat-eater with voracious Class III and IV waves, a bit of excitement that proves to be the river's last hurrah. Over the remaining seventy miles or so, the water slows to the pace of a Sunday afternoon in August. Below Avery, all manner of craft, from kayaks to inner tubes, bob along in bouncy but easy rapids. By the time the river passes St. Joe City, the only waves come from powerboats. This is the stretch touted as the highest navigable river in the world, where tugs pull great rafts of logs to mills in Coeur d'Alene. Despite the activity, the river is pleasant for canoes and other small boats. In the last six miles, the St. Joe actually meanders *through* a series of lakes, separated from their waters by natural tree-lined levees, which are home to the largest osprey colony on the continent.

The St. Joe is a well-known fishing river, filled with native cutthroat trout among other species. No bait fishing is permitted, and special restrictions on length and numbers have helped the population recover from the overfishing of the past.

Access is simple, as long as snow does not block the roads. A county road follows most of the lower part of the river. Beyond Avery, Forest Service Road 218, generally passable to autos, parallels the river all the

way to the Red Ives Ranger Station. Above that point is the roadless
stretch of river, but a primitive road (F.S. 320) winds over a low summit
to the Heller Creek Campground, where drivers can again follow the
river for a few miles to a point five miles short of St. Joe Lake.

Useful Names and Addresses

A brochure, "St. Joe River Float Trips," is available from **U.S.F.S.
Northern Region Headquarters**, P.O. Box 7669, Missoula, MT 59807
(tel: 406-329-3511), or the **St. Joe National Forest**, Avery Ranger
District, HC01 Box 1, Avery, ID 83802 (tel: 208-245-4517).

Coeur D'Alene River

The Coeur d'Alene divides neatly into two halves. The lower half, from
historic Cataldo Mission to Coeur d'Alene Lake, drifts lazily through a
series of marshes and lakes, all easily accessible to small boats and
loaded with waterfowl. Once a conduit for mine wastes from Wallace
and Kellogg, new regulations have greatly improved the water quality.
Especially in the spring, birdwatchers will find this trip worth the
effort, although the proportion of various species changes depending
upon who is migrating through and who is nesting at any given time.
Up to two thousand whistling swans and ten thousand Canada geese
mix with snow geese, harlequin ducks, buffleheads, scaup, mallards,
widgeons, blue- and green-winged teal, cinnamon teal, goldeneyes and
many more, including perhaps the largest nesting population of wood
ducks in the Northwest; also herons, bitterns, Virginia and sora rails,
spotted sandpipers, various hawks, bald eagles, osprey and river mammals such as otter, beaver, muskrat and mink. There are numerous public access points.

The upper river is only slightly more active, except in the spring when
snowmelt hurries it along. Canoes and rafts can float this 55-mile
stretch most of the season until the end of July, after which only the part
below Shoshone Creek has enough water. For information, check at the
old Mission (now a State Park), the Idaho Fish and Game office on
Thompson Lake, or Forest Service and Bureau of Land Management
offices in Coeur d'Alene.

Priest River

Below Priest Lake, this river winds a varied course through 44 miles of
broad meanders, marshlands and swift stretches, all of it floatable by
canoes and rafts, although canoeists may want to portage the Class III
Binarch Rapids and Eight Mile Rapids during periods of high water.

After mid-July, the current slackens and boats must be dragged in shallow places.

Blackfoot River

The Blackfoot flows west from the Continental Divide north of Helena, joining the Clark Fork near Bonner. For almost forty miles, starting at Landers Fork six miles east of Lincoln, the river is gentle, meandering through ranchland in country favored by waterfowl and deer. There's a mild whitewater stretch between Bear Creek Flat and the Clearwater River Junction. From there, the river is easily accessed and scouted from U.S. Highway 200.

Dearborn River

The Dearborn, draining the Scapegoat Wilderness on the east side of the Divide, winds a serpentine course through a canyon below the U.S. Highway 287 bridge. This two-day float to the Missouri River is a popular run for canoes before the middle of July.

Flathead River

The Flathead, both above and below Flathead Lake, is big, mostly gentle canoe water. Of its three forks, the North, Middle and South, the last two begin in wilderness areas not accessible by road (see page 248 for information on running these stretches). Only the last few miles of the South Fork, from Cedar Creek to Hungry Horse Reservoir, can be reached by car. U.S. Highway 2 parallels the Middle Fork from a point near Essex, where the river emerges from the Great Bear Wilderness. Some of this is good kayaking water, easily accessed and scouted from the highway. Other parts, depending on level, are comfortable for open canoes. The North Fork of the Flathead rates as one of Montana's loveliest rivers. It begins in Canada and forms the border of Glacier Park for 58 miles to its junction with the Middle Fork. A gravel road, not visually intrusive from the river, parallels it all the way. The water is emerald green, cold and filled with fish. The mountains of Glacier roll along to the east as its rivers augment the flow. Not a quiet water trip, it is feasible nonetheless for canoes, with several portages and care to avoid logjams.

Kootenai River

West of the Flathead Valley flows the Kootenai River, down from Canada, across the corners of Montana and Idaho, and back into British Columbia where it joins the Columbia River. Much of the Kootenai is backed up by the Libby Dam. What remains is a short stretch of mixed water below the dam, most of it suitable for open boats, with whitewater stretches just above and below Kootenai Falls, which lies below Libby. After Troy, and all the way to Canada, the river is big, powerful Class I water—popular with all sorts of boaters. The Moyie River, an Idaho tributary, is more lively. During spring runoff, it provides some Class III kayaking water between Copper Creek and the Meadow Creek Bridge (harder water below Meadow Creek in a tight canyon) ebbing to Class II canoe water for a brief period before the water is too low to run at all.

Swan River

The upper Swan River above Swan Lake is small but scenic and floatable for its entire length. Like many small rivers in forest country, however, logjams spanning from bank to bank can be a serious hazard during times of high water. Below the lake lies a short two miles of rapids; after that the river is placid.

CHAPTER SIX

Canadian Rockies Region

THE CANADIAN ROCKIES are simpler in structure than the American end of the range. They average only 80 km. (50 mi.) wide, bordered on the east by the Great Plains and on the west by a distinct geographic feature, the Rocky Mountain Trench, a deep, straight, glacier-carved valley which runs from northern Montana all the way to northern British Columbia. Every range east of the trench is part of the Rockies; mountains to the west are not. Through the southern half of the trench flow the Columbia and Kootenay rivers, draining in opposite directions, and then joining west of the Columbia Mountains. These, which include the well-known Selkirks, Cariboos, Purcells and Monashees, are not part of the Rockies. Although this guide includes portions of them, it's important to point out the distinction; residents of the Purcells consider it a serious faux pas to equate their mountains with the Rockies.

The heart of the Canadian Rockies is found somewhere within the Banff-Jasper area, where the range achieves its scenic climax. Mount Robson, on the north corner of Jasper Park, has the highest summit and an appearance worthy of its status, but even so it is one of the many superlative peaks which shoulder against each other for hundreds of linear miles.

The geology of these mountains is also simpler than that of Colorado. They are built of the same layered deposits dating into Precambrian times more than 600 million years ago, deposits of ancient sea bottoms and shorelines. For a time, the western part of the continent

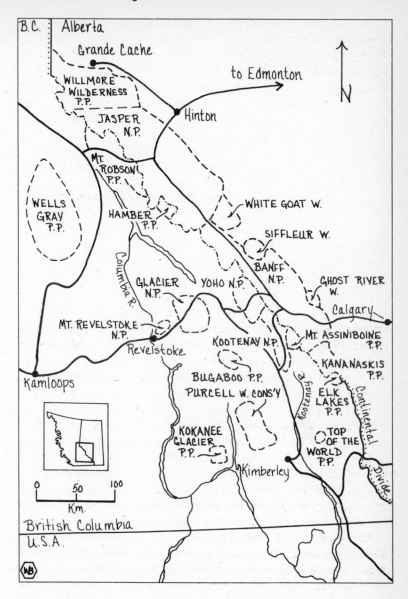

was under water, its coast in the area of today's Great Plains; then the situation reversed itself, and the middle portion of the continent was flooded. This was a period of relative geologic quiet, during which life in the seas evolved from the simplest of plants and animals to more complex forms. Shelled animals appeared, as did fish. They began to live out of the water—first plants, then animals. All of these developments are recorded in the orderly layers of sand- and mud-stones.

Changes began happening around 200 to 150 million years ago, as the continental plates of North America and Eurasia began pushing apart. Mountain building progressed from the western edge of the continent, gradually at first, but with periods of intense activity. As the edge of the continent was lifted above the seas, erosion began its work, scouring off the uppermost layers, exposing the harder metamorphic rocks, which make up the B.C. interior ranges today. It took a long time for the seas to drain away completely. As they did, migrating slowly eastward, erosion continued to deposit material along the swampy shoreline. In the swamps grew a profusion of plants and animals that one day would become coal.

About 70 million years ago, the Canadian Rockies came into being, as a result of the same episode, the Laramide Orogeny, that lifted the entire range. They were thrust upward along a fault which created the Rocky Mountain Trench. East of the trench, like parallel corrugations, 80 km. (50 mi.) of mountain crests appeared where the land had been virtually flat. The uplift was not perfectly clean; a great deal of folding, bending and fracturing took place, as we can see from the tilt and warp of the once horizontal strata. Following uplift came erosion, by wind, water, frost, and gravity and, finally, by glaciers, to create the landscape as we see it today.

History

When President Thomas Jefferson sent Meriwether Lewis and William Clark on their historic expedition to explore the Northwest and find a trade route to the Pacific Coast, repercussions were felt in the British colony of Canada. The North West Company, based in Montreal, Quebec, saw in the American expedition a threat to its own trading ambitions. Fearing American dominance of the Pacific Coast, the company decided it was time to expand across the Rockies.

The key figure in its efforts was David Thompson. He was a surveyor and map maker, and an extraordinarily competent explorer. During his career, he traveled extensively west of the Rockies, as far south as North Dakota, and north to the sub-Arctic. In 1810, he was sent to explore the Columbia River, believed by his company to be the best chance for a water route from the Rockies to the ocean. He had explored that country several years earlier but had failed to recognize the Columbia in its upper reaches. What confused him, understandably, was the Great Bend of the river. He had no way of knowing that the Columbia, which rises at Columbia Lake near Canal Flats, British

Columbia, flows hard and purposefully northward for some 240 km. (150 mi.) before turning abruptly to the south, and then with no further indecision, makes for the Pacific Ocean between the states of Washington and Oregon. The reason for the detour is the immovable Selkirk and Purcell ranges; in effect, the Columbia probes its way north until it finds a weakness which allows it past the mountains.

In 1810, Thompson knew better, and although a variety of problems delayed him, he did finally reach the mouth of the Columbia in 1811, by way of a prodigious midwinter crossing of Athabasca Pass in today's Jasper National Park. As subsequent trade to the interior developed, brigades from west of the Divide would meet their colleagues from the east at a spot just east of Athabasca Pass (a tarn called the Committee's Punch Bowl by Sir George Simpson) to exchange furs for trade goods. This route was abandoned in 1826, but it says much about the stamina and determination of the fur traders that even today a foot trail is the only way over Athabasca Pass, and not a trivial one either.

As a result of the fur trade, travel routes were developed, but just as had happened in the United States, it was the search for gold that provided the major impetus in the settling of the Rockies by whites. However, in the Canadian West, the first big push came not from the East, but from the Pacific Coast. It was many years before the prairie provinces saw the wagons and plows of settlers.

The rush came from the direction of San Francisco in 1858. The California gold excitement had come and gone in the decade just past, and the Colorado rush was still two years away. The nascent city of Saint Francis and the nearby Sierra foothills were packed with prospectors, gold-seekers and arguments about where the next strike would be found. There had been rumors of gold in many places, including the Fraser River Valley up north in British territory, but none was substantial enough to trigger a rush.

Meanwhile, James Douglas, governor of the Crown Colony of Vancouver Island, had collected, in the course of doing business, a considerable quantity of gold dust from various prospectors working interior streams. Nervous about having to protect this gold, he decided to send 800 ounces of it to the San Francisco Mint. Instead of mineral dust, it might have been gunpowder tossed on the embers of gold fever. The rush was on. All available ships were chartered. Into the town of Victoria, a heretofore quiet and orderly British colonial capital with fewer than five hundred residents, came the mobs of prospectors: Americans, Britons and an assortment of Europeans, 30,000 of them by the end of summer, 1858. The price of a building lot jumped overnight from a few dollars to more than $3,000.

It lasted only a year, but then, just as the Fraser rush began to fade, news of the Cariboo bonanza took its place. The stories were as fabulous as any others in the Rockies at that time, whether referring to Colorado, Montana, California or British Columbia. "Doc" Keithley and George Weaver kicked off the Cariboo rush when they found placer gravel with quarter-pound nuggets lying in the shallows. Later, J.C. Bryant took 96 ounces of gold, worth $1,543 then (and over $300,000 now), from a single pan. Some claims netted over a million 1860 dollars. The town of Barkerville swelled to a population of 10,000, with stores selling flour at $300 per barrel, boots for $50 a pair, one dance with a saloon girl for $10.

The prices reflected not only the amount of gold available, but also the distance from sources of supply. Ships brought most goods from California, but some traveled all the way from the East Coast or England. Unloaded in Victoria, everything was carried inland 800 km. (500 mi.), first by packhorse over rough trails and eventually by wagons following a stage road famous for its spectacular cliff-hugging route up the Fraser River Canyon. By the end of the 1860s, about $100,000,000 in gold had been mined. Through all the excitement, the rule of British law was maintained. To be sure, the Canadian frontier was a rough and tumble place in those years, but it was spared the violence that prevailed in the American gold fields.

The situation was entirely different on the plains, where a virulent sort of lawlessness and greed finally became such a sore that official notice of the eastern slope was inevitable. In 1869, two unprincipled scoundrels, John Healy and Al Hamilton, set up a trading post just north of the U.S. border on the plains. They traded with Indians, but instead of useful goods, they provided a concoction they called whiskey; it was really a vile mix of grain alcohol, water and such unlikely ingredients as Tabasco and sulfuric acid. It had terrible effects on drinkers, who went on a rampage and destroyed the establishment when told there was no more to be had. The traders, undaunted by that first loss and encouraged by the obvious demand, built a stronger, more easily defended log fort with small windows in the walls. With characteristic frontier lack of subtlety, they called the new building Fort Whoop-Up. Furs and anything else the Indians had to sell were passed in; rot-gut was passed out (and so, after a while, were the clients). The scene was a scandal; stripped of all valuables and dignity, Indians offered their wives and daughters. Despite the walls, some fifty whites were killed at the fort in the early 1870s. But Healy and Hamilton profited: in their first six months of business, they took in $50,000 worth of goods.

Although Fort Whoop-Up was the most notorious, it was not alone.

Others included Fort Stand-Off, Fort Slide-Out and numerous one-horse, fly-by-night businesses. The whiskey trade flourished to such an extent, causing so many deaths and arousing such bitterness among the Plains Indians, that the stir finally reached Ottawa, where the government of Prime Minister John A. Macdonald established a frontier police force: The North-West Mounted Police, called today the Royal Canadian Mounted Police. The formation of the "Mounties" was either an act of blind foolishness or of pure genius. On the U.S. side of the border at that time, the American Army, replete with Civil War heroes, military expertise and thousands of mounted soldiers, was bungling the job of keeping the U.S. frontier peaceful. How could a mere 300 Canadians, most of them complete strangers to the West, expect to do any better?

What they accomplished was a frontier miracle. Somehow those few red-coated, well-disciplined men were able to impress the whiskey traders, and subsequently the Plains Indians, that they represented legitimate authority. The whiskey trade came to an abrupt halt in the first year of the police presence, 1875. Soon a series of treaties were signed with the Cree, Blackfoot, Blood and Piegan tribes. These treaties resembled those forced upon Indians in the United States, but for the most part, they were upheld. Canada had Indian wars, but on nowhere near the scale of the wars in the United States. The difference between the way matters were handled in the two countries is well illustrated by the events of 1877. After the Battle of the Little Big Horn, where Custer and his men met their deaths, thousands of Sioux, including the famous chief Sitting Bull, fled north to Canada. There, they met the Mounties, who numbered approximately the same as Custer's dead soldiers, and who never drew up into any sort of aggressive battle array. The Mounties simply stated that in Canada the law was supreme, and there would be no disorder. Somehow they prevailed.

From the 1880s, settlement of the region proceeded much the same as it did in the United States. The Canadian Pacific Railway spanned the nation in 1885, the final spike hammered at Craigellachie in the British Columbia Selkirks on November 7. Large groups of immigrants poured in from the East and from Europe. They joined others coming from the West Coast, including significant numbers from Japan and China. Prairie towns grew up as transport and supply centers for ranchers, farmers, miners, loggers, road builders and others. Parts of the Rockies were set aside as national parks to encourage tourism. Toward the end of the century, the Klondike gold rush in faraway Yukon Territory drew prospectors from all directions, even through the unlikely gateway of Edmonton, which quadrupled in size as a result, and continued to grow with the discovery of the Peace River Valley's great agricultural potential.

The scene today is one of continued growth, becoming always more diverse. The cities of Calgary and Edmonton, despite a recent cycle of boom and bust associated with energy development and changes in the world economy, rise skyward in clusters of glass and steel office buildings. Oil and gas exploration shares the eastern slope with coal developments. In the interior of British Columbia, towns and cities which have for decades based their economies on mining and logging struggle to diversify as mines run out or become unprofitable, and as logging becomes more expensive. Communities turn to tourism, agriculture and light industry to replace their old dependence on primary resources. The story is the same all over the Rockies, and it's probably a healthy transition for the area's economy.

Useful Names and Addresses

Tourism British Columbia, 1117 Wharf St., Victoria, BC V8W 2Z2 (among other things, they provide a complete guide to accommodations in the province); **MAPS BC**, Surveys and Mapping Branch, Ministry of the Environment, Parliament Buildings, Victoria, BC V8V 1X4 (tel: 604-387-1441); **MAPS Alberta**, 2nd Floor West, North Tower, Petroleum Plaza, 9945 108th St., Edmonton, AB T5K 2G6 (tel: 403-297-7389); **Hostelling International—B.C. Region**, 134 Abbott St., #402, Vancouver, BC V6B 2K4 (tel: 604-684-7101); **Hostelling International—Southern Alberta**, 1414 Kensington Rd. NW, #203, Calgary, AB T2N 3P9 (tel: 403-283-5551); **BC Parks**, Box 118, Wasa, BC V0B 2K0 (tel: 604-422-3212).

A variety of vacation planning publications is available from **Travel Alberta**, P.O. Box 2500, Edmonton, AB T5J 2Z4. Information phone number across Canada and the U.S. (including Hawaii) is 800-661-8888, or 403-427-4321.

A Climber's Guide to the Interior Ranges of British Columbia, by William Putnam, comes in two volumes, published by the Alpine Club of Canada and the American Alpine Club. *A Climber's Guide to the Rocky Mountains of Canada*, by William Putnam and Glen Boles, is also available in two volumes (the south volume covers the border to Howse Pass) from the same publishers.

BANFF NATIONAL PARK AND SOUTH

Banff is the cornerstone of Canada's national park system. It was the first to be established, and events here had a strong impact on the growth of the national park philosophy throughout Canada and the world. We look at it today as a nature preserve, a remnant island of wildness in a sea of development and change. But a century ago, it represented the opposite; in 1885, most of the continent was wilderness, and the park facilities, so far removed from cities and farms, were seen as outposts of civilization. It seems ironic today, but Banff was conceived in the spirit of development, not conservation, and was born as a by-product of national expansion—a child of the Canadian Pacific Railway.

The same was true of parks and resorts all over the West—Yellowstone, Glacier, Sun Valley, the Grand Canyon and Jasper among them. Even before the transcontinental railroads were completed in both the United States and Canada, promoters were hard at work finding ways of encouraging passenger travel. They quickly learned that western scenery was a saleable commodity, that people would pay money simply to come and look at the mountains and to walk around in them. The visitors required not only transport to the Rockies, but also hotels, trails and other facilities. The railroad companies could provide all of this, but to make the venture really successful, they wanted to protect themselves from competition. This is where the parks came in. If the government owned the land and declared it a nature preserve, then development could be restricted. The railroads, of course, would obtain permits to build what they considered the proper sort of facilities in approved places, and would be assured that both the scenery and their commercial monopolies would remain intact.

This is reflected in Banff's history. The Canadian government made the first move in 1885, when it established a 26-sq. km. (10-sq. mi.) park encompassing the Cave and Basin Hot Springs, thus ending a heated controversy among rival claimants to ownership of the springs. The government called this park the Hot Springs Reserve and meant to operate it along the lines of a European spa. Meanwhile, William Cornelius Van Horne, the American who was largely responsible for construction of the Canadian Pacific Railway, began building a resort in the vicinity. He named the growing settlement after Banffshire, the Scottish birthplace of the railroad's president. Two years later, in 1887, the reserve was enlarged to 670 sq. km. (260 sq. mi.), and renamed Rocky Mountain National Park. However, people commonly called it Banff, after the C.P.R. town at its heart, and eventually, as the park was enlarged to its current size of 6,640 sq. km. (2,564 sq. mi.) in 1930, this became its official name.

For the first forty years or so, Banff was a destination for the well-to-do, for those who could afford not only the train fare, but also the lodging costs and, perhaps most importantly, the time away from work for a holiday. They came to the Rockies for scenery, elegant accommodations and genteel exercise. They dressed formally for dinner and wore only the

Moraine Lake in Banff National Park occupies the Valley of the Ten Peaks. To the north and west lie the equally spectacular valleys of Lake O'Hara and Lake Louise.

latest sporting fashions on treks along the trails and up the mountains in the company of imported European guides. For them were built most of the early facilities in the prime locations—the Banff Springs Hotel and Chateau Lake Louise. Their interests and desires established a tradition for the use of national parks as recreation grounds. As a result, Banff and other Canadian parks have not only trails and grand hotels, but tea houses, ski areas, golf courses and tennis courts as well.

It's not that the parks were closed to less wealthy people by any conscious policy, but they may as well have been. If you couldn't afford train fare and lodging, you had precious few alternatives. What changed the situation was the development of the automobile, and specifically, the Model T. Henry Ford, through the revolution of mass production, made it possible for a family of average income to own a private means of transport. Suddenly, middle class people could afford to go anywhere there were roads. If they wanted, and many did, they could carry camping equipment, thereby freeing themselves from the expense of hotels and restaurants. All they needed was gasoline for the car; certainly no one cared if they dressed for dinner or not.

James B. Harkin, appointed in 1911 as the first commissioner of Canada's parks, recognized the change. Motivated by his personal belief that the parks should be open to all Canadians, he lifted the existing ban on automobiles and pushed for the development of roads through the Rockies.

To say that Harkin's democratic ideas were successful is a vast understatement. By 1920, the Banff-Lake Louise road was finished. Three years later, the Banff-Windermere Highway opened. In 1940, the ribbon was cut on the Banff-Jasper Highway. And it continues today. The main east-west road is the Trans-Canada Highway, carrying huge volumes of traffic and freight in addition to a year-round flood of park visitors. Massive transport trucks compete with bicycles and motorhomes for space. During heavy use periods, vehicles back up on the east side of Banff townsite for miles. The government, in an attempt to accommodate the ever-increasing flood of traffic, is currently widening the road from two to four lanes. With these superhighways, the temptation to see the park from the seat of a vehicle is one which most visitors succumb to. But it is good to remember the thoughts of James Harkin; despite strongly favoring the construction of main routes, he restricted side roads, because "it is only from the trails that one can get into real intimacy with the peaks." Even Henry Ford would have agreed.

The Rockies in the area of Banff are roughly 80 km. (50 mi.) wide, sharply defined on both their east and west slopes. On the east, the rolling plains beat against the base of the range, uncompromised by foothills, like the sea against a fortress island. The western slope plunges just as abruptly into the Rocky Mountain Trench, the glaciated valley separating the Rockies from their older neighbors in the interior of British Columbia. The Trans-Canada Highway crosses the range in tandem with the railroad, by following the Bow River through its big interior valley, past Banff and Lake Louise to Kicking Horse Pass. From there it abandons the Bow Valley and crosses to Yoho National Park.

If, however, you turn north and stay with the Bow River, you enter the Icefields Parkway, a 230-km. (143-mi.) drive through the center of the Rockies, following interior valleys in the embrace of parallel ranges all the way to Jasper townsite. The Continental Divide stays to your left all the way, its crest laden with glaciers and snowfields, which feed the rivers and lakes in the valley bottom. The peaks to the east are no less spectacular; behind their towering summits, invisible from the road, stretches the bulk of Banff's backcountry. The road soon reaches Bow Summit and enters a new drainage. At Saskatchewan Crossing, where the Mistaya meets the Saskatchewan River (and the highway is joined by Route 11 from the east), the road continues northward along the Saskatchewan to the Columbia Icefield on the border with Jasper National Park. Most people drive this route in a day or two, hurrying along with their mouths agape, but apparently not aware that mountains just don't get any better than this. Take your time; the nicest campgrounds in the park are found along this stretch of road.

Trails

Banff presents such a lavish array of scenery and recreational opportunities, that it's hard to know where to begin, but one should certainly start with a walk. The park has over 1,300 km. (700 mi.) of hiking trails, and any degree of difficulty is available, from an amble along a lakeshore to a lengthy backcountry hike. Lake Louise and environs is the popular center for hikers, and for obvious reasons. The trails around the hotel might be as crowded as a Banff townsite sidewalk, but within a short distance, you leave the jostling behind, and the farther you go, the happier you become. Few alpine settings in the world rival this valley for the sheer feelings of exuberance it imparts. A shoreline trail, broad and level, leads from the Chateau to the other end of the lake and back. Continuing on that trail up the valley for about two hours of walking, you come to the Plain of Six Glaciers and a fine viewpoint at the base of Mounts Victoria and Lefroy. A teahouse, reminiscent of the park's luxury years, provides lunch or snacks. On the way back, an optional trail branches to the north, climbing to Lake Agnes (another teahouse here), hidden behind a high knob called the Beehive and then returning to the Chateau.

Trails from Lake Louise connect southward to Paradise Valley and beyond to Moraine Lake and the exquisite Valley of Ten Peaks, all feasible as day-trips for strong hikers. You can also drive to Moraine Lake and choose from a number of trails radiating from there. One of the best day-hikes in the Rockies is the one to Eiffel Lake and Wenkchemna Pass. If possible, try to walk this trail in early fall when the larch trees have turned gold and the sharp edge of winter is in the air.

Nearby is the Sunshine Ski Resort. At the top of the lifts (which operate only during ski season), a short walk leads to Sunshine Meadows, filled with wildflowers, dotted with lakes and ringed by superb views of surrounding peaks, including the distant Mount Assiniboine. Trails lead from here over Healy Pass to the outstanding Egypt Lakes area, a backpacking destination reachable by several other routes, which are perhaps more pleasing to the wilderness traveler than the gondola ride. Also from here, a trail sets off southward over Citadel Pass to Mount Assiniboine.

Around Banff townsite, short trails go in every direction. One leads halfway up Mount Rundle (the distinctive angular peak with its steep western slope and eastern cliffs). Another climbs to Cascade Amphitheatre, opposite Mount Norquay's ski area. The Spray River Trail provides a gentler walk, as does the Bow River Trail. You can hike up Sulphur Mountain in about two hours and ride down on the gondola, or (for those with strong knees) ride up and walk down. Another fine view of the valley can be had on a shorter trail (45 minutes) to Stoney Squaw on the flanks of Cascade Mountain.

Outside this central area, trails tend to be longer and less used, except for the short walks at stops along the highways (Bow Summit and Peyto Lake is one of these). Backpackers should consider trips in two regions of the park: anything along the Icefields Parkway, but especially the high country of the Slate Range, Skoki Valley and Ptarmigan Valley; and the south end of Banff, toward Assiniboine and the Spray River. For really remote country and primitive trail conditions, head for the area between and north of the Palliser and the Sawback ranges on the east side of the park.

Other Ideas

Bus tours are conducted throughout the park, connecting to Jasper and other locations. Gondola rides are offered by the ski resort at Lake Louise, and on Sulphur Mountain, overlooking the townsite. Horseback riding, river rafting, guided hiking and climbing trips can all be booked through the Chamber of Commerce (address below). Canoes, bicycles and camping gear can be rented at sports equipment stores in Banff; also, a boat livery on Lake Louise rents canoes.

Banff Townsite

Banff has a bustling business district (a charitable way to put it), where you can buy everything you need and many things you don't. Restaurants, motels, lodges, trinket shops and throbbing discos crowd Banff Avenue and its side streets, mixed together in a commercial bouillabaisse with a few real pearls to be found. You expect to find good sporting equipment shops (there are several), good restaurants (ditto) and good bookstores (at least one, on Banff Avenue), but some other facilities might come as a surprise. The Banff Centre and School of Fine Arts (tel: 403-762-6100) provides a year-long schedule of concerts, dance, theater, films, workshops and seminars. During summer, a continual program is offered by the Banff Festival of the Arts. Many of the events are free of charge, and none is expensive. To get tickets or a schedule, call the festival office at 403-762-6300, or write to the Banff Centre, P.O. Box 1020, Banff, AB ToL oCo. Every autumn in early November, the Centre plays host to the Banff Festival of Mountain Films, one of the best such festivals in North America. Tickets are usually sold out more than a month ahead of time; call 403-762-6351 for reservations.

Another of Banff's treasures is the Archives and Library, Whyte

Banff Avenue and the lower town of Banff. The town celebrated its centennial in 1985.

Museum of the Canadian Rockies. It contains 4,000 volumes, 1,900 pamphlets, 400,000 photos, 1,000 maps and 150 m. (480 ft.) of records, manuscripts, diaries and so forth. The Alpine Club of Canada Library has 2,400 volumes, 450 pamphlets and a large collection of club papers and journals. Founded by Peter and Catharine Whyte in the 1950s to collect art and artifacts from the Rocky Mountain region, the Whyte Museum also collected photos, books and related materials. Its geographic scope is limited to the Canadian Rockies and immediate area; however, the Alpine Club of Canada Library is international in scope.

The mountain archives and its libraries is a dream world of books and papers dealing with the human passion for mountains all over the world, for as long as people have written on the subject.

From the Soviet Pamirs to Kilimanjaro, from Antarctica to the Himalayas, this collection is a joy to browse through. Services of the archives include reprints of photos and photocopies of materials for research purposes. The reading room is open every day but Sunday from May to Canadian Thanksgiving, from 1 P.M. to 5 P.M. Winter hours are the same, with the addition of Thursday evenings. For information contact the Whyte Museum of the Canadian Rockies, Box 160, Banff, AB ToL oCo (tel: 403-762-2291, ext. 335).

On Banff Avenue stands the old Banff Park Museum, which has been kept in its original condition with old-fashioned exhibits—a museum of a museum, really, and a great pleasure to wander through. Interpretive signs explain the history of the museum and how the collections were made.

Banff has a modern hot springs pool called the Upper Hot Springs (cross the bridge at the south end of Banff Avenue, turn left and follow the signs). For 1985, the park's centennial year, the once decrepit Cave and Basin Hot Springs was restored and reopened as the Cave and Basin Centennial Centre, a historic museum with guided tours, access to the cave and interpretive programs—but no bathing. To get there, go to the south end of Banff Avenue and turn right.

Some Useful Information About Banff

HOW TO GET THERE: By air, Calgary is the nearest jetport. Bus lines run from there to the park (**Brewster**, tel: 403-221-8242 or 800-661-1152; **Laidlaw**, tel: 403-762-9102; and **Greyhound** from the city center, tel: 800-661-8747). Also, a shuttle bus runs from the airport to hotels in the city. The only passenger train to Banff is the Rocky Mountaineer Railtour, a two-day excursion from Vancouver (tel: 800-665-7245). Driving to Banff, four highways enter from the east, west and north.

CAMPGROUNDS: Banff has 13 campgrounds, which vary in the services they provide and the fees charged. The simplest have potable water and pit toilets; others have showers, and the most elaborate have hookups for trailers and motorhomes. Prices range from $10 to $22 in this order: Rampart Creek, Mosquito Creek, $10; Waterfowl, Two Jack Main, Castle Mountain, Protection Mountain, $13; Lake Louise Tent, $14; Tunnel Mountain Village I, Two Jack Lakeside, Johnston Canyon, $16; Lake Louise Trailer, $18; Tunnel Mountain Village II, $19; and Tunnel Mountain Trailer, $22. Backcountry camping is $6 per person per night (or $42 per season), and permits are required. Campgrounds open and close on a staggered schedule from early May to late September.

Winter camping is permitted at Lake Louise, Mosquito Creek and Tunnel Mountain Village (electrical hookups). There is no reservation system.

LODGING: The choice is wide. A list of lodgings can be obtained from the **Banff/Lake Louise Tourism Bureau**, P.O. Box 1298, Banff, AB ToL oCo (tel: 403-762-8421). At the top of the scale are the **Banff Springs Hotel** and **Chateau Lake Louise** (although both hotels offer a range of prices). Moderately priced motels are located in both Banff and Lake Louise, and budget travelers will be interested in the excellent system of hostels (address on page 274). Lodging reservations should be made well in advance during summer months.

USEFUL NAMES AND ADDRESSES: The main park information center is in downtown Banff (224 Banff Ave., tel: 403-762-1550), open every day with lengthened hours in summer. Another information center is at Lake Louise (the highway junction, not the lake itself, tel: 403-522-3833). Warden offices are found at Banff (tel: 403-762-1470) and Saskatchewan River Crossing. The park administrative offices are at the south end of Banff Avenue (tel: 403-762-1500). The mailing address is: **Parks Canada**, P.O. Box 900, Banff, AB ToL oCo.

YOHO NATIONAL PARK

Yoho, a Cree Indian word which, if loosely translated, means "Wonderful!", is an appropriate comment on the upper valley of the Kicking Horse River, which, we can assume is kicking its heels in exuberance. The park is small in comparison to its neighbors—a compact 1,300 sq. km. (500 sq. mi.)—but crammed into those boundaries is a fine collection of wonders. They include 28 peaks over 3,000 m. (9,800 ft.) (the highest being Mount Goodsir at 3,562 m. (11,686 ft.), several icefields, numerous separate glaciers, deep forested side valleys and expanses of tundra meadows set with turquoise alpine lakes. Banff Park adjoins Yoho in the east, while Kootenay National Park lies immediately south. The Kicking Horse Valley bisects the park and provides a route for the Trans-Canada Highway and the tracks of the Canadian Pacific Railway.

Four hundred kilometers (250 mi.) of trails traverse the park, with most activity centered on three popular areas, Emerald Lake, the Upper Yoho Valley and Lake O'Hara. Longer trails up the Amiskwi and Ottertail rivers see less use and penetrate the more remote parts of the park.

The beauty of Lake O'Hara surpasses anyone's ability to exaggerate. Because it lies just over the Divide from that more famous (and crowded) alpine basin, some call it the flip side of Lake Louise. But that suggests a secondary status, which simply doesn't apply. It makes no sense to try rating one place against the other. One thing, however, can be said with certainty: O'Hara alone is worthy of a person's entire vacation, a judgment with which many people agree. What saves it from becoming another Lake Louise is that vehicles are not permitted access. You must either walk in or ride a shuttle bus up the 11-km. (7-mi.) road. Room on the bus is limited, and a fee is charged; reservations are necessary. Demand usually outstrips the number of seats for reasons that are obvious once you arrive. Once at the lake, you have the option of camping (reservations required) or of staying in the Alpine Club of Canada Hut (simple shelter, no services provided) or the private Lake O'Hara Lodge, both of which are often booked months in advance. In winter, the valley is open for people willing to ski the distance; lodging is available in both the A.C.C. hut and the lodge.

In addition to Lake O'Hara, more than twenty-five other lakes, including Lake Oesa, Lake McArthur, Morning Glory Lakes and Opabin Lakes decorate a series of cirque basins. Rising above them in a splendid array of layered rock, blue ice and snow are the same two mountains that dominate the skyline above Lake Louise—Mounts Victoria and Lefroy—in addition to Yukness Mountain, Mount Schaffer and the Wiwaxy Peaks. Trails interconnect throughout the cirques, which hold the lakes and traverse high across the mountain flanks, making this an ideal place to day-hike or climb from a base camp.

Yoho Valley is more accessible and no less rewarding. Visitors are allowed to drive as far as 380-m. (1,247-ft.) Takakkaw Falls, from which trails ascend to the alpine basins of Yoho and Little Yoho. As in the O'Hara Valley, the trail system is extensive and interconnected, allowing a variety of routes beneath the encircling crest of ice-capped mountains. One of the most satisfying is the High Line Trail, from Twin Falls to Yoho Lake, a long day-hike from the trailhead, but parts of it can be cut off by taking intermediate trails. Three backcountry campsites are located in the valley, as well as the Twin Falls Chalet, a private lodge (reservations necessary). At the trailhead is a walk-in campground and a youth hostel.

Yet a third area worthy of attention is Emerald Lake, accessible by auto, and the starting point for its own system of trails, including the very fine circle from the lake to Yoho Pass and back via the high traverse of Wapta Mountain to Burgess Pass. It can be done as a stiff day-hike. Another rewarding destination is Hamilton Lake, about 850 m. (2,790 ft.) above Emerald Lake at the base of Mount Carnarvon's south face.

Yoho has five campgrounds, three of which accommodate vehicles. These are Hoodoo Creek and Chancellor Peak, a short distance from the west entrance, and Kicking Horse, 5 km. (3 mi.) east of Field. The others, at Lake O'Hara and Takakkaw Falls, are for walk-in use. The Lake O'Hara Campground has 30 sites—5 are open on a first-come, first-served basis, and 25 can be reserved. The maximum stay is four nights. The bus (fee charged) operates four times per day, depending on season; call 604-343-6433 for reservations. Backcountry campers must obtain a permit, available at information stations and the park operations center. A quota system is in effect, and during summer, the popular campsites are often filled.

The town of Field provides essential services, including lodging, gas and groceries. Information centers are located near the west entrance and a short distance up the Yoho Valley road. In addition, the park operations center is a few minutes' drive west of Field.

Useful Names and Addresses

For more information, contact **Yoho National Park,** Box 99, Field, BC V0A 1G0 (tel: 604-343-6324). **Alpine Club of Canada** (tel: 403-678-3200). **Lake O'Hara Lodge,** Box 55, Lake Louise, AB T0L 1E0 (tel: 604-343-6418; off-season 403-678-4110).

KOOTENAY NATIONAL PARK

Kootenay National Park consists of two long, deep valleys. The Vermilion River drains the upper valley, compressed between mountains of the Continental Divide on the east and those of the Vermilion Range on the west. At its lower end, the river punches dramatically through the Vermilion Range to join the Kootenay River, which continues south until it finds a way into the Rocky Mountain Trench beyond Canal Flats. One of the interesting features of local geography is that the Kootenay actually begins some 150 km. (93 mi.) north of the Columbia River headwaters; the two great rivers flow parallel to each other, in opposite directions, separated only by a narrow chain of mountains for all that distance.

Kootenay's boundaries encompass 1,406 sq. km. (543 sq. mi.) of these two valleys, extending to the crests of the ranges on both sides. The park had its beginnings as a road-building project around the turn of the century. The area near Windermere Lake in the Rocky Mountain Trench showed agricultural promise, and developers knew that to take advantage of the good growing conditions, a road would be necessary to transport the produce. Accordingly, construction began in 1911, funded mainly by British Columbia, but was interrupted by World War I. After the war, as a way of raising funds for the project, R. Randolph

Bruce, a Windermere mine owner, developer and eventually Lieutenant Governor of British Columbia, suggested that the province offer land for a national park in exchange for federal funding. The federal government agreed to this, the land was transferred, and the road completed to the Banff Highway in 1923.

Kootenay is bounded by Yoho Park on the north, Banff Park on the east and Assiniboine Park on the southeast. Its mountains are the same broad, sedimentary masses of layered, loose rock as those found in the neighboring parks, and rise on the same grand scale. The park's west entrance surely ranks as one of the most dramatic mountain gateways in the Rockies. From the town of Radium, the highway twists through the narrow gorge of Sinclair Creek, past the famous hot springs, and then climbs purposefully to Sinclair Pass. It looks like any other scenic mountain road until, suddenly, it breaks out high on the slope of the Brisco Range overlooking the lush green Kootenay Valley, a classic of glacial erosion threaded by the silver gleam of the Kootenay River and bounded on its far side by the high peaks of the Vermilion Range.

At its opposite end, the road climbs to the headwaters of the river at Vermilion Pass through the remains of a 24-sq. km. (9-sq. mi.) forest fire, which burned in 1968. The silvery, weathered trunks of standing dead trees cover the slopes, while in their thin shade new growth vigorously pushes up to replace the old. Park managers have recently come to view forest fires like this one as natural forces, which have always had a place in the ecology of wild areas. Indeed, as they study the effects of fire on a wilderness, they find that fire is important to the overall health and diversity of a forest. Vermilion Pass is an interesting place to see how a mountain ecosystem recovers from apparent devastation.

Other places of particular interest include Marble Canyon, a deep, smoothly polished gorge below Vermilion Pass with a nature trail along its rim. Farther down the valley, another nature trail leads a short distance to the Paint Pots, a source of ochre, which Indians used to paint their tipis and bodies. Near the Simpson River junction is an animal lick frequented by the park's large mammals. Even mountain goats can be seen at the mineral licks at the base of Mount Wardle within several feet of the highway, causing summer traffic jams. At the west entrance is Radium Hot Springs, a developed mineral pool and bath, a pleasant stop for anyone in need of a soak.

Trails all begin from the highway, most of them ascending side valleys to alpine basins, or crossing passes into neighboring parks. In the northwest, trails enter two parallel valleys drained by Ochre Creek and Tokumm Creek. Both are superb hiking areas. The Rockwall, the sheer eastern face of the Vermilion Range, towers above the Ochre

Creek Trail, which leads eventually to the Ottertail River and Yoho Park; as counterpoint to the valley route, a 50-km. (31-mi.) high line trail skirts the very base of the Rockwall between Floe Lake and upper Helmet Creek. The trail along Tokumm Creek, through Prospectors Valley, takes hikers to superb Kaufman Lake in the shadow of the same mountains that form the dramatic skyline above Moraine Lake in Banff Park.

Another long-distance route begins at the junction of the Simpson and Vermilion rivers, leading by way of Surprise Creek and Ferro Pass to Mount Assiniboine; or turning north, to the Simpson Pass and Egypt Lakes area in Banff Park. Shorter hikes include the climb to Stanley Glacier near the east entrance, a distance of about 4 km. (2.5 mi.). The trail to Floe Lake, in the shadow of the southern Rockwall, is about 10 km. (6 mi.) long and worth every step. The lake gets its name from floating bergs, which break from the glacier on its western shore, but its most noteworthy feature is the stupendous face rising 1,000 m. (3,280 ft.) above the water. You might also consider the Kindersley Pass area, in the upper part of Sinclair Creek; the trail to the pass is strenuous, but very scenic and feasible as a day-hike for strong hikers.

Backcountry permits are required and available at two seasonal locations: West Gate Information Centre, open daily from early June to mid-October (tel: 604-347-9505), and Kootenay Park Lodge, at Vermilion Crossing. In the off-season, contact the park administration office (see below).

Some Useful Information About Kootenay

CAMPGROUNDS: Kootenay has three auto campgrounds. **Redstreak** is near the west entrance (accessed from the business strip in Radium). **McLeod Meadows** is midway through the Kootenay Valley. And **Marble Canyon** is near Vermilion Pass.

BOATING: Boating in nonmotorized craft is permitted on the Vermilion and Kootenay rivers. Raft trips are available on the Kootenay, Kicking Horse and White rivers from **Kootenay River Runners**, P.O. Box 81, Edgewater, BC V0A 1E0 (tel: 604-347-9210).

GENERAL INFORMATION: Seasonal information centers are located at the West Gate and at Kootenay Park Lodge. The town of Radium provides basic services, including gas, lodging, campgrounds, meals and groceries. The hot springs pool is open all year with generous hours.

USEFUL NAMES AND ADDRESSES: For more information, contact **Kootenay National Park**, Box 220, Radium Hot Springs, BC V0A 1M0 (tel: 604-347-9615).

MOUNT ASSINIBOINE PROVINCIAL PARK

Few individual mountains strike the imagination as strongly as Mount Assiniboine, a Matterhorn-shaped snaggletooth of layered rock, 3,618 m. (11,870 ft.) high. The mountain lies in the very heart of the Canadian Rockies, surrounded on three sides by Banff and Kootenay national parks. And if things go as they should, the country to the south will soon become Pass in the Clouds Provincial Park. From various high points in all directions, travelers can see Assiniboine's distinctive shape towering above anything in its neighborhood, but to get closer, no matter which access one chooses, involves a walking trip of at least a day.

The park measures 386 sq. km. (149 sq. mi.), with not a single acre below 1,524 m. (5,000 ft.) high. Shimmering lakes lie surrounded by rolling meadows or steep cliffs. Trees grow thinly in higher areas. During autumn, large groves of alpine larch do for these mountains what aspens do for the Colorado Rockies, painting whole valleys with brilliant sweeps of color. Much of the terrain is alpine meadow rich with wildflowers. It all adds up to a wilderness landscape as fine as any place in the Rockies. The names of neighboring features express the emotion of those who visit the mountain: Marvel Lake, Lake Gloria, Wonder Pass and Sunburst Peak; the meaning behind Og, Gog and Magog lakes is more obscure. The mountain itself stands in the southeast corner of the park, on the border of Banff, shoulder to shoulder with a hulking group of other peaks all above 3,000 m. (10,000 ft.). In combination, these high peaks support a number of icefields and glaciers, which feed the lakes below. Most of Assiniboine's waters drain away through the Mitchell River, which leaves the park rather hurriedly toward the south. However, the bulk of the park's land is drained by the Simpson River and its tributaries, which flow west into Kootenay National Park and the Kootenay River.

The meadows of the park provide grazing for elk, moose and mule deer, while mountain goats and bighorn sheep inhabit the slopes above timberline. Wolf, wolverine, badger and coyote live here but the chances of seeing them are slight.

Most hikers head for Lake Magog, a gorgeous piece of water at the very base of the mountain. They set up base camps (in designated sites) and make day-hikes from there. Also at Lake Magog are four cabins, which can be used for a small fee per person per night, and a private lodge (see below). The routes are of various lengths and start on all sides. One of the most commonly used trails originates at the end of Spray Lakes Reservoir in Kananaskis Country. To get there, take the Smith-

Dorrien-Spray Trail, a well-maintained gravel road running between Canmore, Alberta, and Highway 40 in Kananaskis Provincial Park. At the north end of Spray Lakes Reservoir, a clearly marked but rough road turns and follows the western lakeshore to the trailhead. Note that this route takes you through Banff National Park, and camping permits (obtainable only in the town of Banff) are necessary if you plan to stay overnight in the park.

Another fine choice of a trail begins at the Bourgeau parking area at the base of the Sunshine Village Ski Area's gondola lift. The trail skirts lovely Sunshine Meadows and parallels the Continental Divide over Citadel Pass to Lake Magog. The third important trailhead is on Highway 93 in Kootenay National Park at the junction of the Vermilion and Simpson rivers, clearly marked on the east side of the road.

Assiniboine's popularity among wilderness skiers is growing. In part this is because of the Naiset Cabins, on Lake Magog, which can be used in winter by reservation through the Parks Division in Wasa; they hold a total of 29 persons. The traditional way in is through Sunshine Village, taking two days to make the trip. Route-finding is not trivial, and avalanche danger is a serious hazard. Certainly, this is not for inexperienced people. The other way in is via Spray Lakes Reservoir; during some years, the road from Canmore has been plowed, permitting skiers to cross the frozen lake and follow the summer trail. This route is less exposed to avalanche danger.

One other option should be mentioned for those so inclined. On Lake Magog, a private lodge, the Assiniboine Lodge, offers meals and overnight accommodation. On two days a week, Fridays and Sundays, helicopters are permitted to carry freight and visitors to the lodge and other places. Information can be obtained through the Parks Division Office in Wasa.

Useful Names and Addresses

For topographic maps, order sheets 82 J/13 and 82 0/4 from **MAPS BC**, address on page 274. For more information, contact the Parks Division Office in Wasa, address also on page 274.

ELK LAKES PROVINCIAL PARK

Elk Lakes Provincial Park embraces 57 sq. km. (22 sq. mi.) of alpine wilderness, most of it above timberline, heavily glaciated and very scenic. The park lies tucked against the Continental Divide, where it traces a tight loop along the south border of Alberta's Kananaskis Provincial Park. Three large glaciers—the Pétain, the Castelnau and the Elk glaciers—occupy the western third of the park, draining by way of Pétain Creek and Nivelle Creek into Upper Elk Lake, which in turn channels its waters into the Lower Elk Lake, about half the size of its neighbor. Several other small lakes, Frozen Lake and Fox Lake among them, sit below the Divide to the north. All of this stands in splendid isolation; the nearest road dead ends a quarter of a mile from the border, and it takes a long drive to get even that close.

Elk Lakes is home to a small population of large animals, but generally they stay away from this high region dominated by rock, ice and snow. Neither are the lower elevations, covered mostly by a forest of lodgepole, alpine fir and Engelmann spruce, capable of supporting many grazing animals. Publications of the Provincial Parks Division fail to mention even the occasional presence of elk, saying that even bighorn sheep and mountain goats are uncommon.

Obviously, because it has no roads, Elk Lakes is a hiker's park. Trails, generally not well maintained, lead to popular destinations such as Upper and Lower Elk Lakes, Pétain Basin, Fox Lake and neighboring Kananaskis Park. In addition, a number of routes are feasible for experienced hikers. One of these crosses Coral Pass into the drainage of Cadorna Creek and could be used as a way into the Pass in the Clouds Area (see page 290). The trails all begin at park headquarters. To get there, take Highway 3 to Sparwood and turn north on Highway 43 to Elkford. The road is paved for 35 km. (22 mi.), but then turns to gravel and gets rougher the farther one drives. This road is specifically not recommended for Cadillacs, low-riders and trailers, but otherwise, ordinary passenger cars can usually make the trip. The total distance from Sparwood is 122 km. (76 mi.), or about two and a half hours of driving.

Camping is restricted to three areas: the park entrance; Lower Elk Lake, a walk of 1.6 km. (1 mi.); and Pétain Creek, on the west end of Upper Elk Lake. The two higher sites make for good base camps from which day-hikes can be taken. In addition, climbers are allowed to camp at the headwaters of Pétain and Nivelle creeks. Otherwise, camping is prohibited. Wood fires are not allowed anywhere in the park.

Useful Names and Addresses

A map of the park (1:50,000 scale, with contour lines) can be ordered from **MAPS BC**, Ministry of the Environment, Parliament Buildings, Victoria, BC V8V 1X4. Additional information can be obtained from the Parks Division in Wasa (address on page 274).

PASS IN THE CLOUDS (PROPOSED) PARK

If you look on a large-scale map, even a provincial highway map, you'll notice that there's a huge chunk of the Rockies, from Crowsnest Pass north to the borders of Banff and Assiniboine parks, which is not included in any park boundaries. Much of this terrain has been logged, often with brutal carelessness for other needs and values. One splendid area remains untouched, however, along the North Fork of the White River and the headwaters of the Palliser River, both of which are tributaries of the Kootenay. Several large valleys separate craggy, glaciated ranges made of steep, upended limestone slabs. Mount King George, Mount Queen Mary and Mount Prince Henry, a royal alpine family if ever there was one, dominate the area with a crown of glaciers. However, higher peaks (Mount Abruzzi, Mount Joffre, Mount Cadorna and others) form a long divide, which separates the Elk and the White river drainages. The Pass in the Clouds lies north of Mount Abruzzi on this divide, and provides a route for hikers to cross from one river valley to the other. Conservationists would like to see the whole area, from Assiniboine Provincial Park on the north and almost to Elkford on the south, become the Pass in the Clouds Provincial Park—a splendid idea despite the current political climate best described as inclement. Whatever the outcome, anyone interested in solitude and willing to follow a topographic map instead of trail signs should consider this as prime country.

Access is from two directions: the Elk River road, which goes north from Sparwood on Highway 3, and the Kootenay River road, which runs east from Canal Flats on Highway 93. The Elk River road ends at Elk Lakes Provincial Park, but if you're headed for the White River Valley, stop at Cadorna Creek and follow a rough trail to its headwaters and over the pass. The route connects with a fairly well used packers' trail along the White River to Joffre Creek (stay on the east side of the creek) and on to the Palliser River. Staying on the trail takes you past the Mount King George group all the way to the Spray River in Banff National Park. Once inside the park, you can loop around back over the divide and down Albert River to the Palliser once again. Another option is to cross the Continental Divide before reaching Banff, going east into Kananaskis by either North or South Kananaskis Pass.

Going in from Canal Flats, you have the option of entering the White River Valley or the Palliser Valley. If you choose the Palliser, there is a creek ford several miles from the road's end (it ends at a drill site). That creek, apparently unnamed, is a feasible route northwest to the slopes of Mount King George and small alpine lakes. Another prime area is the rolling highlands, dotted with lakes, centered on Russell Peak, directly west across the White River Valley from Pass in the Clouds.

Other Area Ideas

Mount Fisher

Mount Fisher stands high above its neighboring peaks, a distinctive, pencil-sharp pinnacle near Fort Steele, easily seen from Highway 95 for miles in either direction. Despite its intimidating (but inviting) appearance, you can get to the summit without technical equipment, if steep slopes and wide open panoramas don't bother you. To get there, find the gravel road that runs southeast down the east side of the Kootenay River from Fort Steele. Follow it about 3 km. (2 mi.) to the Mause Creek Road, which reaches a trailhead 8 km. (5 mi.) up Mause Creek (not the end of the road). The trail climbs steeply for 1,600 m. (5,250 ft.) through two cirques and up the mountain's south ridge.

TOP OF THE WORLD PROVINCIAL PARK

The Top of the World Provincial Park is in fact the top of the Kootenay Range of the Rockies, northeast of Kimberley and Cranbrook. The park boundaries include 88 sq. km. (34 sq. mi.) of high alpine plateau, a limestone karst topography, mostly over 1,800 m. (6,000 ft.) in elevation and surrounded by higher peaks. On the west stands the Hughes Range, whose craggy slopes are favored by mountain goats. The Van Nostrand Range stands to the east; it includes Mount Morro, which at 2,906 m. (9,533 ft.) is the highest point in the park. Fish Lake, Sparkle Lake and Dolomite Lake lie in the shadow of the Hughes Range on the west side of the park and drain to the north through the Lussier River, a tributary of the Kootenay. Several other streams—Coyote, Galbraith and Summer creeks—originate in the park, all of them eventually finding their way to the Kootenay.

Subalpine elevations in the park are forested, mostly by Engelmann spruce and subalpine fir with some lodgepole. Near timberline, the hardy alpine larch predominates. The meadowlands around Mount Morro are filled with wildflowers in the summer and resplendent with the gold of larch trees in the fall. No roads enter the park, and maintained trails are limited to about 24 km. (15 mi.), but this is not a problem because the alpine meadows make for easy off-trail walking.

Two ways into the park are commonly used, both from the north side. A trail enters via Coyote Creek, and after about 3 km. (2 mi.) reaches

Coyote Creek cabin and campsite. From here, it is an easy walk to the alpine meadows on the slopes of Mount Morro. A trail also crosses to Fish Lake about 3 km. (2 mi.) west. The Fish Lake area is by far the most heavily used part of the park. It is reached easily along a gentle 6-km. (4-mi.) trail from a good access road. The fishing is reportedly good, for both cutthroat and Dolly Varden trout. Campsites have been designated at the lake, and toilets are provided. From here, a number of day-hikes are possible. Sparkle Lake and Wildhorse Ridge can be reached by two separate routes, which set off from the lake's west shore. On the north shore, near where the Coyote Cabin Trail meets the Lussier River Trail, a third trail heads southeast up the slope to Summer Pass and beyond to the meadows around Mount Morro.

Camping is allowed in five locations: near Coyote Cabin; near the south boundary in the headwaters of Galbraith Creek; just inside the park on the Lussier River Trail; at Sayles Meadow, halfway to Fish Lake; and at Fish Lake itself. Camping is prohibited elsewhere. The cabins at Coyote Creek and Fish Lake can be used by hikers and skiers. The Fish Lake cabin sleeps 25; firewood and a cookstove are provided.

To get to the park, drive to Skookumchuck, about 50 km. (30 mi.) north of Cranbrook on Highway 93/95. The turnoff is marked for the Premier Lake Provincial Park, at the top of a hill as the highway climbs up from the Kootenay River. Drive 8 km. (5 mi.), turn left on a gravel road, and turn right after another 1.5 km. (1 mi.). This road crosses the Lussier River and climbs past Ram Creek Hot Springs until it again meets the Lussier River, which flows around a sharp bend to the north. Turn right, upstream, and follow the river to the trailhead, a total distance from the highway of a little over 40 km. (25 mi.).

An alternate road in begins 5 km. (3 mi.) south of Canal Flats. The turn is clearly marked for Top of the World Park. The road joins the Lussier River near Whiteswan Lake Provincial Park and continues to the same trailhead, a distance of 52 km. (32 mi.) from the highway. Hikers interested in going directly to Coyote Creek should check with the B.C. Forest Service (office in Canal Flats, among others) about the condition of the Coyote Creek road. Those interested in skiing to the park should check on which roads are being plowed for logging operations; and remember that logging trucks, especially in winter, can be extremely dangerous to encounter.

Useful Names and Addresses

A map of the park can be ordered from **MAPS BC** (address on page 274; order sheet 82 G/14W). For more information, contact the Parks Division at Wasa, address on page 274.

PETER LOUGHEED PROVINCIAL PARK

Peter Lougheed Provincial Park lies south of Banff along the east side of the Divide. The park forms the heart of a larger wild area called Kananaskis Country and touted by Alberta as the playground of the province, "a year-round multi-use recreation area." And, it should be added, resource development area. Logging, grazing, oil-and-gas drilling and mineral exploration are permitted in the areas outside the provincial park. The entire region covers some 4,000 sq. km. (1,540 sq. mi.) of mountains and foothills. Recreation possibilities include everything from wilderness activities to golfing, fishing, and snow skiing. Peter Lougheed Provincial Park is the site of Nakiska, a ski resort developed from the ground up to accommodate the 1988 Winter Olympics. A network of cross-country ski trails has been built beside the downhill development.

Several roads provide access to the region, two of which bear description. Highway 40, an extension of the Forestry Trunk Road, which parallels the Rockies from Grande Prairie all the way to Crowsnest Pass, is paved in this stretch. It turns off the Trans-Canada about 80 km. (50 mi.) west of Calgary and follows the Kananaskis and Highwood river valleys—a splendid scenic drive. Travelers should note, however, that it fades to gravel and dirt south of Kananaskis Country, making it a long, rough alternate to the main route between Calgary and the border. In addition, the south part of the road, along Highwood River, is closed in winter. The other road begins at Canmore on the edge of Banff Park (drive into Canmore's business district, cross the Bow River, turn right and follow signs up the steep slope to the Canmore Dam). It passes the Canmore Nordic Centre, then continues along Spray Lakes Reservoir and joins Highway 40 in the provincial park.

Two campgrounds are located along Highway 40 north of the park; none on the paved section south. Within the park are six campgrounds, all of them in the central lakes area, which is served by a dead-end network of roads. A lavish information center stands near the entrance to the lakes area. Special attention has been paid to facilities for handicapped and elderly people at the William Watson Lodge and Campground. Lodging and campsites for overnight or day use can be reserved by calling 403-591-7227 or writing to the provincial park, address below. Park waters are open for boating and fishing in accordance with provincial regulations.

Hiking opportunities are many. Backpackers should consider trips to either North or South Kananaskis Pass; both routes lead over the Divide into the spectacular wilderness of the Pass in the Clouds area. A trail running southward connects with trails in Elk Lakes Provincial Park. Toward the north end of the park, the Burstall Lakes Trail leads to the Spray River Valley in Banff Park; and from the upper end of Spray Lakes Reservoir (outside the park), the popular trail to Assiniboine begins.

Useful Names and Addresses

For more information, contact **Kananaskis Country**, Suite 412, 1011 Glenmore Trail, SW, Calgary, AB T2V 4R6 (tel: 403-297-3362); or **Peter Lougheed Provincial Park**, P.O. Box 130, Kananaskis Village, AB T0L 2H0 (tel: 403-591-7222). Alberta operates an information center just off the highway in Canmore. Other centers are along both described entrance roads at their north ends.

JASPER NATIONAL PARK AND NORTH

In the entire length of the Rockies, Jasper is the largest national park. It covers 10,800 sq. km. (4,200 sq. mi.), extending on the east side of the Divide from Banff Park to a point north of Mount Robson. Less than eight percent of that expanse is in valley bottoms; all the rest is mountain slope, alpine meadow, rock or glacier. Above all, glaciers: the Columbia Icefield, which is the largest of several, measures 325 sq. km. (125 sq. mi.). From the icefield, the Athabasca River and its tributaries drain northward through the center of the Rockies, past Jasper townsite, and on to the plains and Hudson Bay. Everything that has been said about the mountains of Banff apply to those of Jasper. The grand march of the Rockies continues through both parks, complete with all the splendid accouterments of the alpine and subalpine environment: glaciers, snowfields, turquoise lakes, vast meadows covered with mountain wildflowers, frowning cliff faces, soaring peaks, streams, rivers, waterfalls, cascades and herds of wildlife. All superlatives apply.

If, after hours of gaping, the grand scale of the landscape becomes hard to comprehend, you can turn your attention to smaller details—a pond, a grove of trees, a streamlet, a flower, a deer in a meadow. Similarly, if short trails near the road, crowded with people, become tiring (the Angel Glacier, for one), you can always set off on something longer. On remote backcountry treks, you could be gone for two weeks or more without having to retrace your steps. On the other hand, you can find a place of personal solitude much closer than that, simply by walking a few hundred yards from any road or trail. The opportunities for this are everywhere, along riverbanks, meadow verges, lakeshores and ridgetops.

History

The park is named for Jasper Hawes, a factor for the North West Company, who established Jasper House in 1812 near the north end of Brulé Lake on the Athabasca River. Two years earlier, during the winter of 1810-11, the great geographer David Thompson had crossed Athabasca Pass on his way to the mouth of the Columbia River. He had gone that way because the Piegan Indians, a branch of the Blackfoot, determined to prevent guns and other trade goods from reaching their enemies in the interior, had blockaded the more southerly Howse Pass. This new way, up the Athabasca and Whirlpool rivers, became the major trade route across the Rockies for nearly two decades. During that time, and for years afterwards, Jasper House was an important supply station for travelers into the region. In the 1820s, after the merger of the rival Hudson's Bay and North West companies, the post was moved upstream about 25 km. (16 mi.). It retained the name Jasper House even though Mr. Hawes had long since disappeared, drowned, it was said, in 1813 while trying to float the Fraser River on a wooden raft. When the national park was established, the name Jasper was chosen over Athabasca, although the transient fur trader certainly had far less to do with the making of the park then did the river.

Another early fort was built by William Henry, who accompanied David Thompson in 1811, to this place near what is now called Old Fort Point at Jasper townsite. The post was intended to be a supply base and grazing ground for the men and horses of the North West Company, and served that purpose for a short time, eventually falling into disuse in favor of Jasper House a few miles downstream. According to fashion, trappers called this post Henry House after its founder, and perhaps we should be grateful that it was not used as the basis for naming the park.

During that winter of 1810, David Thompson had spent nearly a month drying meat and building snowshoes and sleds for his midwinter crossing of the Rockies, a journey which apparently seemed to him a perfectly natural thing to do. True to form, he and his companions not only discovered the pass, but also continued down the other side, arriving on the banks of the Columbia near Big Bend on January 26, 1811. The snow there was too deep for traveling, so they built rude huts and crawled in for the winter. Thompson sent a small party back over the pass for supplies, and at that point, all but two of his men decided there were better places to be and deserted him. Thompson, not to be deterred, continued on in the spring.

For 15 years after that, until Yellowhead Pass replaced it, Athabasca Pass was an important trade route for the fur brigades. Again in the

A natural causeway of wind-driven sand separates Jasper Lake on the left from Talbot Lake on the right.

1860s, the pass saw traffic as gold-rushers came this way en route to the Cariboo placer fields. A story is told of the Belgian missionary, Father Pierre Jean DeSmet, the same man who established St. Mary's Mission in Montana's Bitterroot Valley in the 1840s. He arrived at the foot of the pass, and, too heavy to continue on snowshoes, fasted for a month to lose weight.

In 1907, anticipating the construction of the Grand Trunk Pacific Railway over Yellowhead Pass, Canada declared the upper Athabasca basin a national park. The town of Jasper grew up a short time later, founded in 1911 during actual construction of the railroad. The site was a logical choice, on the junction of the Athabasca and Miette rivers, at the base of the climb to the pass. Construction work picked up again in 1915, when the tracks of a second railroad, the Canadian Northern, were laid parallel to those of the first. Train traffic remains heavy through the park, but Jasper's modern economy depends more upon tourism than on freight hauling. On any given summer day, the town comes alive with visitors. Climbers and hikers mix with groups of souvenir shoppers. Rafting companies pull trailer loads of their inflatables down the main street. Motorhomes vie with bicycles for parking space. In winter, skiers, attracted to the slopes of Marmot Basin or to the many cross-country opportunities in the area, replace summer visitors.

Jasper's activity (and any visit to the park) revolves around the information center, a venerable stone structure surrounded by a lovely shaded park across from the train station. Maps, books, hiking information and backcountry reservations can be obtained here, along with a wealth of general advice on seeing the park. One entire wall is taken up by small scale topographic maps fitted together to cover the park—an excellent aid in planning a hike, or any other activity.

On these maps you can quickly get a feel for the park's geography, which is strikingly similar to that of Banff Park. The only east-west highway, Route 16, enters the park by way of its major river valley, the Athabasca, and continues, in tandem with the railroad tracks, over the Continental Divide to another major drainage. It is the only feasible way to go, because the park's mountain ranges all trend north-south, and the Athabasca has cut the only path across their grain. Running parallel to them, however, again following the major river, the Icefields Parkway carries travelers through the heart of the ranges, over Sunwapta Pass and into Banff. Short spur roads ascend side valleys to points of interest, notably Sunwapta Falls, Mount Edith Cavell and the Angel Glacier, Maligne Lake, Celestine Lake and Miette Hotsprings. For a distance south of Jasper townsite, an alternate road, 93A, attracts drivers who wish to go more slowly.

Jasper has about 1,000 km. (620 mi.) of hiking trails, which cover only a portion of this immense park. They include the North and South Boundary trails, each one nearly 200 km. (125 mi.) in length, but even so, the bulk of Jasper is traversed only by game trails. A permit system similar to that of Banff is in effect, with quotas set for each area. Hikers can reserve up to a third of a trail's capacity; after that, it's first come, first served.

Several backpacking areas stand out. The North Boundary Trail, with various options along the way, leads from Celestine Lake all the way to Mount Robson. It's not easy to shorten this trip, although some hikers choose to begin at Rock Lake in the Willmore Wilderness; at least a week is needed, unless you retrace your route. From Maligne Lake, the very popular Skyline Trail climbs to the crest of the Maligne Range and traverses it through meadow and bowl, over windblown and barren passes for 44 km. (27 mi.). It might be hard getting a permit for this trail in midsummer, so try to call ahead, and keep an option in mind.

That option is not likely to be the Tonquin Valley, for which hikers also line up at the permit desk. You get there by one of two routes, or make it a loop trip, beginning either on the road to Marmot Ski Basin or from the Mount Edith Cavell Road. Tonquin Valley is a high open area cradling the superb Amethyst Lakes and overlooked by an imposing, craggy wall of quartzite pinnacles called The Ramparts; precisely on

Spirit Island stands near the narrows of Maligne Lake in Jasper National Park.

the opposite side of The Ramparts are the Fraser River headwaters, a fine hiking area in Mount Robson Park, but with primitive trails where there will certainly be fewer people.

Farther south along the Icefields Parkway, you might consider trails to Geraldine Lakes or Fryatt Creek, both protected by long hikes on the west side of the Athabasca River, and therefore beyond the reach of casual trekkers. The trail to Fortress Pass along the Athabasca River, and the one that follows the historic route along the Whirlpool River, both lead to remote places via long walks. A bridge built recently over the upper Athabasca eliminates the more hazardous of the two fords, which have previously kept some hikers away from Fortress Pass.

For day-hiking, ask at an information center for the brochure "Day Hikes in Jasper National Park." It lists walks of various lengths in the townsite vicinity, at Miette Hotsprings, Maligne Lake, Columbia Icefield and at the base of Mount Edith Cavell.

Some Useful Information About Jasper

CAMPGROUNDS: Jasper has ten campgrounds distributed along the Icefields Parkway and the highway from Jasper townsite to the east entrance. The price range is similar to that of Banff Park, with fees starting at $7.25 and going up depending on services. The simpler sites are at Snaring River, north of town, and Mount Kerkeslin, Honeymoon Lake, Jonas Creek, Columbia Icefield and Wilcox Creek, all to the south of Athabasca Falls on the Parkway. Pocahontas, at the east entrance, and Wabasso, about 16 km. (10 mi.) south of Jasper townsite, have running water and wheelchair access, but no showers. Whistlers and Wapiti, with over 1,100 individual sites between them, have showers and trailer hookups; they are located immediately south of the townsite. Season varies among the individual campgrounds. Some open in the middle of May and close with the first serious snowfall. Wapiti Winter Campground offers heated restrooms and electrical hookups. Other camping areas can be found east of the park, both in private campgrounds or Alberta Forest Service and provincial sites (Wildhorse Lake, Obed Lake and Roundcroft along Highway 16, others on Route 40 toward Grande Cache). The best guide to these is the map "Alberta Forest Service Recreation Areas." It covers the entire province and can be picked up free of charge at Alberta Information Centers (there's one in Hinton) or ordered from Alberta Tourism, Parks, and Recreation.

LODGING: Jasper Park lodging is of a wide variety. Motels line the streets of the townsite, and many houses display Bed and Breakfast signs. A hostel is located a few miles from town up the Maligne Canyon road, with several others along the parkway; some of these are open through the winter (see page 274 for addresses). **Jasper Park Lodge** is an expensive 442-room accommodation on the shores of Lake Beauvert across the river from the townsite (Jasper Park Lodge, Jasper, AB T0E 1E0. Tel: 403-852-3301; 800-441-1414 from the United States except Illinois; 800-942-8888 from Illinois).

ACTIVITIES AND EQUIPMENT RENTALS: Bicycles and other equipment can be rented at a variety of sports shops. Boating is permitted on most park waters; powerboats on Pyramid Lake only, battery-powered electric motors permitted on any lake not closed to boating. Whitewater rafting on the Athabasca River by several companies, including **Jasper Raft Tours** (tel: 403-852-3613). Car rental agencies offer cars between Banff and Jasper, often with no drop-off charge. During winter, Marmot Basin attracts downhill skiers, and cross-country terrain is everywhere. The Icefields Parkway is kept open. A ski-in lodge operates in the backcountry at Tonquin Valley (Box 550, Jasper; tel: 403-852-3909).

GENERAL INFORMATION: **Jasper Tramway** runs to the top of The Whistlers, a mountain that provides a fine overall view; get there by driving up Whistlers Road just south of town, or take the shuttle bus from the town square. Jasper laundromats provide a twist on the traditional set-up; they have coin-op showers in addition to washers and driers. Information centers are located in Jasper townsite and at Columbia Icefield, the latter open only in summer.

USEFUL NAMES AND ADDRESSES: For more information, maps or reservations, contact **Jasper Tourism & Commerce**, 632 Connaught Dr., P.O. Box 98, Jasper, AB ToE 1Eo (tel: 403-852-3858). **Canadian Parks Service** can be reached at P.O. Box 10, Jasper, AB ToE 1Eo (tel: 403-852-6176).

MOUNT ROBSON PROVINCIAL PARK

Mount Robson at 3,954 m. (12,972 ft.) is the highest peak in the Canadian Rockies, and despite its being nearly 610 m. (2,000 ft.) lower than Mount Elbert in Colorado, it stands tall in the pantheon of the world's mountains. The derivation of its name is uncertain; it could be a contraction of Robertson, an early Hudson's Bay Company factor, or perhaps it was named for John Robson, who served as British Columbia Premier in the late 1800s. Its original Indian name seems much more appropriate: *Yuh-hai-has-hun*, or "The Mountain of the Spiral Road."

It might also be called the Mountain of the Dead-End Road. Most other mountains in the world (unless sheer altitude is their major defense, as in the Himalayas) have at least one easy way up, a walking route. However frightening a face they may present on one side, many of the most formidable of the world's climbing mountains have gentle backsides. This includes the Eiger, Yosemite's Half Dome and Colorado's Longs Peak. Their summits can be reached by anyone in good health and with the desire to put forth a day's worth of effort.

Not so with Robson, which shows a fierce countenance from whichever angle you choose to look at it. Most of the time you can't see it at all. Notorious among climbers for its unpredictable and abominable weather, Robson gathers clouds the way a Texan buys oil wells; when no one else in the neighborhood has any, Robson could stand to loan a few out. Even in good weather, none of the routes to the summit could be called easy, nor can any party at any time of the year be certain of getting to the top until they are actually standing on it.

The first known attempt on Robson was made in 1907 by the two Coleman brothers and their companion, Reverend Kinney. They failed that year and again a year later. Subsequently, other parties made attempts, but it was not until 1913, the year of the park's establishment, that the famous climber Conrad Kain, in the company of Colonel W.W. Foster and A.H. McCarthy made it to the top. Even today, the mountain frequently turns back well-equipped, experienced groups of climbers.

To be sure, Mount Robson dominates the provincial park, but there is much to this 2,178 sq. km. (838 sq. mi.) of alpine wilderness. Located on the west side of the Continental Divide, it adjoins Jasper National

Park (although Mount Robson itself, by the irony shared by so many of the Rocky Mountain monarchs, is off to the side of the Divide). Numerous streams pour off the snowy Divide through splendid alpine basins and valleys both broad and narrow. They all end up in the Fraser River, which carves the park's central drainage; Moose River and Robson River are the two main tributaries.

The Yellowhead Highway traverses the park on its way from Jasper townsite to Prince George; this is the only road in the park. Any other travel must be done by foot or horseback. Ninety-seven kilometers (60 mi.) of trails are quickly swallowed by the much larger wilderness. By far the best known and loved trail follows the Robson River past Kinney Lake and the Valley of a Thousand Falls to the shores of Berg Lake. From its waters, the north face of Robson rises 2,400 m. (7,800 ft.) in one great wall. The centerpiece of this magnificent sight is Berg Glacier, which continually launches icebergs—hence the name—into the lake.

The distance to Berg Lake from the highway is 22 km. (14 mi.), and involves a stiff climb above Kinney Lake. Designated camping sites are strung along the route. As of now, there is no limit on use, but a fee is charged to cover the extensive improvements that have been made to the trail. These include shelters at selected locations. The Berg Lake Trail continues northeast over Robson Pass to connect with Jasper's North Boundary Trail and many miles of additional hiking. Persons intending to camp overnight in Jasper must obtain a permit from the national park's backcountry office in Jasper townsite before making the trip.

Sturdy hikers can make a loop trip from Berg Lake by heading over Robson Pass, re-entering Robson Park by way of Moose Pass, and following the Moose River back to the highway—a long trip around the Robson massif, a goodly part of it off maintained trails. Otherwise, hikers might choose to follow the Moose River as far as time and ambition allows, perhaps to Resplendent Valley on the east side of Robson and Resplendent Mountain. The shortest access to an alpine area is provided by the Fitzwilliam Trail, east of Lucerne Campground; but even this is a stiff climb and 11 km. (7 mi.) in distance. Robson may not be an ideal place for day-hikers, but it provides many days of hiking.

The park has three auto campgrounds, two at the west entrance near the beginning of the Berg Lake Trail (Robson Meadows and Robson River) and one close to the east entrance (Lucerne). In addition, Mount Robson Motor Village, at the west entrance, provides gas, meals and a commercial campground with showers. The Mount Robson Ranch, in the same area, has lodging, camping and horses for rent. Boating is permitted on the two large lakes, Yellowhead and Moose lakes. A contour map (1:125,000 scale) can be ordered from MAPS BC, address on page 274).

Useful Names and Addresses

For more information, contact **Mount Robson Provincial Park**, Box 579, Valemount, BC V0E 2Z0 (tel: 604-566-4325).

WILLMORE WILDERNESS

The Willmore extends from Jasper to the north, occupying some 4,597 sq. km. (1,774 sq. mi.) of remote and little-traveled country. Except for the grand glacier-crowned country in its Southwestern corner, the landscape is not spectacular in an alpine sense. It is, nonetheless, scenic in the way of all remote mountain areas, and rich in wildlife, including bears, wolves, moose, elk, bighorn sheep, mountain goats and endangered woodland caribou.

Approximately 666 kilometers (414 miles) of trails run through Willmore, some of them connecting with Jasper's trail system to the south. One trail in particular is a short route to the base of Mount Robson from the east side. Except for the well-traveled trails, the routes shown on maps of the area might be unreliable. Many trails have disappeared from disuse or lack of maintenance. This means that backpackers who plan to leave the major trails should be prepared for genuine, undeveloped wilderness—and should check their planned routes with the Alberta Land and Forest Service ranger stations in Hinton or Grande Cache.

Access points to the Willmore are distributed along its north and eastern boundaries, served by Highway 40 between Hinton and Grande Cache, a mining town of about 5,000 people. Campgrounds and recreation sites where camping is permitted can be found all along the road and near each of the three main trailheads. The first of these, Hells Gate, is located on the Smoky River at the end of a well-marked gravel road a half mile beyond the Smoky River bridge, just beyond Grande Cache. From the town, which is perched on the mountain side above the river, you can see well up the drainage. High mountains, their flanks densely forested, rise on either side. But the highest of all is out of sight; the glaciers of Mount Robson itself contribute the first droplets of the Smoky River, some 97 km. (60 mi.) by air from Hells Gate.

The river valley, it seems, should provide a natural route for a trail to Robson, but in fact it does not. The trail, which begins at Hells Gate, follows the river and does connect with others going via different paths to Robson, but the condition of these is unreliable.

The trail from Big Berland follows the Berland River, crossing it many times without benefit of footbridges; this is not a trail for high-water season. East of there is the most commonly used trailhead of all,

The Smoky River Valley provides a northern gateway into the Willmore Wilderness north of Jasper National Park.

at Rock Lake. Its popularity stems from the shortcut route it provides to the North Boundary Trail in Jasper National Park—the well-used, maintained trail to Robson.

A more obscure entry point can be reached via the Kakwa Wildland Provincial Park, itself an area of high rocky ridges and easy bushwhacking. Take the road from Grande Prairie to Lick Creek; from there (4x4 only) to Kakwa Falls Day Use Area, and from there by trail following the South Kakwa River to Trench Creek and over the Divide into the Willmore.

Ranger stations for the Edson Provincial Forest are located in Grande Cache at the upper end of Shand Street, and in Hinton near the Weldwood Pulp and Paper Mill.

Useful Names and Addresses

Contact the **Willmore Wilderness Park,** c/o Alberta Land and Forest Service, P.O. Box 239, Grande Cache, AB T0E 0Y0 (tel: 403-827-3626).

HAMBER PROVINCIAL PARK

Hamber is one of the most isolated of provincial parks. No road comes near from any direction. Comprising 247 sq. km. (95 sq. mi.), it is essen-

tially one deep valley tucked on the west side of a meander in the
Continental Divide and dominated by Fortress Lake, about 26 sq. km.
(10 sq. mi.) in extent. To get there requires a fair degree of legwork. On
the west is the approximately 130 km. (30 mi.) long expanse of
Kinbasket Lake (once a lake, now a much-enlarged reservoir behind
Mica Dam) on the Columbia River, which effectively prevents access
from that direction.

The first to leave written record of Fortress Lake was Dr. A.P.
Coleman, who topped Fortress Pass in 1892. In his book *Canadian
Rockies*, he described the sight: "Suddenly there opened out before us
the most marvellous lake imaginable. We were above its east end, and
could see it stretching for eight or ten miles to the west in a valley completely surrounded by heavy forest, sloping up to purplish cliffs and
mountain-tops with snow and glaciers. The water was turquoise blue,
shading round the edges into green, and a creek [Chisel Creek] entered
it from a glacier on the other side, forming a delta and sending out two
plume-like currents of milky water that almost reached our shore. Forest
and glaciers and mountains were perfectly reflected in the lake."

The only way in is from the east, on a 22-km. (14 mi.) trail from
Jasper National Park. The trail starts at Sunwapta Falls on the Jasper
Parkway, where a footbridge (used by most people to view the falls)
crosses the Sunwapta River. Until recently, the trek involved two significant fords, impassable much of the summer due to high water; now a
suspension bridge crosses the bigger of the two, the Athabasca, but the
second, the Chaba, can be trouble enough. This is not a place to worry
about seeing crowds.

Useful Names and Addresses

For more information, contact **Hamber Provincial Park**, Provincial
Parks Branch, Box 579, Valemount, BC V0E 2Z0.

OTHER AREAS

In the region of Banff and Jasper parks, there are a number of de facto
wild areas and designated wilderness regions, which have no developments except an occasional trail, and primitive trails at that. They adjoin
the park boundaries, effectively enlarging them and serving as needed
buffers between wild lands and developed lands. Following is an outline
of the larger ones. For complete information on these, obtain the book
Eastern Slopes Wildlands: Our Living Heritage, from the Alberta
Wilderness Association, Box 6398, Station D, Calgary, AB T2P 2E1.

The book includes maps and trail guides. Maps and information for wilderness areas in the province can be obtained from: **Environmental Protection**, Natural Resources Service, Recreation and Protected Areas Division, Outdoor Recreation and Operation Systems Branch, 8th Floor, 10405 Jasper Ave., Edmonton, AB T5J 3N4 (tel: 403-427-7009).

White Goat, Siffleur and Ghost River Wilderness Areas

On the north side of Highway 11 as it enters Banff National Park is the White Goat Wilderness Area, Alberta's largest provincial wilderness. Trails follow rivers and high ridges through an area dominated by the 3,000-m. (10,000-ft.) White Goat Peaks. Access is from the Icefields Parkway or up the Cline River (a 40-km route that tops out at 2,164 m.) from Highway 11. Cataract Creek Valley is known for its hanging glaciers, waterfalls and alpine meadows.

The Siffleur Wilderness stands to the south and across Highway 11 from the White Goat Wilderness. A hiking route enters from Banff via Dolomite Pass. Rangers advise that most routes were cleared as seismic cutlines, which means they don't make perfect trail sense; map and compass are essential here.

Finally, down near Canmore is the Ghost River Wilderness, which like the others augments Banff along its eastern flank. Covered by subalpine forest and alpine tundra, Ghost River provides winter range for bighorn sheep and mountain goats; its meadows are said to support a variety of butterflies unusual in Alberta. Among its other attractions are alpine lakes, deep gorges, glaciers and ice-smoothed bedrock. Some trails are quite rough, having been put in as seismic lines or bulldozed firebreaks. One reportedly feasible route crosses into the region from Banff via Aylmer Pass or Carrot Creek Summit; from the east, logging roads and trails make their way up the Ghost and South Ghost rivers.

NORTH OF JASPER

Roads abandon the Rockies north of Jasper, swinging widely to the east and west. Travelers in the area of Beaverlodge, Alberta, see the mountains on the distant horizon in a few places, gleaming with snow but beyond the roads. From the west side, in British Columbia, intermediate ranges hide the Rockies. Access by car, in the few places traversed by passable road, is long and arduous.

A long distance to the north, where the range begins in a line of broad, pyramidal peaks, the Alaska Highway again approaches the mountains, passing through Muncho Lake and Stone Mountain provincial parks. Because this area is so hard to approach, and even experienced wilderness travelers may wish the services of an outfitter, guide or packer, I've included at the end of this section a list of outfitters who work in the region.

Stone Mountain Provincial Park

Stone Mountain Provincial Park includes 257 sq. km. (99 sq. mi.) of wide open landscape characterized by broad-shouldered, barren mountains and wide river valleys. The highest peak is Mount St. George (2,261 m./7,419 ft.). On the slopes of it and the other mountains in the park roam stone sheep and Osborne caribou, clear signs that this place is well into the north. The Alaska Highway cuts the park in two, climbing Summit Pass, the highest point on the road. Hiking is for the most part a matter of cross-country bushwhacking, with one short trail to Little Jade and Sky lakes at the base of Mount St. George.

A long suggested route follows MacDonald Creek to the south boundary of the park, then over the Divide to Wokkpash Lake; from there, down Wokkpash Creek (a river in size), which flows through a spectacular region of hoodoos, all the way to the Racing River and an abandoned road which eventually returns to the Alaska Highway. An alternate trip follows the Wokkpash only part way and turns to cross the Divide and return via MacDonald Creek.

Useful Names and Addresses

For information, contact **BC Parks**, Peace Liard District, #250—10003 110 Ave., Fort St. John, BC V1J 6M7 (tel: 604-787-3407).

Muncho Lake Provincial Park

Muncho Lake is a bit farther north on the Alaska Highway, past the community of Toad River (gas station, motel, cafe). The park surrounding the lake, on both sides of the highway, contains 884 sq. km. (340 sq. mi.) of the Terminal and Sentinel ranges of the Rockies. Few trails exist here, although the open nature of the country makes them unnecessary in higher areas. Wardens warn of problems with bears, however, which means travelers should not hike alone. The majority of visitors stop here because of the lake, which has two campgrounds and fishing for Dolly Varden trout, grayling and whitefish.

Useful Names and Addresses

For more information, contact the **Parks Branch** in Fort St. John, address above.

Less than eight percent of Jasper National Park is in valley bottoms; all the rest is mountain slope, alpine meadow, rock or glacier.

Kwadacha Wilderness Provincial Park

The Kwadacha Wilderness, on the Continental Divide, includes nearly 170,000 ha. (68,000 a.) of spectacularly remote country, dominated by the great limestone mass of Mount Lloyd George (2,916 m./9,568 ft.) and the Lloyd George Icefield. The glaciers fill a slew of alpine lakes and feed several sizeable rivers. The wildlife list is a virtual catalog of North American large mammals. No roads exist; access is via walking or bush plane only. An abandoned fire road (bridges out and badly eroded in places) follows the broad valley of the Racing River, near the hamlet of Toad River, to its headwaters below Churchill Peak in the Kwadacha. Most of the western side of the park has burned recently, choking the already rugged country with down timber and brush. None of the trails are maintained.

Useful Names and Addresses

For information, contact the Provincial Parks Branch in Fort St. John, address above.

Guides and Outfitters

A list of guides and outfitters operating in the region can be had from the Northern BC Guides Association and Outfitters, Box 6370, Fort St.

John, BC V1J 4K6; or the Guide Outfitters Association of British Columbia, P.O. Box 94675, Richmond, BC V6Y 4A4 (tel: 604-278-2688). These groups represent licensed guides, who run hunting camps as well as trailrides and recreation trips. Generally they hold exclusive permits for certain hunting territories, but they can arrange non-hunting trips in the parks and other areas.

Also operating in the region are packers and outfitters who, although not guides, are able to provide outfits and wranglers, or food drop-offs, for people who know where they want to go. Their names are included in the materials available from the above addresses.

COLUMBIA MOUNTAINS

The ranges of the Columbia Mountains—the Selkirks, Monashees, Purcells and Cariboos—were laid down as sediments 1,600 to 800 million years ago, highly metamorphosed by heat and pressure. Then 160 million years ago, they were subject to a period of uplift, which progressed from west to east, making them almost 100 million years older than the Rockies. Other significant differences separate them from their younger neighbors as well. The rock of these mountains is much harder than the Rockies, a fact reflected by the more precipitous landscape. One sees less talus, more stable cliffs and deep valleys below tightly packed, glacially sharpened peaks. The difference in atmosphere caused by the deep, narrow valleys of the Columbia Range is striking when compared to the generous spaciousness of the Rockies' broad valleys.

Located where the dry continental climate meets wet Pacific air, the Columbia Range is also much wetter than the Rockies. Winters are cold enough to produce low-density, dry snow at elevation, and wet enough to collect immense quantities of it. This snow is world famous among skiers, who pay great sums to experience the deep powder of the range via helicopter and snowcat. Rogers Pass, a notorious collector of snow, averages 10 m. (33 ft.) per year. A short distance away, at a weather station on Mount Fidelity, the average is almost twice that.

Every Canadian schoolchild knows about Rogers Pass from history lessons. It was here that the Canadian Pacific Railway fought its hardest battles against the prodigious western mountains. It was through news accounts of disasters in Rogers Pass that most Canadians learned about the deadly hazards of avalanche. In time, the railroad went underground, through a long tunnel, to escape the "white death." The modern highway which crosses the pass is frequently closed in winter despite one of the most vigorous avalanche control efforts in the world.

During summer, the Columbia ranges experience extended dry spells, but glacial runoff and snowmelt keep the mountains from ever becoming truly desiccated. Valley bottoms often support dense rainforests in whose shade grow luxuriant tangles of brush and herbs. The timbered slopes climb steeply to the level of glaciers and snowfields, often with no transition zone. This means rewarding but rugged country for hikers, on no-nonsense trails.

Glacier National Park

Glacier National Park, in the Selkirk Range of the Columbias, is a prime sample of British Columbia's interior range topography. The park encompasses 1,350 sq. km. (513 sq. mi.) of narrow valleys cut into hard rock between lofty peaks. Mount Dawson, at 3,390 m. (11,123 ft.), is the park's high point, with many other summits nearly as high. In fact, half of the park's land lies above 1,800 m. (6,000 ft.), and about a quarter of that is continually covered by ice and snow. Most of the park's moisture falls during winter months, with accumulations sufficient to support more than one hundred glaciers. Even during summer, the weather is frequently rainy, and snow can fall at any time.

Topographically, the park is split by Rogers Pass (1,330 m./4,341 ft.), which carries Highway 1, the Trans-Canada, across the Selkirks. From 1885 until 1916, it also carried the Canadian Pacific Railway through the mountains, but severe winter weather and continual deadly avalanches eventually forced the trains underground through the 8-km. (5-mi.) Connaught Tunnel. Between 1885 and 1911, avalanches killed 200 people in the stretch of rail that was abandoned. The highway was opened in 1962 with the expectation that modern techniques and science could defeat the dangers of moving snow. To a large extent, this has proved to be true; yet two people have been killed here, and the highway is frequently closed during winter storms.

On the north side of the pass looms the Hermit Range, rising with astonishing swiftness to a line of peaks named Cougar, Bagheera, Catamount, Ursus Major, Ursus Minor, Grizzly, Sifton, Rogers and others. South of the pass, the Sir Donald Range, Asulkan Ridge and the Dawson Range make up a more complex landscape covered by a huge amount of ice through which the high peaks thrust their summits: Dawson, Selwyn, Cyprian, Augustine, Castor, Pollux, The Rampart, The Witch Tower, Twisted Rock, Uto, Perley, Sir Donald and others. On their east slope, the mountains are chopped off in a clean line, as if with a celestial cleaver, to form a straight north-south rampart 1,800 m. (6,000 ft.) above the Beaver River Valley. The western slope is less tidy,

Mount Sir Donald. The route to the summit up the left-hand skyline has been a popular alpine climb since the CPR established its route over nearby Rogers Pass.

drained by a network of very deep mountain canyons leading into either the Illecillewaet or the Incomappleux rivers.

Glacier Park is noted for rain and snowfall. Rogers Pass receives an annual average of 1,493 mm. (59 in.) of precipitation, of which nearly 10 m. (33 ft.) comes in the form of snow. The Christiana snow research station at Mount Fidelity on the west side of the park records an annual average of almost 17 m. (56 ft.) of snow. It's interesting to see the difference between the towns of Golden and Revelstoke, on opposite sides of the Selkirks. Golden averages 469 mm. (18 in.) of precipitation, whereas Revelstoke gets 1,081 mm. (43 in.). Measurable precipitation occurs on 187 days per year in Revelstoke and only 68 days in Golden. For park visitors, this means that on any given day, the chance of rain is equal to the chance of sunshine.

The 160-km. (100-mi.) trail system here was originally designed for climbers who came to stay at the Glacier House Hotel near the pass. As in other parks, the Canadian Pacific built this hotel to encourage travel on its lines—a successful endeavor until the tunnel diverted rail traffic from the pass area. That the trails were climbers' routes explains why so many of them appear to climb steeply above timberline, only to dead-end at the base of glaciers and cliffs. Hikers were expected to view the trail's end as the climb's beginning.

The Glacier House burned in 1925. In its place one now finds the Illecillewaet Campground, which remains the best base camp for hikers. An energetic walker could easily fill a week's time with day-hikes from here, most of them high above timberline in the land of snow and ice and bare rock. A complex of trails ascends the heights and valleys of the Sir Donald Range; on the other side of the highway, a smaller number of routes climb the Hermit Range. Some of these connect with long-distance cross-country trails suitable for hikers without climbing experience. However, those wishing to strike off from the ends of access trails must have the skill and equipment for glacier travel. One of the most rewarding backpacking trails is the Copperstain Trail (16 km./10 mi.), which begins in the Beaver River Valley but climbs to the meadows of Bald Mountain (really a broad, flat-topped ridge) with easy bushwhacking and miles of open, scenic country. In 1994 an old trail in the south end of the Bald Hills was reopened, making a loop trip possible from the Copperstain drainage, along the alpine ridge of the Bald Hills, down into the Beaver Valley. The trail from the Beaver Valley into Glacier Circle, a spectacular glaciated cirque, has also been upgraded recently.

Glacier Park is not renowned for its wildlife. Large grazing animals such as elk and moose avoid the high Selkirks because of their paltry meadows and deep winter snows. The creatures that are truly at home in such an environment are the hibernators and burrowers, such as marmots, pikas, ground squirrels and bears.

The park has two campgrounds: Illecillewaet, the nicer of the two, with 58 sites just below the pass on the west; and Loop Brook, 2 km. (1 mi.) west of Illecillewaet.

An elaborate visitor center is located at the pass; it's open all year, daily in summer and usually Thursday through Monday in winter. Its museum has interesting dioramas and scale models of Rogers Pass and the days of railroading over this demanding route. Films are shown, and naturalists give advice on trails and park activities; get backcountry permits here or at the Warden Office across the road. A highly useful little booklet, "Footloose in the Columbias," describes trails in both Glacier and Revelstoke parks. The visitor center also sells maps, but they are sometimes out of stock; hikers should plan ahead. Also on the pass is the Glacier Park Lodge, providing accommodations, meals and gas.

Mount Revelstoke National Park

Mount Revelstoke is a minor peak in the Columbias, with one important distinction—visitors can drive their cars to its summit, thus gaining easy access from low-altitude interior rain forest to the rarefied world of timberline and tundra. The road climbs from 600 m. (1,969 ft.) to 1,920 m. (6,299 ft.) in elevation, just below the 1,938-m. (6,358-ft.) summit of Mount Revelstoke and very close to timberline. From the top parking area, several trails lead through subalpine forest and gently rolling meadows, which have become famous for their summer wildflowers, to a handful of alpine lakes. The walking is easy for the most part, and the rewards seem all out of proportion with the effort expended.

A small network of short, essentially level trails allows easy wandering around the summit meadows to Heather Lake and other features. A longer trail, but still easy walking, strikes off northeast toward the Clachnacudainn Range, whose high peaks form the backbone of the park: Klotz (2,643 m./8,671 ft.), St. Cyr (2,597 m./8,520 ft.), Coursier (2,646 m./8,681 ft.), and others, surrounding the large Clachnacudainn Icefield. However, these peaks are not the trail's objective—it leads to several lakes. Miller and Eva lakes, which take about two hours to reach, are at about the same elevation as the parking lot, making them the favorite destination of day-hikers. The trail might be gentle, but the surrounding terrain is anything but. The view from Eva Lake is of towering cliffs and snowfields. A little more effort takes you over a low pass to a spectacular view of the lakes set in their cirques some 350 m. (1,148 ft.) below. Beyond them, the deep valley of Clachnacudainn Creek falls away into green haze. Camping is permitted at Eva and Jade lakes.

An entirely different view of the Columbia Range environment can be found in the valley bottoms. Two short, nearly level nature walks lead through interesting botanical areas. Both of these are located along Highway 1 where it passes through the park east of Revelstoke. The Skunk Cabbage Trail winds for 1.2 km. (.75 mi.) through a swampy area rich in bird life and known for the extraordinary size of the flowering skunk cabbage, which seem to have found their ideal habitat here. The second nature trail, Giant Cedars, provides a peaceful, fragrant stroll in the deep shade of ancient western red cedar trees.

The park has no campgrounds, nor other facilities beyond roads and picnic areas. Backcountry registration is voluntary. Register at the Revelstoke office (address below) between 8:30 A.M. and 4:30 P.M. or in advance by mail. Commercial campgrounds and a full range of services are available in the city of Revelstoke, at the base of the mountain.

Useful Names and Addresses

The administrative offices for both Glacier and Mount Revelstoke national parks are located in the city, at Third Street and Campbell Avenue, upstairs. Visitors can obtain information, maps and assorted publications at this office. The address for both parks is: Superintendent,

Glacier and Mount Revelstoke National Parks, P.O. Box 350, Revelstoke, BC V0E 2S0 (tel: 604-837-7500).

Purcell Range

The Purcells rise west of the Rocky Mountain Trench, extending from northern Montana to near Golden, British Columbia, at the same latitude as Lake Louise. Low and tree-covered along the U.S.-Canada border, they emerge from timberline farther north in a series of splendid alpine areas. One, the soaring Bugaboos, is a world-famous rock climbing area. Yet it is only one small section of a very fine mountain range.

The Purcells are distinct from the Rockies geologically. Some 175 million years ago, long before the uplift of the Rockies, these older mountains stood against the midcontinent oceans, passing through cycles of erosion and uplift, eventually witnessing the rise of their upstart neighbors to the east. They are made primarily of much-altered sediments, with graceful granitic intrusions like the Bugaboos and the Leaning Towers. High peaks range between 3,000 and 3,300 m. (10,000 and 11,000 ft.), with Mount Farnham, at 3,457 m. (11,342 ft.), the highest. Valley bottoms are quite low, resulting in spectacular relief. Kootenay Lake, for example, on the west side of the range, is only 535 m. (1,756 ft.) above sea level. Timberline averages between 1,800 and 2,100 m. (6,000 and 7,000 ft.).

Generally, the range is steeper and wetter on the west slope; the trench is near desert, receiving only about 38 cm. (15 in.) of precipitation per year. By contrast, the west side gets almost 125 cm. (50 in.).

Access is easiest (or to be more accurate, less difficult), from the east, along the Rocky Mountain Trench. In this long valley, with its near-desert conditions and relatively warm winters, a number of sizeable communities thrive at the foot of the two great mountain chains. Cranbrook bases its economy on logging and transport. Kimberley is a mining town, dominated by a huge Cominco lead and zinc mine. Invermere and Golden owe their livelihood to tourism, agriculture and transportation. All these communities are connected by Highway 95 running north-south along the Columbia and Kootenay rivers. These two great watercourses begin at the same divide midway in the trench. The Columbia flows north to get past the Purcell and Selkirk ranges, reaching the latitude of the Columbia Icefield before finally finding a way back to the south. The Kootenay flows the other way, south into Montana. At Libby, it rounds the south end of the Purcells and then heads back into British Columbia, where at Castlegar the two rivers at last meet.

From the trench, several roads, of varying reliability, penetrate deep valleys in the Purcells. No road here can be implicitly trusted. The area is subject to summer floods, which regularly take out sections of roadbed, bridges and culverts, or simply cause impassable erosion. The situation may necessitate patience—or a long walk.

As of now, no road crosses the range between Cranbrook and Golden. Developers announce perennial plans for new highways at the lower passes (St. Mary Valley for one), but low is a relative term and so far the Purcells, armed with ferocious weather both winter and summer, have successfully defied the bulldozers. This is not to say they have frustrated logging, which despite economic ups and downs, continues apace wherever trees can be taken. In the Purcells, logging operations provide their usual mixed benefits. Roads provide access for recreationists, but the country remaining desirable for recreation shrinks accordingly. Clear cuts, which because of their tangled devastation are impossible to walk through, appear suddenly where, weeks before, a winding footpath followed a tumbling mountain stream. This makes it essential for anyone traveling in areas not specifically protected by park status to check on trail conditions with local people. The best source of current information is the B.C. Forest Service.

The other reason to check with them is to find out about logging trucks. These immense, heavily laden vehicles may well be the most serious hazard of exploring backroads in all the western mountains. A truck coming down-grade with 27,000 kg. (30 t.) of logs chained to its trailer has little maneuverability and no way to stop suddenly. The drivers know that if they hit the ditch or otherwise come to a quick stop, those logs are likely to come straight on through the cab. Therefore, it is important for travelers to pay attention to warning signs and to keep a close eye out for trucks. Ask at a forestry office. Failing that, drive up the roads in the morning and drive down them in the afternoon. Turn off the car engine and listen occasionally. Trucks coming downhill use compression brakes, which make a terrifically loud noise.

There are three main access roads from the east. From Spillimacheen, north of Invermere, a 46-km. (29-mi.) route follows Bugaboo Creek to Bugaboo Glacier Provincial Park. Second, from Invermere, the Toby Creek road, paved as far as Panorama Ski Resort, continues on, touching the northern border of the Purcell Wilderness Conservancy. Farther south, between Kimberley and Marysville, a forestry road runs west then north to St. Mary's Alpine Park and the South end of the wilderness conservancy.

From where the roads end, one soon learns that none of this country is readily accessible. Trails are not well marked (if at all) in large parts of the range. With the exception of a few well known, well-traveled and occasionally maintained trails, this remains wilderness country providing significant challenges and rewards.

Bugaboo Glacier Provincial Park

Bugaboo Glacier Provincial Park and Alpine Recreation Area encompasses an unusual series of toothlike, granite spires thrusting in clean expanses of gray rock above the largest icefields in the Purcells. The spires range between 2,700 and 3,300 m. (9,000 and 11,000 ft.), with the highest being the north tower of Howser Spire, at 3,399 m. (11,150 ft.). The area was officially recognized in 1969, in two administrative units. The park is 3.6 sq. km. (1.4 sq. m.) along the headwaters of Bugaboo Creek, the main access. The recreation area, nearly 260 sq. km. (100 sq. mi.), surrounds the park, the spires and the icefields.

The spires originated as volcanic intrusions, magma forcing its way some 70 million years ago into the much older metamorphosed sediments, which comprise most of the range. Sheersided and spectacular, they have attracted generations of climbers from all over the world. These faces have the reputation of Yosemite as a place of clean, aesthetic rock-climbing routes. Conrad Kain, a famous early mountaineer and guide, climbed the south ridge of Bugaboo Spire in 1916, a route that he claimed was the hardest he had made in Canada. Over the succeeding years, as equipment and techniques were refined by later climbers, the other difficult routes were deciphered and climbed by people such as Fred Beckey, Layton Kor, Yvonne Chouinard and Ed Cooper. The spires continue to provide new challenges. Climbers are continually accomplishing previously unclimbed routes or climbing the old routes with better style and less equipment.

The emphasis in the Bugaboos has always been climbing, and hikers unprepared for glacier and off-trail travel will find few trails to their liking. There are, however, two hiking routes well worth the strenuous effort they require. One is the standard 5-km. (3-mi.) climber's approach to Boulder Camp, at the base of Snowpatch and Bugaboo Spire, where the Parks Division maintains the Conrad Kain Alpine Hut. The second trail begins at the Canadian Mountain Holidays (C.M.H.) lodge on the recreation area boundary and climbs over the ridge to Cobalt Lake (also 5 km./3 mi., and 760 m./2,500 ft. of elevation gain).

To get there, drive 27 km. (17 mi.) north of Radium Hot Springs on Highway 95 to a well-marked gravel road. This road passes the C.M.H. lodge at 45 km. (28 mi.) and ends 1 km. (.6 mi.) farther at a public parking lot. There is no camping at the end of the road, and only limited tent sites near the Conrad Kain Hut. A Forest Service campsite is located on a short spur road, which leads south at the recreation area boundary; another site is roughly halfway between the highway and the park. The Conrad Kain Hut accommodates 50 persons between May 1 and

September 30. Propane stoves for cooking are provided, but everything else must be carried in. A fee ($5 per night in 1984) is charged.

Useful Names and Addresses

Maps can be ordered from **MAPS BC**, Ministry of the Environment, Parliament Buildings, Victoria, BC V8V 1X4; order maps 82 K/15 and 82 K/10, in the 1:50,000 series. For more information, contact the Parks Division in Wasa, BC (address on page 274).

Purcell Wilderness Conservancy

The Purcell Wilderness Conservancy occupies a central position in the range and measures roughly 30 by 45 km. (19 by 28 mi.). Except for the Earl Grey Pass Trail, developed routes are virtually nonexistent. It should be mentioned that most of this country is crossed by foot trails, which are laid out and maintained to some degree or other by area trappers and guides. These trails are rarely marked in any way, and not at all advertised, but wilderness travelers can assume that if a place is worth visiting, there is likely to be a way of getting there. At the south end of the conservancy is the St. Mary's Alpine Provincial Park, a magnificent collection of alpine lakes and mountains, which, like the rest of the range, is accessible only on foot by those willing to bushwhack, follow thin trails by map and compass, and expend considerable effort.

Earl Grey Pass

The Earl Grey Pass Trail crosses the Purcell Wilderness Conservancy on a well-maintained 61-km. (38-mi.) route, which can be done in four days of hiking. A week allows for a relaxed trip and opportunities for exploration of this lovely high country. Earl Grey Pass is 2,195 m. (7,200 ft.) high, surrounded by glaciers and high peaks, which include Mounts Toby, Christine and Cauldron. The two trailheads are Hamill Creek on the west, at 914 m. (3,000 ft.), and Toby Creek on the east, at 1,372 m. (4,500 ft.). The trail itself is equipped with shelters and tent platforms, which along with the superb scenery of the Purcells, accounts for its popularity. Hikers walk from either direction, making the complete traverse, or return the way they came to avoid the long car shuttle.

To find the eastern trailhead, drive to Invermere and follow signs for the Panorama Resort. The road follows Toby Creek past the resort for a total of 32 km. (20 mi.) to a junction with Jumbo Creek, where the trailhead is located. Hikers can reach the pass from here in one day, making the return trip a reasonable two-day overnight. The western trailhead is north of Argenta on Kootenay Lake. The trail follows the

Hamill Creek Valley on an old road through a climax forest of western hemlock and cedar. Some of these trees are 1,000 years old. For information, contact the Parks Division in Wasa, address on page 274.

St. Mary's Alpine Provincial Park

St. Mary's Alpine Provincial Park surrounds an exquisite alpine basin on the south border of the Purcell Wilderness Conservancy. Its borders include 91 sq. km. (35 sq. mi.) with 29 lakes, rugged ridges and sharp mountains perched between 600 and 900 m. (2,000 and 3,000 ft.) above the surrounding valleys. Like the dinosaur plateau in the movie "The Lost World," there is no easy way to reach it. In fact, there are no established trails at all.

To get there, the best way is up the St. Mary River Valley, served by a road that begins between Kimberley and Marysville. After 34 km. (21 mi.) on this road, you reach the forks. The right fork leads up White Creek, a very rough four-wheel-drive road, which might be best ridden on mountain bikes. At last report, this road was next to impassable. The left fork follows the St. Mary Valley. Most wilderness users will choose the central fork, which follows Dewar Creek. Three hiking options exist farther along the road: at 8 km. (5 mi.) from the forks, a rough road can be driven or walked; at 15 km., (9 mi.) another side road climbs part way up the slope; and at the end of the road (the Wilderness Conservancy Boundary), a trail continues toward Dewar Hot Springs (beyond which are the Leaning Towers pinnacles); a branch of that trail follows Wesley Creek and feasible routes to the northern part of the park. Once the alpine basin is attained, bushwhacking remains moderately difficult.

A contour map covering the park (sheet 82 F/16, 1:50,000 scale) can be ordered from **MAPS BC**, address on page 274; additional information is available from the Parks Division in Wasa, whose address is on page 274.

Useful Names and Addresses

Exploring the Purcell Wilderness, by Anne Edwards, Pat Morrow and Art Twomey, is an excellent guide to the Purcell Range, filled with little bits of information one would never think to ask about. For example, it cautions that in the Purcells, porcupines, or bristle pigs, are a real hazard to car tires; the authors recommend that hikers surround their cars with chicken wire to protect tires and hoses, especially in the White Creek area of the St. Mary drainage. This should serve as another testimonial to the value of picking up local guidebooks.

British Columbia Forest Service offices are located in Cranbrook, Canal Flats, Invermere, Spillimacheen, Golden, Revelstoke, Lardeau and Kaslo. The Fish and Wildlife Branch has offices in Cranbrook and Nelson. Maps either 1:125,000 scale (half-inch to the mile) or 1:50,000, are available at some of these offices and at area sporting goods and book stores; or they can be ordered from **MAPS BC**, address on page 274.

Kokanee Glacier Provincial Park

Located in the Selkirks north of Nelson, this park takes its name from the Kokanee Glacier, the largest glacier in the area. The word *kokanee* is a Kootenay Indian name for the brightly colored land-locked salmon, which are found in certain drainages throughout the region. The same fish provide the spectacular run up MacDonald Creek in Montana's Glacier National Park every fall—renowned for the hundreds of bald eagles that gather to feed on the easily caught salmon. The Montana fish swim up from Flathead Lake; the salmon of Kokanee Creek come from Kootenay Lake.

The park was established in 1922. Its boundaries encompass about 32,000 hectares (79,000 acres). From its center, dominated by the Kokanee Glacier and some delightfully named surrounding features— Giants Kneecap, The Battleship, Esmeralda Peak, The Keyhole, and Joker Lakes—radiate a cluster of watercourses, which carve alpine basins and deep, thickly forested valleys as they descend. Those which fall eastward drain to Kootenay Lake; the others contribute to the Slocan River, which also ends up in the Kootenay system.

Several other glaciers, and a complex of mountain-capped ridges, set off the separate sections of the park. In the northeast, behind the sharply incised Sawtooth Range, Clover Basin, Queens Basin and Scranton Basin are popular among hikers. On the west side, the Enterprise Creek drainage also boasts alpine lakes and open flower meadows with well-supplied clearwater streams. In all, the park has more than thirty lakes. The terrain is often rugged, but more often characterized by the rounded shapes of glaciated granite. The rock is part of the Nelson batholith, an igneous intrusion which was eventually stripped of overlying sediments. The same geologic feature explains the mineral areas of the Kootenay region in general; just about all the surrounding towns grew up around lead, silver and zinc mining. A colorful history of steamboats on the lakes, connected by short "portage" railroads, is not far in the past.

Campsites in the park are designated, and hikers are requested to use them. In addition, three cabins are available. One is a venerable Kokanee institution, the Slocan Chief Cabin, at the foot of Kokanee Glacier. It was built in 1896 by builders who knew what they were doing. No sight could be finer on a sleeting autumn day than this lovely log structure, perched comfortably on a knob surrounded by conifers. It sleeps 12 persons. During summer, a ranger lives nearby. In winter, reservations must be made with the Parks Division; a fee is charged year-round, $10 in summer, $25 in winter. The other cabins are Silver Spray Cabin and Woodbury Cabin, which sleep eight persons each; same fees as above. Both are in the Woodbury Creek drainage.

Six separate roads provide access to the park. Two of these are commonly used. One begins 21 km. (13 mi.) north of Nelson on Highway 3A, and follows Kokanee Creek to a parking area and cabin on Gibson Lake, 16 km. (10 mi.) from the highway. The second main entrance road begins on Highway 31A, 5 km. (3 mi.) from the town of Kaslo, and ends 25 km. (16 mi.) later at Joker Millsite; this is the only road that actually penetrates the park for any distance, and it provides the shortest access to the Kokanee Glacier area.

Useful Names and Addresses

Topographic maps can be ordered from **MAPS BC** (address, page 274). For more information, and reservations for winter use of the Slocan Chief Cabin, contact **Kokanee Glacier Provincial Park**, Site 8, Comp. 5, R.R. 3, Nelson, BC V1L 5P6 (tel: 604-825-9509).

Wells Gray Provincial Park

Wells Gray Provincial Park, named for a former BC Minister of Lands, and established during his tenure in 1939, is an immense wilderness area in the Cariboo Mountains across the North Thompson valley from Mount Robson. The park measures about 5,200 sq. km. (2,000 sq. mi.; the size of Delaware and twice the size of Rhode Island). It contains mountain ranges capped by glaciers, five large fjord-shaped lakes, numerous smaller ones, a significant wildlife population and virtually no human developments. The highest mountains, and the glaciers, are located in the northern half of the park, or along its eastern boundary, formed by the crest of the Cariboo Mountains.

Murtle Lake, in the central-east portion of the park, is claimed by some to be the most beautiful wilderness lake in British Columbia. Its shape forms a narrow, eccentric curve surrounded by mountains which, although not snow-covered and craggy, are high enough to have alpine meadows and stunted subalpine forest. The only way in is by portaging 3 km. (2 mi.) from an access road. The other big lakes—Mahood, Clearwater, Azure and Hobson—are also many times longer than they are wide. Access roads reach the banks of Mahood and Clearwater. Azure Lake can be reached by paddle or motor; the last mile or so of upriver paddling against stiff current can be avoided by a portage.

Getting to Hobson Lake involves a portage of 13 km. (8 mi.).

The entire park drains into the Clearwater River, which rises in the icefields at the far northern corner of the park, and flows south through three of the lakes and over a series of spectacular waterfalls on its way to a junction with the North Thompson River. The best known of these falls is Helmcken, where the entire river, in one concentrated gush of water, free-falls for 137 m. (449 ft.) into a bowl-shaped plunge pool. Others in the area, and accessible by road, are Dawson Falls on the Murtle River, Canim River Falls and Spahats Creek Falls. Waterfalls accessible by foot are too many to count.

Wells Gray is used mostly by boaters of various persuasions, whether they prefer motors or paddles, whether interested in fishing, sightseeing or both. Numerous hiking opportunities can be found, but most of these are best done in conjunction with a boat trip on one of the lakes. Otherwise, a few trails suitable for backpackers lead to small lakes and mountain tops along the Clearwater River road.

Access can be had by way of three roads, two from Highway 5 in the North Thompson valley, and the third from 100 Mile House on Highway 97, the Cariboo Highway. Most visitors enter from Clearwater on Highway 5. Consider stopping at Spahats Creek Provincial Park along the way; a deep gorge and waterfall can be seen from overlooks near the road. There is also a campground here. The road is paved past the park entrance and information station to Helmcken Falls. From there it is gravel to its end at Clearwater Lake. Campgrounds are located at both Dawson Falls and Clearwater Lake.

The second access is primarily of interest to Murtle Lake canoeists. A 22-km. (14-mi.) road leaves Highway 5 at Blue River; from the end of the road, a 2.5 km. (1.5 mi.) trail leads to the lake. Last is the road from 100 Mile House to Mahood Lake. The road actually turns off at Mile 97, and bumps along for 88 km. (55 mi.) to the lake and a campground.

Some Useful Information About Wells Gray

CAMPGROUNDS: The park has four campgrounds, two at Clearwater Lake, one at Dawson Falls and one at Mahood Lake.
LODGING: Two private lodges offer accommodation, meals, boat rental and limited supplies. Their addresses: **Helmcken Falls Lodge,** Box 239, Clearwater, BC V0E 1N0 (tel: 604-674-3657). **Mahood Lake Resort,** Mahood Falls Post Office, BC V0K 2A0 (tel: 604-393-2220).
USEFUL NAMES AND ADDRESSES: A contour map (1:125,000 scale, sheet PS-WG3) can be ordered from MAPS BC, address on page 274. For more information, contact the Area Manager, **Wells Gray Park,** RR2, Box 4516, Clearwater, BC V0E 1N0 (tel: 604-587-6150).

Index